Su

Other Periscope Publishing books by
the author:

The First Submarines
Submarines at War 1939-1945

Submarines at War
1914-1918

Richard Compton-Hall

Periscope Publishing
Penzance

First Published by Macmillan London in 1991 as
"Submarines and the War at Sea 1914-18"

Republished in 2004 by
Periscope Publishing Ltd.
33 Barwis Terrace
Penzance
Cornwall TR18 2AW
www.periscopepublishing.com

A CIP record for this book is available from the
British Library

ISBN No 1-904381-21-9

Printed in England by Anthony Rowe Ltd,
Eastbourne

Contents

Contents

Acknowledgements

I am grateful to the Trustees of the Royal Navy Submarine Museum, Gosport, for permission to use the Museum's unique photographic collection for reproduction in this book; and also to the Museum's archivist, Mr Gus Britton, for assistance in locating some of the records and library references.

I am, above all, grateful to my wife, Eve, both for patient, invaluable assistance in putting the book together and for expert criticism; and also to Graham Dobbin who has generously given much help.

My thanks go to many people, all good friends of the Submarine Museum, who have offered advice or assisted with extensive research: in particular, Paul Kemp of the Imperial War Museum; Brian Head; Selwyn Mee; Nicholas A. Lambert; David Stanley; H. E. Boakes; and Jak Mallmann Showell. Michael Wilson's excellent book, *Baltic Assignment* (Leo Cooper, 1985), saved me a lot of work in tracking down facts for chapter 8: his *Destination Dardanelles* (Leo Cooper, 1988) was also very useful when I revised the manuscript.

The layout of HMS *E-II*, most successful of the 'E' class, totalling fifty-six boats with few variations in design.

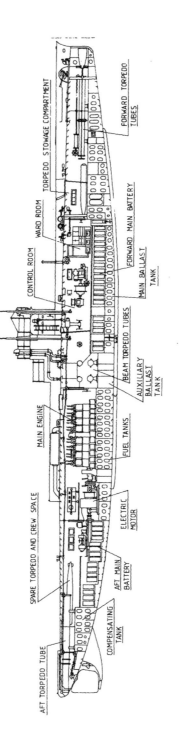

FORWARD TORPEDO TUBES

TORPEDO STOWAGE COMPARTMENT

WARD ROOM

FORWARD MAIN BATTERY

MAIN BALLAST TANK

CONTROL ROOM

BEAM TORPEDO TUBES

AUXILIARY BALLAST TANK

MAIN ENGINE

FUEL TANKS

SPARE TORPEDO AND CREW SPACE

ELECTRIC MOTOR

AFT MAIN BATTERY

COMPENSATING TANK

AFT TORPEDO TUBE

Author's Note

Ranks and Equivalents

Controller of the Navy: The (British) Sea Lord on the Board of Admiralty responsible for material and hence, subject to the Treasury, finance

First Lord of the Admiralty: The civilian head of the Royal Navy

First Sea Lord: The naval head of the Royal Navy

Grossadmiral: Admiral of the Fleet (British)

Admiral: Admiral

Vizeadmiral: Vice-Admiral

Kommodore: Commodore

Kapitän-zur-See: Captain

Fregattenkapitän: Junior Captain (no direct equivalent)

Korvettenkapitän: Commander

Kapitänleutnant: Lieutenant Commander

Oberleutnant-zur-See: Lieutenant

Leutnant-zur-See: Junior Lieutenant (no direct equivalent)

RA (S):   Rear Admiral (Submarines): nowadays Flag Officer Submarines (FOSM)

SNO: Senior Naval Officer

Sub: Sub-Lieutenant

Measurements

cable: For practical purposes, 1 cable = 183 metres (200 yards)

fathom: 1 fathom = 1.83 metres (6 feet)

knot: Speed is expressed in knots: nautical miles per hour (see nautical mile)

nautical mile: The length of a nautical mile differs slightly in different latitudes but can be taken, nearly enough, as 1853 metres (6080 feet) or, for practical purposes, 1829 metres (2000 yards). Where it is obvious that a reference is to sea-going distances, nautical miles are sometimes expressed as n. miles or simply miles.

Introduction

This book looks closely at the Great Underwater War from below – from the viewpoint of submariners themselves. Although major issues are confronted it tells mainly of tactics rather than strategy, of people rather than politics.

The focus is unashamedly on the Royal Navy's submarines. British records are markedly more full, frank and uninhibited than surviving German chronicles because the Royal Navy had no need to conceal, camouflage or falsify documents after the First World War; papers were not destroyed or altered for political reasons. Moreover, little use has previously been made of the comprehensive collection of letters and documents in the Royal Navy Submarine Museum's First World War archive which has been a prime source (cross-checked elsewhere) for research. The tales which emerge, the greyish humour and strong, quite often quirky, personalities are revealing and form an excellent basis for comparison with other participants in the deadly game played out beneath the sea.

It has been commonly assumed in the past that one submarine or *Unterseeboot* was much like another but they differed in construction, propulsion and weaponry. Climate and geography, as well as purpose, also demanded various methods of operation. The received whims of political masters – who could be cynics, hypocrites or pragmatists – were changeable or liable to alternative interpretations by the servants at sea and, most important of all, the temperament and ability of captains and crews varied widely among and within the several submarine services.

The years from 1914 to 1918 witnessed a revolution in naval warfare. That point has been made frequently enough in standard histories; but little attention has been paid to how the undersea pirates went about their business. There is seldom a word about individual captains' strengths and weaknesses, and how good or bad their weapons were, the engineers who sweated over recalcitrant machinery, the trimming officers and hydroplane operators who miraculously kept the ordered depth in heavy weather, the cooks who somehow produced hot meals in a heaving hull, the torpedomen who reloaded ton-weight weapons in record time, and all the other unrecorded crewmen on whom a captain necessarily depended.

The intriguing question of why some submarines were successful while the great majority were not has scarcely been asked, let alone resolved. The account that follows endeavours to find the answer. To an extent it is subjective; academics may not care for that, but practically any warfare is subjective, a personal matter for those involved. After all, it is the whys and wherefores of actions by men on the spot – even if they are later shown to be misinformed or wrong – which win or lose battles.

The decisions made by Allied submarine captains and German U-boat commanders were entirely personal because communications with shore headquarters were unreliable or non-existent at that time. A boat was on its own at sea. It was prudent to assume that all ships and aircraft would be hostile towards any submarine discovered: positive self-identification as a friend, before being urgently attacked, was very difficult and emergency signals such as flares were not dependable. Whereas a surface vessel could easily identify itself and expect assistance from a consort if the engines broke down, seek medical advice from a doctor on board a big ship, or check its navigational position with, perhaps, the Flotilla Leader, a submarine could not. A submariner, of any navy, learned quickly to be self-sufficient and self-reliant, with a thorough understanding of the complex workings of his boat. Some technical understanding is also necessary for us now to appreciate what happened and why when submarines first went to war.

We must deal with usage and development of what might be called the tools of the trade. The Royal Navy's Submarine Service was popularly known as The Trade at a time when trading was anathema to the ruling classes – no occupation for a gentleman. It was a name, coined when submarines were still in their infancy, that reflected a curious mixture of admiration, envy and lofty scorn for officers and men who necessarily acquired mechanical skills known only to specialists in the surface fleet. The full implications of that nickname, and their consequences, will become apparent later.

In relating events as they unfolded for submariners during the First World War, geographical areas have been treated separately because each encompassed particular aims, and submariners had to use particular tactics to achieve those aims. This allows chronological continuity in, say, Baltic affairs but it means jumping about in time from chapter to chapter as well as switching back and forth between the submarines of opposing nationalities. Nevertheless, this treatment will – I hope – make the underwater facts of life more accessible than the usual straight chronology. Where relevant, dates are included in chapter headings; and focusing mainly on British boats should also assist in making clear the sequence of events.

In 1916 Rudyard Kipling wrote a telling little poem about 'The Trade':

> They bear, in place of classic names,
> Letters and numbers on their skin.
> They play their grisly blindfold games
> In little boxes made of tin.
> Sometimes they stalk the Zeppelin,
> Sometimes they learn where mines are laid
> Or where the Baltic ice is thin.
> That is the custom of 'The Trade'.
>
> Their feats, their fortunes and their fames
> Are hidden from their nearest kin;
> No eager public backs or blames,
> No journal prints the yarns they spin
> (The Censor will not let them in!)
> When they return from run or raid.
> Unseen they work, unseen they win.
> That is the custom of 'The Trade'.

Kipling's jingoistic style was typical of the times, and reflects the attitudes of the First World War. Certain phrases may grate on the ear or sound absurdly like *Boy's Own Paper* ripping yarns but they take us back to a navy imbued with schoolboyish enthusiasm and an England riddled with class distinctions – factors which had their effect on the conduct of the war, not least by creating a certain *naïveté* or credulousness at high level. Gentlemen of all nationalities were always expected to 'play the game' with a 'straight bat'.

In Germany, society was even more sharply divided into aristocracy, middle class and working class, which became one reason for Germany's collapse. Britain's strength, on the other hand, lay not only in the resilience and fortitude of her people but in their ability to adapt to new situations, and as the war progressed the borderlines between the classes began to blur.

Society was reflected in microcosm among submarine crews, but shared danger, hardship and dependence on one another for survival bonded men together. Submarine life was a great leveller. Where, rarely, class intruded, morale – and hence performance – was poor.

However, ratings ('the lower deck' in British terms) were themselves snobbish. In the two major navies they were proud to serve a 'true gentleman' provided that he stood up to their definition of that term and did not treat them like inferior beings. They did not in the least begrudge him gentlemanly privileges or comforts (a relative term in submarines), but they resented a pretender with airs and graces which they felt were not his proper due.

Generally speaking, the public-school system and the Royal Naval College (where cadets started at the age of thirteen) both served the Royal Navy well, although scientific education was scant. The more sheltered young officers, with a gentle background, lacked the maturity which a tough, unrelenting struggle at home forced early on the men. Yet public schools, the RNC and gunrooms for midshipmen were harsh on youngsters – cold plunges and beatings were commonplace – and the abominable conditions in a submarine came as no great shock.

Submarine service brought out the best in officers and men: characters strengthened rapidly. Nor was it difficult for discerning captains to get rid of undesirables, at least until wartime losses began to mount, especially in the U-boat arm. The most dreaded punishment for a British submariner was to be reverted to General Service – meaning the surface navy – not only because of the loss of extra pay but also because of the disgrace of being proclaimed unable to accept the informal but rigorous discipline demanded underwater.

Class was much more significant in the Russian Navy, where officers of any description were almost universally hated and feared. Very few Russian crews, therefore, were truly efficient or stood up to the tests of war. Elsewhere, submarine companies established mutual trust and tolerance during the initial patrol. When they did not, ineffectiveness was predictable and disaster a strong possibility.

It is, of course, impossible to portray all the personalities involved, although a fair number will be sketched. The careers of certain British officers are touched upon quite frequently because they exemplify the characteristics of successful submariners and help to show that men and morale were more important than machinery and materials. That is the justification for this book's personal approach to the first Great Underwater War.

R.C-H.
Royal Navy Submarine Museum
Gosport
Hampshire

PROLOGUE

The Inevitable Path

At 3.45 p.m. on 5 September 1914, on a fine sunny day one
month after war had broken out, the 25-knot light cruiser HMS
Pathfinder suddenly blew up in her own home waters just off
the Scottish coast at the entrance to the Firth of Forth.

Damage-control methods at the time were rudimentary and
little practised. The explosion below the bridge touched off
ammunition in the forward magazine. Most of the men forward were killed outright and there were heavy casualties
elsewhere. The Captain, Martin Leake, was blasted into an
upper-deck meat-safe and a sailor was blown into the aftermost
funnel.

In the wardroom the 'almighty crash' was followed by a
breathless silence for several drawn-out seconds. Then the
crockery in the pantry fell to the deck, the lights went
out, and the deck shuddered underfoot as bulkheads below
started to give way. Boats were jammed in their crutches or
shattered. In moments the base of No. 2 funnel was awash
(No. 1 had gone) and the water was filthy with a scum of coal
dust and oil.

Barely four minutes after the initial detonation the 2940-ton
patrol leader plunged bow down. For a little while her stem
rested on the seabed and her stern, cocked up at an angle of
60°, hung as if suspended above the surface. Then, slowly
at first but with gathering speed as more bulkheads carried
away, the whole hulk slid to the bottom.

There were many non-swimmers in the company (the Navy
had been lax about instruction) and no lifejackets. Although
the destroyers *Stag* and *Express*, both '30-knotters', raced to the
spot, only a dozen of *Pathfinder*'s 268 officers and men survived
to relate their unprecedented experience.[1] Leake, of course,

1

was the last, as far as he could determine, to leave the sinking ship: his loyal Secretary or 'Scratch', Assistant Paymaster Alan Bath, stooped to unlace his master's boots before both officers jumped.

The ship was poorly prepared for underwater attack, but by no means exceptional in that. When the Fleet first heard the news by wireless, at 4 p.m., it was assumed that she had run onto a mine; but *Pathfinder's* Chief Boatswain's Mate, the 'Buffer', had seen what he rightly took to be a periscope and the track of a torpedo. Indeed the latter was still faintly visible when the ship went down. His hail from the forecastle to the bridge was promptly answered by the Officer of the Watch[2] who put the helm hard over and rang the engine telegraphs to full astern starboard and full ahead port in order to speed up his emergency turn towards the sighting. His prompt action was too late. The engine-room watchkeeper at the throttles disbelieved the port telegraph order – full astern would have been understandable – and, assuming that someone on the bridge had lost his head, did not obey. But, in any case, the engines would not have saved the ship: at the miserable economical speed of 6 knots – the best she could do on patrol for five days a week with small coal bunkers – manoeuvring was sluggish and it would have taken ten minutes to work up to full power.

Thereafter the minimum speed for HM ships on patrol was fixed at 15 knots, but on this occasion there was no way of avoiding the carefully aimed 'eel' fired from what was then considered an abnormally long range of about 1200 metres (1300 yards). It was the first time anywhere that a submarine torpedo warhead had struck home.

Some grisly details emerged. The *Stag* lost her main circulating water supply: a diver found the inlet blocked by a man's leg. The Royal Navy was starkly confronted with its first glimpse of real modern warfare as opposed to peacetime simulation.

About half a mile away a slender, stick-like object – known as the 'Asparagus' by U-boat men – was protruding 2 metres (6 feet) above the surface, unnoticed now among the confusion and the breaking crests of a gathering sea. Kapitänleutnant Otto Hersing, at the conning-tower periscope of *U-21*, grimly observed the carnage, while his Engineering Officer in the control room below struggled to keep correct depth with the boat altering course away under full wheel which tended to pull the stern down.

The standing U-boat orders were to watch the hit, note any countermeasures adopted and judge whether a second shot was necessary. Then a U-boat captain was advised to lower his periscope, proceed to the greatest possible depth – usually 45 metres (148 feet) but later extended to 60 metres (200 feet) – and preserve silence in the boat. 'The Higher Command', the instructions emphasised, 'must know with certainty when a ship is reported merely as hit, whether she has to be reckoned with for the future or not.'[3]

The hit had undeniably been lucky. The U-boat school taught its pupils to shoot at 200 metres (220 yards), increased to 300 metres (330 yards) on active service. At 1200 metres (1300 yards), with a 38-knot high-speed torpedo setting, the running time was just over one minute. If the enemy speed was estimated only 2 knots wrongly the 'eel' would miss 63 metres (207 feet) ahead or astern of a 113-metre (370-foot) target; and the little gyro-compass in the torpedo itself might well 'wander' slightly to add (or subtract) another 12 metres (39 feet). The vagaries of underwater weapons will be emphasised later, but at 6 knots HMS *Pathfinder* was a sitting duck.

There was no need to consider another torpedo in this case; but retribution could now be expected from the Eighth Flotilla which Leake had been commanding in the wearisome task of guarding the entrance to the Firth. Hersing duly went deep and, with only a few metres beneath the keel, *U-21* stole quietly away into open waters. The hunters, with no underwater detection devices and no aircraft to support them, searched in vain.

Hersing, twenty-eight years old and the son of a Strasbourg University professor, was remarkably inexperienced as a submariner. He had commissioned the newly built *U-21* less than eleven months earlier and, apart from undergoing the U-boat

Command Course, had never served in a submarine before. Nevertheless, he knew a lot about torpedoes, having been a Watch Officer in three surface torpedo-boats.

It was thus a relative newcomer who struck the first underwater blow. Others were quick to follow from both sides of the grey North Sea – or the German Ocean as the Kaiser's *Volk* called it. *U-21* herself, with Hersing left in command by the Staff for no less than twenty-one patrols spanning three strenuous years, went on to claim thirty-six victims in all, including two battleships and two cruisers. Moreover – perhaps the clearest proof of speedily acquired professionalism – he and his crew lived to tell the tale.

The loss of HMS *Pathfinder* to a U-boat was more of a shock to the Admiralty than it should have been but, true to her name by ironic fate, the luckless cruiser demonstrated, by her sinking, the path along which naval warfare would inevitably progress.

PART I

WAYS AND MEANS

CHAPTER 1

'The Trade'

The newspapers described the month of July 1914 as 'freakish'. They were referring to the thermometer which rose to a sweltering 128°F on the first of the month. But not only the weather was abnormal: the Royal Navy, albeit in a financial straitjacket, was preparing for war. First Lord of the Admiralty Winston Churchill had substituted an economical test mobilisation for the usual costly Summer Grand Manoeuvres. The exercise was completed on 25 July, and the Fleet was in an exceptionally high state of manpower-readiness while most of the battleships were concentrated in home waters.

At the same time Churchill pictured the German High Sea Fleet gathering in serried, heavy lines off Norway. But the Admiralty took scant note of the secretive submarine flotillas arming themselves in the Baltic – or, for that matter, those of The Trade which had nearly three times the German number of boats. Battle fleets were the essence of naval warfare, or so the admirals on both sides believed. British pride in the Royal Navy's magnificent battleships and prejudice against submersible craft abounded.

At the beginning of the century submarines were 'a damned un-English weapon'. The upper-deck executive officers who volunteered to descend into smelly, oily little 'submergibles', to get their hands dirty and delve into intricate machinery, were looked down upon – figuratively as well as literally – by their contemporaries pacing the spotless quarterdecks above. The consequence was that British submariners withdrew into a tightly knit clan. Looking like 'unwashed chauffeurs' (a popular epithet) they were prone to talk shop to a tedious degree at table and the officers were not, on the whole, popular outside what was virtually a private navy. They therefore seldom took opportunities to explain their trade to admirals and their staffs, and it was not surprising that the senior officers, who ultimately controlled submarines from shore but had no direct experience of them, were slow to recognise their full potential. Misemployment and unsuitable equipment were apt to result, and the effects of what was something like a chip on the average submariner's shoulder were evident.

The rumbustious, mercurial Admiral Jacky Fisher was almost alone when he foresaw in 1904 'the immense impending revolution which submarines will effect as offensive weapons of war'.[1] Until about 1910 this elderly admiral, who had joined the navy as a lad in 1854 during the Crimean War, never formulated any firm plans for offensive underwater operations for the Royal Navy. In the early days he probably saw British (as opposed to enemy) submarines mainly in a defensive role, protecting harbours with the gunnery system he had created, thereby freeing the big ships for a battle of leviathans on the high seas. Nevertheless, his support was invaluable to the developing Trade.

For three or four years before the war, however, when diesel engines conferred range and reliability, Fisher was advocating a British submarine offensive across the North Sea and predicting that the German enemy would reciprocate. At the same time he opposed the view that submarines should conduct such an offensive in consort with the Grand Fleet, evidently recognising the submarine as an independent weapon system, a weapon of stealth.

Few officers dared disagree with Fisher, whatever he said; they were either 'in the fishpond' or in outer darkness as far as promotion was concerned. But one like-minded admiral, Sir Percy Scott, was subjected to some violent criticism when, on 2 June 1914, in the month of Sarajevo, he wrote a letter to the *Daily Mail* concluding '. . . as the motor has driven the horse from the road, so has the submarine driven the battleship from the sea'. He followed this two days later with a letter to *The Times* containing the following controversial but equally prophetic paragraphs:

- that as we had sufficient battleships, but not sufficient submarines and aircraft, we should stop building battleships and spend the money voted for their construction on the submarines and aircraft we urgently needed.

- submarines and aircraft had entirely revolutionised naval warfare.

- that if we were at war with a country within striking distance of submarines, battleships on the high seas would be in great danger, that even in harbour they would not be immune from attack unless the harbour was quite a safe one.

- that probably, if we went to war, we should at once lock up our battleships in a safe harbour, and the enemy would do the same.

- that submarines could deliver a deadly attack in broad daylight.

- that battleships could not bombard an enemy if his ports were adequately protected by submarines.

- that the enemy's submarines would come to our coasts and destroy everything they could see.

Five admirals rushed into print: Fremantle described Scott's letter as a mischievous scare; Briggs said Scott had not gone thoroughly into the matter; Bridgeman (late First Sea Lord) referred to submarines as inaccurate and undeveloped weapons (and this two months before war was declared); Beresford (Fisher's implacable enemy) stated flatly that submarines could only operate in the daytime, that they were highly vulnerable, and that a machine gun could put them out of action. The unkindest cut came from Bacon, the very man who had started the submarine service in 1901. He was 'astonished' at Scott publishing views 'with an authoritativeness which could only be justified by an accuracy of knowledge which it was difficult to see that he had at his disposal': he pointed out the great problems in navigating a submarine. The *Hampshire Telegraph* reported that Lord Sydenham 'regards Sir Percy Scott's theory as a fantastic dream and considers that Sir Percy Scott does not appear to have grasped the logical results of his theories'; and the *Pall Mall Gazette* told its readers that 'Sir Percy Scott's ideas approached the boundaries of midsummer madness', while the *Manchester Courier* recommended that the forecasts 'may safely be relegated to the novel shelf'.

There was a score of other snide comments in the press which showed what the country at large and, by inference, the Admiralty thought about submarines with war so close ahead. The views were summed up by Mr Hannon, Secretary of the Navy League, who warned that Scott's statements were 'premature, ill-advised and calculated to do serious harm to the cause of maintenance of British supremacy at sea'.

It is reasonable to suspect that these declarations were less than objective and that they arose from wishful thinking. The fact was that if submarines belonging to an enemy were successful the mighty British fleets would be in grave danger, just as Scott warned. It is odd that Scott did not also consider the danger to vital seaborne supply lines for the British Isles but then, surely, warfare could not be waged against non-combatants in an age when, in England anyway, gentlemen 'played the game' (cricket, of course) and boxers never 'hit below the belt'.

In pre-war Germany there was a strong lobby against *Unterseeboote* or *U-Boote* – U-boats as they became known in English to distinguish them clearly from relatively good and honest Allied submarines. In August 1914 the Imperial Navy had neither the capability nor, it was claimed, the intention of launching a submarine offensive against merchant shipping. The balanced-fleet construction policy of Grossadmiral von Tirpitz precluded a major U-boat development programme. As for Kaiser Wilhelm II, big guns were his notion of prestige in 'my navy'; the destiny of the German Empire lay on the sea, not under it. In any case, by 1914 he had convinced himself, with typical arrogance, of the need for a short preventive war to be fought with the existing fleet. But the High Sea Fleet with twenty battleships, three battle-cruisers, six cruisers and seven destroyers[2] was unmotivated because it was to be held in check – and there is nothing worse for a sailor's morale than inaction. The problem was that German 'dreadnoughts', by far the best type of battleship with 280- or 300-mm (11- or

12-inch) guns as their main armament, numbered only thirteen against twenty in the Royal Navy armed with bigger 300- or 340-mm (12- or 13.5-inch) guns. On the other hand the German giants were better protected by armour. The ten German 'pre-dreadnoughts', however, were inferior in all respects to the nine British equivalents. The Imperial Navy had some confidence in its gunnery prowess but a massed action with the Royal Navy's Grand Fleet would, in theory at least, see the German ships at a marked disadvantage.

Unfortunately for the Kaiser, Grossadmiral Alfred von Tirpitz, Minister of Marine from 1897 and architect of the High Sea Fleet, was a slow and reluctant convert to the U-boat. Born in 1849 (eight years after Fisher), he joined the then small Prussian navy as a cadet in 1865 and later specialised in torpedoes. This specialisation might have led him to promote submarines in due course, had he not become wholly occupied with the idea of a balanced fleet centred on 'dreadnoughts'. These were built in direct competition with Britain where Fisher had originated them, and thereby started an arms race.

Growing flotillas of German surface torpedo-boats attested to Tirpitz's appreciation that rapidly improving torpedoes might prove an excellent weapon against the Grand Fleet, but his reasoning was comparative rather than absolute. It was based on the torpedoes being so much better than those available in the Russo-Japanese war of 1905. He gave no objective thought to what might be the best weapon-carriers in a new era. Also, he considered submarines unnecessary for protecting the fortified and easily mined German Bight. Although U-boats might, if developed and refined, help to shorten the odds currently in favour of the Grand Fleet, he could agree only to their being built at a rate compatible with battleship and battle-cruiser construction.

Tirpitz was already sixty years old before the first practicable U-boats (U-3 and U-4) were completed in 1909, and it was at least another two years before the infant U-Bootswaffe started to show its paces. Nor were reliable U-boat diesel engines at sea until 1913. It is therefore hardly surprising that the conservative *Grossadmiral*, not known for his flexibility, was unable to enthuse about the new underwater arm in the short time that existed between its inception as a fighting force and the outbreak of war. When, in 1925, the revisionist *Kapitän-zur-See*, Lothair Persius, reviewed the Reich's generally poor naval wartime record, he blamed it largely on the neglect of submarine construction. 'Before the war,' he asserted, 'Tirpitz had fought all U-boat construction hand and foot.'[3] This harsh view was not shared by the wartime *Führer der Unterseeboote* (FdU) Hermann Bauer, who, during his years as submarine adviser in the Reich Marine Office before he took up his wartime duties, described Tirpitz's approach as cautious but favourable. U-boats were not in fact sufficiently advanced before the war to merit mass production, and their ultimate purpose – the destruction of British commerce which the French *Jeune Ecole*, the young school of new French strategy, had advocated many years earlier – was envisaged by only a few.

'The thought of cutting England off from her sea supply by means of submarines,' said Bauer a quarter of a century later, 'had in no manner been considered, since such a submarine war against English sea trade would not have been in conformity with the London Declaration.'[4] That claim, made so long after the event, is suspect: by 1915 the German Naval Staff was openly pressing for ruthless and unrestricted U-boat warfare to terrorise neutrals. Indeed the German *Jeune Ecole* had earlier called for attacks on seaborne trade by U-boats, but that call was rejected in the light of the strategic doctrines of Rear Admiral A. T. Mahan USN. These prevailed, and led to submarines being described in Britain at the turn of the century as 'the weapon of a weaker power':

It is not the taking of individual ships or convoys, be they few or many, that strikes down the money power of a nation: it is the possession of that overbearing power on the sea which drives the enemy's flag from it, or allows it to appear only as the fugitive: and by controlling the great common, closes the highways by which commerce moves to and from the enemy's shores. This overbearing power can only be exercised by great navies.[5]

Nevertheless, a campaign against British shipping was to be conducted at the outset by armed surface raiders. The underlying logic of *Handelskrieg* – war on trade – was accepted; but despite the initial great successes of the *Emden* and *Karlsruhe*, the cruiser forces only sank fifty-two merchant vessels over a period of five months for the loss of nine of their number – an unsatisfactory exchange rate of six to one.

Critics after the First World War repeatedly asked what would have happened if, say, 100 U-boats had been available and employed on commerce raiding from the very beginning of the war. The question was answered by the two respected historians Gibson and Prendergast:[6] 'If Germany *had* possessed one hundred submarines in 1914, the majority of these boats would have been crudities like *U-1* to 4 or unreliable craft such as the "Desiderata" (*U-5* to 18) boats.' In other words the boats that might have been built would have been styled operational – that is, *Frontboote* – but they would scarcely have been capable of a sustained offensive against Britain's trade routes.

Germany, unlike Britain, had no co-ordinating War Cabinet. The Kaiser, commanding a chaotic system, was solely responsible for the conduct of the war: he decided upon what was termed a strategic defensive policy as far as the big ships were concerned, the Chancellor having repeatedly urged that the High Sea Fleet should be kept intact throughout the war so that Germany might wield an imposing political weapon during peace negotiations.

The Emperor outlined his strategy in the German Ocean under three headings,[7] only one of which mentioned U-boats, and then almost in parenthesis:

1. Our object is to damage the British Fleet by means of offensive advances against the forces watching or blockading the German Bight, and also by means of a ruthless mining and, if possible, a submarine offensive, carried as far as the British coast.

2. When an equalisation of forces has been obtained by these measures, all our forces are to be got ready and concentrated, and an endeavour will be made to bring our Fleet into action

under favourable conditions. If a favourable opportunity for an action occurs before this, advantage is to be taken of it.

3. War is to be carried on against commerce as laid down in the Prize Regulations [i.e. humanely]. The Commander-in-Chief High Sea Fleet will determine to what degree this warfare is to be carried on in home waters. The ships allocated for war against commerce in foreign waters [surface raiders] are to proceed as soon as possible.

Only twenty-eight German U-boats were commissioned between 1906 and August 1914. Twenty-one boats were fully operational when war broke out, but some of the earlier ones were described as crude and unreliable. Peacetime training of their officers and crews was criticised as cautious to the point of timidity, and boats were not trusted beyond sight of land without an escort of surface vessels. The British, however, did not know this. The Admiralty's reckoning was that thirty-three U-boats had been built and that twenty-eight of these were capable of independent offensive patrols; another twenty-eight were said to be already building. This compared with seventy-four submarines in the Royal Navy (with another thirty-one building and fourteen ordered or projected) of which, initially, only eighteen – the 'D's and 'E's – were oversea (that is, offensive) boats.

If the German view from above was that submarines were purely defensive and largely experimental, a handful of junior and middle-ranking officers had other ideas. It must also have been apparent to the less hidebound German militarists, long before the war, that Britain's merchant fleet was the jugular that had to be severed, and if U-boats could be made effective they would provide the cutting edge.

In August 1914 the German U-boat men, although still unappreciated in Berlin, rapidly revised their cautious peace-time policy under the dynamic and aggressive leadership of the remarkably junior Korvettenkapitän Hermann Bauer.[8]

It may seem surprising, in the light of the concept's widespread unpopularity, that Britain acquired such a large submarine fleet before the war. It grew not so much from a perceived requirement for more boats (although keeping up with the German Joneses – and indeed the French – was politically important) but because of technical advances. One class followed another (alphabetically from the 'A's which succeeded the primitive 'Hollands' of 1901–2 through to the 'E's) with little strategic direction from the Admiralty. Successive types were simply better and safer, and built predominantly for a coastal defensive role even if the bigger boats were seen within The Trade as capable of ranging further afield or co-operating with the Grand Fleet.

In all this, the current Inspecting Captain of Submarines (who headed the Submarine Service) had a remarkably free hand: nobody further up the ladder had the evidence, let alone the experience, to gainsay his advice. And although the civil servants in Whitehall mustered their customary objections, they knew next to nothing about submarines either.

British submarines should, in theory, have been a little better prepared for war than the German U-boat men because they had engaged in more frequent exercises against the fleet. Fleet manoeuvres offered a degree of practice in the new art of underwater warfare and at least taught commanding officers how to avoid collision with surface ships; but they involved false assumptions and unjustified claims of success by submarines and their opponents alike. They were scarcely indicative of wartime operations, and their supposed results tended to mislead the navy as a whole. Of course, it is easy to criticise the lack of realistic training now; but the submarine services were young – barely in their teens – and there was much to be learned while trying to operate safely.

Nevertheless, peacetime torpedo-attack training in The Trade should and could have been significantly improved. There were no proper attack instruments (other than local inventions) until halfway through the war: submarine captains generally fired by eye alone after working, if they could, into a position four to six points (45° to 67.5°) on the target's bow. No attempt was made in basic exercises to estimate or plot enemy course or speed: the capabilities of the most usual practice target – a tiny torpedo-recovery vessel of the 'Pygmy' class – were so well established that its deflection angle, or aim off, was known as 'The Magic Number'.

There was no formal training for submarine command in the Royal Navy (although the more methodical Germans had a school), and a new captain learned how to attack, if he learned successfully at all, by trial and error at sea. It was said, and evidently believed, that 'if a captain was a good shot at partridges etc. he probably became a good attacker in quick time'.[9]

Practice attacks were quite often fudged. For example, Archibald Cochrane of *E7*, who hated exercises, used to dive on sighting the target, wait a few minutes (according to visibility), then order 'up periscope, surface' without the least attempt to steer an attacking course or simulate firing. In a rare instance of allowing his First Lieutenant to carry out an exercise off Harwich in early 1915, well into the war and before proceeding on patrol, Number One duly dived the boat and ordered 'up periscope'. The following exchange then took place:[10]

CAPTAIN: 'Down periscope. What the Hell are you putting it up for?'
NO. 1: 'To see the target and find out what course to steer . . . '
CAPTAIN: 'Steer so and so.' [the usual course]
       A pause followed. A little later:
NO 1: 'May I up periscope and have a look at her?'
CAPTAIN: 'Don't be a bloody fool. Wait two minutes and then surface.'

Cochrane went on to gain distinction with *E7* in the Dardanelles, but it is significant that his successes were achieved either with the 100-mm (4-inch) gun or, when firing torpedoes, against targets in harbour.

His First Lieutenant, Oswald Hallifax, was subsequently appointed to command *B5*, an elderly training boat based at Fort Blockhouse, from November 1915 to October 1916. He was never permitted by the Squadron Captain to make a practice attack during this time and was told to confine his activities to basic instruction although two out of the three training boats were despatched every morning at daybreak to St Helen's Fort in the Portsmouth approaches, where they were required to torpedo the German High Sea Fleet if it hove in sight.

It was no wonder that impractical but supposedly safe orders and lack of realism had long persisted in the light of a long list of serious submarine accidents. From March 1904 to July 1914 the Royal Navy had suffered eight (seventy-nine men killed), France eleven (fifty-seven killed), Russia five (seventy killed), Italy one (fourteen killed), Japan one (fourteen killed), the USA one (two killed) and Germany one (three killed).

Until the end of 1910, when Roger Keyes, soon to be given the courtesy title of Commodore, was appointed Inspecting Captain of Submarines, it was mandatory for a submarine on exercises to be accompanied by a ship flying a large red flag, like the man who was obliged to walk ahead of the first motor cars carrying a similar emblem to give warning. That was obviously absurd: if The Trade could not manage by itself it might as well pack up.

Keyes headed the submarine service during the critical years from 1910 to 1915, but had never served in a submarine. The Industrial Revolution had caught up slowly with the Royal Navy and Keyes had grown up in the age of sail. He was already too old at twenty-nine when the Royal Navy's first boat was launched in 1901 and, anyway, he had no technical flair. Nor, in Admiral Jellicoe's words, was he 'blessed with much brains': painfully aware of his own limitations he kept a copy of Rudyard Kipling's inspiring poem 'If' pinned above his wash-basin. He was a seaman pure and simple – although Churchill, always attracted to an adventurous spirit, described him as 'a brilliant officer, with more knowledge and feeling for war than almost any naval officer I have met'.[11]

Churchill was writing to Fisher, who thought that the Inspecting Captain of Submarines was 'very shallow' and determined to get rid of him. In the end he succeeded. Keyes went on to other things, where he reached great heights, but not before he had indelibly impressed his own offensive ardour

17

on The Trade. Fisher undoubtedly had a point: the object of his dislike, often burdened by political and commercial machinations, did not always direct the submarine service well where technicalities were concerned, but in the all-important matter of morale he displayed superb leadership, and chose excellent men to assist him on his Submarine Development Committee.[12] He allowed his commanding officers a great deal of latitude and that counted for much. They sailed for the first war patrols to devise their own methods uninhibited by rule-books, which was all to the good because no worthwhile rules had yet been established.

Keyes, like many other British leaders, came from a well-to-do Anglo-Irish family, and enjoyed useful connections in London. Despite his shortcomings in an alien atmosphere of submersible engineering he was backed by valuable experience in destroyers, intelligence and the diplomatic world. From the start of his career he had contrived to be in the thick of things and now he brought to The Trade a refreshing breeze of salt air, candour and a wish for submarines to be in closer touch with the rest of the fleet. It was the last point which prompted Admiral Sir Arthur Wilson, First Sea Lord in 1910, to offer him the post of Inspecting Captain. It was also Wilson – 'Old 'ard 'eart' to the lower deck – who sourly suggested, as Controller of the Navy ten years earlier, that crews of submarines captured in wartime should be 'treated as pirates and hanged'. Now he was changing his tune, but only on the understanding that submariners would fall in line. Keyes had been hesitant about accepting the appointment, but the Naval Secretary's well-chosen remark that Wilson wanted an officer with good prospects of making the Admiral's list clinched the matter.

Thus from the start Keyes was necessarily, in conflict with Fisher, an exponent of 'fleet submarines' – boats with sufficient speed and seaworthiness to act with the Grand Fleet. The sequel to such complex employment was dire; but at heart the Inspecting Captain from the surface navy was a practical realist. He not only rid the more advanced submarine exercises of handicaps like the red flag but did his best, with a good team under him, to promote submarines by direct communication with the members of the Admiralty Board as well as with naval and civil departments.[13] It was uphill work.

In 1910 Keyes found that the boats at sea, with the possible exception of *D1* (the first of a new class equipped with diesels superseding hazardous short-range petrol engines and an important step forward), were indeed fit for no more than local defences, acting as mobile minefields – a substitute, in fact, for defensive mining which was exactly how the German Navy viewed its U-boats. *D1* showed her paces during the annual naval manoeuvres, and people started to think a little more about the advantages of diesel power. In addition, the usefulness of submarines for scouting and reporting enemy movements by radio (with which *D1* was first to be fitted) began to be apparent.

Two years later, in 1912, Lieutenant Geoffrey Layton, commanding *D2*, made a stronger point by entering the Firth of Forth and making his way unobserved past the patrols. In spite of all the navigational difficulties in a narrow fairway beset by strong tides, he slipped submerged beneath the Forth Bridge and torpedoed his own depot ship anchored off Rosyth Dockyard. The warning of things to come, made clear by Keyes to the Admiralty, was not heeded. Max Horton in *D6* repeated the exploit, torpedoing two ships a little while afterwards, but still the admirals declined to take note. Winston Churchill admitted that until the end of September 1914 (which is when U-boats threatened the Firth) 'no one seriously contemplated hostile submarines in time of war entering the harbours of either side and attacking ships at anchor'.[14]

The first submarine exercise against a fleet protected by destroyers was not conducted until September 1912, when the First Battle Squadron and a destroyer flotilla steamed through an area occupied by the Dover 'C'-class Submarine Flotilla (all petrol boats) to the west of Portland Bill, clear of merchant shipping routes. Here there was plenty of water for the boats to go deep, below the anti-submarine screen flung out ahead of the main units, and let the destroyers – clearly audible through the hull – speed overhead and away before rising to periscope depth to attack the heavy targets. The destroyers were too far away from the ships they were intended to protect and Keyes, who was embarked in C32, was able to enjoy the excellent lunch which the Captain, Clement Head, wisely provided for his master while still at safe depth. The little 'C' boats pressed home their attacks at close range and surfaced over the flattened noses of the torpedo collision heads floating in the wake of the disappearing Battle Fleet.

Keyes was impressed. But as trials progressed towards devising effective anti-submarine formations for the fleet, he allowed the boats to take risks which must have been against his better judgement. He was particularly worried, with good reason, when the submarines operated in shoal water with insufficient depth below the keel of a big ship to pass beneath it. Destroyer captains who had never worked with submarines before were quite liable to simulate gunfire and rush at a nearby periscope with a good chance of ramming the submerged submarine – a favourite wartime tactic but dangerous in early exercises. Still, it kept the submarine commanding officers on their toes while they learned to take rapid evasive action and the experience was to stand them in good stead when the real fighting started.

Meanwhile, submariners, when they eventually surfaced to claim a prize, were continually frustrated by being told that their periscopes had been fired at and that they were 'sunk'. When the Captain of *A8* rose alongside the flagship and hailed the Commander-in-Chief with a cheery 'Sir, I claim thee', the Admiral merely roared with laughter and shouted back, 'Boy, put your toy away. We have been watching you for a long time and could have sunk you many times with our six-inch guns.' The Admiral was an unrepentant liar but claims by the destroyers were often dubious as well. It was galling for a boat which reckoned it had made a successful torpedo attack – and easily escaped afterwards – to be ordered to hoist the 'out of action' flag and return to harbour.

The following year the senior umpires appointed for the manoeuvres were resolute that the submariners should not win. The destroyer men were believed, the submariners were not. During one tactical evaluation eight submarines were put out of action, and an invaluable opportunity to gain experience on both sides was lost. Keyes was compelled to submit that 'the time has arrived to face the question, if we are to prepare ourselves to deal with the submarines of an enemy. I am convinced that there will be a very rude awakening if tactics which were common during the most recent manoeuvres are repeated during actual warfare'.[15] There were still admirals who affirmed that submarines were only playthings – and that was at least partly the fault of The Trade's early disinclination to express itself.

Although neither the anti-submarine forces nor the submariners were prepared for warlike conditions on 4 August 1914, the lack of realistic peacetime training did not prevent most crews from adapting quickly to real fighting when the time came. For submarine combatants everywhere – British, German, Austrian, Italian and American – the transition was made easier because of their basic efficiency and professionalism; peace or war, they had constantly to battle against the greatest enemy of all: the unrelenting sea.

Offensive wartime operations were usually initiated by the submariners themselves who seized opportunities and exploited them enthusiastically. No tactical advice could be expected from above: ingenuity, improvisation and self-help featured largely. The commanding officers who were determined, in Nelsonian fashion, to 'engage the enemy more closely' succeeded; those who stood off or were unimaginative failed.

CHAPTER 2

Living in a Can

It is astonishing how well the Tradesmen coped – given purpose and leadership – with primitive weapons and equipment amid appalling discomfort of a kind which is difficult to appreciate today. To realise what 'living in a can' was like – 'existing' would be a better word – is an essential preliminary to any account of how men fought in those distant days. Without some idea of their conditions, so far removed from the modern nuclear navy, it is impossible to judge their actions and reactions fairly.

Nowadays a submarine scarcely ever surfaces at sea. Inside, albeit cramped and crowded, it is tight, warm and stable in the depths, virtually unaffected by the sea or weather above. But during the First World War (and the Second) submarines had to spend a great deal of time on the surface in order to run their diesel engines, both to recharge batteries and shift position, because endurance on electric motors was limited. Consequently, whenever the sea got up, water sluiced down the conning-tower hatch only a few feet above the surface, while the long thin hull pitched and rolled abominably. It was impossible to prevent water slopping around the control room and into the bilges where it mixed with oil from inevitable leakages, scraps of food and vomit from seasick sailors.

There was always an overwhelming smell of diesel fuel at sea or in harbour, and it clung to clothing, so that if anybody wanted to find a submariner ashore he had only to follow his nose. But oil was not the only smell. Unwashed bodies in unchanged clothing – nobody ever undressed at sea – made a notable contribution to the stench, together with the revolting bilges, spilled fat on the galley stove and, of course, the insanitary, reeking heads or WCs. The latter were in short supply and in some of the earlier boats there were no built-in toilet facilities. Where heads were installed it was not just a matter of pulling the plug after use: they had to be pumped out by hand or discharged by high-pressure air through a complicated series of valves and levers, at a maximum depth of 10 metres (30 feet). It was not safe to do this by daylight in enemy waters because air bubbles were revealing at the surface; and when it was permissible to blow the heads, often only when the pan had been used several times in order to conserve air, it was all too easy to make a mistake, an event known graphically as 'getting your own back'. This was an unforgettable experience and it happened to most trainee submariners. For some reason officers suffered most – perhaps they were less accustomed to working valves. It was common to see a young sub-lieutenant propelled stern first into the passageway wiping worse than tears from his eyes. Just to be on the safe side, cautious operators used to crouch on all fours below pan level before commencing flushing operations.

Mercifully, the human nose becomes desensitised quite quickly when exposed to pungent effluvia. But a stranger – a depot ship officer, for example – would feel as though his senses were being physically assaulted if he climbed down into a submarine immediately after its return from patrol.

Not surprisingly, unless a captain recognised the importance of regular habits, the more sensitive souls in a crew, especially the officers, were apt to dope themselves (opium pills were favoured in the U-boat arm) to avoid the necessity of using the heads at all even on short excursions. Alternatively, on longer patrols, they perched on the bridge rails when on the surface at night and did what they had to do on to the ballast tanks below. 'Lucky blighter!' exclaimed a captain to his navigator sitting precariously alongside him on one such occasion when he heard a thud: 'Not so lucky,' replied the navigator, 'that was the deck watch.' In British 'C' boats, where heads were omitted in the design, an extra-large bucket for the use of all and sundry was brought up from below and placed on the casing beneath the overhang abaft the bridge, providing, of course, that the sea was calm and the enemy was not expected to turn up.[1]

Foul breath, caused by rotten teeth, trench mouth and cheap tobacco, was normal. In short, submariners were not nice to know. Nevertheless, despite the unpleasant odours exuding from their persons (or perhaps because of them) the girls in port found them highly attractive – the more so because of their extra submarine pay. The latter (to compensate for 'hard lying', not danger) put 60 per cent on top of a young lieutenant's salary and more than doubled the meagre daily rate of one shilling and eightpence paid to an Able Seaman.[2]

Officers, better placed than ratings in all navies to make themselves presentable in fairly good depot ship accommodation before going ashore, were prone to take full advantage of the supposed glamour surrounding their occupation. Moreover, an officer could entertain ladies on board his boat in harbour, legitimately or sometimes illicitly. A certain amount of privacy could be contrived in the wardroom or in the Captains's screened-off hutch in the bigger boats; and it was not difficult to arrange, with the connivance of duty crewmen, for a close liaison not to be interrupted. Twosomes in boats alongside a depot ship were not encouraged by watchful staff officers, but by judiciously shutting a submarine's heavy bulkhead doors their investigations could be delayed while the lady of the day departed up the conning tower or out of the after hatch. This was not always as easy as it sounds because it was usual for a member of the oldest profession to signify that she had reached the peak of her career (thereby being available to officers only) by carrying a small white poodle everywhere, which could prove an encumbrance on a narrow, vertical steel ladder.[3] A tryst could have been more comfortably enjoyed in a nearby hotel – there were plenty of venues in all naval ports where the landlords were not too particular – but there is evidence to suggest that the submarine atmosphere, with all its unpleasantness, was considerably more effective as an aphrodisiac than the whelks and winkles recommended by ratings and the oysters by officers in the surface navy.

That small advantage aside, submarine accommodation

offered no more than the barest of bare essentials. All boats were squalid to a greater or lesser degree, depending mainly on their size; but the little 'A', 'B' and 'C' classes could only be described as noisome. The larger 'D' and 'E' classes were a trifle better. Living conditions were certainly not ideal in the German U-boats either, but were, on the whole, less horrible than in British submarines.

German leather clothing, to say nothing of warm under-garments, was superior to anything the Royal Navy produced for another forty years or more. The best that the Admiralty felt able to issue to submariners were leather boots, white roll-neck sweaters or 'frocks'[4] and a limited number of oilskins for bridge watchkeepers. All such issue clothing was strictly accountable and had to be paid for if lost. Wives, girl-friends and naval tailors, like the expensive but credit-tolerant Gieve, provided items like scarves, pullovers and thick socks.

Bunks in British boats were few and far between. Those that there were had to be shared by a process of 'hot bunk-ing', whereby a man off watch turned into the warm 'pit' just vacated by his relief. Many of the crew kipped down as best they could on the steel deck with a filthy blanket wrapped around them and an improvised pillow which was sometimes a tool chest, a box of tinned food or a sack of potatoes. Even in the comparatively roomy 'D' and 'E' classes only the captain had a regular bunk: in HMS *D8* it was a long drawer pulled out from beneath the chart table. The Second Captain (First Lieutenant) lay on two spare torpedoes with the space between filled with duffel coats and cotton waste; and the Third Hand bedded down underneath the electric oven. The latter was a welcome innovation when it first arrived (in 'D' boats) because until then a couple of hot plates were the only means of heating food or the severely rationed fresh water.

Washing was normally out of the question: Leading Stoker Haskins of *E14* noted laconically in his diary for 1 March 1914 that at 6.45 p.m., after an exciting action, 'we had a wash – the first for seven days and we certainly needed it'. Another ten days passed before Haskins noted that he was 'allowed to wash', by which time the need must have been extreme. In warm climates and often at some risk of being surprised by the enemy, considerate captains surfaced for 'Hands to bathe' whenever they could, with non-swimmers attached to heaving lines.

The Admiralty's mentality with regard to creature comforts was reminiscent of the early nineteenth century rather than the twentieth. A great deal more could have been done to alleviate the suffering of submariners at small expense, in return for enhanced efficiency. For example, better protection than a canvas 'dodger' around the bridge would have enabled lookouts to be much more alert. The lack of attention to welfare on board was not just due to ingrained Admiralty meanness dating back to the days of Samuel Pepys: there was an extraordinary lack of imagination among naval and civilian officers responsible for design, and very few of them ever experienced conditions at sea. And, as in other respects, submariners themselves did not state their case coherently in the right quarters. Things were not much better in the US Navy, but American habitability was to improve dramatically in time, so much so that a British officer remarked wonderingly of American 'pigboats': '. . . their design seemed cleaner than ours. In order to dive they must have had the same machinery . . . but it was not so much in evidence.'[5]

Meanwhile, the daily issue of an eighth of a pint of rum to all Royal Navy ratings and a capacious wine locker (mainly stocked with spirits) in the wardroom – which came to be abused more and more in many boats as the war ground on – afforded a temporary lift, just as it had in the days of sail.

Nothing was done, at Admiralty level, to improve matters in the Royal Navy until Winston Churchill, who had been First Sea Lord since 1911, enquired closely about submarine crews after hearing (from prisoners-of-war taken from a captured U-boat) that German U-boat men were given special rations and leave following each patrol. Living conditions were not altered, but from the summer of 1915 British submariners were able to enjoy tinned soup (one tin between two men) and delicacies such as Harris's pre-cooked bacon (each slice neatly separated by greaseproof paper) *or* a can of Palethorpe's sausages (also pre-cooked) and a tin of fruit for four. A tin of sardines was sometimes provided as a treat at tea-time, at the rate of four 'whales' per man. Better still, each crew was sent on forty-eight hours' leave after every second patrol. None of these awards was generous, but the way in which they were welcomed demonstrated just how poorly submariners had been treated until then.

The Germans, on the other hand, had a well-deserved reputation for thoroughness in all things, which contrasted with the casual do-it-yourself British approach to life below. It will be helpful to look at a U-boat in 1914 through German eyes. The outstandingly successful but primitive *U-9*, commanded by Kapitänleutnant Otto Weddigen (of whom more later), had Johannes Spiess as First Watch Officer (Second-in-Command). Spiess left comprehensive accounts of the boat and its devastating activities, translated in a US Intelligence document.[6] We can visualise *U-9*, from Spiess' own words:

Far forward in the pressure hull, which was cylindrical, was the forward torpedo room containing two torpedo tubes and two reserve torpedoes. Further astern was the Warrant Officers' compartment, which contained only small bunks for the Warrant Officers (Quartermaster and Machinist) and was particularly wet and cold.

Then came the Commanding Officer's cabin, fitted with only a small bunk and clothes closet, no desk being furnished. Whenever a torpedo had to be loaded forward or the tube prepared for a shot, both the Warrant Officers' and Commanding Officers' cabins had to be completely cleared out. Bunks and clothes cabinets then had to be moved into the adjacent officers' compartment, which was no light task owing to the lack of space in the latter compartment.

In order to live at all in the officers' compartments a certain degree of *finesse* was required. The Watch Officer's bunk was too small to permit him to lie on his back. He was forced to lie on one side and then, being wedged between the bulkhead to the right and the clothes-press on the left, to hold fast against the movements of the boat in a seaway. The occupant of the berth could not sleep with his feet aft as there was an electric fuse-box in the way. At times the cover of this box sprang open and it was all too easy to cause a short circuit by touching this with the feet. Under the sleeping compartments, as well as through the entire forward part of the vessel, were the electric accumulators which served to supply current to the electric motors for submerged cruising.

On the port side of the officer's compartment was the berth of the Chief Engineer, while the centre of the compartment served as a passageway through the boat. On each side was a small upholstered transom between which a folding table could be inserted. Two folding camp-chairs completed the furniture.

While the Commanding Officer, Watch Officer and Chief Engineer took their meals, men had to pass back and forth through the boat, and each time anyone passed the table had to be folded.

Further aft, the crew space was separated from the officers' compartment by a watertight bulkhead with a round watertight door for passage. On one side of the crew's space a small electric range was supposed to serve for cooking – but the electric heating coil and the bake-oven short-circuited every time an attempt was made to use them. Meals were always prepared on deck! For this purpose we had a small paraffin stove such as was in common use on Norwegian fishing vessels. This had the particular advantage of being serviceable even in a high wind.

The crew space had bunks for only a few of the crew – the rest slept in hammocks, when not on watch or on board the submarine mother-ship while in port.

The living spaces were not cased with wood. Since the temperature inside the boat was considerably greater than the sea outside, moisture in the air condensed on the steel hull-plates; the condensation had a very disconcerting way of dropping on a sleeping face, with every movement of the vessel. Efforts were made to prevent this by covering the face with rainclothes or rubber sheets. It was in reality like a damp cellar. [The Captain of one British D-boat used an open umbrella to protect his slumbers.]

The storage battery cells, which were located under the living spaces and filled with acid and distilled water, generated gas [hydrogen] on charge and discharge: this was drawn off through the ventilation system. Ventilation failure risked explosion, a catastrophe which occurred in several German boats.[7] If sea water got into the battery cells, poisonous chlorine gas was generated.

From a hygienic standpoint the sleeping arrangements left much to be desired; one awoke in the morning with considerable mucus in the nostrils and a so-called 'oil-head'.

The central station [control room] was abaft the crew space, closed off by a bulkhead both forward and aft. Here was the gyro compass and also the depth rudder hand-operating gear with which the boat was kept at the required level similar to a Zeppelin [presumably if the electrical system in the conning tower was not working or if the tower was overcrowded during an attack]. The bilge pumps, the blowers for clearing and filling the diving tanks – both electrically driven – as well as the air compressors were also here. In one small corner of this space stood a toilet [*Klosett*] screened by a curtain and, after seeing this arrangement, I understood why the officer I had relieved recommended the use of opium before all cruises which were to last over twelve hours.

In the engine room were the four Körting paraffin engines which could be coupled in tandem, two on each propeller shaft. The air required by these engines was drawn in through the conning-tower hatch, while the exhaust was led overboard through a long demountable funnel. Astern of the gas engines were the two electric motors for submerged cruising.

In the stern of the boat, right aft, was the after torpedo room with two stern torpedo tubes but without reserve torpedoes.

The conning tower is yet to be described. This was the battle station of the Commanding Officer and the Watch Officer. Here were located the two periscopes, a platform for the Helmsman and the 'diving piano' which consisted of twenty-four levers on each side controlling the valves for releasing air from the tanks. Near these were the indicator glasses and test cocks [to show tank levels].

Finally there was electrical controlling gear for depth steering [which was installed after building: operating the hydroplanes by hand in the control room was 'the work of an athlete' and the operator had to strip to the waist]; a depth indicator; voice pipes; and the electrical firing device for the torpedo tubes. [There was also a steering wheel with a compass in the tower besides similar fittings in the control room and on the bridge.]

Above the conning tower was a small bridge which was protected when cruising under conditions which did not require the boat to be in constant readiness for diving: a rubber strip was stretched along a series of stanchions screwed into the deck, reaching about as high as the chest. When in readiness for diving this was demounted, and there was a considerable danger of being washed overboard.

The Officer on Watch sat on the hatch coaming, the Petty Officer of the Watch near him, with his feet hanging through the hatch through which the air for the gas [paraffin] engines was being drawn. I still wonder why I was not afflicted with rheumatism in spite of leather trousers. The third man on watch, a seaman, stood on a small three-cornered platform abaft the conning tower; he was lashed to his station in heavy seas.

This was the general arrangement for all seagoing boats at that time of the Types 'U-5' to 'U-18' with few exceptions. [A post-war note by Spiess states that all but two of these boats are now lying at the bottom of the sea.]

Spiess did not mention one piece of equipment which conferred considerable operational benefits. This was a simple air purification plant (for removing carbon dioxide) allied to oxygen bottles which helped to prevent a man from becoming drowsy when submerged for a long period. Another notorious cause of doziness, alcohol, was forbidden in U-boats from one hour before diving; but many accounts suggest that even this quite liberal regulation was often lifted when the boat was safely submerged. Most British submarines were eventually equipped with carbon dioxide absorption units but there was seldom any way of providing oxygen in the early days: matches refused to strike when a boat had been submerged for twelve hours.

The effects of carbon dioxide – heavy breathing and depression – were made worse by the steady build-up of pressure from high-pressure air leaks compounded by venting internal tanks, torpedo tubes and the heads after blowing. When the boat did at last surface it was a prudent precaution to hold on to the Captain's legs when he opened the hatch: there was a real danger of him being shot out like a human cannonball and lost over the side. At the same time a dense fog formed down below due to the pressure being suddenly released in a saturated atmosphere.

When the engines were started the fresh air coming down the tower was greedily gulped, but nausea was a common reaction, especially for those climbing up to the bridge. Internal odours became even more offensive with the drop in pressure before the engines cleared the air. A foul stench was sucked out of the heads apparatus; wet bilges generated marsh gas and battery gases were also more noticeable. Random samples taken of bilge water in one British boat were found to contain 87 per cent sulphuric acid from battery cells which had splashed, leaked or overflowed.[8] The much-needed fresh air was soon accompanied by torrents of sea water when the boat picked up speed in a seaway. The bilges would be topped up and have to be emptied with buckets and pump-suctions; carefully dried electrical machinery would inevitably be wetted so that the little earth lamps glowed brightly and electric shocks were commonplace; and sickness renewed its assaults on cold exhausted bodies. On patrol, the cycle of foul air when submerged and sodden misery on the surface repeated itself day after cheerless day, with seldom a chance of doing business with the enemy.

The effect of prolonged discomfort on an individual naturally varied with his temperament, susceptibility to seasickness and response to danger. Action was by far the best morale booster, assuming that the crew had faith in their captain; but phlegmatic characters, so long as they were not in a position where rapid decisions were called for, were a great help in steadying the nerves of others. Martin Niemöller gave a nice picture of the stolid, rather elderly second-in-command or First Watch Officer (*Eins WO*) Oberleutnant Rohne in the slow, unhandy 'floating coffin' minelayer *U-73*.[9] The weather was abominable, the crew had more or less given up eating as 'devoid of purpose' and the engineer 'seemed doubtful of a happy issue of things'. But Rohne, sitting wedged on the Captain's bunk at what should have been breakfast time for all, was a splendid example of imperturbability. Oblivious to lockers breaking loose from bulkheads and gear crashing to the deck, he could be observed heartily enjoying a *Frühstück* of black bread spread with butter and tinned liver sausage, covered with a layer of marmalade and topped with an assortment of mixed pickles.

Besides common internal disorders, accidents and injuries were bound to occur. Here, too, the Germans were better served in having somebody qualified in first aid and basic medicine on board, and occasionally on long cruises even a doctor. In a British boat the Captain, First Lieutenant or Coxswain – none of them trained for the purpose – decided among themselves who would do the doctoring. A small medical handbook (with no particular application to submarines) was provided, mainly to discourage amateur operations or other drastic types of treatment. It stressed the benefits of fresh air and exercise and underlined the importance of choosing female companionship ashore with care. Venereal disease was not then as rife as it became later and – in the Royal Navy anyway – its more virulent form appears to have been more the perquisite of officers than ratings. The penalty of a serious sexually transmitted disease in The Trade was a terse note in red ink at the bottom of a man's service record: 'Discharged – syphilis'.

It was not until after the war, when many reports were collated by Rear Admiral (S) (the Head of the Submarine Service had by then been elevated from Commodore), that the British Admiralty realised that quite modest and inexpensive improvements to living conditions could result in substantial operational advantages. All that was needed was to make life below a little more tolerable so that crews would perform better.

In paying more regard to habitability and clothing, the German underwater arm had the operational edge on The Trade. Admiral Jellicoe remarked gloomily in 1914 that 'for a [British] boat to keep the sea for five or seven days was a considerable achievement'. Later, the boats did longer than that but one of the most experienced of the Royal Navy's commanding officers remarked, at the conclusion of the war, that 'U-boats used to spend thirty days at sea – two, three or even four times the length of British submarine patrols – but their living conditions were only a little better'. The 'little better', though, made all the difference. All the same, that CO, who seems to have agreed with the general opinion held on high that British crews (often coming from a very poor background) could cope whatever, went on to opine that 'in our boats the endurance was limited by the engines and not by the health of the crews. There should, however, be sleeping accommodation and all boats should have better washing facilities'. Another well-known CO, belonging to the old, hard school which did not believe in pandering to the lower deck, contented himself with recommending that 'dishcloths should be provided for Ship's Companies as well as anything that can be provided to make messing more cleanly and civilised'. Added together and digested by submarine staff and naval architects, minor recommendations of this kind were in due course adopted, but it took a long time to shake off the wartime image of The Trade (although the title itself, with its rather disreputable connotations, fell into disuse before the Armistice was signed).

German U-boat officers were not prone to philosophise in the stark world in which they found themselves losers after 1918, but Admiral Sir Reginald Bacon, who had been the first Inspecting Captain of Submarines at the beginning of the century, claimed to represent the view of British submariners in a speech made between the wars: 'I will end by giving you an expression of opinion about life in general in submarines. I always feel it is a strange thing to like, but if you do like it, which most do who take it up, you like it very much indeed.' Given the abysmal quality of life below, this was an astonishing thing to say; but that it was rare for anyone, anywhere, to request a transfer to surface ships suggests that Bacon may have been correct.

CHAPTER 3

Mechanics

The means of diving, surfacing, propelling and controlling a boat under water were simple and basically similar in all submarines. However, most (but not all) German U-boats were mechanically superior to British and other boats in several significant respects. The comparative systems need some description to account for apparent anomalies discussed in later chapters.

Buoyancy and Depth

Submariners have always been indebted to the principle discovered by the Greek mathematician Archimedes in the third century BC: if the weight of a body submerged in water equals the weight of the water it displaces, the body will tend neither to rise nor sink. In other words it is neutrally buoyant. If, on the other hand, it is heavier than the water it displaces it will go down and become more negatively buoyant as it goes down because external water pressure steadily increases with depth and compresses the body which consequently displaces less. Of course, if the body is positively buoyant, weighing less than the water it displaces, it will rise and stay on the surface.

The problem for submarine designers in the early days was to devise a safe method of destroying positive buoyancy so that the submarine could dive and move to a state of neutral buoyancy at any given depth on an even keel; then it would remain submerged without bobbing up to the surface or plunging to the depths. The solution was to equip a boat with large tanks along its length with a volume such that, when flooded, they brought it to the desired neutral condition and when empty gave it sufficient buoyancy to stay afloat.

These 'main ballast tanks' could be either inside or outside the pressure hull – the submarine proper – which was always circular in cross-section to resist pressure. In both cases water was admitted through flood holes at the bottom and the air, which provided buoyancy on the surface, was released through vents at the top. The flood holes on external tanks were usually open except in cases where they were sealed by Kingston valves for additional safety or so that the tanks could be used for carrying extra fuel. Thus, the only action normally necessary to fill the ballast tanks, assuming that relevant Kingstons had already been opened, was to open the 'main vents' at the top. Submarines like the British 'D' and 'E' classes, with this arrangement allied to long blisters running about two-thirds the length of a boat, were known as saddle-tank types. So-called double-hull or partial double-hull boats, such as the British 'G' and 'J' classes and the large ocean-going German boats, had external tanks wrapped virtually all around the pressure hull: their form was suited to high speed on the surface and a double-hull provided a large reserve of buoyancy, but these tanks took longer to flood and so the submarine was slower to dive.

The single-hull pattern was preferred by the Irish-American John Philip Holland; double-hull designs are credited to the French Laubeuf and the Italian Laurenti, the latter restricting his double-hull to the middle portion of his boats.

All the early boats – the British 'A', 'B' and 'C' classes, for example – had internal main ballast tanks and were therefore single-hull or 'spindle-hull' types. Their fat cigar shape, unhindered by external bulges, was good for submerged performance and hence ideal for coastal defence; but a long thin hull was best for long-range 'oversea' operations. In a single hull the volume of the tanks was necessarily small because they took up much-needed space inside the submarine, and positive buoyancy on the surface was therefore low. Every tank had to be fitted with a Kingston valve to shut it off when full, otherwise sea pressure submerged was exerted not only on the pressure hull but also on the relatively weak walls of the ballast tanks which had to be flat or concave. Moreover, it could never be certain that Kingston valves would provide an absolutely pressure-tight seal.

On the whole, saddle tanks were preferred in all but the German navy. Today, the very fast and manoeuvrable Western nuclear submarines have an uncluttered pressure hull extended forward and aft by light ballast tanks which continue the streamlined shape. Soviet designers, on the other hand, favour double-hulls for survivability because they provide a high degree of protection against anti-submarine weapons (which do not then detonate directly against the pressure hull) and allow an exceptionally large amount of reserve buoyancy which is available in the event of action damage. Considerations of this sort are not new: the First World War laid down firm foundations for subsequent developments.

While tanks were being flooded (that is, filled) at the order to dive by klaxon ('hooter') or some other kind of diving alarm, the propulsion was changed over to the electrical motor(s), while the hydroplanes forward (or on the conning tower amidships in the early classes) and 'diving rudders' aft (styled 'after hydroplanes' later) were set to dive. Water flowing over their surfaces drove the submarine down at an angle until the requisite depth was reached. The operators then worked the planes to maintain that depth – to within 30 cm (1 foot) or so – or change depth as ordered. All this was quite easy as long as the submarine was neutrally buoyant, but it seldom was because it was difficult to calculate the weight (that is, to 'trim' a boat) precisely and then allow for alterations due to stores and fuel being consumed, torpedoes being fired, changing sea-water densities, the movement of men forward and aft and so on. A boat was therefore equipped with at least three – and often many more – internal trimming and compensating tanks: basically, there was one right forward, one right aft and one amidships. Water could be flooded into these tanks or pumped out, and it could also be pumped or blown from forward to aft and vice versa to correct the longitudinal trim. The First Lieutenant (Second Captain) in British boats, or the Engineer Officer in German, French and American submarines, was responsible for calculating the initial quantity of water in the trimming tanks and for 'catching the trim' on diving; thereafter the Officer of the Watch took over.

Trimming was an art rather than a science. Some officers learned it quickly (assisted by heavy hints from the Coxswain or Petty Officer on the after planes), while others never did become expert and were the recipients of continual wounding remarks.

Far from flooding in water to go deep, it had to be pumped out to compensate for compression but some boats were given special internal tanks which could be flooded to give temporary negative buoyancy and then blown quickly when they were in a particular hurry to dive or go deeper. Such a tank came to be known as Q-tank in British submarines and Negative tank in American boats.

The maximum operational diving depth, with a fair margin of safety, varied considerably between classes but it was generally about 30 or 60 metres (100–200 feet). German U-boats were able to dive deeper than almost any others throughout the war. Their standard test depth was 60 metres (200 feet) but they frequently went well below this to avoid the attentions of anti-submarine craft, and proved that the hulls could withstand the sea pressure of 9 kg per square cm (130 lb per square inch) at 90 metres (300 feet). The 'E' boats, which bore the brunt of the war in the Royal Navy, were deemed safe by the designers at 60 metres (200 feet) with the proviso that 'it was impossible to be quite sure on this matter without actual trials'. In 1917 E40 struck the bottom in 53 fathoms of water – 97 metres (318 feet) – but the only problems were leaks in the engine-room hatch and stern tubes. French and Italian designs were claimed to be capable of 45 metres (150 feet) but British constructors were doubtful about this, as they were about their own 'G' class designed for 60 metres (200 feet) but normally limited to 30 metres (100 feet): the 'H', 'L' and 'R' classes were originally specified for 75 metres (250 feet) but advised operationally not to go below 45 metres (150 feet). In fact L2 once went to 90 metres (300 feet) by accident and survived with only a few leaks. British commanding officers seem to have been left in some doubt about what was safe and what was not: instructions were vague and continually changing, not least because hulls were never formally tested below 30 metres (100 feet) during the war.

The Germans, who could not risk taking new boats out of the Baltic into deep water for test dives, built a pressure dock containing a huge reinforced steel cylinder for proving hull strength. This was invaluable throughout both world wars.

With an eye to emergencies and starting with the last in line of the 'C' class, some British boats were fitted with one or more drop keels weighing about 10 tons each, which could be quickly slipped to obtain positive buoyancy. A number also had mushroom anchors which could be dropped and raised from inside the submarine. These came to be used quite frequently for hovering in shallow areas where bottoming (the more usual tactic to save battery amps) might have been uncomfortable.

Control submerged

At the beginning there was much controversy about whether a submarine should dive on an even keel or at an angle. Simon Lake, the famous American designer, was a firm believer in diving and depth-changing on a more or less even keel. The Irish-American John Philip Holland, arguably the father of all modern submarines, took the opposite view and 'steered his boat down and up on an incline by the action of horizontal rudders placed in the stern'. Lake's principle of having both bow and stern hydroplanes eventually won the day because they were much better for control than Holland's single set of 'diving rudders' aft. Nevertheless, Holland's method of pitching a boat to dive or change depth became universal, and so a combination of the Lake and Holland philosophies came to be adopted.

The British 'A' boats, first laid down in 1902, were deployed only for defensive purposes in the war. The following is a first-hand account[1] of the very slow diving procedure in HMS *A6*:

Trimming a submarine in those early days was about a day's work. We did a standing trim as it was called. Having got to the diving area off Sandown Bay, the petrol engine was stopped and the crew went to Diving Stations: being very confined they sat alongside the valves etc. they were responsible for. The conning-tower hatch was closed and the captain stood on a moveable shelf hooked on to the conning-tower ladder with his head in a sort of dome like a diver's helmet in the top of the hatch. This dome had glass scuttles round it and water was admitted to the ballast tanks of the submarine until the buoyancy was so far reduced that the surface of the sea came up to the level of the scuttles. The submarine had then a matter of a few pounds' buoyancy, and by going ahead with the main motors was forced underwater by the after planes at an angle of five degrees down by the bow. Taken down to her depth the after planes maintained such depth by angling the boat now up or now down as required. [A-boats were fitted retrospectively with depth-control hydroplanes either on the conning tower – where they were ineffective – or at the bows.]

The whole procedure of trimming was most tricky because, when buoyancy was reduced, the submarine became more and more horizontally unstable and would take up most alarming angles unless promptly anticipated. There were trimming tanks forward and aft, interconnected, by which water could be blown from forward to aft or vice versa. This was often too slow a method to correct a sudden desire of the boat to stand on her head or stern, so we generally had the fattest member of the crew available to dash forward or aft as necessary until the water passing from one trimming tank to the other could correct the angle and release the human ballast for his next dash!

Sometimes, when nearing the end of the trim when little buoyancy was left, a wave bigger than the rest would plop on top of the conning tower and the boat would sink – so water had to be blown out of the ballast tanks and a new start made. We didn't realise in those days that by going ahead we could gain control of the boat. It was all rather like someone learning to swim and being afraid of putting his head under water.

Speed was of course the means of controlling a submarine submerged when it was a little out of trim, but this used more precious amps from the battery. An Officer of the Watch who continually speeded up was not popular.

According to British instructions for diving and maintaining depth (similar in other navies):

When diving at a steady depth, the Second Coxswain at the foreplanes keeps the submarine at the depth ordered, using 'Dive' or 'Rise' helm as required. The Coxswain uses the after planes so as to keep the submarine horizontal. Thus, supposing the submarine is above the depth ordered, the Second Coxswain puts on 'Dive' helm, which will force the bow down, and the Coxswain will put on 'Rise' helm to check the angle: both planes are now in the same direction, that is leading edge down; and the submarine is being forced down nearly horizontal. When at the required depth, the Second Coxswain eases his helm, letting the bow rise under the effect of the after planes; the Coxswain, when he sees this, eases, and if necessary reverses, his helm and the submarine arrives at the proper depth horizontal.

When attacking in good weather conditions, with a fine trim and with the submarine proceeding on a straight course at slow speed up to moderate submerged speed, this method whereby the coxswains are working independently, one to maintain depth and the other to keep the submarine level, should result in the variation of the depth line not exceeding one to one-and-a-half feet. The amount of helm on the planes under such conditions should not exceed ten degrees as larger amounts lead to varying resistances on the submarine and so affect the speed while causing unsteady diving.

Under bad weather conditions, if cooperation is lacking or the planes are not skilfully used, the submarine will 'porpoise' considerably and either break surface, betraying her position, or go deep and lose sight of the target.

When at watch diving stations it should, whenever possible, be the practice to use the planes 'in hand' [rather than in electrical or hydraulic power]. It will make for steadier depth-keeping if the hydroplane operators, through the personal exertion required, realise that it is better to use a little helm as soon as the slightest alteration in the depth or angle is noticed, and not wait until too late when more exertion will be required to obtain the necessary larger angles of the plane.

Whenever practicable a submarine should always be controlled on one set of planes only. This readily teaches each plane operator the relation between the depth needle and the angle, and trains them to dive the submarine when one set of planes is out of action.

For a German novice's view of submerging we can turn again to Oberleutnant Johannes Spiess when he first went to sea in 1912 as IWO of the famous *U-9*. At that time diving was 'somewhat of an event,' he said, 'since the boat was not quite technically reliable and the manoeuvre was very troublesome, taking over five minutes'.[2] He continues:

All new submarines found the business rather awesome. The reassuring clatter and rumble of the engines ceased immediately when the diving alarm sounded, to be replaced, amid a sudden silence, by the loud rush of air escaping from the ballast tanks and an unfamiliar string of orders while men raced to their diving stations. Then the boat passed through a period of dubious stability as it settled, down by the bow, into its element and this was worryingly evident to a seaman accustomed to relative stable surface ships.

The commanding officer of *U-9*, Kapitänleutnant Otto Weddigen, had achieved a reputation for efficiency on peacetime exercises, and Spiess was congratulated on going to the boat for his first submarine posting. Weddigen was an excellent teacher and allowed his junior officers great freedom of action: Spiess felt 'more like a younger comrade than a subordinate'. There was certainly much for the U-boat men to learn about the capabilities of their craft which were widely underestimated. As late as December 1913 it was a matter for congratulation that six U-boats remained secured at buoys in the Helgoland Bight for a whole week of winter weather, and the crews were accorded great respect on their return to Wilhelmshaven for what was believed to be a world record. Whatever the British Admiralty may have thought, most of the men in *Unterseeboote* were unskilled at their trade before the war, and so all the more credit is due to them for accomplishing so much so soon when they embarked on war patrols.

Considerable precautions were taken during Kiel week in June 1914 to prevent visiting British ships, taking part in the event as unwelcome but obligatory guests, from learning the true state of affairs. Parts of the bridge superstructures were removed to confuse an estimate of displacement, engine exhaust funnels were laid flat, radio masts were taken down, and the boats were assigned to outlying berths to make a count difficult. All this was amateurish counter-espionage, but the Germans were also ill-informed about British submarines. A paltry 40,000 marks (£2000) was allocated to the German Navy's share of the Secret Service, a sum equal to 1.3 per cent of the 3 million marks appropriated for building a single U-boat at the time. (The cost of a U-boat more than doubled during the war: in 1914 it was 4110 marks per ton but by 1918 it was more than 9000 marks per ton.)[3]

On his 1912 introductory Baltic cruise in *U-9*, Spiess wrote:

It is an exciting moment when one stands for the first time in the conning tower and notes through the thick glass of the small ports how the deck becomes gradually covered with water and the bow slowly sinks. Have all the openings been properly closed and is the pressure hull tight?

In the clear sea water, when the sun is shining, the silvery air bubbles sparkle all over the boat's hull and rise as in an aquarium. I was always interested in observing the surface of the water from below after diving as it looked like moving glass. Under favourable lighting conditions it is possible to see about twenty metres under water, but we were never able to see the bow of the boat. At times, when the boat was lying still on the bottom, we could observe fish swimming close by the ports of the conning tower, attracted by the electric light which was shining through.

To put a submarine on the bottom without undue shock requires a certain amount of expert handling on the part of the Commanding Officer. The boat is brought down by the horizontal rudders until contact with the ground is slowly made; and then, after stopping the motors, the regulating (i.e. compensating) tanks are flooded until the boat is heavier by several tons and remains anchored of its own weight – that is, provided there is no heavy seaway or strong tide.

Although largely forgotten in the present nuclear age, bottoming was such a favourite tactic on all sides that it deserves some comment. It rested the battery and the crew while making a boat difficult to detect with hydrophone listening devices – because complete silence could be kept – although it became extremely uncomfortable when bottom sweeps came into play. It was imprudent to attempt bottoming where the seabed was rocky or very muddy but there were plenty of areas where bottoming was safe. The British orders[4] will serve for all:

Sitting on the bottom

1. Obtain a good trim and pull up the log [a little propeller device to register speed, which could be lowered through a small tank in the bottom of the boat] proceeding at slowest possible speed and stemming any known current.

2. Stop the motors when within forty feet of the bottom and watch the depth gauge. Trim should be adjusted to obtain very slight negative buoyancy.

3. Allow the submarine to sink to the bottom horizontally or slightly bow down, checking her by blowing a little main ballast if movement is too rapid.
   Note: The bump should be such as to be imperceptible (sic).

4. Admit more water into an empty internal tank so as to ensure that the submarine will remain stationary.

5. Keep a careful eye on the battery tank and all glands.
   Note: If the submarine takes the bottom beam-on to a tideway she will at once list over until she has swung fore-and-aft to the direction of the tide.

Coming off the bottom

1. Go to diving stations (i.e. not 'watch diving').

2. Put the motors' armatures in parallel for maximum power.

3. Pump out the internal tank flooded before bottoming.

4. Blow midship main ballast tank.

5. As soon as the submarine is clear of the bottom (10 or 15 feet) go ahead and flood main ballast again.

6. Correct trim at about 60 feet.

7. Listen on hydrophones and, if clear, come to periscope depth, adjusting speed as necessary.

   Note: If the submarine starts bumping on the bottom come off at once. Submarines should never bottom on mud if it can be avoided, and the softer the mud the more the danger of choking hull outlets, and of suction effects on the hull.

One custom relevant to control was mandatory throughout the underwater services everywhere. It was underlined, with heavy type, in the German U-boat instructions: 'All orders or replies given for flooding, diving, blowing etcetera are to be repeated in order to ensure that the order or reply has been correctly understood.' Submariners still strictly adhere to this practice today.

Propulsion

A submarine employed one or more air-breathing engines on the surface for propulsion and also to charge the batteries by driving the main electric motor(s) for generating power. There were several variations on the theme, made possible by an arrangement of clutches connecting the engine, electric motor and propeller on a single shift. A tail clutch between the motor and the propeller enabled the former to be used as a generator without turning the screw; and an engine clutch between the engine and the motor permitted the engine to be disconnected on diving at which time the motor, supplied by the battery, took over. If a boat had two shafts the arrangement was identical on both sides, but it was quite common on the surface – especially in German boats – to use one electric motor for propulsion and run the engine on the other side, with the tail clutch disconnected, for charging and 'floating the load', thus making up a form of diesel-electric propulsion.

Very small submarines like the British 'B' class and German 'UB-1' type were grossly under-engined and had to remain stationary on the surface to provide sufficient power for a charge. This was a severe handicap in enemy-controlled waters because diving took a long time from stopped, and several boats were 'jumped' by anti-submarine units as a result.

Trying to avoid surfacing to put on a charge, more than one British commanding officer devised a crude air-intake pipe sticking up above the sea for running an engine at shallow depth. The experiments, foreshadowing the proper German *Schnorchel* of the Second World War, were frowned upon and dangerous but they worked, more or less. For example, Lieutenant 'Paddy' Ryan of *C3* had an extension fitted to a small cowl ventilator for diving on the petrol engine with this up; and Guy D'Oyly Hughes in *E35* had a wooden plug made in the depot ship *Vulcan* to fit the conning-tower lid.

E35's plug (not the best substitute for steel) was pierced with a 15-centimetre (6-inch) hole in the centre to which was riveted a short copper collar; on to this was shipped a copper tube 1.8 metres (6 feet) long. On the underside of the plug were two screwed eyelets fitted with short rope lanyards and clip-hooks which secured the whole to the conning-tower ladder when the plug was put in place. While on anti-submarine patrol, *E35* ran her main engines and charged batteries with the funnel at shallow periscope depth even during heavy weather. A tarpaulin was slung from the conning-tower lower hatch to the beam torpedo-tube well. Water came down with the air (just as it did when the conning tower was open on the surface) but it could be removed from the well by the ballast pump. D'Oyly Hughes, notorious for enjoying risks (as will be seen later), was hazarding his submarine with the device because it lessened the integrity of the vital upper lid; but he may have been right in believing he would have been in more danger on the surface with submerged U-boats in the vicinity.

Unlike the Royal Navy, the German fleet never had petrol (gasoline) engines, but used paraffin and then diesel oil. Until the completion of HMS *D1* with diesel engines in 1909 – a major step forward – all British boats were fuelled by petrol, which not only caused continual fires and explosions, but also made men drunk on the fumes. This was deemed an advantage by certain stokers who claimed to enjoy the effects despite the appalling hangovers that followed, but there were times when an entire engine-room crew became totally irresponsible at sea and nobody considered that a joke. In such a state a man would be liable to switch on an electric motor and thereby ignite the petrol vapour. On one occasion in C6 the Captain and the head of The Trade himself, Commodore Sydney Hall, were both observed half-seas over while the boat was refuelling, arguing violently about who was the drunkest until they were forcibly removed into the fresh air.

In the first generation of petrol boats three white mice could be found because, as a postcard of the day explained, 'being extremely sensitive they notify the slightest escape of gasoline by squeaking'. The useful little creatures had been omitted from the complement long before war broke out, thereby reputedly saving the King's navy their allowance of one shilling a day for food and keep. They were not very reliable sentries anyway because they were stuffed so full of food by sailors that they remained comatose throughout their service careers. Nor did they 'notify' the presence of dangerous hydrogen gas evolving from lead-acid cells.

Before *U-19* was commissioned in 1913 with the first MAN diesels the German navy depended upon Körting paraffin engines, which required a tall, heavy exhaust funnel to be erected before the engines could be started. Fuel consumption was very high and such quantities were burned in the cylinders that vast volumes of billowing white smoke belched out of the exhaust making a boat horribly conspicuous. At night, showers of sparks and even flames were clearly visible. The funnel also had to be lowered and stowed before a Körting boat could dive, which added considerably to the time required to disappear. It was therefore customary, when sighting a hostile vessel at long range, for the U-boat to stop the paraffin engine, lower the funnel and make the first part of its approach on the surface, running on her electric motors. Naturally, the Captain dived for the attack (unless the target was unarmed) but the prolonged run on motors made unnecessary inroads

46

into the battery capacity available for subsequent submerged operations. Limitations like these make the successes achieved by boats like *U-9* seem even more remarkable.

The French favoured steam propulsion on the surface, but it proved unsuitable for North Sea weather. Lieutenant Deville, Commandant of *Archimède*, found the steep seas a startling revelation after the coastal service he had been used to. *Archimède*, laid down in 1907, displaced 577 tons on the surface with a healthy 273 tons of reserve buoyancy. She was supposedly an exceptionally seaworthy submersible of a type that Laubeuf, the retired Engineer-in-Chief of the French Navy and then the most renowned European architect in the submarine field, was constantly advocating in the Press as being vastly better than the all-electric harbour-protection submarines unique to France. But Laubeuf, who had such great influence on design, must be held at least partly responsible for the fact that boats like *Archimède* were simply not up to the stresses of patrolling in the open sea.

On 17 December 1914 *Archimède* was on patrol off Helgoland when a gale blew up. Deville reluctantly decided that he would have to return to harbour, but hardly had he altered course westwards when a big wave struck the funnel – always the most vulnerable part of a steam-powered submarine. The funnel was partially displaced and could not be lowered sufficiently to shut the watertight hull valve, and Deville was unable to dive. Water poured down the aperture and had to be baled out by the crew who passed buckets from hand to hand. Lieutenant Godfrey Herbert, the British Liaison Officer on board, was much admired by the French *matelots* for taking his turn with the bucket-chain. He displayed a degree of cheerfulness not expected from an Englishman. When one of the crew helpfully remarked '*Il fait très mauvais temps, Monsieur,*' Herbert replied, in schoolboy French, '*Oui, mais après le mauvais temps vient le beau temps.*' This immensely encouraged the dispirited crew who shouted the catchwords in chorus whenever a particularly heavy deluge of water threatened to defeat the efforts of the bucket brigade.

Submarines with funnels were too vulnerable, but the Royal

Navy failed to learn the lesson. Notwithstanding Admiral Jacky Fisher's pronouncement in 1913 that 'the most fatal error imaginable would be to put steam engines in a submarine', The Trade forged ahead with the disastrous *Swordfish* and the 'K' class a couple of years later.

It was with great gratitude that the navies of the world welcomed Herr Rudolf Diesel's invention of 1893, which was much the same as the compression-ignition engine patented in Britain three years earlier by Herbert Akroyd Stuart. The American submariners did not commission their first two diesel boats, *E1* and *E2*, until February 1912, three or four years after the major European navies. Coming from a country where the Cadillac and Oldsmobile companies were sufficiently confident to mass-produce motor cars, they had suffered remarkably few breakdowns, explosions or so-called gas-jags – intoxication – with gasoline engines.

Although American submariners had their technical problems and they were not too good at tactics, they were particularly adept at making repairs at sea (as the Society of Engineers noted rather significantly) and they were especially interested in the effects of sea-water density on buoyancy and trimming. Trials off Annapolis showed that a submarine could 'sit' on the layer caused by a marked temperature change at whatever depth. It was an ability that became extremely useful and which led to the further discovery that a boat could hide acoustically beneath such a layer. However, the excuse of density variations offered by Lieutenant Hincamp USN to explain why a large number of practice torpedoes was lost in Chesapeake Bay sounds a little thin.[5]

Endurance and speed varied enormously between different types in different navies, but most diesel submarines could make between 12 and 16 knots on the surface, and their range was markedly better than surface ships. For instance, the modest *U-19* of 637/837 tons – the first German diesel boat – could go for more than 4000 nautical miles at her full speed of 15.4 knots, 5300 miles at 9.5 knots or 7600 miles at 8 knots; and subsequent types had up to 50 per cent greater range than that. The maximum speed, again taking *U-19* as a fairly typical example, was 9.6 knots although that could be maintained for only one hour before the batteries were drained. At 5 knots submerged, a more meaningful figure, she could go for 80 miles without recharging.

The diving time for *U-19*, from the normal surface condition with diesels running, was 75 seconds, but successive types (other than the really big boats) were able to reach periscope depth in 30 or 40 seconds. The 'UC-80'-class boats at the end of the war, displacing 480/560 tons, held the all-time record of 15 seconds. These figures compare with 65 seconds for the renowned *U-9* even after the clumsy exhaust mast had been lowered.

Practically all the German U-boats had the edge on the workhorse British 'oversea' 'E' class which had a reasonable top speed on the surface of 14 knots and 9 knots submerged (for one hour) but a considerably more restricted surface range of 3000 miles at an economical 10 knots.

There was good reason for the disparity in endurance between German and British submarines. To The Trade, 'oversea' meant the German coastline: from Portsmouth to Wilhelmshaven was only 620 nautical miles, and it was much less from ports on the east coast. U-boats, on the other hand, would have to deploy around Scotland to the Atlantic or the Irish Sea – implying a range of 5000 to 6000 miles – although 2000 or 3000 miles would be enough for operations in the English Channel. Since the comparatively long-range *U-19* and her three sisters were ordered in October 1910, the suspicion arises that the U-boat arm, if not the Kaiser, envisaged a war on trade – *Handelskrieg* – in the approaches from the Atlantic long before it was openly discussed (or admitted by post-war German apologists).

General Construction

When British submariners looked closely at German boats immediately after the war they exclaimed at the simpler, lighter but more robust diesels, their smaller electrical fittings, their standardisation of equipment (for easier maintenance and training), their more efficient ventilating systems and a host of minor technicalities which they reckoned were better. One distinguished British officer said that British diesels looked crude by comparison, and another remarked ruefully:

U-boats of each class are built absolutely to a properly designed drawing. When examining a certain type of U-boat and finding out the position of certain pipes, fittings etc., they would all be found in another boat of the class in the same position. In our submarine construction this is not the case. Our submarine builders are allowed to, and do, place any fittings, leads, pipes, ventilating trunks, etc. where and how they please. There are no properly designed drawings, with the result that the submarine takes longer to build than she should. The result of this is also seen in the rush to complete the submarine, where each separate trade tries to take the easiest place to put whatever fitting or pipe that has to go into the submarine, and there is no real authority to say where such a fitting or pipe should be placed.[6]

The submarine captains gathered in the smoking room of their depot ship, HMS *Maidstone*, were particularly incensed by the apparent lack of coordination between the major building firms Vickers and Yarrow. Lieutenant Commander Leir (*E4*) thought that 'a little friendly chat between the two might be fruitful and fortunate – for the submarine officers'.

Sheer carelessness by British ship-builders was not unknown. For example, on 18 September 1917 Lieutenant Commander Hervey-Macleay of *E27*, built at Yarrow on the Clyde, wrote to Mr H. G. Parker, Engineer in Charge of Construction, with a long list of complaints at a time when three years of war and twenty-six previous boats of the same type should have provided ample experience for shipyards everywhere. While generally good confidential reports on Hervey-Macleay by his Captain (S) included a comment that he was 'tactless and required subduing from time to time'[7] (and *E27*'s unofficial motto was 'The Devil looks after his own'), the letter is revealing for all that:

We have just found a nasty thing, it was discovered by smell. That after well across the boat at 41-42 sta. had never been cleaned out before they put in the main line cross-connection pipe, and contained a wonderful collection of things, including an empty petrol can, sacking, sweat rags, and all sorts of pieces, and to finish the thing there was about two foot of rotten shavings and water down the sounding machine drain. You will be glad to hear that we were quite right about that stern cap, and Noble was wrong, it should have had grease caps on the hinge of it, as the thing has jammed closed and has taken a great deal of oil and persuasion to open it, but is all right if it is worked every day.

Since starting this I have found that the bottle wells are in the same state as the other well. We have also found some half-finished meals under the bunks and no paint! By the way, please do not repeat this, as it is only for your information.

The Williams Janney [steering motor] holding up coil, that arrived about two days before we sailed, was connected up the wrong way and was a source of great annoyance for a long time until we found out what was wrong. Incidentally, I have got rid of the Petty Officer TGM [Torpedo Gunner's Mate] also my RNR Sub: so we may be able to get ahead a little now. But up to date we have found nothing to compete with the torpedo stowages, the after one is nearly as bad as the others.

Will you ask Dadd, by telephone, if he will write and let me know if there is any hope of getting any of the stores that I told him were short, as they want me to sign for them, and I am refusing, I wrote to him, but have had no answer yet. . . .

Anyhow you can console yourself that we have far and away the best arranged and finished boat here. . . .

The Captain's last comment is indicative of the state of affairs.

Supervision during the building and fitting-out period seems to have been markedly poor in some yards. Perhaps it would have helped if senior naval management had been given some submarine instruction: the Engineer Captain at Sheerness expressed his interest in the business of submerging while visiting a boat, but asked the First Lieutenant where he got the water to fill the main ballast tanks.

Doubtless alcohol among a dockyard workforce was responsible for some of the shoddiness. The British government was worried about the high level of drinking during the war[8] and introduced a 'no treating' rule with fines for those who broke it. The law brought scant results, however, and 'Squiff' Asquith, Prime Minister until December 1916, hardly set a good example, although King George V dutifully gave up spirits for the duration. Naval officers are not on record as emulating the Sailor King in this respect, and submarine sailors were not slow off the mark when the pubs opened; the temptations when a boat was building or in refit were manifold.

The results, in the shape of the submarine hardware, were not always ideal; but thorough captains made the best of what was sometimes a bad job. In fact, thoroughness was agreed to be the hallmark of a first-class commanding officer. Time and again it was listed as a prime requisite in both the British and German navies. Above all, though, a good captain acknowledged his indebtedness to the engine-room staff: on them the success or failure of a patrol largely depended.

Meanwhile, the British Admiralty was not prepared to tolerate criticism of dockyards or design. As late as 1934, sixteen years after the Armistice, a thoughtful and constructively critical paper prepared by Engineer Captain George Villar RN who examined the shortcomings of the 'E' class, resulted in that 'most energetic and exceptionally efficient officer'[9] being put on half pay for several years before being re-employed on relatively mundane duties when the next war came.

It was to be repeatedly demonstrated throughout the First World War that the German U-boat arm enjoyed notable mechanical advantages, not because more money or talent was available but simply because designers and shipbuilders were thoroughly painstaking, well organised, rational, and willing to listen to the users of their products.

CHAPTER 4

Finding the Enemy

Today, submarines detect their prey with sonar equipment designed to hear sound under water at ranges of up to 100 miles or more. Complex electronic support measures (ESM) enable them to 'hear' enemy radar and radio emissions, and sophisticated periscopes are capable of viewing by night as well as by day. Boats at sea have reliable radio communication circuits and are seldom out of touch with base. In other words, they know what is happening over an extremely wide area. Their principal problem is to sort out the mass of data continually coming in.

It was not like that during the First World War, when the first essential in finding the enemy was for a commanding officer to know where he was himself. But in wartime, with artificial aids to navigation like lights and buoys often removed, with no chance to take a sight for days on end, harassed by the enemy, with compasses often 'acting queerly', a submarine went 'by Guess and by God'. That was the frank phrase coined by British navigating officers, often the captains themselves, to describe the erratic ways and means available for finding the way. Virtually blind, frequently having to estimate their position by dead reckoning, with unknown tidal streams and currents to contend with, they guessed and prayed inwardly that they guessed right: the rest was in the hands of Providence. Alas, Providence frequently failed them.

A compass was obviously the prime requirement, but none could be wholly trusted. The German Anschultz gyro may have been a little more robust than the British Sperry first installed in early 1915, but all gyros were apt to topple or deviate wildly when rolling in heavy weather, or 'go off the board' under counter-attack. The first wave of German

U-boats was particularly liable to gyro error – up to 90 degrees in the otherwise trustworthy *U-9*.

Some boats had no more than a magnetic projector compass outside the hull or in the conning tower. It was prone to all kinds of vagaries: the light inside fused at the slightest provocation; the optical tube leading to the control room fogged with damp; and it was impossible to compensate accurately for deviation on a compass subject to a continually changing magnetic field. When the engines were started to drive the electric motors as dynamos they produced some strange effects on the compass card because the cables leading to the batteries forward and amidships were not magnetically screened; despite the compass-correcting coils which eventually came to be fitted, this anomaly was enough to persuade a captain to charge batteries on the surface by day when he could see where he was, rather than by night when a boat would have been much less detectable. Untrustworthy compasses were also one of the reasons for submarines sometimes being towed, or at least escorted, by surface ships out towards their patrol areas during the first months of the war.

Most boats carried a portable liquid compass as a standby. This was stowed in the conning tower and brought up to the bridge when necessary, complete with a binnacle similar to that supplied for use in picket boats. This instrument later came to be known as Faithful Freddie and saved many a submarine navigator from bewilderment.

A naïve little note was appended to the instructions for British officers concerning the care of compasses: 'It is a very good thing to be always checking your compasses one by the other while at sea. They are not very likely to all go wrong at the same time.' Unfortunately, that is often exactly what they did. When electrical supplies to the gyro failed an alarm bell rang. Amid the shattering hammer-blows of depth-charges, with lights going out and water jetting in, the classic response to the gyro alarm was a fairground cry in the control room to 'Give the gentleman a bag of nuts, Maria'; but the system, as long as it was supplied with power, gave no indication of error. All the navigator could do was to check the instrument against the sun, which was not apt to shine much on a wintry North Sea.

Another vague factor was distance run through the water. A log, typically of the Forbes type lowered down to project beneath the hull, depended upon a tiny propeller which revolved a set number of times for each nautical mile travelled. This was connected to a commutator which transmitted electrical signals (usually 100 per mile) to a distance recorder as well as to a magneto-generator which generated current proportional to the speed at which the log's propeller revolved and hence the speed of the boat. At any rate that was what it was intended to do, but it was prone to fouling by seaweed, and nobody ever succeeded in calibrating it over the full range of speeds. Its readings had to be recorded in the handwritten control-room log – the diary in which all incidents were recorded and upon which Boards of Enquiry and Courts Martial based their findings – but a prudent navigator treated them with the distrust they deserved.

Celestial sights were taken on the surface whenever possible (nowadays the periscope embodies an instrument for the purpose) but it was a miserable performance in anything but calm conditions, and there was always the danger of being surprised by the enemy. The sextant was continually soaked by spray and had to be wrapped in a towel between sights while the navigator tried to retain his balance on the swaying, jerking bridge. In rough weather, with such a low height of eye, it was very difficult to judge the true horizon and bring down the observed sun, moon or star accurately on to it. Even though they were treated with reverence, the chronometer and deck watch might not show the exact time; if it was wrong by even a few seconds substantial errors would be introduced. Then, if some reasonably satisfactory sights were obtained, there were no rapid reduction tables of the kind available today: it could take an hour or more to work out the position with the aid of an Almanac and five-figure logarithms from the Haversine Tables, not a welcome task when officers were standing 'watch and watch', two hours on and two hours off. The American and German navies sensibly employed Quartermasters (specialised Senior Ratings) who as a rule were outstandingly good – better than many navigating officers in British boats with the honourable exception of RNR officers from the Merchant Navy (in boats lucky enough to have Third Hands) who were generally quick, skilled and accurate.

In short, navigation – like trimming – was more of an art than a science; and the best of artists had very poor materials to work with. The following example of a British navigational error illustrates the potential consequences.

The loss of HMS E17

During the first watch (8 p.m. to midnight) on 5 January 1916, HMS *E17* (Lieutenant Commander J. A. G. Moncrieff, later Sir Guy of that Ilk) was running on the surface at 12 knots, bound for the Helgoland Bight. It was a black night, and a light to moderate south-westerly wind was blowing over a moderately rough sea. Judging from fishing-vessel lights sighted, visibility was good. Moncrieff felt justified in turning in.

Shortly after one bell in the middle watch (12.30 a.m.), the wind freshened and the sea commenced to rise although visibility was apparently unimpaired. At 12.55 the First Lieutenant, who was on watch, called for a messenger to shake his relief, the navigator Lieutenant C. V. Groves RNR.

Throwing off his blanket, Groves went to the chart and pricked off the position by DR (Dead Reckoning). Significantly, there was no mention in the various accounts of him working out the EP (Estimated Position) which would have involved applying tidal stream and the effects of wind to the DR: he was probably anxious not to be late in relieving Number One. He then struggled into oilskins and stepped over recumbent bodies to check the gyro and its switchboard. Everything seemed normal.

Groves climbed up the ladder inside the bronze walls of the conning tower (bronze for the sake of the magnetic compass fixed halfway up) but could see nothing at first, when he emerged on to the bridge. (The captain had unwisely allowed bright lighting in the control room to be left on during the hours of darkness rather than dimming it or changing over to red lighting for the benefit of relief watchkeepers' night vision.) However, after a few moments his eyes became accustomed to the darkness and he glimpsed what appeared to be ships' wakes right ahead and on either bow. 'Hello,' he remarked to Peploe, the First Lieutenant, 'are those destroyers ahead?' Almost simultaneously Peploe picked up the white streaks himself, recognised them as breakers, and shouted down the voicepipe: 'Hard-a-starboard,[1] out clutches,[2] full astern both.' The order was too late. The submarine hit the shoal at speed and heeled heavily over to starboard. *E17* was aground on the Dutch island of Texel.

The Captain arrived on the bridge to find the motors going full astern, but to no effect. Everything was tried, but manoeuvring only resulted in turning the boat broadside to the sea which carried her still further on to the shore. Pounded violently by waves breaking over the bridge, the conning tower hatch (which had been closed but not clipped) flew open, allowing quantities of water into the boat, on to the main switchboard (which soon caught fire) and, before long, into the battery cells.

Smoke now filled the submarine, and deadly choking chlorine gas, from salt water mixing with sulphuric acid in the cells, started to make itself evident. The hatch had to be shut and clipped to prevent even more water coming in. Conditions were far from pleasant.

At 2.45 a.m. it was decided that nothing more could be done until high water at daybreak, by which time the weather might have moderated. Confidential books and charts were put in the galley electric oven and burned. Three officers and fifteen sailors sat on the battery boards and tore up the signal books, intending to heave them over the side at the first opportunity. There was little hope of salvation and German seaplanes invariably commenced their work at dawn. Most of the crew lay down and went to sleep, as is the habit of submariners in adversity, but a few played cards and laid bets with the gunlayer as to his (slim) chances of bringing down the seaplanes when they appeared.

At 6.30 a.m., at first light, a look through the glass scuttles in the conning tower revealed sand dunes and grass patches less than 45 metres (50 yards) away. With a high tide approaching, preparations were made for a final attempt to get the boat off. When all was ready the Captain, Navigator, Coxswain and Signalman went up to the bridge. Moncrieff ordered fuel tanks to be blown and once more put the motors to full astern. Oil smoothed the sea but the submarine would not move. Prospects were not improved by the brief appearance of a large cruiser but this hauled off to the southward after a few minutes.

At 8.24 a.m. *E17* at last slid clear into deep water and motored astern until 3 miles from the shore. The engines were then started and a course laid for home; but at this point, just when hope was glimmering, the rudder was found to be jammed and both propeller shafts were obviously bent. By using one motor to steer and the engine on the other side to propel, *E17* crabbed her way for a couple of miles in a westerly direction only to find, when a rain squall cleared, three destroyers close inshore and two more to seaward. The cruiser then reappeared. All these ships, presumed to be German, were converging. Another sudden squall offered a respite but it did not last. The cruiser broke through the rain on the port beam with a bone in its teeth, a wicked-looking bow wave clearly signifying an attempt to ram.

There was no choice but to dive, although the boat was in no state to do so. Moncrieff sang out, 'Flood all externals!' and the submarine plunged, very fast indeed, massively heavy and 43 degrees down by the bow. The upper lid could not be shut before yet another torrent poured down as the sea closed over the bridge. At 16 metres (53 feet) the after bulkhead, weakened by the earlier pounding, gave way. Water rushed in with full force up to the engine room bulkhead. The Chief LTO (Electrician)[3] could be heard shouting, 'Port motor burnt out, sir,' as Moncrieff ordered main ballast to be blown. Now the submarine see-sawed violently with angles up to 55 degrees before levelling off and breaking surface.

Moncrieff had no intention of surrendering. The torpedo tubes were made ready and there, stopped and broadside on just 365 metres (400 yards) off, lay the cruiser. Just as he was saying to himself 'a beautiful shot', he saw the Dutch colours broken at the cruiser's gaff. It was the *Noord Brabant* – neutral and welcome because *E17* was sinking quickly and the end was near. It came at 10.58 a.m.: the submarine slid down stern first, almost vertically, with an eerie wailing sound. Two boats rescued all thirty-three of the crew who were interned in Holland for the rest of the war. Nobody had anything to be ashamed of, except, of course, bad navigation.

Search

There were many other instances of getting lost, albeit seldom with such dramatic results; at the beginning of the war the 'E'-class oversea boats were ill-equipped to undertake the voyages that their named implied. They then had no Forbes Log, no sounding machine, no gyro compass, no compass repeater on the bridge (so the helmsman could, and sometimes did, steer the wrong course unnoticed), no high-power periscope, no wireless telegraphy (W/T) and no depth gauges that registered below 30 metres (100 feet). The two dozen volumes of navigational treatises packing the wardroom bookshelf were not much assistance without the basic tools of the trade.

If a submarine got itself into more or less the right patrol position, how did it discover the enemy? There was of course no radar, and on the surface the lookouts used binoculars. These were far better in U-boats than in British submarines where the instruments were heavy and prone to internal condensation. The Officer of the Watch and his lookouts were always tired; they had to cling – or be lashed – to precarious platforms; and no waterproof clothing, not even the best gear issued to U-boat men, entirely kept out the waves which constantly broke over exposed bridges.

Consequently, a surface watch was inefficient; and after long days of boredom and discomfort motivation was non-existent. As a rule the captain – if he was on the bridge – made the first sighting (although his eyes were probably not as good as those of the younger men, he was more determined than anybody else to find a target). Funnel smoke on the horizon, especially from merchant steamers, was usually the first indication of a target: coal-fired warships were nearly always smoky and it was impossible to convince merchant skippers of the danger they ran from not attending more carefully to their boilers.

Hydrophones or 'mechanical ears' were fitted as fixed hull plates on the newer submarines, but were of little use because their receiving oscillators were small, amplifiers were weak and noise from the submarine itself masked all but the loudest sounds. Pre-1916 U-boats had a carbon microphone fixed to the pressure hull on either side, in such a way as to make the whole boat act as a sound receiver. Three pairs of microphones were later installed, two pairs in the ballast tanks and one forward. One microphone in each pair was tuned to 700 cycles per second (Hertz) and one to a much lower frequency. The W/T apparatus was employed as an amplifier and 20-mile detection ranges were claimed. Any noise in or around the hull rendered the system useless: a boat had to be silent to hear anything, and that was not easy because all submarines in those days were veritable rattle-traps.

A supposedly directional pair of matched hydrophones, 12 centimetres (5 inches) in diameter and tuned to 900 cps, was provided for British boats from 1916 after trials on the elderly B3. The operator, drawn from the telegraphist branch with (HL) standing for Hydrophone Listener after his name, listened intently to the noise from his right and left headphones to determine – vaguely – the direction in which the source lay. A practised man with a musical ear might say what he was listening to; but guesswork must have played a large part in his pronouncement. Only a torpedo, whirring and whining viciously, was unmistakable.

Rotating uni-directional or bi-directional hydrophones, mounted on the casing forward of the bridge and unique to the Royal Navy, started to appear in 1918. They showed promise, but it was a promise that had no time to be fulfilled before the war ended.

Underwater communication devices, notably Fessenden gear at the bows, were quite widely fitted for passing messages between adjacent submarines. The American firm that produced the Fessenden, operating at 540 cps, claimed it could be used for search, but that was a sales gambit: the maximum range on a noisy target was in the order of 3 miles. To judge a bearing the submarine had to alter course until a 'null point' was reached, indicating that the noise source was ahead. Nevertheless, Fessenden was often used for exchanging information while dived, although why two submarines should have been on patrol within the necessary 2 or 3 miles of each other is not clear: there were no 'pack tactics' as such. When transmitting Morse code on Fessenden, the power at low frequency was such that the deck in the fore-ends vibrated alarmingly. The receiving submarine listened on one of its normal hydrophones.

Fessenden was eventually abandoned because, although it offered such a short range itself, it could be heard many miles away by the enemy. On the night of 28 October 1918 HMS *G2* heard the German equivalent in the North Sea, homed in and sank what transpired to be the large minelayer *U-78*. Why the U-boat was blurting out on the surface is not known: perhaps the captain was trying to detect mines (there were many in the eastern part of the German Ocean) or telling other U-boats, hidden on submerged patrol, that he was a friend.

All in all, underwater listening devices were not much assistance, and a captain relied almost entirely on his periscopes when dived. There were usually two of these, one for search (magnification 6×) with a head about 9 centimetres (3½ inches) in diameter and the other for attack (magnification 1½× to give the appearance of normal vision) with as small a head as possible. This was the standard arrangement but there were variations, particularly with regard to positioning in a boat. For example, while in British submarines (apart from the earliest ones) periscopes were in the control room and were lowered into deep wells below the deck, U-boat commanders conducted their attacks in an enlarged conning tower or kiosk above the control room where the attack periscope, and sometimes the search periscope as well, were situated.

Periscope ranges were measured by vertical and horizontal graticules inscribed with one-degree and five-degree markings. If the height – of the funnel, say – or the length of an enemy ship were known, the angles subtended could be converted into distance. However, attacking ranges were so short that experienced commanding officers believed that their own estimation by eye was good enough, besides being much quicker: it was extremely unwise to expose a periscope for more than a few seconds when close to the enemy.

Periscopes were long, 7 metres (23 feet) in an 'E' boat, and expensive at about £600 apiece (about £12,000 in today's money), although this was only a small fraction of what a modern instrument costs. (A complete 'E' boat cost in the order of £106,000, the equivalent of £2.3 million today which is one-fiftieth of the price of the latest British Type 2400 diesel-electric boat commissioned in 1989.)

The problem for periscope designers was twofold. Firstly, light had to be passed down through a very long thin tube without too much loss. Secondly, the tube had to be watertight and resistant to vibration. Not surprisingly, the technology of the time did not permit these aims to be met very well. Desiccation – drying out the tube by pressurised dry air – was difficult; the top window quickly got dirty (the British used duty-free gin to clean it), especially if there was any oil on the surface, and vision was frequently faulty.

Primitive periscopes (otherwise known as optical tubes, hyposcopes or cleptoscopes) were still installed in the older British boats when war came. Mistakes could arise when a captain was struggling to see a target: besides being constantly blurred, the horizon rotated when the instrument was trained around. On the beam it appeared vertical, and astern it was horizontal but upside down. This was held by some to be a useful aberration because it indicated relative bearings; but on one well-known (pre-war) occasion Lieutenant Ferdinand

Feilman, commanding an 'A' boat in the Solent off Portsmouth, was trying to view an up-ended target when he glimpsed what he thought was the target's red flag. When he had turned and brought his tubes to bear he fired a torpedo. Unhappily, the flag turned out to be a very large pink parasol under which the wife of a retired colonel was sitting on Alverstoke beach. Ferdie made a perfect shot and the torpedo hit the shingle, running up alongside the terrified lady: the colonel sued the Admiralty for damages. However, Feilman (like not a few of his contemporaries) became fond of the bottle and it may well have been more than mechanical tilting and condensation which confused his vision on that day.[4] Later, returning from patrol in an 'E' boat, the same man reported of his target: 'I'm not sure what range it was but I couldn't see the bow or the stern!' He probably fired at the destroyer *V-186* when analysis showed the range to be an absurdly short – and dangerous – 180 metres (200 yards). Ferdie's only victim during the war was the Zeppelin *L7* which his gunlayer in *E31* shot down and sank.

Somebody in The Trade composed a Submarine Alphabet. Two lines are relevant:

> P is the periscope used by the Captain
> M is the perpetual mist it is wrapped in . . .

By the time Lieutenant Norman Holbrook won the first submarine Victoria Cross in December 1915 for sinking the Turkish battleship *Messoudieh* at the entrance to the ancient Hellespont, some of the boats, like his *B11*, had what was called an 'erecting eyepiece' on the solitary periscope in the conning tower. It was worked by a man turning a handle to keep two pointers in line, the result being that the horizon would tilt jerkily back to normal alignment as the periscope was rotated. A Staff Officer blandly asserted that 'frequent use accustomed one to this' but, in moments of stress, it was sometimes difficult to estimate where the crooked-looking objects in the prism really were.

The Captain of *E23* (Turner) said that 'examination of a Hun periscope from a German U-boat showed it was

100 per cent better than British instruments', whereupon marked improvements were initiated for the latter. Actual modifications came slowly, however.

Communications

An ability to receive messages from headquarters and other friendly forces was an important factor for finding the enemy; and communications were, naturally, linked with finding out about the enemy. Intelligence was extraordinarily well developed during the war, more so in the King's Navy than the Kaiser's, thanks to the Marconi wireless company working closely with Admiral Sir Reginald Hall, chief of the Naval Intelligence Department. Hall was the dominant figure responsible for attacking German ciphers from the famous Old Admiralty Building Room 40 OB. The Royal Navy desperately needed to know when the German High Sea Fleet put to sea in time to enable the British Fleet, normally based at Scapa Flow, to intercept it. If the German Commander-in-Chief's wireless communications could be intercepted it would be obvious when the Fleet was passing through the Kiel Canal towards the disputed North Sea. Eventually, a system of identifying significant signals, linked with direction finding (D/F) equipment, was devised: during the last part of the war it became invaluable not only for predicting High Sea Fleet movements but also for determining where U-boats were operating.

The W/T transmitting apparatus on board submarines was mostly weak and unreliable: it was the Paulsen arc or spark-tube as a rule with a theoretical 300-mile range although valve sets – more delicate and subject to vibration but able to transmit out to 450 miles – were installed in some later classes. There was no way by which wireless messages could be received underwater: very-low-frequency (VLF) shore transmitting stations, whose signals could penetrate 3, 6 or even 18 metres (10, 20 or 60 feet) below the sea, were a long way in the future. For most of the war a high-frequency aerial had to be brought up and rigged on the surface, but various kinds of HF aerial, usually raised on an elbow joint, came to be permanent fittings in due course. Leir, in *E4*, flew a kite with the wire 'string' acting as an aerial: he was proud of sending a signal 170 miles with the device. A kite became quite common as a W/T accessory because it was soon realised that the aerial more than the wireless transmitter governed range, with the equipment and frequencies in use at that time.

Submarines were ordered to keep watch on assigned frequencies at specific times laid down in individual patrol orders. For example, during one British operation in the North Sea in 1914, the boats were required to listen out between 4.20 and 4.30 p.m. and again between 5.20 and 5.30 p.m. Even then it was not certain that signals would get through, and the sending station had no means of knowing whether its messages were being received. Later on a system of signal interception was used with some success: typically, the depot ships at Harwich and in the River Tees exchanged signals on the submarine wavelength (which ensured that the messages were actually audible) at stated intervals, and the boats on patrol were enjoined to surface in order to receive them.

Messages were not normally receipted because submarines did not transmit on wireless at sea unless they had something very important to say – a report of significant enemy movements for instance – because W/T transmissions might be heard by German listening stations. A boat could then be located by crude direction-finding apparatus, and distance could be judged from the strength of the signal.

Pigeons, on the other hand, were extensively employed in the Royal Navy for submarine-to-shore communications. They were thoroughly reliable except when overfed (like the earlier white mice in petrol-engine spaces) by pet-loving sailors. A bird in trim flew at an average speed of 30 m.p.h. Some were faster, but due allowance had to be made for wind. On one recorded occasion in 1915 *E6* (Talbot) released four pigeons (each with the same message) from off Terschelling at 4 a.m. The wind was 15 knots south-south-easterly and the birds had to fly 130 miles west-south-westerly to their traps. Their owner duly found them on arrival, removed the messages, took one to the local post office and telegraphed it to the Admiralty. It was decoded in Whitehall, retransmitted in a different cipher to HMS *Maidstone* at Harwich, again decoded and read by Captain (S) at 3.30 p.m. On that occasion *E6* had become temporarily entangled in an anti-submarine net off the Ems, got clear and sunk the enemy destroyer sent to finish her off. Talbot was anxious that other submarines should be warned of the nets as quickly as possible: pigeon post duly obliged.

It is impossible to say how many submarines, on all sides, lost their way – thereby getting themselves into trouble or missing the enemy – or were unable to receive and send crucial messages, but it must have been a very large number. Some captains were much better at navigating than others and made sure that their W/T and detection equipment was on top line, but no submarine anywhere could have got everything right all the time.

CHAPTER 5

Mouldies, Bricks and Deadly Eggs

Submariners said many things about torpedoes and few were complimentary. 'The only use of *Holland'*, declared Admiral O'Neil USN of the US Navy's first submarine in 1900, 'is to discharge torpedoes and no weapon is more erratic!' O'Neil was a gloomy prophet but many people came to agree with him when underwater weapons underwent the ultimate test of war. 'Tinfish', 'fish', 'kippers' or 'mouldies', as they were called in the Royal Navy, were skittish enough in peacetime, as Rear Admiral Arnold Forster (who had been the Royal Navy's first submarine captain in 1901) remarked: 'In the old days many of the torpedoes were distinguished and known by pet names. Those that were inclined to get out of hand were not allowed to run often, and then only when the omens were good. They still have their lucky and unlucky days.' At the time this was said an analysis of pre-war British submarine attacks indicated that hits out of the total fired amounted to 76 per cent. It was admitted that the percentage on active service would have been considerably less because mechanical failures were for some reason omitted from the analysis, and in war targets would take avoiding action.

During the first full year of war (1914–15) only 28 per cent of British 'mouldies' hit; the French figure (from a mere five submarine torpedoes fired) was 20 per cent. During approximately the same period, German U-boats hit with no more than 12 per cent of their 'eels' against British warships but 52 per cent against less evasive French warships. However, U-boats attacking merchant ships – much easier targets – hit 63 per cent. Merchantmen did not vary their speed (the prime requisite for a torpedo fire-control solution) and usually steered a straight course.

Presumably because of the German aptitude for thoroughness in all things, U-boat torpedoes seem to have been more mechanically reliable than Allied weapons. When practice torpedoes failed and sank they were salved, and personnel who had made gross errors were duly punished. 'Prepping' (the British term for preparing a torpedo for firing) was the responsibility of shore or depot-ship torpedo staff; submariners at sea then had to carry out subsequent maintenance and make adjustments.

A comprehensive analysis of British attacks, recently compiled,[1] arrives at some intriguing and hitherto unsuspected figures. In tabular form:

	1914	1915	1916	1917	1918	1914–18
Torpedoes fired	32	184	76	151	174	617
Torpedo hits	3	64	6	15	13	101
Torpedo mechanical failures claimed	9	49	26	18	42	144
Approx hitting percentage of torpedoes fired	9	35	8	10	7	16
Approx percentage of mechanical failures of torpedoes fired	28	27	34	12	24	23

With regard to the table:

• The year 1915 was the prime year for more experienced British captains because they had more targets than at any other time.

• Torpedo mechanical failures cited were by no means all proven as such. The beginning of 1918 saw another group of 'old stagers' arriving on the scene with surfaced U-boats as their primary objective, but the latter were exceedingly difficult targets and the largest available salvoes were fired against them.

• The much better torpedo mechanical performance in 1917 points to an outstanding team in the parting shop of the depot ship HMS *Maidstone* at Harwich where most of the 'tinfish' were 'prepped'.[2] There is no particular Torpedo Lieutenant or Gunner (T) serving uniquely during that period in HMS *Maidstone* (the principal 'Torps' officer was there throughout the war), so the expertise and dedication of senior ratings can be inferred. It is also possible that, for a while, lower torpedo speed settings were used, leading to greater reliability.

• An overall torpedo hitting rate of 16 per cent was not surprising in the light of the difficult and mainly small targets more often encountered by the British than the Germans.

Several odd factors determined hits, misses and failures. The usual British torpedo discharge pressure of 17.5 kilos per square cm (250 pounds per square inch) at a firing depth of 11 metres (36 feet) was too high. It created a lot of splash at the surface, thereby warning the enemy, and it swung back the pendulum that assisted and stabilised depth-keeping, forcing a fish deep for several hundred metres. 'Run unders' were common at ranges out to 550 metres (600 yards) but a torpedo recovered by the time it had run 700 metres (800 yards). For this reason close attacks by British boats often failed, but they succeeded in German U-boats where discharge was smoother. The Royal Navy ultimately decided that 1100 metres (1200 yards) was the optimum firing range and held to that until straight-running torpedoes were abandoned in favour of 'intelligent' (or 'smart') weapons in the 1980s. In Germany Commander Holtzapfel, President of the Torpedo Experiment Committee, declared that even if torpedoes were fired in salvoes (as they were by both sides against warships) it was useless to fire at ranges beyond 3000 metres (3280 yards).

High-speed settings of 40 knots or more tended to make a torpedo roll. This again upset the pendulum and depth, as tests from HMS *Vernon* at Portsmouth demonstrated. A speed of 35 knots was formally recommended in 1917, allowing a fish to run for 4500 metres (5000 yards), but Ross Turner in *E23* had already decided on much lower speeds for his bow torpedoes. On 19 August 1916 Turner fired beam and stern torpedoes with standard speed settings at the battleship *Seydlitz* from

700 and 4000 metres (800 and 4500 yards) respectively: both shots missed. But when he later fired two bow torpedoes with 18-knot settings – slow but sure – from 1100 metres (1200 yards) at the battleship *Westphalen* he scored a hit. He may have hit the damaged ship again with another bow salvo set to 12 knots from 1400 metres (1500 yards) two hours afterwards. But torpedoes crawling along like this risked missing if the target zig-zagged, even if they do seem to have been more dependable: submariners in general preferred a higher speed.[3] The speed setting for the German type G torpedo was 38 knots, but there was no mention of roll problems. High discharge pressure was almost certainly the culprit in the Royal Navy.

On the British side there was yet another reason, initially, for deep running. Due to an oversight, peacetime practice 'mouldies' on which wartime depth settings were based carried exercise heads which were 18 kilos (40 pounds) lighter than warheads.

German 'eels' occasionally suffered from a more subtle malaise. Depth-finding depended primarily upon a device which Robert Whitehead, the inventor of practicable torpedoes, called 'The Secret'. A hydrostatic valve on the body of the torpedo acted against an internal spring which could be adjusted for the requisite depth. When the pressure of water overcame the spring a connecting rod angled the horizontal rudders so that the torpedo came up. Contrariwise, if the spring overcame the hydrostatic valve the torpedo was directed downwards, but when the spring and valve were in equilibrium, meaning that the torpedo was at the correct depth, the horizontal rudders kept the torpedo level. Unfortunately, Whitehead's Secret became unbalanced if insidious air pressure, arising from high-pressure air leaks inside a boat submerged, found its way into the balance chamber which contained the mechanism. When that happened, as it could during a long dive before the difficulty was resolved, air pressure augmented the force of the spring against the hydrostatic valve. Consequently, the torpedo 'thought' it was shallower than it was. The danger, clearly pointed out in the Most Secret German

Handbook *Torpedo Firing From Submarines* (1915), was entirely forgotten by 1939 when exactly the same failures were experienced in the U-boat arm, with similar puzzlement.

Meanwhile, in London, the ferocious First Sea Lord Admiral Fisher aimed a heavy salvo at anyone connected with HMS *Vernon*, the Navy's torpedo establishment, during the four years preceding the war: 'I hope to get a good many officers disgraced for it!' Fisher went on to express a desire to have Charlton, the Assistant Director of Torpedoes from 1911 to 1914, 'blown from a gun' and swore to have the senior officers hanged or shot; but despite a certain laxity among British torpedo experts it is not certain that all the complaints from commanding officers about their fish running too deep were justified.

On 10 September 1914 Ernest Leir in *E4* fired a single 460-mm (18-inch) fish at *U-23* on the surface off Helgoland. He noted in his Log that 'judging by the gesticulations on the bridge' the torpedo had run beneath its intended victim, but experience was to show that a single shot of this kind had a low probability of hitting; and bubbles from the exhaust (clearly denoting a torpedo's track) did not immediately indicate a torpedo's position relative to the target because they took some time to rise to the surface. Indeed, if the wake was visible abreast the bridge the torpedo itself had very likely passed ahead, whether or not it was running at the correct depth.

Nor were the German U-boat commanders believed when they reported that they saw the track of bubbles actually touching the stern of the target, implying a hit amidships or thereabouts frustrated by an underrun. The staff of the U-boat school at Eckernförde coldly remarked that this could not be in accordance with the facts: 'with a height of eye of 10 centimetres [4 inches – the amount of periscope exposed] immediately in line with the track of bubbles you cannot form any correct idea of lateral distance. Even in the case of observers on board the target ship there may be differences of opinion amounting to 10 or 15 metres.' The school staff, confident 'that the depth keeping of our torpedoes can be relied upon' [by 1916], was sure that 'the shots in question must have been misses for direction, unless the torpedoes passed underneath the target owing to being fired at too close range [under 170 metres (185 yards)] or owing to incorrect depth setting.'

The Germans took the precaution of fitting double detonators to warheads. Many a British 'mouldy' with only one detonator – and that not dependable – ended its run with a thud rather than a bang.

The extremely close range, by today's standards, from which torpedoes were often fired was thought to be advantageous in securing hits; and, with torpedo speeds usually in the 30- to 40-knot bracket, there was no time for the target to take avoiding action. Close range was sensibly recommended for German torpedoes but it was chancy for British weapons. As Captain Arthur Waistell, commanding HMS *Maidstone* in 1914, observed (not knowing about the pendulum effect):

at 300 yards range and under, the percentage of misses is higher than at 400 yards. This is probably due to the necessity of more attention being paid to the safety of the submarine, particularly if firing a bow tube and, in a minor degree, to the change of bearing of the target being more rapid.

Leaving aside the unrecognised torpedo-depth problem which nullified so many efforts, it required extremely fine judgement to bring a submarine to a firing position, deemed ideally to be seven points on the target bow (about 80 degrees – just forward of the beam) at such a precise and short range entirely by eye and without the periscope being seen. It is no wonder that only a small proportion of submarine captains perfected their art.

As the war progressed, so did anti-submarine measures and a target's ability to evade by zig-zags and 'dazzle' paint or camouflage. The latter could be very confusing, making it extremely difficult for a captain to judge angle-on-the-bow (inclination and thereby target course) or estimate range. Neither, if some kind of disguise was added to the *ensemble*, could he be

sure of the potential victim's length, height, draught and tonnage characteristics which were crucial for graticule-ranging
and torpedo-depth settings.

Commanding officers were very aware of the technical
ability required for their job. C. G. Brodie, returning to
submarines after a spell in big ships, was conscious of not
having kept up with technology and was 'wondering if I'd lost
my good eye at the periscope – my sole justification for command.' A good eye was certainly essential even when crude
attack instruments had been evolved to calculate deflection
angle and approach courses – largely thanks to Lieutenant
Commander Martin Nasmith in the Royal Navy – but much
more was required.

Charles Little (one-time captain of *D1* and Flag Officer
Submarines in 1931) lamented that the war encroached on
the traditions of The Trade:

I am a great believer in the *complete knowledge* of all the details
of a submarine in any of her proper officers. In the old days an
officer had a *far* greater knowledge of his vessel than any of the
crew. Quick entry and training, necessitated by rapid construction
during the war, has to some extent encroached on this old tradition
and I have noticed that officers are inclined to rely too much on the
knowledge of their men, a habit which must be stamped out or it will
become worse and worse. For instance, I have been ordered as Sub
of a submarine to go and steady the diving wheel when the Coxswain
was in difficulties and as CO I have taken the wheel myself for a short
period if time permitted. How many submarine officers can now
dive their submarines better than their Coxswains? I wonder! The
same applies to an equal or superior practical knowledge than the
ERA [Engine Room Artificer] has. This *can* be taught; if the engines
knock badly, run unevenly or smoke badly, the officer must be able
to correct the ERA. It is only the advent of the Engineer Officer in
the Submarine Service which has robbed the submarine officer of
his supremacy in this respect.

Minute attention to and knowledge of every detail is essential for the best results in a submarine where, more than in
any other vessel, awkward situations and rapid decisions are so
frequent.

The successful submarine CO has the qualities indicated above, a complete knowledge of attacking and of the practical manoeuvring of the vessel together with the gift of handling his men and all the ordinary attributes of a successful naval officer: these last are very, very desirable.

Among submarine captains everywhere 'aces' are never likely to be plentiful. An analysis of attacks conducted by German boats, for example, shows that 4 per cent of the commanders sank 30 per cent of the shipping that went down to U-boat torpedo and gunnery attacks; and during the Second World War 2.2 per cent sank 31 per cent. The lesson taught by this – but evidently not learned after either of the world wars – was that only a small proportion of the boats listed in a navy's Order of Battle is likely to function as advertised.

The influx of new and prospective commanding officers demanded training devices – so-called Attack Teachers – at submarine bases and in depot ships because operational submarines could not be spared for basic attack instruction. Charles Little thought that the Lewis Teacher[4] was a wonderful instrument:

One of its best features is that it encourages Smoking Room discussion of attack and elucidation of various situations, making the novice familiar with these and avoiding the dilemma into which the young commanding officer often gets at an awkward juncture, with the consequent deep safety dive and loss of attack.

'Smoking Room discussion' was invaluable: there was no other way of disseminating war lessons quickly, and tactics had to change and adapt to fresh situations continually.

Enemy zig-zagging and the employment of anti-submarine screens often made short-range shots impossible, and it became necessary to fire from outside a destroyer screen at ranges exceeding 900 metres (1000 yards) and sometimes, in the case of high-speed targets which could not be closed in time, from 3500 or even 4500 metres (4–5000 yards). At these much longer ranges the hitting probability for submarines with only one or two tubes was very low. Four tubes were needed for difficult (usually meaning warship) targets and six would have been better; but only the British 'R' boats, commissioned in 1918 and specifically designed for anti-submarine work, could fire six fish in one salvo.

The principle of torpedo-fire required a submarine to be pointed like a gun towards the future position of the target when the torpedoes crossed its track. In a rapidly changing situation it was often impossible to turn the submarine in time to put it on course for the required deflection angle (DA) or aim-off. Stern tubes were a partial solution, allowing the captain to turn away if that required the least alteration of course; beam 'broadside' tubes, fitted on many British boats, were another. The latter had the great advantage, for short-range attacks, of not obliging the captain to continue closing the target during the last moments before firing. A much better answer, however, which U-boat men adopted, was pre-angling torpedoes in the bow or stern tubes, so that they took up their required hitting track after discharge. Fish in 'the beamery' of an 'E' boat could also, theoretically, be pre-angled 90 degrees but submariners evidently thought that this would be asking too much of British 'mouldies'.

Most German U-boats had only two bow tubes until about halfway through the war when four became usual; but British submariners were able to welcome a fair-sized bow salvo with the excellent American-designed 'H' class, built for the Royal Navy by Vickers in Canada in the spring and early summer of 1915. The popular 'H' boats had four 450-mm (18-inch) bow tubes and were very handy submerged. Production continued during the war at the Fore River yard, USA. It says much for American expertise that some of these boats continued to serve during the Second World War. The British submarines with adequate armament and fire-control equipment which followed the 'H' boats – the 'J', 'K', 'L', 'M' and 'R' classes – unfortunately had few opportunities to engage German ships because, towards the end of the war, the latter so seldom put to sea.

When the chance of a long-range salvo against a worth-while target did present itself, the torpedoes were fired one after another at carefully calculated intervals along the same track so that the target's own movement created, in effect, a linear spread. Supposing that two hits were required to sink, say, a cruiser and four fish were available: the first might deliberately be fired to miss ahead (on the basis of estimated target speed across the line of sight), the next a quarter length inside the bow, the third a quarter length inside the stern and the last to miss astern. This kind of spreading allowed for target-speed errors in the order of 3 or 4 knots provided that the torpedoes ran true, but it was customary in The Trade to expect one failure in a salvo.

Making sure that the 'mouldies' performed properly (at £900 apiece) was a worrisome business for torpedomen who were anyway keeping watch and watch – two hours on and two hours off. The old torpedoes had been driven by compressed air alone at around 30 knots out to no more than 1800 metres (2000 yards). They were simple weapons and required little attention, but wartime 'Heater' torpedoes in which fuel was ignited with compressed air – to drive a radial engine or, in the US Navy, provide steam for a small turbine – required servicing at sea.

Maintenance did not compare with 'prepping' but, strictly speaking, it involved withdrawing every torpedo from its tube daily – a hideous performance in itself when rolling on the surface. It is doubtful if any submarine obeyed instructions to the letter.

Reloading after a shot was also an arduous and lengthy procedure. The Germans benefited from better arrangements but in many British boats (although not the American-designed 'H' class) there was not enough space in the reload racks for a waiting torpedo to carry a warhead: this had to be attached just before reloading in an exceedingly confined space cluttered by personal belongings and spare gear.

A torpedo tube was sealed at one end by a bow cap and by a rear door at the other. It was obviously important not to open both at the same time because, even on the surface in harbour, the tubes were underwater. There was an indicator to show the position of the bow cap (which was electrically or hydraulically operated in all save the earliest boats) but no positive interlocks. Loading and reloading operations were supervised with great care. They still are: memories of the HMS *Thetis* disaster in 1939 remain fresh in mind after half a century.[5]

When a torpedo was home and the rear door shut, the tube was flooded from an internal water round torpedo (WRT) tank so that, when the bow cap was opened, water would not rush in and make the submarine heavy forward. The fish itself weighed between 635 kilograms (1400 pounds) and 1.3 tons depending on size and type. Whatever the weight, it was heavier than the water that completely filled the tube immediately after firing. It was therefore necessary to admit an extra amount of seawater to another tank right forward at the crucial moment to compensate. In due course, this came to be done automatically, but it was more usual for one of the torpedomen to hold open an inlet valve for a given number of seconds. The practice continued in American boats long after automation was adopted elsewhere.

It was also important not to let discharge air escape from the tube. The air for firing each tube was stored at a calculated pressure for a given depth in a bottle of specific capacity. In theory the quantity of rapidly expanding air was just sufficient to launch a fish on its way (the engine was started by a trip-lever in the tube as it moved forward) but not enough to bubble out against the external pressure of seawater rushing in. In practice the discharge or splash was nearly always visible on the surface, especially in British boats due to the high firing pressure. Methods of 'swallowing' the air before it could escape were not perfected during the war, but German discharge was less of a giveaway.

Until the middle of the war practically all French submarine torpedoes were carried externally in Drzewiecki launching systems and/or cradles. These left the torpedoes exposed to the sea which, besides being bad for *torpilles*, limited a boat's diving depth to 30 metres (100 feet). The Polish engineer's arrangements were far from satisfactory, but the Russians followed suit in several of their boats with equally unhappy results.

French attack capabilities were poor to moderate. Having made an early start in the nineteenth century in the submarine field, it might have been expected that *les sous-marins* would be performing well by 1914, but they did not consolidate their promising beginnings. In 1905 the Entente Cordiale, the special Anglo-French relationship, was revived after years of hostility, and the original objective of the submarine force – to sink British merchant shipping – became redundant. Since *Albion* was no longer *perfide* fresh objectives had to be devised, although these never became entirely clear; and impetuosity was allowed to seize upon exciting but unproven equipment while overriding the need for painstaking trials and tactical evaluations.

The Gallic fascination with complexity and experimentation resulted in a wide variety of submarine types, power plants and systems with consequential training and maintenance difficulties. Steam propulsion (for speed on the surface) was hazardous, and armament was considered after hull design rather than before it, hence the disastrous external torpedo-launching gear.

French submarines were not well fitted for the tasks they were given when war came, but the best *commandants* were able to work quite effectively with sub-standard *matériel*. A small, select band operated with distinction in the Adriatic; and *Curie*, one of the diesel 'Brumaire' class, captured at Pola after penetrating that well-defended base, became one of the best boats in the Austrian Navy. She was renamed *U-XIV* after being re-equipped with good motors, a new battery and an 88-mm ($3^1/_2$-inch) gun.

The last word on torpedo attacks can be left to Captain Waistell, commanding HMS *Maidstone* at Harwich, who wrote in 1917 before statistics for that year were complete:

It is difficult to deny that for some time past the percentage of hits with torpedoes from submarines has fallen short of reasonable expectations, even if allowances are made for the fact that submarines have been the most frequent targets . . . it is very difficult to assign the cause to *matériel*, much as one is inclined to do so.

During the last year, 720 torpedoes have been landed from these submarines for their three-monthly overhaul: only one was found unfit to run.

If, therefore, it is considered that the percentage of hits is unreasonably low and that it is not due to defects in the torpedoes themselves, one is forced to the conclusion that it is in some way due to personnel, or especially to the captain of a submarine, as the attack is entirely centred in him.

The Submarine Service breeds a particularly fine type of officer, but it cannot perform miracles; and a fully trained submarine officer cannot be produced during war in half the time which was taken under peace conditions, especially when the facilities for training are so considerably reduced.

The effects of dilution, restricted exercise areas and shortage of training submarines were just as evident in the German navy.

Guns

Guns on submarines did great execution throughout the war. They were generally small on British boats: those firing shells weighing 5.5 kilos (12-pounders) were the most common although these were sometimes replaced by 75-mm (3-inch) HA (high angle, anti-aircraft) weapons; and 100-mm (4-inch) guns were fitted on the bigger boats towards the end of the war. About 100 rounds of ammunition were carried, and more for portable 1-kilo guns (2-pounders) or machine guns. U-boats, according to size and purpose, were equipped with 88-mm (3.5-inch), 105-mm (4.1-inch) or, on the big U-cruisers, 150-mm (5.9-inch) guns. The Austrians paid more attention to light anti-aircraft armament while the French, almost exclusively, fitted 75-mm (3-inch) general-purpose weapons.

A 100-mm (4-inch) weapon was the best calibre for most British purposes: the ammunition was not too heavy to hand up the tower for rapid fire; and 16-kilo (35-pound) 'bricks' did a lot more damage than 5.5-kilo (12-pounder) shells. The 5.5-kilo (12-pounder) guns fitted on 'D' boats (and probably other classes) were twenty years old and emphatically not designed for submergence. However, it was accepted that the first round cleaned out the barrel although it could not be used for a spotting correction. The big 150-mm (5.9-inch) guns on U-cruisers were best of all, but their mountings were heavy and shell-handling presented special problems.

Getting a gun into action quickly after surfacing was the nub of the business. It was essential to disable the enemy before he could retaliate in kind. Surprise was the essence. The bigger the gun, the further the submarine could stand off; and it was seldom that the German U-cruisers with two 150-mm (5.9-inch) guns came under counter-attack. One submersible ocean raider achieved spectacular results during a long cruise from January until April 1918, during which she sank twelve vessels by gunfire in the Bay of Biscay and around the Canary Islands before making for home by a dog-leg past the Azores and sinking an unlucky thirteenth. She also fired at another dozen vessels without sinking them and herself came under attack three times, but only when imprudently close to land. There was no threat to a surfaced submarine from the air in remote areas.

Multiple sinkings by U-cruisers would not have been possible with torpedoes because the number carried was limited. In any case, small targets like schooners would have been difficult to hit even if they justified the high cost of an 'eel'. Convoys with adequate escorts debarred U-boat gunnery, but defensive armament on unescorted merchant ships was not much of a deterrent.

Gunnery was not only used against ships: shore bombardment was a sport which British submariners enjoyed. HMS *H1*, under Lieutenant Wilfred Pirie in the Sea of Marmara in 1915, was probably the first submarine to engage shore targets and shipping in harbour. 'We penetrated', said Pirie, 'into all sorts of places and destroyed shipping. We even shelled a railway and destroyed two troop trains. We shelled an embankment and blocked the line, then caught the trains as they came along. It was the funniest thing you can imagine to see a train try to hide between the trees but we caught her and smashed her to blazes. Three ammunition wagons blew up with terrific explosions.

'The soldiers, of course, got out and took cover and fired tons of ammunition at us but we were out of range. Altogether we sank 1 gunboat, 5 steamers (one of 3000 tons) and 17 large sailing ships, and destroyed 3 trains and 1 railway embankment.'

The Germans formulated orders for weaponry which would have seemed unduly thorough and wordy on the English side of the North Sea, but they ensured consistently good results. The Trade, though, was reluctant to abide by a gunnery rule book save in 'M'-class monitors with their huge 300-mm (12-inch) guns which had an obvious potential for self-destruction if misused. Submariners detested anything to do with Whale Island, the Naval School of Gunnery. In fact, a number of officers had joined The Trade to avoid not only the world of gas and gaiters but also the boring company, in big ships, of gunnery specialists who were reputedly deafened by their own excesses. Guns – and demolition charges placed by a boarding party to finish a ship off – were used to good effect but with a degree of informality by British captains, who depended largely on the expertise of individual gunlayers.

Deadly Eggs

Mining had a major influence on the war at sea, and submarines were much involved with it. Developments and strategies were quite complex, and it may be less confusing to deal with them piecemeal, illustrating each point as it arises, rather than adhere to a strict timetable.

Until the end of the nineteenth century marine mines were also called torpedoes and the terms were interchangeable. Admiral David G. Farragut USN gave his stirring war-cry – 'Damn the torpedoes! Captain Drayton go ahead! Jouett full speed!' – when US ships entered a minefield, not a submarine zone, during the Battle of Mobile Bay on 5 August 1864. But by 1914 no admiral echoed Farragut's sentiments. Caution was the watchword where deadly eggs were thought to have been laid because the lessons of the Russo-Japanese war of 1904–5, which featured extensive minelaying around Port Arthur, were still fresh in mind. In that small arena the losses from mines on both sides amounted to three battleships, five cruisers, four destroyers, four lesser craft and numerous damaged vessels. In fact, the outcome of the war may well have been presaged by Admiral Makarov's death when his flagship was mined while sailing to engage an attacking Japanese force. Morale in the Tsarist navy never recovered.

Both Germany and England took careful note of the effects of mines in the Yellow Sea, and they engaged in mining operations on a large scale. The Royal Navy established war zones by minefields which required most North Atlantic shipping, and all ships sailing to the Baltic, to enter British ports for clearance and routeing. Mining thus theoretically assured Great Britain's control of neutral shipping over the most important areas.

The extensive fields of 'Elia' and 'Service' mines laid in the Channel during the winter of 1915–16 were, however, ineffective against U-boats, even in those shallow waters. German post-war analysis suggested that nearly two-thirds of British mines used against German submarines between 1914 and 1916 were defective: their detonators failed to function, their depth-setting gear was inaccurate, their moorings were not strong enough to survive winter gales and their explosive charges were too small to be sure of a kill. They were also apt to come to the surface at low water, revealing themselves to a U-boat commander as innumerable little black dots which could be avoided; and in German waters, particularly off Helgoland, they were easily swept.

Russian mines were, by contrast, thoroughly reliable and no German U-boat willingly entered the Gulf of Finland where the hidden menace was disposed most thickly: 2200 mines had been laid across the entrance on the eve of hostilities. Although U-boat commanders went where they were told, officers who had any say in the matter steered clear of Russian operations altogether – simply because of the minefields, it was said,[6] although the weather was probably another good reason.

In January 1915 Admiral Fisher, the First Sea Lord, had to tell Churchill that England had only 4900 mines ready, but that a shipment of more reliable contact mines from Russia was awaited to strengthen anti-submarine defences at Scapa Flow. The Royal Navy thereupon applied itself with belated vigour to improving the mining art. Sensitive Herz horns linked to an electrical circuit (long fitted to Russian and German mines) began to replace clumsy mechanical detonators in 1916; stronger and better variable-depth moorings were employed for anti-submarine barriers; and larger charges of TNT were packed into the units. Nevertheless, only 1500 mines out of 20,000 stockpiled by April 1917 were fit for laying when the need was greatest.

Towards the end of the war British minefields were con-centrated in areas such as the English Channel which were constantly traversed by U-boats. 'Listening buoys', moored at intervals and ideally 5.5 metres (18 feet) above the seabed, were capable of picking up a submarine's propeller beat. They were connected to manned stations on shore – the forerunners of today's SOSUS system – where the 'audible spoor' was tracked until it led directly to a group of mines. Then – according to theory and as believed by U-boat men – an electric button would be pressed to explode them. Some mines could them-selves incorporate a 'magnetophone' which was designed to detonate the 225-kilo (500-pound) charge at the closest point of approach of a U-boat.

The systems were imperfect to say the least, but, together with nets and anti-submarine vessels, they did act as a deterrent. The first shore-controlled minefields making use of hydrophones and magnetophones were not laid until mid-1916: they accounted for two U-boats and possibly two others, and they damaged another two.[7]

It was clear from the start that, despite the numerous bad eggs, a submarine had no real defence against mines although British hydroplane fairings and jumping wires over bridge superstructures helped to deflect mooring wires. The Germans adopted similar measures and added saw-tooth netcutters to their bows. As the British mining effort intensified, the danger to U-boats mounted steadily. Losses due to mines totalled forty-four by November 1918, 24 per cent of the 178 boats lost from all causes and six more than the number which went down to underwater bombs (*Wasserbomben*) or depth-charges as the Allies called them.

The effectiveness of anti-submarine mines depended on where they were laid. A vast field of 70,117 mines stretching 230 nautical miles from Scotland to Norway and 35 miles deep, was laid, primarily by the 'Yankee Mining Squadron',[8] between June and October 1918. Costing $21 million ($450 million at today's prices) for the 'eggs' alone, the 'barrier of death' was supposed to shut off 'the U-boat breeding ground' and twenty German submarines were said to have been claimed by it. In fact the total was three, and that at a time when U-boats were traversing the belt at an average rate of 42 transits per month.[9] The field was in the wrong place: U-boats could pass through it on the surface virtually unimpeded by anti-submarine forces. The huge effort would have been better devoted to covert lays – by submarines – off German bases.

Naturally, mines were a menace to surface ships. On the German side, laid predominantly by U-boats, mines accounted for 682,000 tons of British shipping sunk and 432,400 tons damaged – 10 per cent and 6 per cent respectively of losses and damage by direct U-boat action.

As for warships, Admiral Sir John Jellicoe, Commander-in-Chief of the Grand Fleet, recognised a significant factor only two weeks after war was declared:

There is, of course, an element of considerable risk in traversing the North Sea with the Battle Fleet. It does not appear that mines are laid yet, but at any moment they may be, and even with mine-sweepers ahead, which can only be done at ten knots speed, there is no certainty they will be discovered before a ship hits one. An objection to having the mine-sweepers ahead is that *the slow speed this entails on the Battle Fleet makes it an easier prey to submarines*. [italics added]

The Admiralty believed, correctly, that enemy naval strategy would depend upon mines, torpedoes and submarines to tilt the balance against superior British surface forces. Jellicoe continued to be apprehensive about the Battle Fleet being 'disabled by underwater attack before the guns opened fire at all', and mines as well as submarines were constantly on his mind. His fears were to be justified, not initially in the North Sea as he presumably expected, but in the Dardanelles where a tiny but well-placed field in March 1915 'altered the whole course of history'.[10]

The great strategic value of mine warfare, as demonstrated in the Dardanelles, was confirmed to the German naval staff early in the war. Recognising that submarines were the most secretive of minelayers, the first U-boats specifically built for the purpose with external chutes, *UB-12* and *UC 1-15*, had already been ordered. Successive programmes would demand another 197 increasingly capable types.

In the event, little more than half that number – twenty large and seventy small or medium-sized German minelayers – were actually completed. The boats were good value for money with small economical crews: the 'UC's had between thirteen and twenty-nine men according to class. Nevertheless, only a trifling effort was made later when far-reaching results could have been expected off the eastern American seaboard. No more than fifty-eight 'pineapples' were planted in six ports after the entry of the United States into the war in 1917. What might have been achieved by a wholehearted minelaying offensive was indicated by that paltry number sinking the armoured cruiser USS *San Diego* and four merchantmen, and damaging the battleship USS *Minnesota*. Moreover, several ports had to be closed for substantial periods until hastily prepared minesweepers declared them safe.

Germany's reason for not pressing home her submarine mining advantage in American waters was simply that the large boats *U-71* to *U-80* and *U-117* to *U-126*, which could carry worthwhile loads of thirty-six and forty-eight mines respectively, did not have the necessary range. The middling boats of around 500 tons from *UC-16* onwards were good for about 7000 miles and might have squeezed in a little more fuel, but each could carry, in six chutes, only fourteen or eighteen mines altogether. By the time that ten 1160-ton boats of the *U-117* and *U-122* classes were complete in 1918, with stern-tube laying gear, Germany's plight was such that dockyard refits to increase their range beyond 6000 miles were impracticable. The Kaiser's staff, desperately hoping that the United States would be kept out of the war by diplomacy, had failed to provide a contingency plan for mining on the other side of the Atlantic where the effects could have been devastating.

By mid-1915 Grossadmiral Tirpitz was able to bring his first operational minelaying submarines into play in the European theatre. They contributed significantly to British shipping losses, mostly in the English Channel before the Royal Navy's anti-submarine measures became reasonably efficient. The 'UC'-type boats made their initial patrols from Flanders in the summer using 'E' (standing for *Ei* or egg) mines with Herz Horn firing gear. These weapons were dependable, each charged with 150 kilos (330 pounds) of TNT. They were equipped with hydrostatic depth-setting devices and, although restricted for a while to waters no deeper than 100 metres (330 feet), they were eventually modified for laying in 300 metres (nearly 1000 feet).

Although the Russians were enthusiastic proponents of mine warfare they employed few submarines for mining. Covert lays were seldom necessary because minefields in the Baltic – their principal naval theatre – were defensive and in waters under their own control. No more than six of the forty-two Baltic boats were equipped with mines, and these were discharged from torpedo tubes. However, *Krab*, the world's first purpose-built submarine minelayer (and a mechanical abomination), was designed for offensive operations in the Black Sea. Russian submarine-laid mines do not appear to have claimed any victims except the Turkish gunboat *Issa Reis* which was damaged in a field laid by *Krab* in the Bosporus; but by early 1915 four of the eight German cruisers in the Baltic had been disabled by mines laid from surface vessels.

It was always difficult to know exactly whose eggs were hatched. That was one reason why minelaying was an unpopular occupation in the Royal Navy: there were no visible rewards. Worse, mining took boats into dangerously shallow waters where they had to leave tempting torpedo targets undisturbed for fear of being discovered.

HMS *E24* (Lieutenant Commander George Naper) was the first British minelaying submarine. On 4 March 1916 she embarked a load of twenty mines, all in chutes within the saddle tanks, at Harwich and sailed for the mouth of the Elbe River. The cargo shook and rattled unnervingly when the sea got up, and nobody was anxious to retain it for longer than necessary. But Naper had difficulty in finding the assigned 15-metre (8-fathom) patch north of the river mouth. Visibility was extremely poor and navigation even more hit-and-miss than usual, literally so: Allen, the First Lieutenant, wrote privately that 'the submarine navigated largely by bouncing off shallows, charting the depth at the time . . .' It was no way to treat a score of explosive cylinders stacked outside the pressure hull, and the lay was almost certainly inaccurate – a danger to both sides. The other 'E'-class minelayers that followed were probably, on occasion, equally vague about the position of their lays although their officers were not so frank in saying so. The German 'UC'-boats, with a sounding device worked from inside the hull, had a less haphazard approach to navigation.

It was not absolutely necessary to build a submarine specifically for minelaying because certain types of moored mines were designed for launching through standard torpedo tubes. Most British boats, all German and some Russian submarines had that capability. But, as Captain J. S. Cowie RN (the acknowledged expert) remarked some thirty years later, 'the restriction thus imposed on the size and shape [of mines] prevented a high standard of efficiency being achieved.' Minelayers with chutes (usually angled at fifteen degrees to the vertical with two or more mines, one above the other, held by retaining catches) had ordinary torpedo tubes as well so that they could engage in offensive operations when clear of the mining area. The six British E-boats fitted with mining chutes (externally in the ballast tanks)[11] sacrificed their beam tubes to compensate for weight (not much of a sacrifice by the middle of the war because very close-range attacks were becoming rare) but kept their one stern and two bow tubes.

The losses among minelaying submarines were huge; it was fortunate for French and Austrian submariners that their navies declined to participate. HMS *E24* hit a mine and was lost with all hands on her second minelaying patrol. In July 1918 *E34* (Pulleyne), having torpedoed *UB-16* two months earlier while returning from a lay to Harwich, never came back from her twenty-fourth minelaying operation off Vlieland, probably because she strayed into a field laid in the vicinity by *E51*. If that was so, at least one of the automatic 38-day sinking plugs must have failed to function. Five 'UC' boats were blown up by their own mines, eight ran on to enemy mines (one in a mined net) and thirty-nine were lost from other causes on minelaying patrols.

CHAPTER 6

The Enemy All Round –
Anti-Submarine Measures

A submarine, like a buccaneering ship of old, was prey for anyone, anywhere, at any time. Not even supposedly friendly ships or aircraft could be trusted because unreliable submarine navigation and communications too often resulted in barging matches between team-mates and not a few own goals.

During the first few months of war there was little or no organised anti-submarine (A/S) activity. Destroyers had been devised and originally named as torpedo-boat destroyers (TBDs),[1] intended to safeguard a fleet of heavy ships from torpedo attack, not by submarines but by small, fast craft of the kind envisaged by the French *Jeune Ecole* in the late nineteenth century.

The far-sighted French journalist Gabriel Charmes declared that giant battleships no longer reigned supreme but would be replaced by myriads of tiny craft, *la poussière navale*, mere specks of dust – in other words torpedo boats; and Admiral Aube led French thought towards submarines as ultimately the best torpedo carriers. Writing in 1879,[2] the admiral agreed that armoured ships had had their day: a new navy was needed to fight a running battle and wage war against commerce (*guerre de course*). Scarcely anybody paused to consider what might be done in practical terms about submarines belonging to another side, although Britain was concerned about the implications of developments across the Channel.

The idea of underwater warfare was not new even then, nor was the logical progression from submerged explosives to submersible vehicles. Both sprang from the American Civil

War which (although fought almost entirely on land over the abolition of slavery) profoundly affected the naval art by demonstrating that a semi-submersible[3] with a primitive 'bursting charge' on the end of a pole – a spar torpedo – could sink an armoured warship. Indeed, the concept, in true submarine deterrent form, had clearly been grasped by David Bushnell with his *Turtle* during the American War of Independence some ninety years earlier.[4]

Nevertheless, although torpedoes and mines worried surface admirals, submarines were virtually an unknown quantity until the First World War. Very few influential people had contemplated the new threat seriously during the long years of peace at sea. Where amateurish anti-submarine methods had evolved, with scant money and little enthusiasm, they were directed almost entirely at harbour defences or in the shallow waters of the Channel and North Sea where fleet action might be expected.

Thus, for the lack of anything better and for quite a long time, submarines themselves were the dominant actors against their own kind in the open sea, with British boats taking the initiative. By the end of the war submarine duels had accounted for at least seventeen German U-boats by torpedo fire (or perhaps nineteen because there were two uncertain cases), about ten per cent of the U-boats lost. The U-boats were, of course, on the surface when attacked. Depth-charges – delayed-action underwater bombs – dropped by surface ships on submerged German submarines sank twice that number, but only started to take a notable toll after 1917.

On the other hand, U-boats sank only four British submarines by direct action and one by a submarine-laid mine. The imbalance was due to differing employment and did not reflect the comparative skills of the two principal opponents. It is not known if any U-boats, of the forty-four sunk by mines, ran on to 'eggs' laid by British boats.

Gunfire and ramming were the favourite A/S tactics for surface ships in 1914, although damage to the rammer almost always necessitated a lengthy docking for repairs. Gunnery

could be disconcertingly accurate, as Nasmith in *E11* discovered when he torpedoed the Turkish gunboat *Pelenk-i-Dria*
in May 1915 in the eastern Marmara: his 'mouldy' struck home
but the gunboat opened fire even as she was sinking, and
accomplished the remarkable feat of hitting *E11*'s periscope
with her first round.[5]

Any shot which hit the pressure hull was almost bound
to sink a submarine or at least prevent it from diving, so
submarine captains approached armed targets with caution,
submerged whenever possible. This was where decoys or Q-
ships came into play. Sixteen U-boats were sunk by gunfire
(not including Q-ship action) but the *coup de grâce* was
generally delivered after a boat was forced to the surface
by depth-charges. Fourteen boats went to the bottom after
being rammed. A submarine was frequently subjected to all
available methods of attack in any one action, and it is difficult
to be sure whether a shell, a sharp bow, a depth-charge, an
explosive sweep or sheer panic following a 'hammering' was
finally responsible for a boat's destruction.

Besides *ad hoc* methods adopted in chance encounters at
sea, there were two distinct but related lines of approach to
A/S warfare before escorted convoys were introduced. The
first was to hunt for submarines and the second was to lay
traps for them.

So far as hunting went, no submariner worth his salt
admitted, before the war, that he could be detected visually.
In the event, sightings of periscopes and surfaced submarines
were quite frequent but A/S forces could not count on them.
Some kind of underwater detection system had to be devised,
and sound was the obvious, probably the only, answer.

Hydrophones – artificial ears – were constructed to listen
passively for the distinctive noises a submarine made underwater. Active echo-ranging was not seriously considered
until towards the end of the war although Professor R. A.
Fessenden's electromagnetic oscillator, developed for the
American Submarine Signal Company, detected an iceberg
at a range of 2 miles on 22 April 1914. The equipment owed
its existence to the sinking of the *Titanic* two years earlier, but

its use in submarines was confined to underwater signalling. 'Asdic', the acronym first used for underwater detection gear in July 1918,[6] was not available in the active mode.

Everything depended upon the science known as ultra-sonics and passive hydrophones. The latter were usually designed for a frequency range between 400 and 1000 cycles per second (Hertz). They were non-directional (or omni-directional if that sounded better) until 1917, when directional hydrophones started to be fitted on surface ships and sub-marines of the Royal Navy.

The notable talent of Lieutenant Hamilton Harty RNVR (later Sir Hamilton, conductor of the Hallé Orchestra) was enlisted to tune the equipment and match pairs of hydrophones. Any-body with a musical ear was an asset to underwater sound research, but one man deserves immortality, not so much for possessing perfect pitch but for checking it with a precisely tuned cranium. Sir Richard Paget was convinced by 1916 that the key to hydrophone design was to establish propeller frequencies. Accordingly, he arranged to be suspended by his legs over the side of a boat in the Solent while a submarine circled him. After a suitable period submerged (and before he actually drowned) this devoted scientist was hauled up humming the notes he had heard whereupon, safely back in the boat, he related them to the standard G-sharp which he obtained by tapping his skull with a metal rod.

The 'central clearing house' for warlike scientific and technical inventions, including anti-submarine warfare as a primary task, was the Board of Invention and Research (BIR) established by A. J. Balfour who had succeeded Churchill in May 1915 at First Lord of the Admiralty. It was obvious that ideas for effective U-boat countermeasures had to be sifted and coordinated by professionals. Admirable though the gesture was, Vice-Admiral Sir David Beatty's circular letter in May 1915 to all personnel in his battle-cruiser squadron calling for suggestions, and offering prizes of £5, £10 and £15 for the best, did not produce results. None of the sixty-four replies received was practicable. The Navy did not lack imagination – quite the contrary – but there was simply no scientific application of thought. While the BIR was deliberating and when thirty-one anti-submarine research centres got to work, it became apparent that naval officers and civilian scientists had a totally different approach to the problem.

On the one hand, those relatively few officers who mastered the art of modern warfare (in spite of an outdated naval education) were pragmatic and wanted to use whatever was immediately available. On the other hand the scientists resolutely refused to produce any hardware which had not been subjected to systematic research and development. Among other things the BIR, officially formed on 5 July 1915, was supposed to sort out these differences and ensure an effective, harmonious solution to the U-boat peril.

That the BIR never came close to its objective and that it was disbanded in late 1917 was largely due to Balfour's inept decision to appoint Admiral Lord Fisher as its first chairman. Fisher had been forced into premature retirement in April 1915 when, as First Sea Lord, he had disagreed with Churchill's Dardanelles campaign and behaved irresponsibly. When the offer to return to a prestigious post came two months later, the forceful but no longer always rational old seadog seized the opportunity of getting back into the war. Fisher's chairmanship of what might have been a most productive agency, served by eminent scientists, physicists (including Sir Ernest Rutherford) and engineers, was a disaster. His outspokenness, by no means always based on scientific fact, and his cruel criticisms were often counter-productive. When he should have been seeking to win support and loyalty he turned senior officers and distinguished scientists against him – and hence against the BIR which soon became known as the Board of Intrigue and Revenge.

The business of the Board was apportioned to six separate sections, Section Two dealing with submarines and wireless telegraphy (W/T). On the face of it this was an odd combination, but it stemmed quite logically from the relationship between wireless waves and underwater sound waves. In fact, Section Two investigated submarine detection methods far in advance of relatively simple acoustics: these included anomalies in the earth's magnetic field, which did not bear fruit as MAD (Magnetic Anomaly Detection) for twenty-six years, thermal variations in sea water caused by the outflow of propulsion plant coolant (known today as thermal scarring) and optical detection below the surface. The latter came to nothing then, but is currently being researched with blue-green lasers.

No possibility was wholly ignored. Remote dowsing was seriously considered by Sir William Barrett, supported by the well-known psychic researcher Sir Oliver Lodge who was also on the Board, but members only agreed to defray Sir William's expenses: no fees were to be paid for these particular experiments.

Some 14,000 suggestions dealing with the submarine menace were submitted by the general public and some of them bordered on the bizarre. For example, Mr Thos. Mills, a rich and successful Australian businessman who returned to England during the war, was convinced that seagulls were the answer to finding U-boats; and he importuned the BIR incessantly on the subject as well as writing to anyone whom he thought had authority or influence. The scheme, detailed in prolix correspondence, was outlined in his comparatively brief initial letter dated 27 February 1917:

I would like to suggest that a decoy should be used to train the sea birds to locate submarine periscopes. Have a small float containing a dummy periscope; the float to contain a quantity of rough food, say dog or cat's flesh or any other food which will float on the water.

The machine to discharge small quantities every few minutes . . . if the experiment was tried first near some port or near where the enemy submarines were working, I believe the birds in about two weeks would be thoroughly trained to fly around a periscope or over the wake of a submarine . . .

The letter was passed to the Admiralty Anti-Submarine Department (ASD) rather than dealt with in-house, almost certainly because by this time the BIR was so disheartened by the Navy's offhand behaviour towards it that even Jacky Fisher was deflated. On 30 March he ended an unwontedly moderate memorandum to the Secretary of the Cabinet: '. . . the policy of certain Departments has been to adopt such a reticent attitude in dealing with the Board as to create a feeling that the efforts of the latter were viewed with – to say the least – indifference'.[7]

It was undoubtedly true that scientists were deprived of access to much information by the Navy. Commodore S. S. Hall summed up the attitude of the Admiralty: 'the only information necessary to be given was that the enemy submarines were in the sea, and that means were required to detect their presence.'[8]

Not surprisingly, men like Thos. Mills were given short shrift. The BIR was particularly plagued by proposals for the use of giant magnets to draw U-boats to the surface. Unfortunately, another idea which contained the germ of a sound A/S tactic was also rejected because the BIR could not see beyond the ridiculous way in which it was framed. This was to pour green paint on the surface of the sea where it would blind a U-boat commander's periscope and – here was the put-off – make him think he was still too deep to see, whereupon he would bring the submarine shallower and shallower until it was fully exposed. The idea of using paint – or oil – to rob a U-boat of its only means of detecting a target when submerged deserved more than a passing thought, at least in critical and confined areas like harbour approaches. Something of the sort is still a last-ditch defence against marauding midget submarines today.

Although it was decided that seagulls were non-combatants, extensive experiments were carried out with anti-submarine sealions. The trials were virtually the BIR's last bid for power. Dr E. J. Allen, Director of the Marine Biological Laboratory at Plymouth, was appointed as the Board's representative and he immediately put himself in correspondence with the self-styled Captain J. G. Woodward, a well-known trainer of performing sealions who had a regular act with the animals in the repertoire of Hengler's Circus. Woodward claimed to have established already that sealions could hear noises in the sea: 'quite weak sounds, such as the tinkle of a bell which is put on dogs' collars, at speeds up to nine knots, and they could tell the direction'. Dr Allen studied the structure of the animals' ears and set himself to compare the underwater listening ability of a sealion with that of hydrophones. He concluded that sealions had better facilities. Accordingly, on 17 May 1917 the Flag Captain at the submarine base Fort Blockhouse, at the entrance to Portsmouth Harbour, was sent orders from the Admiralty:

Sir,

I am commanded by My Lords Commissioners of the Admiralty to acquaint you that they have approved of a series of trials being carried out in the Solent in regard to the capabilities of sealions in tracking submarines.

2. Rear Admiral B. A. Allenby (Retired) is in charge of these trials, and Their Lordships desire that you will place a submarine at his disposal for the trials and furnish him with all necessary facilities for this purpose.

3. Rear Admiral Allenby's requirements for the trials are as follows:

A stable or shed with water laid on, salt for choice.

A *suitable* launch with small boat in tow, which launch could carry a cage with two animals. The launch should be as noiseless as possible. A suitable cage would require to be fitted, with a sloping gangway to be fitted for the animals to climb on board, unless the launch has a low gunwale (3 feet).

A submarine of any class would suffice to train the animals with preliminary trials at anchor on the surface, later submerged. There are no data to enable a definite opinion to be expressed as to how long the training with submarines would continue, but a decision might be arrived at, one way or another, in about a fortnight provided weather conditions were favourable.

4. You are requested to report to the Admiralty by telegraph when this trial will be ready to commence, observing that the sealions will not be ready before 25th instant.

Signed   S. C. Colville, Admiral

Initial experiments were undertaken in the Glasgow Corporation swimming bath, then in the open-air pool at Alexandria

Park, Glasgow, then in the pool at Great Smith Street, Westminster, and finally in Bala Lake on the Welsh estate of Sir Watkin Williams Wynn. It is clear that the renowned Captain Woodward realised from the start that he was on to a good thing: he was only too glad to supply sealions 'which were available in very large numbers' to the Admiralty.

The final trials, involving an actual submarine, were conducted in the Solent in accordance with the Admiralty directive: they progressed at commendable speed. Some distinguished gentlemen were involved including Sir Richard Paget (of the G-sharp cranium) who, ever resourceful, devised a muzzle made of wire with a small trap-door in front through which the animals could be fed. This prevented any sealion so equipped from catching fish and thereby being distracted from its duty.

Several beasts were chosen for the experiment, foremost amongst them being Millicent, Billiken, Queenie and Dorande. The last-named was getting on in years, short-sighted and heard of hearing; but dim vision made him less prone to pursue fish and he was able to work unmuzzled. Dorande was, in fact, so nearly blind that there was some difficulty in teaching him to jump accurately on to the launch; but with loudly shouted directions he soon managed quite well. He was the most reliable worker in the team and was quite happy to tow a large cigar-shaped float so that his course could be followed by eye from above.

The animals were encouraged to chase the target submarine by rewarding them with herrings but on one occasion the fish were bad. The failure of Billiken, following a hot spell, was attributed to this: he was off colour and disinclined to chase submarines for quite a while thereafter.

The project collapsed when the BIR went out of business, which was probably just as well. But such was the awe in which the Admiralty held Chairman Fisher that it was not until 1931, when Fisher had been dead eleven years, that Their Lordships enquired from Rear Admiral Submarines 'whether any reports and photographs were readily available about the matter at Submarine Headquarters, Gosport'. They were not.

The severely practical German navy wasted no time on outlandish anti-submarine detection methods. It followed the mainstream of British thinking without diversions.

Despite hydrophones of one kind and another, the most reliable A/S detection method on both sides remained, throughout the war, a sharp visual lookout for periscopes and torpedo wakes. Time and again a brief glimpse, reported smartly to the bridge, led to the immediate prosecution of an attacking submarine – often by ramming but later in the war with a string of depth-charges. At the least, an alert lookout could initiate an emergency alteration of course to avoid torpedoes. It was difficult to convince merchant seamen of this, but naval crews quickly realised that binoculars spelled the difference between life and death. Nevertheless, it was largely a matter of luck if an urgent counter-attack succeeded: when a submarine had gone deep hydrophones were the only answer for finding it and then, of course, it was no use trying to ram it or use guns. Underwater explosives were the only solution, and various systems were devised before depth-charges became effective.

For Q-ship decoys, however, gunnery remained the anti-submarine weapon because the concept depended upon enticing the enemy to the surface. Q-ships were usually converted tramp steamers or trawlers, although some were specially constructed. Churchill, typically, was much taken with ambushing the enemy by subterfuge. In his words,[9] 'These vessels carried concealed guns which, by a pantomime trick of trap-doors and shutters, could suddenly come into action. Great ingenuity was shown by the Admiralty Department in developing this idea, and the use of these vessels afterwards afforded opportunity for some of the most brilliant and daring stratagems in the naval war.' To say that they were brilliant is rather too much, but daring they certainly were, and the theatrical performances put on by the crews were worthy of professional thespians.

The ploy was simplicity itself. The Q-ship plodded along in a known U-boat hunting ground to invite attack. The nervous strain on the crew during weeks of waiting must have verged on the intolerable. When a torpedo duly exploded in the little ship's guts (which were stuffed with buoyant materials) a 'panic party' took to the boats in disarray to convince the marauder that all was up with his victim. Meanwhile, hidden armament was manned and, as soon as the submarine surfaced to inspect and finish off its prey, the guncrews dropped the disguise and sprang into action. A dozen U-boats succumbed to decoys between 1915 and 1918; and the men who accounted for them richly deserved their medals.

A quite different kind of decoy consisted of a trawler and submarine partnership, with the latter dived on the end of a tow rope which incorporated a telephone line. HMS C24 (Taylor) put paid to U-40 with this gambit on 23 June 1915, 50 miles south-east of Aberdeen. The trawler *Taranaki* sighted U-40 and engaged the attention of the enemy while telephoning C24 who immediately tried to let go her end of the tow. At this critical juncture the cable refused to slip and the trawler had to free her end instead: that left 180 metres (100 fathoms) of heavy tow rope dangling from the submerged submarine's bows. By desperate pumping, C24's First Lieutenant managed to recover the trim and the Captain was able to get into a firing position without the cable becoming wound up in the propeller. The sight of the trawler's crew abandoning ship so engrossed the lookouts on the bridge of U-40 that they failed to see the periscope nearby. A single torpedo from C24 finished the business: only the three men on the U-boat's bridge survived. Exactly a month later C27 (Dobson), towed by the trawler *Princess Louise*, repeated the trick and put a fish into U-23.

Nets, another kind of trap, often had explosive charges attached to them and these were detonated either by remote control from shore or by direct contact like mines. Minenets, or plain nets with anti-submarine vessels in attendance, destroyed six U-boats. Explosive sweeps towed back and forth over an invisible submarine's supposed position (possibly suggested by the shaking of net-buoys earlier) sent another five boats to the bottom.

The simplest type of barrier was the Bircham Indicator Net,

a light flexible curtain of thin steel woven into 2- or 3-metre (6- or 10-foot) meshes and supplied in lengths of 180 metres (200 yards). It had been tested on one of the Royal Navy's own submarines. The lengths were laid, clipped together and supported by glass buoys in long lines across particular channels. The disappearance of a buoy, or the automatic ignition of a calcium light, immediately betrayed an entangled submarine to the armed vessels that kept watch – a 'mosquito fleet' of yachts, trawlers and drifters – and enabled them to follow the trail.

The Admiralty ordered more than 1000 miles of netting at the beginning of 1915, and by 13 February 17 miles of the Dover Straits were barricaded. The theory was excellent but the practice was disappointing. The tiny ships on guard were mostly commandeered and many had crews who were untrained or unenthusiastic, particularly in steep seas. They were often unable to maintain a proper watch, and bad weather wreaked havoc with the nets. U-boat commanders who might know a net's position from intelligence reports had been expected to slip beneath it and run on to rows of deep mines which could be planted below; but, sadly for the defenders, they usually chose to break through on the surface by night.

Depth-charges or 'ashcans' were by far the most lethal A/S weapons. But their development, with variable depth settings and an integrated attack system, was slow during the first two years of war. The effective Type 'D' was not issued to the fleet until March 1916. The tactical difficulty was twofold. Firstly, enough depth-charges had to be dropped over a sufficiently wide area to allow for errors in estimating the submarine's position; and secondly – a matter of pure guesswork – the right depth for them to explode had to be selected immediately before they were released.

The lethal range of an Allied 140-kilo (300-pound) depth-charge was no more than 4 metres (14 feet), although at twice that distance it might disable a submarine and at 18 metres (60 feet) it would have a telling effect on a crew's morale.[10] Bearing in mind that a submarine making 5 knots covered

460 metres (1500 feet) in three minutes – and that might be in any direction – the scale of the problem becomes apparent. Even if hydrophones did hear a U-boat the beat only gave an approximate bearing with no indication of range. In other words they could detect but not positively locate the enemy below. In the circumstances it is surprising that depth-charge attacks succeeded as well as they did.

Depth-charges were in short supply for the first three years of the war. Even by July 1917 the weekly supply from armament factories was only 140. Admiral Sir John Jellicoe (who became First Sea Lord in November 1916) insisted on strenuous measures to increase the rate of production, and under his goad the weekly output rose to 800 by the end of 1917 and continued to mount rapidly. During the whole of that year between 100 and 300 depth-charges were used each month on average; but during the last six months of hostilities in 1918 no less than 2000 depth-charges per month were expended. In 1916 two or perhaps three U-boats were sunk by 'ashcans', in 1917 twelve and in 1918 twenty-four. The first submarine victims – *UC-7* and *UB-44* in July and possibly *UC-19* in December 1916 – left no survivors. It was apparently not until May 1917 that *U-49* (Hartmann), surviving an attack, brought back positive intelligence about the capabilities of a fully developed British *Wasserbombe*.[11] (For the record, two disguised armed trawlers, *Gunner* and *Quickly*, were the first A/S vessels to use depth-charges in anger on 20 July 1915 off the Bell Rock: they claimed to have sunk a U-boat but history denies them that honour.)

Depth-charge throwers gave the hunter more of a chance than rolling ashcans over the stern because valuable seconds were saved, and not having to pass right over the submarine meant that hydrophone contact was not necessarily lost at the moment of attack. For the same reason some ships were equipped with howitzers for throwing a small bomb to explode 12 or 18 metres (40 or 60 feet) below the surface. Similar shells were provided for 190-mm (7.5-inch) guns and even some of the little 5.5-kilo guns (12-pounders) had 'bricks' which exploded underwater.

Any of these would have been more effective than the gadgets busily constructed by the Forth torpedo-boat crews at the beginning of the war. Each device consisted of a copper-wire noose with 29 metres (16 fathoms) of line and a wooden buoy, the idea being to lasso a periscope. The lasso revived a project seriously considered in 1904; but, as one of the officers concerned was heard to mutter, it was like putting salt on a rabbit's tail. It was the same group of torpedo-boats which was ordered to clear away starboard anchors at sea, ready for letting go on top of an enemy submarine.

Absurdities like these sprang from pre-war evolutions arranged and judged by umpires so that surface ships always won. For example, ten years before the war – the time span required to turn an impressionable young officer into the captain of a destroyer or the captain of a destroyer into an influential admiral – the Channel Fleet destroyers 'sank' fourteen submarines with no loss of a surface ship. Before the advent of depth-charges 87.5 per cent of destroyer claims were allowed, but not a single submarine attack was adjudged successful. Nor was the inhibiting effect of a submarine presence taken into account. Jacky Fisher had something to say about that: 'These manoeuvres are the most misleading manoeuvres ever devised by man! There were the destroyers calmly laying over the submarines (so utterly out of the question in actual war), fishing for them as if they were trying to catch whiting!'[12]

However, the 1912 and 1913 manoeuvres had clearly demonstrated that a large destroyer screen around a battle fleet, with all ships zig-zagging at high speed, was effective in defeating submarine attacks; and if there were not enough destroyers a horde of smaller craft speeding about on unpredictable courses would do almost as well. Always escorted while underway at sea, none of the 'dreadnought' battleships went down to submarine attack. Only the 'pre-dreadnought' *Formidable*, unescorted and inexplicably steering a straight course at slow speed, was sunk, by *U-24* on New Year's Day 1915.

Alas for Britain's supply routes, the Admiralty was fixated on protecting the Grand Fleet. Escorted convoys of merchantmen were historically sound: they were advocated by junior officers at the beginning of the war, and strongly recommended by Mediterranean commanders from 1915. Yet a convoy system was not properly organised until the spring of 1917. The delay cost Britain dear.

When convoys were at last marshalled and shepherded, the prime problem for German U-boat captains was an empty sea. Hitherto merchant ships could be found here, there and everywhere, but now they were formed into groups which might or might not pass through a U-boat's area. Since there was no way of predicting a convoy route with certainty there was no way of concentrating U-boats in a convoy's path. It was the dearth of opportunities more than the efficacy of convoy escorts that made the convoy system so difficult for the U-boats.

However, convoying did bring together in one place the various anti-submarine measures, and these immediately began to take effect. No longer, in the face of escorts, could a U-boat captain choose the place, time and range for an attack. No longer could he surface for gun action. No longer, after torpedoing a merchant ship, could he count on escaping before warships arrived on the scene. An escorted convoy took action to the U-boats, and in that sense convoying was an offensive rather than a defensive strategy.

The related concept of physically obstructing a submarine or distracting it from its avowed intent – all that high-speed destroyers could really do for fast naval formations – led to the employment of airships and heavier-than-air flying machines. Although it was undoubtedly intended from the start that submarines should be attacked from the air, strategists realised that the greatest rewards would be early warning of enemy boats (allowing prospective surface targets to evade) and the discouragement of submarines which wanted to make speed on the surface.

Six U-boats were destroyed by airborne attack (all in 1917) and a few British boats had some narrow escapes. The captain of HM Airship *NS6* was right in believing that aircraft, as a rule, only saw a submarine 'when he is caught napping or been careless . . . .'. In clear water, though, a submarine could be seen from above at a considerable depth: in July 1915 the captain of *E18* was mortified to find that a German zeppelin was still able to track him when he went to 20 metres (70 feet); and on 15 September 1916 the French *Foucault* was sunk by Austrian aircraft after being spotted at 15 metres (50 feet) where her *commandant* thought himself safe. Usually, however, the sea was too murky in the principal areas of conflict for airborne units to pursue a fully submerged prey: their value, in today's much-favoured word, was deterrence. As an eastern Mediterranean squadron intelligence summary put it: 'Aircraft attacks on submarines are most disconcerting . . .'.

Airships and zeppelins were more of a potential menace to submarines than aircraft because their endurance was far greater. A zeppelin could hang on to a contact, and it was very difficult for a submarine to shake it off. One of the monstrous cigars was sighted in 1917 by *G13* at sunrise off Horns Reef. The captain, George Bradshaw, over-confident after sinking *UC-43*, gleefully elected to shoot it down. Accordingly, he ordered gun-action stations: the boat surfaced and the gun's crew tumbled up in record time to bring the 'disappearing' AA gun up and into action from its stowage in the casing. Five rapid rounds caused the 'zepp' to drop her tail steeply and start weaving erratically, but she soon regained an even keel and came roaring back to take up a strategic position dead astern of the submarine where the gun could not bear. *G13* was thereupon forced to dive – and fortunately Bradshaw got her down before the enemy could drop a bomb on the temporarily defenceless boat. Throughout the day any attempt to surface was greeted with bombs. This happened so many times that, by the evening, Bradshaw thought the enemy must be out of stock. Deep, and wondering whether it was yet dark, he casually asked the telegraphist hydrophone listener, who was still wearing his headphones, what the time was. The 'Sparker', stunned by the amplified noise of bombs over several hours, was in no shape to answer anything: 'The time, Sonny, what is the time?' Bradshaw demanded again. 'The time, sir, is slow ahead, sir.'

When the submarine returned to periscope depth the zeppelin had gone and *G13* was able to surface safely, but the incident was a good example of how a continual threat from the air could wear down a submarine and its crew.

Observation balloons or blimps were not much use for A/S work. It was impossible for men in tiny swinging cages to maintain an alert watch continuously, nor were they by any means sure whether they were looking at a friend or foe. One blimp mistook HMS *C9* for a U-boat in a practice diving area north of Spurn Point and dropped a bomb. It missed – of course – and the pilot politely apologised by Aldis lamp. Some British submarines were fitted to tow blimps themselves, the idea being to slip the tow and go into an attack when the blimp reported a target. Nothing came of the scheme but the German U-boat arm was to revive it, successfully, with manned kites during the Second World War.

Persistence was the governing factor in all kinds of A/S warfare, and if bangs could be created during a hunt so much the better. Vice-Admiral de Robeck, writing from HMS *Lord Nelson* in the eastern Mediterranean in February 1916, spelled out the point to amplify an Intelligence Directive:

Every occasion should be taken to attack submarines, with depth-charges, lance bombs, etc. Even if the chances of inflicting vital injury are small, the explosion of a charge in the vicinity of a submarine may react unfavourably on the personnel – *a very important consideration.*

Experience amply confirmed the advisability of anti-submarine units attacking again and again despite the chances of a kill being slight. Naturally, reactions varied according to the temperament of the submarine crews and of the captain in particular. The captain, as always, set the tone and, according to British records, there were several who cracked completely. One brief extract from a confidential report about a commanding officer[13] in The Trade will be enough: '. . . was very queer after a severe depth-charging . . .'. Who can blame him? It was not pleasant to be in charge of thirty or forty fellow beings locked up in a steel cylinder and subjected to repeated hammer-blows for hours on end, knowing that at any moment the hungry sea could rush through a started rivet or a split seam. The greatest enemy was literally all round.

PART II

THE ACTION

CHAPTER 7

Opening Shots in the
North Sea (1914)

The Admiralty, London

Commodore Roger Keyes hated the Admiralty. He was no match for the civil servants or the politically minded admirals in what he described to his wife as 'that hotbed of wickedness and intrigue'. The old building was stuffy and plagued by flies. He could not open the window because the multitude of papers on his desk flew about and even more flies came in. He longed for the sea and persuaded the Board that his supposedly administrative appointment as head of the Submarine Service would become, in the event of war, an operational sea-going command. He was personally to control the Eighth 'Oversea' Submarine Flotilla ('D'- and 'E'-class boats) based at Harwich, and would operate under the orders of the Commander-in-Chief Home Fleet. Best of all, two fast destroyers, *Lurcher* and *Firedrake*, would be attached to the flotilla and he would fly his broad pennant on one of these whenever he went to sea. Until then he had an alternative office, much more frequently used, in a hideous hutment erected on the old sailing brig HMS *Dolphin* at Fort Blockhouse, Gosport, where the alma mater of submarines had been established in 1905.

When Keyes read the Sunday papers at his Fareham home on 26 July he became convinced that war was imminent. Typically, he took matters into his own hands: he cancelled all leave, by telephone, for the submarine flotillas and took the early train to London to see the Chief of War Staff and the First Sea Lord. Both were much relieved that Commodore (S) had anticipated an order now being sent to the whole fleet. The submarines were fully manned and ready to proceed to their war stations at once: Keyes urged that the 'oversea' flotillas should be moved out into the North Sea and that the Dover Patrol flotilla of 'C' boats should be brought to readiness, on station, immediately.

That evening Keyes and his wife attended a dance at Goodwood. Several officers were recalled to duty while the party was in progress: the submariners among them came up to Eva Keyes to be wished God-speed. The commodore was reminded of the Duchess of Richmond's ball before Waterloo. Amid the glitter of naval uniforms it was doubtless rather romantic; the totally unromantic squalor of wartime submarining was yet to come.

The flotillas were ordered to deploy the following day, but on Wednesday Keyes learned that, owing to a blunder by the staff, the Eighth Flotilla had been sent to the Humber instead of its proper war station at Harwich. It was not until 10 p.m. that Keyes was able to track down a preoccupied Commander-in-Chief and ask for the error to be rectified. He was told, laconically, to 'do as you like'. He managed to catch the midnight train to Grimsby, arriving next morning by the workman's train at Immingham where he hoisted his broad pennant in the depot ship HMS *Maidstone* and led the flotilla to Harwich with the other depot ship HMS *Adamant* in company. He was thankful to reach port safely on the 31st because he expected a pre-emptive attack en route, but he was even more thankful to be in a ship, in command, and out of the Admiralty.

Commodore Reginald Tyrwhitt, commanding some forty ships of the First and Third Destroyer Flotillas, together with the attached light cruisers *Fearless* and *Amphion*, was also at Harwich. Tyrwhitt was a kindred spirit and shared an intense desire to engage the enemy. The enemy was similarly inclined.

Helgoland

On 30 July the German High Sea Fleet passed through the Kiel Canal into the North Sea followed by the First Submarine Flotilla (*U-5, U-7 to 10, U-15 to 18*), which went straight to the strongly fortified island base at Helgoland and received orders to commence patrol duties in the Bight the following afternoon. The signal to 'take war measures forthwith' was sent on 2 August. As Keyes suspected, in naval parlance the Germans were warming the bell, but the U-boats were not allowed to go far. They simply rode to their anchors among the sandbanks to seaward of the fortress during daylight hours and returned to harbour each evening. Their duty was to give the High Sea Fleet timely warning of the massed naval attack upon the German coast which was fully expected from Britain before war was formally declared. British 'C'-class coastal boats were stationed off the Humber for a reciprocal purpose.

Of course, nothing happened. Nor, after war was declared, did an attack materialise on 4 or 5 August. The British Grand Fleet, now under the command of Admiral Sir John Jellicoe and based at Scapa Flow, contented itself with a broad sweep between Scotland and Norway in the belief that three German transports, seen passing Sprogo Sound at the entrance to the Great Belt on 1 August, presaged a raid on the Shetlands. Still nothing happened.

Harwich

All the 'oversea' boats, nominally eight 'D' class and nine 'E' class, belonged to the Eighth Flotilla. Ten were immediately available and another five of these modern diesel boats would soon be attached. *D1*, however, was by now mechanically unreliable and could not be sent on sorties.

The 'E's, displacing 660/800 tons,[1] had two bow, one stern and two beam torpedo tubes, some of them mounting a 5.5-kilo (12-pounder) gun. They were good general-purpose boats – with major variations within the class – capable of operating in all theatres.

On the evening of 4 August Keyes cleared lower deck of all submariners and addressed the officers and men. He told them that in a couple of hours they would be at war: what they had done in the way of fitting themselves for service by taking war risks during the past three years would now be rewarded.

It was a rather ingenuous statement but the commodore was loudly cheered. 'You must go into this seeing red – it's the only way.' A voice sang out, 'Don't worry sir, we'll give 'em Hell', and an impromptu rendering of 'Rule Britannia' followed, quashed by Keyes who advised, 'Better keep that for the end.'

The crews were prepared for battle in a peculiarly British way. In this great game against the Hun the submarine officers were determined to act like English gentlemen – standfast (navalese for 'except') Max Horton and a few other exceptionally talented and crafty rogues who were not inhibited by public school traditions. And the captains, good or bad, were supported admirably by petty officers brought up in the Victorian and Edwardian navies to a lifetime of utterly dependable service. Together they made an unbeatable team which won loyalty – accompanied, of course, by the usual grumbling – from the sailors and stokers who did the dirty work.

Apart from the Eighth Flotilla, whose 'oversea' title implied offensive operations even if the Admiralty had not yet hoisted in that fact, there were plenty of older boats available for defence at home and abroad. Three were on the China station, three at Malta and another three at Gibraltar. Thirty-four 'B' and 'C' petrol boats were assigned to work with surface patrol flotillas off the principal naval ports, and eight primitive 'A' boats joined the destroyer harbour defence flotillas. The 'B' and 'C' boats based at Dover spent their time secured to buoys laid across the Straits, to conserve fuel and minimise watch-keeping. They had a miserable time but it was hoped, with the boundless optimism so evident at the time, that they could slip their moorings quickly and intercept German warships which might threaten the British Expeditionary Force to France. Anyway, the unpleasantness would not last long because the war would 'be over by Christmas' or – as believed in Berlin – 'before the leaves fall'.

In the Forth, where some 'C' boats had been moved up from Chatham to supplement the outer defences, there was 'horrid excitement'. Everyone was 'fearfully warlike and very keen for a scrap'[2] which was expected somewhere off the east coast.

Meanwhile the French, with forty-five assorted boats and twenty-five building, were slow off the mark, and it was not until October that they suggested sending the fast 17.5/11.4-knot steam-reciprocating *Gustave Zédé* to Harwich. They backed off when Keyes told them about probable German anti-submarine tactics in the Bight because the crew was not sufficiently trained. Instead, the slower but more efficient *Archimède*, also funnelled, eventually arrived at the beginning of December; she was to suffer horribly in the winter gales.

The Helgoland (or German) Bight was a crucial area, embracing as it did all the enemy ports bordering the North Sea. This was why Keyes was content with operational command at Harwich, albeit with only one-fifth of The Trade at his disposal.

At 3.30 a.m. on 5 August, some three hours after Britain's ultimatum to the Kaiser expired, *E6* (Talbot) and *E8* (Goodhart) sailed from Harwich, too early to get a cheer from the depot ship, whose officers had anyway been up until late drinking confusion to the Kaiser – the 'Big Cheese'[3] to punsters who spoke German. But the Boy Seamen from HMS *Ganges* at Shotley turned out on the forecastle and along the foreshore to cheer themselves hoarse as Tyrwhitt's destroyers, the *Amethyst* and *Ariel* (taking *E6* and *E8* in tow) and later four more submarines with Commodore (S) in *Lurcher*, passed down the estuary. Keyes found it all very inspiring.

E6 and *E8* slipped from their tows (by means of an internal mechanism forward) off Terschelling in the evening. Towing, a routine evolution, spared the crews if not the officers. A 'Third Hand' for each boat was soon provided but without him the Captain and Second Captain (First Lieutenant) kept alternate watches. There was not much comfort off watch. The wardroom – a curtained area – did not justify the name, although officers had their own Able Seaman cook who produced delights like kidney and onion pie. But at least the oversea boats had 'heads' – WCs – which the 'A's, 'B's and 'C's did not.

Keyes reckoned that personnel endurance would be low. The first two boats on patrol were ordered not to stay in the hostile waters of the Bight for more than three days: unless they found themselves 'very well placed for offensive operations' they were to return after two. Talbot and Goodhart stretched their orders to the limit but returned from their initial expedition on 8 August with little information save that the Bight was packed with Dutch, Danish and German fishing vessels, some of the latter being fitted with wireless and suspected of being lookouts. However, a further reconnaissance by *D2*, *D3*, *E5*, and *E7*, returning to Harwich on 18 August, and another by *E4*, *E9* and *D5*, returning on 23 August, brought back invaluable intelligence about enemy destroyer movements. So complete were the submarine observations that Commodore (S) was able to form a clear picture of German dispositions in the Bight by night and by day, and he could gauge approximately the time that patrols relieved one another. With this information Keyes felt that an enterprise could be organised to cut off German night patrols on their way home, day patrols on their way out, and 'generally smash up the look-out organisation of the Helgoland Bight'.[4]

Accordingly, Keyes recommended to the Chief of the War Staff that 'a drive, commencing before dawn from inshore close to the enemy coast, should inflict considerable loss on these destroyer patrols. Before the drive takes place, the submarines might take up position close to the enemy's port [Wilhelmshaven] lying on the bottom until a pre-arranged time when they might rise and be in a position to attack the enemy's cruisers proceeding out to attack the drive, or vessels returning which may have escaped through or round the drive'.[5] Keyes felt that German heavy ships would be sure to come out to beat off the raiding force, and they would provide much more satisfactory targets for the submarines than destroyers zig-zagging about at high speed.

HMS *D5* (Herbert) had, in fact, fired two torpedoes at the small German cruiser *Rostock*, on 22 August, during the last scouting mission but they passed beneath the target: they had been set to run as for light practice heads but the submarine's crew blamed a mascot teddy bear that resided in the torpedo compartment for luck, or 'joss' as sailors who had served on the China station called it. Immediately after the abortive attack, Herbert came upon a man with teddy in one hand and a knife in the other. 'I'll teach you to be *good* joss', the seaman growled and then proceeded to slit the furry throat, letting the sawdust stuffing trickle out into a bucket below.

Unfortunately this grisly little ceremony did nothing to dispel the evil genius presiding over *D5*, but it typified Herbert's association with misfortune. *D5* blew up on a mine soon afterwards on 3 October; the surviving captain went on, in due course, to take a leading part in the notorious *Baralong* Q-ship action (see page 203) and then to command the steam submarine *K13* which sank on trials in 1917.

Keyes's plan for a drive was broadly adopted. It was to be the first offensive fleet operation of the war, proposed by none other than the Head of the Submarine Service. Keyes was bent on his flotilla working not as a private navy but in wholehearted support of the surface fleet. This tended to mask the potential of submarines operating independently against the enemy, and his strategy certainly risked what would now be called mutual interference – that is, the danger of friendly units attacking each other – but it did ensure that the capabilities of the newer submarines were brought to the fore.

Hermann Bauer interpreted the Kaiser's strategy aggressively, inasmuch as it mentioned submarines at all. HMS *Pathfinder* was the first to suffer the consequences of 'an offensive carried as far as the Baltic coast'. But success was not immediate: two U-boat losses preceded it.

At 4.30 a.m. on 6 August ten U-boats (*U-5, 7, 8, 9; U-13, 14, 15, 16, 17* and *18*) set out from Helgoland, escorted by surface ships, on a pioneering war cruise. Drawn from Bauer's first half-flotilla (commanded by Kapitänleutnant Mühlau), they were paraffin-fuelled 'Desiderata' boats, not the newest but their crews were judged to be more efficient and experienced than those in the second half-flotilla.[6] 'Desiderata' (*U-5* to *U-18*) referred to the desired characteristics agreed in 1907 and supposedly embodied in their design. In fact, even when their Körting paraffin engines held together, the speed and endurance of the 'Desideratas' fell well below the requirement. The group of ten which embarked on the first major U-boat sortie was not representative of the mechanically sound and operationally effective MAN diesel boats, including Hersing's *U-21*, which were coming up behind them in increasing numbers.

In contrast with the Royal Navy's plans (which had not yet matured under Bauer's opposite number Roger Keyes) there was no intention of drawing out units of the battle fleet. On the contrary, the German U-boats were going to seek the Grand Fleet in its own waters. Although it might be further north, the main body was most likely to be found in the middle of the North Sea between the parallels 56 and 57 degrees north: that was 50 to 100 miles in advance of the blockade line which was thought (wrongly) by the German naval staff to have been permanently established between Peterhead and Egersund on the South Norwegian coast.

The intention was to inflict damage on British heavy ships. During the advance light forces, if encountered, were not to be torpedoed unless the circumstances were exceptionally favourable. On the return journey, however, advantage was to be taken of any attack opportunities.

When 80 miles out into the North Sea, the light cruiser escorts *Hamburg* and *Stettin* (first and second U-boat flotilla commanders respectively) together with the destroyers *S-99* and *S-135* (half-flotilla leaders acting as wireless repeating ships astern of the group) turned sixteen points and made off at full speed towards the protection of the big guns and howitzers on Helgoland. The slow and poorly armed little torpedo boat *D5*, the third repeating ship, had prudently retired a couple of hours earlier, 'Returning for coal' according to her signal but doubtless excusing herself in the face of the big British guns expected ahead. The submarines, starting from a fairly accurate position given by the lead escorts, were on their own.

The group was to drive northwards in line abreast, with 7 miles between boats (a little less than maximum horizon visibility from conning tower to conning tower) as far as an imaginary fixed line – *Standlinie* – drawn between Scapa and Hardanger Fjord. It was the archetypal example of a naval staff wishfully thinking that if courses and positions were drawn on the staff chart submarines would conform precisely to them. Neither then, nor at any other time subsequently, did they do so. Sometimes the boats were hopelessly out of position after a while, as in this case, and sometimes they were only a little away; but it was very seldom that they were exactly where the staff expected them to be – and that was so in all navies.

Although German gyros were better than those in the Royal Navy the compasses in 'Desideratas' were grossly affected by rolling and pitching in bad weather. Chronometers for celestial navigation had only just been issued and quartermaster-navigators were unpractised in sight-taking. In short, navigation was very imprecise during this initial cruise. The constant accompaniment of U-boats by surface vessels in peace had concealed difficulties in finding the way, and the submarines soon strayed far from their assigned tracks. An exception was *U-18* with Second Half-Flotilla Commander Spindler embarked for war experience. Uniquely, the plotted positions of this boat matched well with charted movements of British cruiser squadrons which were briefly sighted.

The magnetic clutch on one engine in *U-9* broke loose two days out on 8 August, and Otto Weddigen was forced to limp home. At 3 a.m. on 10 August Weddigen was woken with the news that Helgoland's triple flashing light was in sight, but it turned out to be a light with similar characteristics at Hanstholm on the northern edge of the Jutland Peninsula. *U-9* had been steering north-east while the compass showed south-east, and was now some 220 miles off track, close to being stranded in the Jammer Bight where Weddigen's career would have ended prematurely (with the consequent saving of four British cruisers and four merchantmen) had not the mistake been discovered in time. *U-5* (Lemmer) had to reverse course at about the same time and make for Helgoland with one set of Körtings out of action and the other puffing and smoking, as was its wont.

Pohle in *U-15* had better luck, at first. On the same day, simply because he was inadvertently more than 100 miles west of his proper route, he discovered the battleships *Ajax*, *Monarch* and *Orion* carrying out a battle-practice shoot off Fair

Island. Pohle dived and fired a torpedo at *Monarch*. It missed, but alerted the British ships to an underwater threat hitherto unexpected in these latitudes. At this point Pohle evidently realised his navigational error (probably because he was able to take sights in relatively fair weather) and steered eastwards at best speed on the surface.

At 3.40 a.m. on the following morning the light cruiser *Birmingham*, one of the Grand Fleet's advanced screen, sighted a submarine apparently hove-to in the mist. This was *U-15* again – her number was clearly visible – and Pohle was now having trouble with both Körtings. The sound of heavy hammering could be heard and no proper watch was being kept. Pohle paid the penalty. *Birmingham* opened fire with all the 150-mm (6-inch) guns that could be brought to bear and turned to ram the submarine amidships at full speed, cutting her in half. No bodies came to the surface.

Before the war ended another 198 U-boats and 4716 men were to join *U-15* on the bottom. One of these was *U-13* (Count Arthur von Schweinitz) which failed to show at Helgoland when the others returned on the afternoon of 11 August. The cause of loss was never established but it was almost certainly an internal accident, probably a hydrogen explosion above the batteries.[7]

On the face of it the ten boats – now reduced to eight – had achieved nothing, but the *U-15* incident worried Admiral Jellicoe to the extent that he thought the danger from U-boats to be so acute that the battle fleet could not safely remain in the North Sea. As soon as the British Expeditionary Force had been transported to France he wanted the big ships to be held west of the Orkneys or be confined to secure anchorages, Loch Ewe (adopted as a war anchorage on 11 August) being preferred to Scapa Flow. Jellicoe's unease showed that the presence of submarines, even if no more than suspected, was beginning to be a serious deterrent to traditional naval strategy. However, the Admiralty disagreed, for the moment, with the Commander-in-Chief. Before Jellicoe finally had his way in October the Grand Fleet was to be in the North Sea again.

While the First Flotilla was engaged to the north, four MAN-engined diesel boats from the Second Flotilla (Korvetten-kapitän Otto Feldmann) sailed at 5.30 p.m. on 8 August to attack heavy ships covering the BEF which was predicted, incorrectly, to be landing at Zeebrugge, Ostend, Dunkirk and Calais on the following day. Torpedoes were fitted with net-cutters and strong countermeasures were expected, mainly consisting of explosive sweeps. *U-19, U-21, U-22* and *U-24* were cautioned to keep enough in their batteries to pass through British patrol lines dived and return without surfacing to recharge: they could make 80 miles at 5 knots submerged, a creditable performance for the day.

Many destroyers and light craft were sighted, but no capital ships. The group was back at Helgoland on 11 August when, in fact, the BEF had barely started the massive landing operation. It seems extraordinary in retrospect that German sights were not shifted, at least temporarily, to the troop transports which were bound to affect the course of the war far more than battleships; but intelligence was faulty and the German Naval Staff was anyway wholly concerned with naval matters, obsessed with the problem of the Grand Fleet and not interested in land battles where the Kaiser's soldiers would 'walk over General French's contemptible little Army'. In any case it was believed on both sides at this time that no nation would be so uncivilised as to destroy merchant shipping – which included transports – wholesale. Admiral Scheer declared (after the Armistice) that 'such aggressive ideas were quite foreign to our naval policy',[8] but he was being a post-war apologist. The strategy was certainly – if privily – considered (as previously suggested), and one staff officer had written a paper which calculated that 200 U-boats would be needed for what he termed 'cruiser warfare' against England. The estimate proved remarkably accurate.

After further abortive searches for important units between 15 and 21 August, which threw some light on British patrol procedures but little else, the Staff concluded that 'the British Main Fleet, and probably all war vessels which are worth attacking by submarine, are so far away from Germany that it is beyond the technical capabilities of our submarines to find them. . . . Submarine operations will therefore be abandoned for the present until it can be assumed that the British Fleet has come nearer.'9

This uninspired conclusion proved to be a watershed for German naval strategy which thereafter turned towards a kind of guerilla warfare. Future sorties would have to be moulded with different objectives, and U-boat men had their own plans for those.

Battles in the Bight

Keyes's plan to shake things up in the Bight matured on 26 August. At midnight he hoisted his pennant in HMS *Lurcher*, with *Firedrake* in company, and led two 'D' boats and six 'E' boats eastwards across the North Sea. Everyone was 'on the grin', wrote Oswald Hallifax, Second Captain of *E7*, 'except *D1* and *D4* who are staying behind, poor brutes'. The dangers that lay ahead were plain enough but there was an additional cause for anxiety: when *E5* left Harwich, a man (subsequently arrested and found to be a spy) was seen letting off a carrier pigeon, presumably telling of the flotilla's departure.

Tyrwhitt, with two light cruisers and some thirty destroyers, would constitute the surface force. Participation by the Grand Fleet had been refused and it was therefore a trifle disconcerting when the Light Cruiser Squadron (Rear Admiral Goodenough) and the Battle-Cruiser Squadron (Vice-Admiral Sir David Beatty) fell in with the Keyes-Tyrwhitt team two days later off Helgoland. The change of heart had been signalled but a broadcast on the destroyer radio frequency did not reach Keyes 100 miles from Whitehall: unwisely, the Admiralty message failed to call for a receipt.

The makings of a first-class shambles abounded in the Bight at what came to be called the Battle of Helgoland. Keyes noted wistfully that 'it means so much to a ship to know that, if she falls in with another, it is beyond the shadow of doubt a friend or an enemy; indeed it is the essence of good Staff work to ensure this is possible.' The idea was for light British surface forces to drive inshore, engage the enemy destroyers and tempt German cruisers out to support them, while submarines were to be positioned to seaward, lying on the bottom until a prearranged time. They would then rise, torpedo enemy cruisers coming out to attack the drive and have a second go at them on their way back. 'It will', wrote Keyes thoughtfully, 'require some organisation . . .'.

It was just the sort of boyish, adventurous scheme which Keyes enjoyed, and it appealed equally to the flamboyant Beatty, with his cap perpetually at a rakish angle, flying his flag in HMS *Lion* and leading the battle-cruisers into action. All kinds of difficulties were bound to arise but the great thing was not to be a 'pompous ass' and make much of them. The *Maidstone Muckrag*, the depot ship's internal newspaper, was jocular, in keeping with the popular approach, in its editorial:

War – red, ruddy war is in our midst. You didn't know that did you, Gentle Reader? The green fields are stained with gore. The green seas are littered with lost torpedoes and broken hydroplanes. The roar of battle well-nigh drowns the mild oaths of the Submarine Officers. Truly we live in queer times. No time this for moping or dawdling. Each must do his little bit for the honour of Old England, and the Empire, and the Alhambra, and places like that. It is not given to all of us to penetrate into the lonely Bight of Heligoland.[10] In the language of our brilliant allies, '*Hélas, nous ne pouvons touts faire fondre au bout de la mer Hélas*' (or words to that effect).

What then can *we* do?

The *Maidstone Muckrag* readily supplies an answer to that question. We seek to prove that the pen is mightier than the sword, torpedo or any weapon. The Kaiser does so daily; we shall do so every month. We shall elevate, instruct, and amuse those whose hard lot prevents them elevating, instructing or amusing themselves. What more would you of us? Ring up the curtain. Circulate the gin. Let the revels commence.

The early morning of Friday 28 August was misty and the sea was calm, the worst kind of weather for submarine operations. The eight boats were on station by 4 a.m. with *E6*, *E7* and *E8* on a north–south line 30 miles west of Helgoland,

D2 and *D3* on an east–west line to the south-west, *E4*, *E5* and *E9* in the forefront straddling the island. The submarines were 12 miles apart and all were on the surface by dawn to act as bait. They were in an unenviable position, liable not only to encounter German destroyers but to be attacked mistakenly by British surface units. The submariners, as Hallifax mildly remarked, could expect a few surprises but everybody thought it was 'a jolly good stunt'. (A stunt was something organised by one's own side while a spasm was due to the enemy.)

Spasms were few but surprises were plentiful, arising from unannounced British ships crashing through the submarine lines. It was only by good fortune that no boat was rammed (*Southampton* made a pass at *E6*) and that no British cruisers were torpedoed. Astonishingly, the Great Raid, headlined by the newspapers as such, went much according to plan. British cruisers and destroyers attacked German outpost destroyers and sank one at the outset. Some small German cruisers then arrived on the scene, inflicting damage on the British light cruiser *Arethusa* and some destroyers; but Beatty's battle-cruisers now appeared, and within a few minutes the German light cruisers *Mainz*, *Köln* and *Ariadne* were sinking.

Keyes's wish to create the right atmosphere succeeded: the results of the action were far-reaching. In Churchill's words: 'Henceforward the weight of British naval prestige lay heavy across all German sea enterprises . . . the German navy was indeed muzzled. Except for furtive movements by individual submarines and minelayers not a dog stirred from August until November.'

Churchill was underestimating the U-boats. Underwater wolves had now been set loose and they were hunting outside their own territory. But what effect did the British submarines have on the Battle of Helgoland? The intelligence which they brought back after reconnoitring the broad bay beforehand was essential: without it the raid could not have been timed successfully. But the sum total of their exploits was not impressive. HMS *E6* managed to occupy the attention of four German destroyers, 'including one to stay and hunt her', a practice which declined quite rapidly thereafter; a couple of boats had shots at German destroyers but missed (destroyers have always been difficult targets and attacks were still being made by eye without the benefit of spreading torpedo salvoes); and no submarine succeeded in getting close to the enemy cruisers.

There was gallantry nonetheless. Lieutenant Commander Ernest Leir in *E4* stayed on the surface amid the thunder of big guns to rescue the men from two of Tyrwhitt's destroyers which had been left in boats to pick up German survivors. He also 'collected three German samples to bring back', giving the remaining Germans water, provisions and a course for port. It was a chivalrous but rash act.

A young lieutenant from HMS *Defender*, one of the destroyers concerned, wrote to the *Morning Post*, describing Leir's action as 'the most romantic, dramatic and piquant episode that modern war can show'. He explained:

The *Defender*, having sunk an enemy, lowered a whaler to pick up her swimming survivors; but before the whaler got back an enemy's cruiser came up and chased *Defender*, and thus she abandoned her whaler. Imagine their feelings; alone in an open boat without food, twenty-five miles from the nearest land, and that land the enemy's fortress, with nothing but fog and foes around them. Suddenly a swirl alongside, and up, if you please, pops His Britannic Majesty's submarine *E4*, opens his conning-tower, takes them all on board, shuts up again, dives, and brings them home 250 miles! Is not that magnificent? No novel would dare face the critics with an episode like that in it, except, perhaps, Jules Verne; and all true!

Leir enjoyed the sobriquet of 'Arch Thief' because of a marked proclivity for purloining Admiralty Stores. He was reported to have disposed profitably of 300 tons of lead ballast when *E4* was building at Barrow, hence the boat's punning unofficial motto 'We need no Lead'. A contemporary inserted a 'spoof' letter, which probably contained more than a grain of truth, in HMS *Maidstone*'s monthly *Muckrag* after a visit by Leir to a Naval Air Station:

This particular member arrived, uninvited, in our mess some three months ago, and we have had ample opportunity of studying his characteristics, which, in the absence of evidence to the contrary, we must unwillingly conclude to be representative of the 'Trade' in general.

In the few moments that he can spare from the building of his Submarine, few things appear to interest him more than Air Service Stores. On one occasion, in the confusion caused by an alarm of fire (given, it is believed, by himself), he distinguished himself greatly by making violent and successful efforts to remove several valuable Store articles to a place of safety, namely:

2 Leather Coats, Lined with Fleece
1 Walnut Whatnot
22 $5/_8$ inch Bolts
1 Tube Secotine
1 Copy of *La Vie Parisienne*, the property of the Stores Officer

Besides this kindly and parental interest in Air Service Stores the subject of my letter has shown perhaps an even greater interest in Air Service Motor Transport; he has, with wonderful kindness, tested two Air Service Motor Bicycles to destruction, and in the test on one of these Machines obtained valuable figures as to the impact strength of an organ negligently left in the street by an itinerant musician.

While this Officer's supervision of his submarine and his parental interest in Air Service Stores monopolises the greater portion of his time, he has been able to pay several visits to Portsmouth where, we understand, he is furnishing a château for his family, fitted with hot and cold water and the usual offices, on an economical system.

The manners of this Officer are excellent. Charming to those who have something that he covets, firm and dignified with those who covet something of his – nothing could be more courtly or dignified than the cold contempt with which he treats the monthly presentation of his Mess Bill.

In conclusion we may say that he has done much to cement the bonds of friendship between the Submarine and Air Service and we shall all feel the poorer for his departure, in the latter part of which sentiment we believe the Messman most cordially and enthusiastically joins.

Thieving – for the benefit of one's own ship or submarine – was a recognised pastime, but Leir seems to have been addicted to the habit on a more personal basis. Despite that, he was extremely popular and nothing if not an English gentleman.

Submarines achieved little in the Great Raid, and their presence was a needless danger, both for them and the British surface ships. Keyes was admonished for personally leading his flotilla. The Chief of Staff objected to him embarking in *Lurcher* and 'would not have (him) barging about the Bight on (his) own again, it was too risky . . .'. He protested, but the First Sea Lord, Admiral His Serene Highness Prince Louis Alexander of Battenburg (soon to be ousted because of his Teutonic heritage) endorsed the order: 'the Commodore is not to go in a destroyer, signed L.B. 6/9/14.' The dashing Keyes was disgusted but there was good sense in the decision.

A second raid in September drew a blank. Keyes told the Chief of Staff that he had been regarded during the China Wars as 'good joss'; the Admiralty could not expect fair fortune if he was not allowed to take part in such enterprises. The Chief of Staff was not persuaded.

It now appeared that the enemy was supporting destroyer patrols with submarines instead of cruisers. The Eighth Flotilla boats thereupon stepped up their patrols in the Bight and some interesting duels resulted. *D8* (T. S. Brodie) and a U-boat surfaced simultaneously on one occasion a bare 90 metres (100 yards) apart: both dived immediately (a 'D' boat could reach periscope depth in about half a minute) but nothing could be heard on hydrophones. Theodore Brodie, regarded with great affection in *Maidstone*'s wardroom, was deeply religious. It was his pre-war practice to call the crew together while he beseeched the Almighty to grant them success in an attack, but fortune seldom attended his endeavours. On one occasion, returning to the depot ship, a sailor leaned over the rails and asked a chum on the boat below how they had got on. 'No bloody good today,' the submarine sailor replied, 'the Lord was 'avin' a make-and-mend.'[11] An hour later *D8* rose again to find the enemy doing exactly the same, but too distant for a mutual attack. As Brodie said, 'neither knew what to do with the other'. Numerous encounters of this kind ended in stalemate.

When the weather started to worsen with the autumn gales, conditions became very bad. A north-westerly blowing into the shallow waters of the Bight raised a heavy ground-swell, and a jerky roll of 15 degrees each way was normal when sitting on the bottom at 30 metres (100 feet). Most boats started to 'weep' a little below 24 metres (80 feet) and the crew existed in a state of coma brought on by lack of sleep, seasickness and foul air. It had been better when submarines anchored by mushroom weights (worked from inside) rather than bottoming; they could even do it dived. But that was in good August weather and before enemy patrols became inquisitive.

The glamour, the *Boy's Own Paper* ripping yarns of undersea adventure, were obliterated by stinking, sloshing, oily bilges and hideous overflowing buckets full of garbage, or worse. Dispiritingly, there was nothing to attack, no job to do except keep a boat going. Mostly it was a matter of getting the engines to start at night and endeavouring to keep salt water away from the batteries and electrical machinery, but major physical damage was unavoidable. Canvas screens around the bridges – inadequate at the best of times – tore away, rivets started and had to be plugged, and compasses toppled. *D7* returned to Harwich one day with her forward hydroplanes spinning around like paddles, to be greeted with a volley of jeers from the depot ship. Sympathy for submariners was out of place since they got extra rations, generous submarine pay and 'hard-lying money'.

Boats equipped with W/T had difficulty in keeping wireless sets working and aerials rigged. The danger of mistaken identity was compounded by unreliable communications and flag hoists hard to see. Fortunately, pigeon post was trustworthy albeit no substitute for tactical signalling.

It began to look as though there would never be any action, just unremitting hard labour, and without action the war would drag on and on. On land, the Battle of the Marne from 6 to 8 September marked the failure of both German and French strategies designed to bring the war to a quick close; the 'all over by Christmas' syndrome was forgotten. Things looked no more hopeful in the submarine world.

Then, on 13 September, Lieutenant Commander Horton in *E9* broke the pattern of dismal events. Horton was a remarkable man, first among equals in the Eighth Flotilla, who became arguably the most famous and successful British submariner of all time. Brash, ruthless, intensely ambitious and a showman, Max Kennedy Horton was officially reported in 1907 as *'good at his boat and bad socially'*. The latter criticism presumably referred to the fact that women found him intensely attractive; he probably upset a number of influential husbands. But the worst situations invariably turned out for the best when Max was around: luck, another attribute of good COs, was always on his side. In many ways he resembled Jacky Fisher. He may even have modelled himself on the old admiral.

Max led the rest in the Great Underwater War, and during the Second World War he was to win the Battle of the Atlantic. He brooked none of the slackness permitted by some captains. He smoked heavily but drank moderately, and never succumbed to degrading filth at sea. Hot water for washing was practically unknown in *E9*, as in all other submarines, but Max used to insist on bathing in a small tub surrounded by canvas just before returning to harbour. One day, while engaged in this solitary operation, he unwisely allowed a part of his anatomy to protrude outside the screen whereupon he felt a sharp pinch. It was characteristic of the man that he immediately announced a stoppage of leave for the entire crew until the culprit owned up. The culprit did own up – he was a Petty Officer who refused to be quashed by the strong personality of Max, and could not resist the opportunity of a physical reminder that Horton was human. He got away with it. And the crew did not mind that their captain was the only one to enjoy clean hot water. The rest of them usually washed, if they washed at all, in the remains of the tea kettle or in cocoa, the only warm liquids available.

Max, scouting the Bight at periscope depth by day and

charging batteries on the surface or lying doggo on the seabed by night, remained unaffected by the appalling conditions and the unappetising belly-binding food; but after five or six days of the usual routine, in worse than usual weather, the Second Captain admitted to being in dire digestive straits. A box of pills consumed on the evening of 12 September quickly – too quickly – put him right. Halfway through the morning watch the atmosphere became oppressive, so Horton ordered the boat off the bottom earlier than planned and came to periscope depth prior to surfacing for much-needed fresh air. The story goes that, on putting up the periscope, he was immediately greeted by the sight of the small German cruiser *Hela* steaming slowly past and put two 'mouldies' into her – all thanks to a box of pills. The tale has gone down in history, but the truth is that Max was just making the best of a good story. *E9* did indeed come to periscope depth, surfacing at 6.30 a.m. for a quick and necessary blow through. But the boat dived again two minutes later and there is no record in Horton's log of seeing a target at this time; it was still dark. However, with dawn approaching he remained at periscope depth and probably sighted *Hela* soon afterwards. He fired both bow tubes at 7.28 a.m. and the little cruiser went down minutes later. The sinking of HMS *Pathfinder* eight days earlier was avenged, but hardly because of Beecham's patent medicine.

The wind had gone down during the night and the early hours were dead calm with patches of fog. When Horton came shallow to see the result of his attack, the periscope was immediately sighted and shelled by destroyers who harried the boat for the rest of the day and much of the night (to no effect: it was 13 September and Max believed that thirteen was his lucky number). Several attempts to recharge the flattened battery were frustrated but he methodically worked the boat clear of enemy ships and brought *E9* safely back to Harwich.

After a spell in harbour *E9* was sent to the mouth of the Ems, a dangerous navigational spot to patrol with flocks of destroyers guarding the narrow channels between sandbanks. No major vessels hove in sight so, on the last day, Max settled for the destroyer *S-116*, hitting her with a single torpedo from extremely close range as she raced past. 'She went up beautifully', he wrote laconically. *E9* came alongside the depot ship at 10.30 the next morning with two small white and yellow flags flying, each bearing the pirate skull and crossbones. His fellow officers, who had been so sadly disappointed on their own patrols, showed no jealousy: 'Horton will be *the* hero of the Admiralty and the halfpenny press now,' said one in his diary, 'I am jolly glad that he does get the luck as he is such a fine fellow and deserves it.' Admittedly this officer was in a generous frame of mind because he also noted, with satisfaction, that he had just paid Gieve (the naval tailor) 'right off'. *S-116* was not valuable and the *Hela* was old; but elements of the German High Sea Fleet were manoeuvring in the vicinity when the cruiser was hit, and the sinking had a profound consequence. The C-in-C, Admiral von Ingenohl, decided that he could no longer exercise his ships in the German Ocean with enemy submarines on the prowl. Rehearsals, necessary to remain efficient, would have to be conducted in the Baltic, and squadrons detached for this purpose would not be immediately available in the prime area of operations.

That aside, it now became Germany's turn to strike one of the most devastating blows of the Underwater War.

Below the belt before breakfast

Kapitänleutnant Otto Weddigen commanding *U-9* (with Spiess as his No. 1) was the flotilla's torpedo expert and his boat was assessed as outstandingly efficient despite the breakdown in August. On 20 September *U-9* left Helgoland to patrol between Ostend and the West Hinder Lightship with belated orders to attack British transports approaching the Belgian coast. Heavy seas delayed the passage but by 22 September *U-9* was off the Maas west of the Hook of Holland. At 5.45 a.m., on the surface just before sunrise, Spiess was on watch while Weddigen and Chief Engineer Schön strolled up and down the narrow slatted casing enjoying the crisp land breeze. Spiess cursed the white paraffin exhaust fumes which were surely visible for miles while obscuring his own view aft. Changing course frequently to clear the arcs he suddenly spotted a mast, then smoke, through his binoculars. Stopping the engines he called the captain to the bridge.

Weddigen did not hesitate: 'Take her down.' The upper-works of three ships soon appeared over the horizon and Weddigen, at the conning-tower periscope by now, identified them as British cruisers of the *Birmingham* class. In fact they were much older ships from the turn of the century – *Aboukir*, *Cressy* and *Hogue* – but they did have four funnels like *Birmingham*, and wishful thinking contributed to the incorrect identification because *U-9* was intent on squaring the *U-15* account. Tension grew throughout the boat as the targets drew on, in line abreast at a stately 10 knots. The predicted range of firing at the closest ship was 500 metres (550 yards): nobody knew the effect of a warhead on the firing submarine at close range and *U-21* had reportedly been shaken by the hit on *Pathfinder* at 1200 metres (1300 yards). (It was later determined that 200 metres (320 yards) was safe, which accorded with Submarine School instructions.)

At 6.20 Weddigen, close enough to make a miss unlikely, barked 'Number One tube – *Los!*' Spiess pressed the electric firing button in the tower and Weddigen ordered the boat down to 15 metres (50 feet) to avoid breaking surface at the moment of torpedo discharge. Human ballast ran forward and then aft again through the narrow passageway to keep the submarine on an even keel while sea water flooded in to compensate for the sudden loss of weight as the torpedo left the tube. A dull thud, followed by a loud crack, came thirty-one seconds later. It was rather an anticlimax, but back at 12 metres (40 feet) Weddigen reported the target settling by the stern with her bow ram rising out of the water. The cruiser, which proved to be *Aboukir*, turned turtle and disappeared at 6.40. But already, with furnishings and kit flung aside while the human ballast continued to gallop backwards and forwards, Number One tube was almost reloaded. By 6.50 the job was done and Weddigen had *Hogue* in his sights, stationary while hauling in survivors. Spiess reduced speed to the minimum for depth control – the range was closing rapidly – while his captain studied the new target carefully. It was definitely an armoured vessel, not a light cruiser: two torpedoes would be advisable to make sure of a kill. Accordingly, both bow tubes were fired at ten-second intervals from a range of just 300 metres (330 yards) – too close for comfort against a stopped target. Weddigen had to order one of the motors astern to help *U-9* turn and clear the massive ship towering over the periscope: the 5-cm (2-inch) diameter top window almost rubbed the side armour before both 'eels' hit, shaking the boat itself severely. At 7.05 *Hogue* vanished beneath the waves.

At this point the Chief Engineer decided that the batteries were drained and the Chief Quartermaster on the after (hand-worked) planes was exhausted: 'How much longer,' the engineer shouted up the tower, 'is this going to go on?' 'We are going to attack,' replied Weddigen coldly as he manoeuvred to bring his stern tubes to bear on the third cruiser, HMS *Cressy*. He was sure that a few more amps could be squeezed out of the 'box', and the planesman could hang on for a while yet.

At 7.17 Weddigen fired both stern tubes from 1000 metres (1100 yards), a long shot but much more comfortable for *U-9*. The torpedo tracks were sighted 180 metres (1 cable) away from *Cressy*'s starboard side. Captain Robert Johnson, who had served in submarines but evidently failed to appreciate the present danger, at last attempted to take evasive action. His order for full speed ahead came too late, although it resulted in only one torpedo hitting. It was probably enough, but to make sure Weddigen fired another shot from a reloaded bow tube at 7.35, and twenty minutes later HMS *Cressy* followed her sisters to the bottom.

The death toll was 1459, greater than that suffered by the whole of Admiral Lord Nelson's fleet at the Battle of Trafalgar. Among the victims were fifteen-year-old officer Cadets and Boy Seamen who should have been finishing their education.

It was sardonically observed that the worst aspect of the multiple disaster was not only that a solitary obsolescent submarine had offended the Queensberry Rules by hitting three ships below the (armoured) belt but that it had done so in the space of one hour *before breakfast*.

U-9 was received rapturously on her return. The Supreme Command granted Weddigen the Iron Cross both First and Second Class, and the entire crew was awarded the Iron Cross Second Class. The Fleet Commander at Wilhelmshaven, His Excellency Admiral von Ingenohl, decreed that an Iron Cross was to be painted on each side of the boat's conning tower; and when, after a short refit, Weddigen took the boat out of the Jade River to Helgoland to prepare for another mission the admiral signalled: 'After *E9* comes *U-9*'.

On 13 October Weddigen sent a fourth cruiser, HMS *Hawke*, to the bottom. Weddigen's earlier exploit had already convinced objective Allied observers that the U-boat threat was real, but the German surface torpedo-boat service attempted to belittle the triple sinking. There was snide comment about exceptional luck, just as there had been over the *Pathfinder* sinking. As late as December, by which time the losses inflicted by U-boats were considerable, Admiral Tirpitz was still hesitant about the value of the underwater arm. Nevertheless, he was swinging in favour of a campaign against British trade. In reply to a question by an American journalist, as to whether the day of large ships was over, he answered:

It is difficult to draw conclusions yet. It is unquestionable that submarines are a new and powerful weapon of naval warfare. At the same time one must not forget that submarines do their best work along the coasts and in shallow waters, and for this reason the Channel is particularly suitable for these craft. . . . It is still questionable whether submarines would have made such a fine show in other waters. We have learnt a great deal about submarines in this war. We thought they would not be able to remain much longer than three days away from their base, as the crew would then necessarily be exhausted. But we soon learned that the larger type of these boats can navigate around the whole of England and can remain absent as long as a fortnight.

All that is necessary is that the crew gets an opportunity of resting and recuperating; and this opportunity can be afforded the men by taking the boat into shallow waters, where it can rest on the bottom and remain still in order that the crew can have a good sleep.

The interviewer added (in his report for the London *Times*) that it was 'an open secret that Germany is building forty new submarines of the 900-ton type'; and that 'In Admiral Tirpitz's opinion a submarine war against British merchant ships would be more effective even than an invasion of England by means of zeppelins.' To the question 'Will the German Navy come out to fight the British Fleet?' Admiral Tirpitz replied, 'Certainly, if the British give us an opportunity to engage them. But can it be expected that our fleet, the strength of which is only about one-third of the British fleet, will seize an opportunity unfavourable in the military sense and challenge the British fleet to fight? As far as we know the British Grand Battle Fleet is lying off the west coast of England in the Irish Sea.'[12]

Despite the *Grossadmiral's* cautious phrasing, all that had been feared at the beginning of the century was coming to pass. With the war only a few weeks old both the British and German battle fleets were severely inhibited by the underwater threat. The seas were no longer 'ours' or 'theirs': no ship, however mighty, had a confident right of passage since it was beginning to look as though the seas and oceans would be ruled from below.

By 7 October, when a U-boat was located in Loch Ewe, that emergency anchorage was declared unsafe. Until Scapa Flow could be made secure the British battle squadrons were obliged to move to Lough Swilly in the north of Ireland. A handful of U-boats had forced the most powerful battle fleet in history to abandon its main wartime base, retreat to a second base and then to a third, each progressively more remote from the principal theatre in the North Sea.

Anti-submarine weapons and tactics, neglected in the years of peace, had urgently to be invented, tested and applied. Major warships – and, soon, merchant vessels – had to be guarded, which meant taking destroyers away from offensive operations. Meanwhile, the British admirals were wondering what would happen if submarine minelayers came into play on a large scale and, most worrying of all, what would happen if undersea marauders turned their full attention to merchant shipping.

CHAPTER 8

Boats for the Baltic (1914–16)

While measures to counter the U-boats were desperately being sought, a depressing stalemate settled heavily over the North Sea. It was to continue, unrelieved by decisive action, throughout the war. There was to be no breakthrough in anti-submarine warfare that would allow the opposing surface battle fleets to operate at will in the way that their creators intended.

The first campaign to bring British submarines to prominence was outside home waters. On 17 September 1914 a meeting took place on board HMS *Iron Duke*, flagship of the Grand Fleet at Loch Ewe, to review the war at sea. It was attended by First Lord of the Admiralty Winston Churchill, Commander-in-Chief Jellicoe with his subordinate admirals, Chief of Staff Vice-Admiral Sturdee and the submarine and destroyer Commodores Keyes and Tyrwhitt from Harwich.

Jellicoe held to his conviction that the Grand Fleet could not venture on ambitious operations of the kind so dear to Churchill's heart. A bombardment of Helgoland followed by a landing to capture the U-boat stronghold was rejected: apart from the risk to important ships it would be impossible to keep the small island secure only 20 miles from German naval bases on the Elbe, Weser and Jade Rivers without immense cost and effort. The reasons for not attempting to capture Helgoland were as unassailable as the island itself; but it is hard to understand why it could not at least have been bombarded from sea with heavy shells.

Where else could the fleet operate offensively against the enemy? On 19 August Churchill had written (without consulting his colleagues) to the Grand Duke Nicholas, the Russian Commander-in-Chief, outlining his plan to sail a substantial force from the North Sea through the Skagerrak and Kattegat into the Baltic. The idea, apparently, was to follow up an attack on the German fleet in Kiel Bay by a landing of troops on the Pomeranian coast. It was a typically impetuous Churchillian proposal in an increasingly stagnant atmosphere. It was well, however, that the Royal Navy declined to play: the results would no doubt have been even more catastrophic than the forthcoming Dardanelles campaign.

The dashing Keyes advised the more practical alternative of launching an underwater offensive in the Baltic. Where battleships could not venture through the tortuous, mined and heavily defended approaches submarines might be able to penetrate. Once inside they could attack German units off Kiel, employing their greatest attribute – surprise – to the full. There would be danger all the way, particularly in the Sound which separates Denmark and Sweden; but Keyes was sure his men were steady. Unfortunately, he proved to be much less sure of the logistics which would ultimately be required: in all probability he never gave a thought to them although he must have recognised that the boats selected could never attempt a return journey after the enemy had been alerted. They would have to stay in the Baltic and operate henceforward from a Russian base. Stores and supplies could only be sent by sea to Murmansk or Archangel and thence, via the inefficient Russian rail system, to Petrograd and on to wherever the submarines might be berthed. But boring difficulties of that nature could, evidently, be considered later: Keyes applied his mind solely to the dangers which the narrow passage to the inland sea presented, and found them acceptable.

Action was the thing, and the First Lord was always in favour of that. A couple of 'E' boats could wreak havoc on units of the German High Sea Fleet which often exercised in the comparatively safe waters of the southern Baltic, as well as disrupting the vital iron ore traffic between the Swedish mines, at Lulea in the Gulf of Bothnia, and Germany. German capital ships were justifiably afraid of Russian mines and operated no more widely in the Baltic than they did in the North Sea. Only light forces, U-boats and minelayers were given free rein; and they had little cause to worry about the Tsar's submarine force which was weak, backward and inefficient. Churchill doubtless foresaw the dispatch of British submarines to reinforce the Russian allies as a shrewd political move whatever else might be achieved.

In the first instance no more than a reconnaissance of the Kattegat was authorised, and Keyes wasted no time in getting an operation underway on his return to Harwich. HMS *E1* (Laurence) and *E5* (Benning) were on their way by 22 September, just five days after the conference. The two boats were towed by the destroyers *Firedrake* and *Lurcher* towards the Skagerrak, where they slipped and made their separate ways around the Shaw at the northern tip of Denmark, into the Kattegat. They were to examine, in particular, anchorages on the Danish east coast. The weather was abominable, *E1* developed engine trouble, and nothing of note was accomplished. German patrols were anchored at Skagen, sheltered by the Skaw, and neither submarine sighted enemy ships. On the other hand, the presence of British submarines in the Kattegat was reported by merchant skippers to German authorities who alerted their forces accordingly. The preliminary scouting, which did not indicate the practicability of passing through the Sound into the Baltic Sea itself, was useless, and surprise in any subsequent operation was jeopardised. It would have been wise at least to scan the approaches to the Sound but the submarines were not so instructed.

So, with no meaningful information about the hazards ahead, with ample evidence that submarines seldom knew where they were (and with good reason to doubt the mechanical reliability of at least one boat), Keyes pressed on with his Baltic plan. It was demonstrative of his inability to cope with detailed staff work that Keyes neglected to ensure that the Admiralty warned the Russians of the arrival of submarines at one of their ports in due course. When two boats did eventually turn up, Admiral von Essen, the Russian Commander-in-Chief at Petrograd, felt obliged to tell the British Naval Attaché that 'he would have been even more pleased had he received timely notice of their coming, or been informed as to whose orders they were intended to be subordinate'. Nor, when the operation was mounted, had arrangements been made for them to receive fuel, stores, torpedoes or ammunition, and nothing was prepared in the way of maintenance and docking facilities.

The boats chosen were *E1* (Noel Laurence), *E9* (Max Horton) and *E11* (Martin Nasmith). The three commanding officers were outstandingly competent and reliable; all were to distinguish themselves and attain high rank later; and all were very different personalities. Laurence, the Senior CO, was serious, reserved and rather imposing; Horton, as we saw in the North Sea, was coldly daring but publicly flamboyant, and arguably dedicated as much to his own advancement as he undoubtedly was to the Service; Nasmith was a calculating professional who had long endeavoured, by devising attack instruments, to make torpedo salvoes more dependent on science than on a good eye or sheer luck.

The trio, Baltic bound, left Harwich on Tuesday 13 October but paused at Gorleston for fuel. They were not – in a last-minute decision by Keyes – to be towed this time. Final departure was due at 5 a.m. on the 15th, but *E11* was delayed by an engine defect until the late afternoon and *E1* suffered another breakdown during the morning, stopping her for an hour. The boats were afterwards unable to keep anywhere near to a timetable which directed them to attempt the passage of the Sound at two-hourly intervals.

Laurence, despite his recalcitrant engine, was the first to reach the Baltic. He had dived frequently to avoid being seen by merchant ships, and he entered the Sound when darkness fell on the 17th. The passage, almost disappointingly easy, was accomplished by 11.30 p.m. There were some German patrol vessels about and at daylight on the 18th, when *E1* surfaced, Laurence found a German destroyer close by. He immediately dived again, without being detected, and continued his way southward. But, a little after 9 a.m., Laurence sighted through the periscope the old cruiser *Victoria Louise* (which he wrongly identified as a more important ship) coming within easy range

137

for a shot from a beam tube at 460 metres (500 yards). The torpedo ran too deep – the old problem – and German lookouts in the crow's nest and on the quarterdeck saw the tracks in time for the Officer of the Watch to take avoiding action. There was no longer any doubt that British submarines were in the Baltic. Within half an hour of the abortive attack, Prince Henry of Prussia, German C-in-C Baltic, was ordering patrols to be stepped up, especially in the Sound between Sweden and Zeeland which was the only navigable passage fit for merchant traffic now that corridors west of Zeeland – the Belts – had been mined. The Sound was less than 10 miles across at its narrowest point at the northern entrance, and islands in its lower reaches, some 60 miles down, made the passage equally restrictive before opening out into the Baltic Sea. Nor was the water deep throughout the channel. With alerted destroyers vigorously hunting the Kattegat as well as the Sound itself, there was scant room for a submarine to evade.

By ill chance merchant shipping was particularly dense in the Kattegat while Horton was cautiously taking *E9* southwards, and a Swedish cruiser was hovering on the submarine's intended track. Horton bottomed for the whole day of the 18th and did not surface until 5.20 p.m. when the sun was beginning to set. He was now so far behind schedule that, accepting the probability of being sighted by the stream of neutral vessels, he continued on main engines while charging the battery. By 11 p.m. *E9* was past Copenhagen and approaching the Drogden Channel where, at 11.47, Horton discerned the black shape of a destroyer only 140 metres (150 yards) away. What followed is best told by the Control Room Log which Horton wrote himself:

Dived very rapidly and struck bottom very hard. Gauge reading 15 feet. [At that depth the periscope standards were not under water.]

19 October. 12.6 a.m. rose to surface. Sighted destroyer on port beam 70 to 100 yards.

12.7 a.m. dived and hit bottom. Gauge reading 23 feet. Continued to dive in SWly direction, the greatest depth at which we could dive being 15 feet.

3.40 a.m. Stevens Cliff three points on the Port Bow. Rested on the bottom in 48 feet.

5 a.m. Rose and dived. Sighted destroyer astern distance three miles.

10.16 a.m. Surfaced. Course as necessary to reach Moen Bank for night.

20 October. 5.40 a.m. Surfaced.

6 a.m. Sighted destroyer to northwards steaming Sly. Proceeded SEly to pass six miles off C. Arkrona.

11.40 a.m. A/c to eastward to proceed to Danzig.

1.25 p.m. Sighted mastheads of a cruiser about seven miles to northward near Bornholm.

5.30 p.m. Dived for night, wind and sea increasing. Depth keeping on one motor very difficult.

11.15 p.m. Starboard motor shorted. Insulation given out. Motor had to be stopped.

21 October. 5.30 a.m. Surfaced. Sea very rough. Wind blowing a gale from NE. Proceeded under GE [Gas or diesel engine] 6–7 knots.

Shaped course for Libau owing to defect in starboard motor. On the surface all day. Course N62E Magnetic.

E9 had made it safely.

E1 had been at Libau since the previous afternoon when *E9* arrived, firing rockets and flying an extra large White Ensign in accordance with Keyes's orders; so the Russians were not as surprised as they had been when Laurence appeared at the harbour entrance. A tug with a Russian navigating officer on board was sent out to help Horton find his way through a German minefield. It was only when he was secured alongside *E1* that he learned that the dockyard had been rendered useless and that fuel, stores and ammunition had been burnt in anticipation of imminent German occupation.

When he eventually received the reports from Laurence and Horton, Churchill wrote in red ink in the Admiralty docket:

These are probably the most skilful submarine pilots in the world. To send these submarines into the Baltic without telling them of the Libau minefield or what they were to do if they did not return [to England] was bad Staff work. The Russians also were imperfectly acquainted with their project and possible arrival.

The First Lord's Minute was restrained because the Admiralty was ultimately responsible for these failures and it would not do for the Head of His Majesty's Navy to acknowledge them too openly, even though Commodore Keyes was the real culprit. It could well be, however, that Fisher, who returned to the post of First Sea Lord while all this was going on, took note of Keyes's inefficiency and intensified his hate campaign against an officer whom he had disliked from first acquaintance.

Meanwhile, luck had again spurned Nasmith in *E11*. Delayed by continual engine troubles and unconvinced that makeshift repairs would see him through, Nasmith found himself hounded by steamers (which he suspected of towing explosive sweeps), a couple of destroyers (one of which attempted to ram) and a supposed U-boat which he attempted to torpedo in the belief that it was *U-3* when it was actually the Danish submarine *Havmanden* (fortunately the 'mouldy' missed). He was also embarrassed by a German seaplane. Harried in the southern Kattegat from the 20th to the 22nd, the crew were exhausted and it was obvious that the Sound was now extremely well guarded. Reluctantly, but rightly, Nasmith returned to Harwich.

A few days before *E1* and *E9* broke through the cordon three German submarines, *U-23*, *U-25* and *U-26*, were despatched to attack Russian cruisers patrolling the mouth of the Gulf of Finland. On 10 October *U-26* missed the armoured cruiser *Admiral Makarov* with two torpedoes but the following day hit a sister ship *Pallada* amidships. The torpedo evidently detonated a magazine: the *Pallada* went down quickly and none of the crew was saved. All Russian heavy units were promptly withdrawn to the east.

But this success by *U-26*, followed by the reported arrival of two British submarines at Libau, threw the German High

Command into a temporary panic. If a U-boat could destroy a Russian cruiser the British boats would be a real danger to German heavy units in the south-western Baltic, traditionally regarded as a German lake. A force was therefore despatched to bombard Libau from the sea. It was a nugatory operation because *E1* and *E9* were by now safely berthed at Revel on the Esthonian coast, 250 miles north-east of Libau in the Gulf of Finland; and 270 10.5-cm (4-inch) shells were exploded on a dockyard that had already been destroyed by the Russians themselves. Furthermore, the cruiser *Friedrich Karl* was sunk en route to the operation by a Russian mine barrier laid off Memel.

The bitter temperatures and ice of the winter months did not altogether prevent *E1* and *E9* patrolling until mid-February 1915. No enemy ships were sunk although Horton claimed (wrongly in the event because the torpedo gyro failed) that he hit a German destroyer.

Engineer Lieutenant Cecil Simpson had sensibly been sent with *E11* – engineer officers were not normally carried in submarines – and he struggled to refit the two submarines as best he could in what was described as a semi-moribund dockyard. Russian torpedoes were adapted to replace the RNTF weapons fired; and the first consignment of spare parts for machinery had arrived on 15 January. But practically everything was in short supply and British clothing was totally unsuited to the sub-zero climate.

The harsh winter took its toll of men and material. Worst of all, the boats ran out of rum and the crews missed their daily ration. Horton asked for vodka. The Russian Navy was officially 'dry' but the request was eventually sanctioned at the highest level. When the Tsar heard of it he remarked: 'If they are so cold, why can't they wear two shirts?' At sea, spray froze on the bridge and men were employed continuously with hammer and chisel to keep the conning tower hatch free of ice. Periscopes and torpedo-tube bow caps also froze solid, main vents refused to open and, when they were at last persuaded to function, they were sometimes jammed open by small pieces of ice. When they did manage to dive – a dangerously slow procedure in the ice-bound Baltic – the British boats found it best to sit on the bottom until the comparatively warm water had thawed out moving parts. That was the only thing of value learned from Russian submariners.

On 31 December 1914 there was cause for celebration. Laurence and Horton were both given their 'brass hats', but the British and Russian Admiralties had a much more important reason for congratulating the two new commanders: the presence of their boats, where Russian submarines had so far failed to operate effectively, was sufficient seriously to disrupt German naval operations and trade. The comparative inactivity of the Russian Fleet had encouraged the Germans to formulate grandiose plans to capture Petrograd by a series of amphibious assaults along the Baltic coast, but a pair of British submarines, obviously well handled, was sufficient to stifle any such attempts. Before long a convoy system had to be adopted to escort valuable merchant shipping across what came by mid-1915 to be known as 'Horton's Sea'.

Unfortunately, though, the British spring assault in 1915 opened with a series of failures. Repeatedly, torpedoes missed or misbehaved. Russian submarines, inspired or shamed by example, became more active but they fared no better. The first success for *E9* came on 5 June when Horton attacked a group of ships which had stopped close to Windau in order to allow two destroyers to embark coal from a collier. Horton realised that if he got into the right position and timed his attack correctly he would be able to fire at the cruiser *Thetis* with a beam tube and aim at three of the other ships, which were very close together, with his two bow tubes.[1] He manoeuvred patiently and bided his time until most of the ships were together in his line of sight. The first torpedo (a Russian model) veered off course, but the second struck the collier *Dora Hugo Stinnes* and the third hit the destroyer *S-148*. The latter was not sunk, but was out of action for a long time.

In July 1915 Russian cruisers ventured out in strength, led by the *Admiral Makarov*, and on the morning of the 2nd they stumbled upon an inferior German squadron in thick fog off Gotland. The Russians had the best of the engagement by damaging two cruisers and a minelayer, and two elderly German armoured cruisers, the *Prinz Adelbert* and *Prinz Heinrich*, escorted by destroyers, were hastily called up for support. Fortuitously, their course led them straight across *E9*'s patrol position. The sea was glassy calm and Horton knew he would have to fire from very close range if the torpedo tracks were not to be seen and avoided. Accordingly, he waited until the leading ship, *Prinz Adelbert*, was only 365 metres (400 yards) away when he fired both bow tubes. He then altered course hard-a-port in order to bring a beam torpedo to bear, but the rapid course alteration (always likely to upset the delicate trim) combined with the discharge of torpedoes forward which had not yet been fully compensated by flooding in water, was too much for the planesmen. *E9* broke surface momentarily, allowing Horton to see a hit abreast the cruiser's forward funnel. As the first lieutenant flooded tanks to regain control a second explosion rang through the hull. Russian 'fish', whatever their faults, did seem to keep the right depth. *E9* hit the bottom while a destroyer rushed overhead.

The *Prinz Adelbert* was badly damaged but not, as Horton believed, sunk: the second torpedo had detonated on the seabed. On return to Revel, on 4 July, Max was decorated with the Order of St George, Russia's equivalent of the Victoria Cross. 'The activity of British submarines in the Baltic', said *The Times*, 'seems to be causing intense displeasure in Hamburg . . . a leading article [was] full of bitter complaints and almost pathetic appeals to Sweden.' But the defects in *E9* had multiplied during this patrol and with *E1* still under repair, all operations had to be halted until the end of the month.

Horton was now a marked man. The Germans plotted to assassinate him, and a 'Mata Hari' was engaged to ensnare him because German intelligence knew all about Horton's predilection for pretty girls. However, they had not reckoned on the degree of charm which he could exercise. At a party one night he was introduced to the lovely young snare and happily agreed to sit down with her at a table discreetly out of the way. Her English was perfect and Max scented an easy conquest. When the waiter came with two cups of coffee he felt a touch on his sleeve. 'Don't drink!' she whispered. 'It might be poisoned. They asked me to put poison in the cup myself.'

Max asked who 'they' were and she told him. He immediately passed on this valuable information and her pro-German employers were rounded up and shot. Horton refused to divulge the lady's name, however. They became close friends: Max was not a man to let danger impede his doings, either professionally or socially. When he left for England in January 1916 – 'urgently required for service in home waters' – he gave his mysterious girlfriend a gold cigarette case with his signature engraved upon it. She later used that signature, which was honoured as a passport in Scandinavia, when she escaped from Russia to England via Sweden and Denmark.

On 30 July Laurence in *E1* had success at last: he sank the transport *Aachen*, one of three ships in company which had been specially fitted out for minesweeping. The Germans believed that a mine was responsible, but they did not make the same mistake when *E1* next went into action.

On 16 August 1915 the Germans made a determined effort to enter the Gulf of Riga through the Irben Straits. Reinforcements for the operation included new battleships and battle-cruisers from the High Sea Fleet. The German army already controlled the southern shores of the Straits; the object was to bombard troops on the right-hand flank and thus assist the army to capture the important port of Riga itself, in a rare example of inter-service cooperation.

A massive force was assembled. Two 'dreadnought' battleships, four cruisers, three destroyer flotillas and various auxiliaries, preceded by minesweepers and net-clearers, duly forced the Straits into the Gulf while eight battleships, three battle-cruisers, five cruisers and three destroyer flotillas acted in support of the attack-group outside the Gulf. The important units from the High Sea Fleet were placed under the command of Prince Henry who was then given a free hand, with the significant proviso that 'adequate precautions against loss are taken'. The navy was prepared to support the army, but only if no risk was involved.

The force inside the Gulf, under Vice-Admiral Schmidt, had little effect on the Russian army. The German admiral's attention seems to have been directed mainly towards the old Russian battleship *Slava* which, with a few destroyers and gunboats, tried to stop the German minesweepers clearing a way through the fields. *Slava* was unsuccessful but, although damaged by gunfire, was able to escape through Moon Sound leading to the open sea at the northern part of the Gulf. The remainder of the Russian fleet showed no inclination to come out from secure bases in the Gulf of Finland. Schmidt, disappointed at being unable to engage worthwhile naval forces, decided to withdraw the way he had come. For some reason the three Russian submarines *Makrel*, *Minoga* and *Drakon*, patrolling in the Gulf itself, took no active part in the affair, but to seaward *E1* and *E9* were keeping watch with the two new Russian boats *Bars* and *Gepard*. Only one of this team, *E1*, found itself in a position to attack; but the single torpedo fired by Laurence, at a ship of the support force as it happened, had notable consequences.

At 8.10 a.m. on 19 August, with visibility no more than 2 miles, Laurence sighted a squadron of battle-cruisers in line abreast. Many destroyers were about but none had anti-submarine detection gear or A/S weapons so it was simply a matter of careful periscope drill and physical avoidance. Laurence fired at the starboard wing ship at 8.20 and immediately went deep to avoid being rammed by a destroyer which passed within a few feet. Fog prevented *E1* from getting off another shot or seeing the result of the first torpedo, but a loud explosion was heard. It was not a very creditable attack because Laurence missed his target, the battle-cruiser *Seydlitz*, and the torpedo carried on to strike the sister 'dreadnought' *Moltke* which was just abaft her port beam. *Moltke* had seen the warning signal from *Seydlitz* and was in the act of turning away when the torpedo struck in the forward torpedo room, flooding that compartment and shipping some 450 tons of water forward. With the 'no risk' instructions to the C-in-C in mind, it was enough for Vice-Admiral Hipper command-ing the support force, and he straightaway shaped course for Danzig with all his ships, including the *Moltke* whose damage necessitated a reduced speed of 15 knots for the force.

The German Riga assault was a failure. It was said that troops had actually been landed in flat-bottomed boats at the northern pocket of the Gulf to take Riga in the rear,[2] but if that was true they were either captured or killed. The German Navy was discouraged and dismayed; just as the admirals always thought, it was a mistake to help the army.

Accounts differ about the effect of *E1*'s attack. Admiral Scheer did not mention it in his story of the High Sea Fleet,[3] but he would not perhaps have wanted to record the failure. It looks, however, as though the single torpedo from *E1* was seen as the final blow to German aspirations in the Gulf of Riga. Plans to turn the Riga flank were abandoned the day after *Moltke* was crippled.[4] The German *Official History* (speaking of Admiral Schmidt) stated that 'as he now received confirmation of the presence of enemy submarines, he came to the conclusion that the advance of the ships would not be in accordance with the Imperial Decree'.

The withdrawal of naval units supporting the German army enabled High Sea Fleet ships to return to the North Sea, but without their support the army was unable to advance. Military operations against Riga were not renewed until October 1917. For all this, it could reasonably be claimed that Laurence was responsible. The German withdrawal also negated the main reason for sending further British submarines into the Baltic. But *E8* (Goodhart) and *E13* (Layton) were ordered there in August 1915, and *E18* (Halahan) and *E19* (Cromie) followed in September.

Francis Goodhart had a similar experience to Horton in the Sound. At the shallowest point a patrol vessel, sighted at 180 metres (200 yards), forced him to dive. *E8* hit the bottom with the conning tower barely under water, and by chance the destroyer raced over the bows which were just deep enough to avoid contact. Throughout the night of 17/18 August Goodhart played hide-and-seek with the patrols, bouncing from time to time along the bottom. At one point his starboard propeller blades were stripped off by a rock, but on coming to periscope depth at 7.15 a.m. he was surprised to find the horizon clear. *E8* was in the Baltic.

Layton in *E13* tried the same tactics, and surfaced after dark to run at top speed down the dangerous defile. All went well until *E13* entered the Flint Channel which formed the final 40-mile passageway into the open sea. Suddenly the Danish island of Saltholm loomed horribly close. Layton slowed to check his Sperry gyro with the magnetic compass, and the navigator, Garriock, jumped down the conning-tower ladder to look at the chart, but too late. The submarine grounded with a grinding crash: the gyro had been 15 degrees in error.

It was a quarter of an hour before midnight and there was some hope of getting off before being spotted, but, despite pumping out all tanks and discharging fuel overboard to lighten the boat, she refused to move. Books, charts and war codes were burned. When dawn broke *E13* was seen by both Danes and Germans. At 5 a.m. HMDS *Narhvalen* closed to hailing distance and informed Layton that he would be given twenty-four hours to refloat the submarine. Layton knew this was impossible and sent his first lieutenant, Eddis, over to *Narhvalen* and thence to the guard ship *Falster* off the west coast of Saltholm Island. He was instructed to arrange a tow within the twenty-four-hour limit and, if this proved impracticable, he was to negotiate terms for internment. The Germans were jamming wireless frequencies and there was no way of signalling *E13*'s predicament to the Admiralty.

The Germans held off in face of the Danish First Torpedo Boat Squadron which arrived on the scene to ensure fair play. Everything seemed peaceful: after all, *E13* was (improperly) in neutral waters. However, at 10.28 a.m. two German destroyers came up from the south at high speed, both flying flag signals meaning 'Abandon ship immediately', but they allowed no time for either the Danes or the British to react. One of the destroyers fired two torpedoes (which did not hit) and raked *E13* with machine guns, shrapnel and HE shells, some of which Petty Officer Lincoln, the senior electrical rating, actually saw passing right through the boat from one side to the other.

The Danish torpedo boats tried to stop the Germans firing, but already the attack had been devastatingly effective: ammunition on board was exploding, salt water in the battery cells was generating chlorine gas, the submarine was on fire and fifteen men had been killed. When the crew abandoned ship and jumped into the water they were met by more machine-gun fire and shells despite the Danish protest. Five men were shot while trying to swim away. It later became known that the authorisation to fire on *E13* in Danish waters was given from Berlin, but the machine-gunning of men in the water was a local decision.

The survivors were interned in the Navy Yard at Copenhagen where they were treated very kindly. Layton gave his parole on behalf of the crew with three days' notice on either side, a 10-mile radius from Copenhagen as the boundary and a few other minor restrictions. The parole lasted twenty-four days and all hands enjoyed themselves with the hospitable Danes. Layton contrived to make some friends on whom he knew he could rely for help if he attempted to escape.

The Danish authorities were understandably upset when Layton eventually withdrew his parole but took no particular precautions. There were, no doubt, many who expected Layton, if nobody else, to try to escape; and it can be assumed that, tacitly, they wished him well. Layton bribed his Danish conscript sailor (who had a grievance against his own navy) and kept up a correspondence with two prospective helpers in the capital. His sailor-servant also procured a suit of Danish sailor's clothes. On the Friday night following the expiry of parole Layton changed into sailor rig, made up a dummy (from coats and a sponge) in his bed, and climbed out of the window down the wall using a hammock-lashing as a rope. A box of cigarettes sufficed for one man not to see him, and money persuaded two others to occupy the attention of sentries.

The friends ashore did the rest. A normal ferry took Layton to Sweden whence the naval attaché arranged transport to Bergen in Norway by which time Lieutenant Commander Geoffrey Layton had become Mr George Perkins, a marine overseer from the United States. At Bergen the British Consul forged an American passport and booked a ticket in a Norwegian mailboat to Newcastle. A number of fellow passengers politely refused to believe that Layton was an

American: one went so far as to say that he put him down as a British naval officer; but nobody interfered. 'George Perkins', still accompanied by one of his Danish friends, arrived safely at Newcastle, caught the 10.20 a.m. train to London and delivered 'certain dispatches' to the Foreign Office. Layton then went on to the Admiralty where, to his surprise, he was greeted 'most cordially'. In due course he became Admiral Sir Geoffrey Layton, GBE, KCB, KCMG, DSO.[5] E13, however, unluckily numbered, was sold for scrap to a Danish dealer.

While Layton was making his way back to England, Horton continued to do battle with the enemy in the Baltic. Four steamers were sunk either by torpedo or by scuttling charges. The last, the *Dal Alfoen*, took a long time to go down. Horton surfaced to finish her off with another torpedo but the Swedish destroyer *Wale* decided to protest. The following exchange of signals then took place:

WALE: You are in Swedish waters.
E9:   I make myself six miles from land.
WALE: I make you five.
E9:   The neutral limit is three miles. Please stand clear while
   I sink this ship.

There was no response to the last message and Horton despatched the *Dal Alfoen* with a torpedo from his stern tube.

Four days later Goodhart in *E8* fired a torpedo from 1200 metres (1300 yards) at the cruiser *Prinz Adelbert* (which had been damaged by Horton in July) and watched her blow up as the magazine exploded. Showers of heavy metal fell all around the submarine and Goodhart had to take shelter at 12 metres (40 feet).

Cromie, in *E19*, suffered two mishaps at the beginning of his first patrol. On leaving Revel he mistook the route out of harbour and crashed through the net defences instead of passing through the gate. No harm was done although the Russians were somewhat aggrieved; but on 2 October *E19* became entangled in a much stronger German anti-submarine net west of Bornholm Island. The charges attached to the wires, which wrapped themselves around propellers and hydroplanes, were fortunately too small to do any real damage, but the cracking explosions did nothing to calm the crew. The submarine was trapped – or so it seemed – and Cromie rallied his men, telling them that if all efforts failed to disentangle the clutching steel fingers he would surface the submarine and explode demolition charges himself. They could swim over to the nearby German patrol ship *Silvana* which he had sighted as his prey before *E19* got into the present mess.

Happily, by using full power astern, blowing and flooding main ballast alternately, *E19* struggled clear despite breaking surface a couple of times and being fired upon by the *Silvana*. It had been an unpleasant two hours but the crew were now convinced that their captain was one of the best. Besides his display of personal bravery he had that one great ability which sailors respected above all else: he could get them out of trouble.

Cromie's targets during that initial patrol were cargo ships. His technique was to stop and scuttle them without, if possible, employing a torpedo. A true gentleman, Cromie did his best to ensure the safety of his victim's crews. Nevertheless, his activities caused at least one diplomatic storm. This centred not only on one target being stranded in Swedish waters but on the German claim that, according to international agreement (not ratified by Britain), its cargo of ores was not contraband. The Royal Navy, now represented by five submarines in the Baltic, had no intention of allowing the iron-ore trade to pass unscathed; the Admiralty paid no attention to the fuss. During October *E19* put paid, by one means or another, to eight steamers plying between Germany and Sweden. In consequence, German shipping was kept in port until four destroyers and other escorts were called back from the North Sea to supplement anti-submarine forces in the Baltic. Fewer ships thus became available for operations against Britain (another unforeseen result of submarine depredations outside home waters).

Cromie was to sink two more submarines in November and December 1915, but it was on 7 November that he scored his greatest triumph, patrolling between Bornholm and the Swedish coast, when he sighted a light cruiser and two destroyers. They had probably been sent to the area with vengeance in mind because Cromie had despatched one of his victims there five days earlier. On their first pass the German ships kept out of range but a few hours later they reappeared on a most favourable course as far as *E19* was concerned. A torpedo, fired at 1000 metres (1100 yards) from a beam tube, hit the cruiser *Undine* amidships. That would have been enough, but Cromie fired a second fish to make sure.

Cromie was already decorated with the Order of St Vladimir for breaking through into the Baltic and the Order of St Anne for his first patrol. Now, on return to Revel, he received the Order of St George and was invited to dine with the Tsar in the Royal train. The British Admiralty was less prompt in acknowledging his feats: his DSO was not gazetted until 31 May 1916.

When Laurence and Horton left for home at the beginning of 1916 Cromie became the Senior Naval Officer, Baltic, and paid a four-day visit to Moscow. His status pleased him greatly and he played the role to the full, but tragedy was to follow from it.

Max Horton, relieved in *E9* by Lieutenant Commander Hubert Vaughan-Jones in January 1916, was glad to leave. Relationships with Laurence, marginally his senior, had deteriorated; Max, as was his habit, had openly criticised him and other British officers. However, Max was beloved by the Russians, not least because he shared their love of gambling and, when it came to a drinking match, he had hollow legs – a physical attribute much admired in Russia at the time. He was poured into a train in what was described as a benign state, swaying gently, while the Commander-in-Chief's band played him out of the station.

Max travelled home via Sweden and Norway to Newcastle, smoking Russian cigarettes incessantly and wrapped, for the latter part of his journey, in a huge sable coat – a gift, needless to say, for Max was not one to spend money unnecessarily. The odours surrounding his person, emanating from strong tobacco and poorly cured fur, were such that he and his

brother, who met him at Newcastle, had a carriage to themselves all the way to London.

On 25 January Horton was appointed to command the new
submarine *J6*, which was to patrol tediously in the Helgoland
Bight with never a sight of a target for many weary months
before he went on to command the revolutionary *M1* with its
300-mm (12-inch) gun. (He was, in fact, to return to Revel in
September 1919 in command of a submarine flotilla when the
British government decided to assist the small peripheral states
against Bolshevik aggression; but that curious and wasted
effort is outside our story.)

Laurence, relieved by Lieutenant Commander Athelstan
Fenner, departed a few days later to command the first-of-class
J1. In this unusual and fast-on-the-surface type of submarine
with three propellers, Laurence was to fulfil the submariner's
dream of hitting two battleships with one salvo. Although out
of context in this chapter, it is fitting to complete the story
of Laurence's brilliant career as a submarine commanding
officer here. HMS *J1*, a difficult submarine to control submerged, with a huge expanse of flat upper deck, was on
patrol off the west coast of Denmark in a heavy swell. It was
impossible to maintain periscope depth except by using high
speed and draining the battery, so the patrol was carried out
at 20 metres (70 feet) with periodical excursions to 8 metres
(25 feet) in order to search the horizon.

At 11.50 a.m. Laurence came to 8 metres (25 feet) and sighted
some ships very indistinctly to the south-west. He altered
course to the east, bringing the sea abeam and making depth-
keeping easier, and soon distinguished four battleships of
the 'Kaiser' class steering north at a range of about 2 miles.
Laurence immediately altered 180 degrees westward, going
deep to do so, and on return to periscope depth observed the
enemy reversing course. At that point *J1* broke surface but was
evidently not seen. When the First Lieutenant took her down
again he over-corrected the trim and dipped the periscope; but,
just before Laurence lost sight of his targets, he noted that the
submarine was precisely lined up – if he fired immediately – for
a shot at the third ship in line. All four bow tubes were ready,

with bow caps open, and he did not hesitate to fire an arbitrary spread, resulting in 5 degrees between torpedoes along the target's new line of advance. At 12.08 a.m., when the first torpedo left the tube, *J1* was under starboard wheel 3600 metres (4000 yards) on the port beam of the third ship in line. Enemy speed was correctly estimated at 16 knots.

Three and a half minutes later a loud explosion was heard, followed by another two minutes afterwards. The results were not observed but Laurence believed that he had hit the third and fourth ships: he was right. The *Grosser Kurfürst* and the *Kronprinz* were both extensively damaged by this remarkable 'left and right'. One battleship was out of action for six weeks, the other for three months. Laurence had learned his trade well in the Baltic.

British successes encouraged the Admiralty to send yet more boats to the inland sea, although it was obvious that the Sound was no longer navigable. So in July 1916 an imaginative scheme was presented to the Admiralty Board for towing four small petrol-engined 'C' boats to Archangel and thence taking them on barges down the river and canal system to Petrograd. The boats were obsolete, but would be capable of harbour-defence duties, as indeed they were around the British Isles, and the Gulf of Riga was well within their limited range.

Commodore S. S. Hall, by now heading The Trade, chose *C26* (Eric Tod), *C27* (Douglas Sealy), *C32* (Christopher Satow) and *C35* (Edward Stanley), and tugs took the little boats in tow at Chatham on 3 August 1916 for their long voyage up to the White Sea. The four little submarines arrived by the overland route at Petrograd on 9 September, just seventeen days after being shipped on barges at Archangel.

Although the 'C' boats, as well as the 'E' boats, still had work to do, and exciting times lay ahead (the tale is continued later), the Baltic heyday was over. German anti-submarine methods improved dramatically from 1916, shipping began to be heavily escorted, prospective targets tended to hug the coastline, Russian military morale started to deteriorate rapidly towards the end of the year, and rumblings of revolution were in the air.

CHAPTER 9

Daring the Dardanelles
(December 1914–January 1916)

When the British Admiralty at last recognised that submarines could go where surface ships could not, thanks
largely to the enthusiasm of Churchill and Keyes, the Board
followed the Baltic venture with a directive in the spring of
1915 for submarines to penetrate the Dardanelles and launch
an offensive in the land-girt Sea of Marmara.

The number of submarines employed in the Dardanelles
campaign was never substantial, but the influence of a few
determined British boats was disproportionately large. On the
German side the lone *U-21* (Hersing) not only sank two battleships off Gallipoli in May 1915 – HMS *Triumph* and *Majestic* –
but thereby inhibited, by the threat of a repeat performance,
Allied seaborne operations for the remainder of the ill-fated
venture.

It was the antiquated little *B11* that led the small procession anticipating future operations. She belonged to one of
the earliest British classes. Launched in 1906 and displacing
only 287/316 tons, her overall length was 43 metres (142 feet).
Maximum speed submerged, with a single shaft, was 6.5 knots
which could be maintained for about three-and-a-half hours
(22 miles); at 4.5 knots she could continue submerged without
recharging the battery for 50 miles. The single petrol engine
could drive her (with coaxing) at 12 knots on the surface for
740 miles. The complement was two officers and thirteen
men; and she had two bow 450-mm (18-inch) torpedo tubes
with two reload torpedoes. The periscope was rudimentary,
usually blurred, and torpedo-fire control facilities were non-
existent.

Ernest William Leir, the 'Arch Thief', justifying the criticism that submarining was 'no occupation for a gentleman' while commanding *C13* in 1908; and ashore, proving that he was a gentleman after all.

To the Commanding Officer and Crew
of
H. M. Submarine E 4.

You have thrilled the hearts and aroused the
deepest enthusiam of your fellow subjects by
your simply magnificent feat of humanity
towards the men of the Defender who had had
to be abandoned whilst they too were
performing a great act of charity. What must
their feelings have been to see you rise like a
beautiful benign mermaid from the waves —
open out your bosom envelope, then in its warm
embrace close up and dive once more, only to
emerge and land them in safety. All honour to
you, and God bless you is the wish of four of
your Country women.

Pormanain   Mary. E. Harvey
Penmaenmawr   Margaret C. Harvey, Junr
North Wales.   Margaret. Harvey.
                                             Muriel. C. Harvey.

August 28th 1914.

Lieutenant Commander Leir's gallantry in keeping *E4* on the surface to rescue British (and three German) survivors during the Battle of Helgoland, on 28 August 1914, was fulsomely recognised by four of his 'Country women'. However, Leir was not Welsh: the family home was Ditcheat Priory in Somerset.

430 N. COMMODORE R.J.B. KEYES BEAGLES POSTCARDS.

WHO COMMANDED THE SUBMARINE FLOTILLA WHEN FIVE SHIPS OF THE GERMAN NAVY WERE SUNK OFF HELIGOLAND, 28th AUG. 1914.

Commander Roger Keyes, head of the Submarine Service, pictured shortly after the Battle of Helgoland.

U-9 (Weddigen) emitting the customary white exhaust from her paraffin engines while completing a lap of honour around the High Sea Fleet after sinking HMS *Aboukir*, *Cressy* and *Hogue* on 22 September 1914.

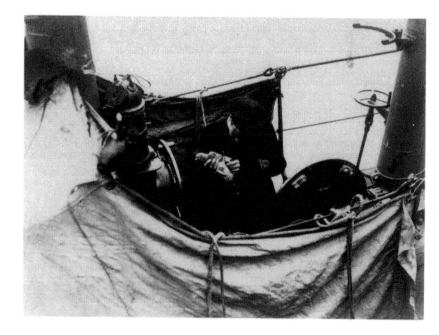

Releasing a carrier pigeon from an 'E' boat, a reliable and reasonably speedy method of communicating with shore.

Loading a moored mine into a Type UC-II boat at Zeebrugge: eighteen mines were carried in six slightly sloping vertical shafts, sloping a little upwards towards the stern, with three mines to a shaft one on top of the other.

Lieutenant von Trapp bringing the Austrian *U-V* into Cattaro in August 1915. Tiny though the petrol-engined boat was (273 tons, 2 tubes, maximum range 48 miles underwater), von Trapp sank the 12,416-ton French armoured cruiser *Léon Gambetta* with considerable strategic consequences.

ВѢЧНАЯ ПАМЯТЬ
ПАВШИМЪ ЗА СВОБОДУ МОРЯКАМЪ
КРЕЙСЕРА ПАМЯТЬ АЗОВА"
ВЪ 1905 ГОДУ.

The ex-cruiser (1888) depot ship *Dvina* reverts, after the Revolution in 1917, to her former name *Pamyat Azova*, which had been stripped from her by the Tsar in 1905 after the crew mutinied.

Russian sentry, suitably protected against the Baltic winter, on board the
depot ship *Dvina* at Revel in 1916.

HMS *E18* (Halahan) returning from patrol to Revel in the winter of 1915. The difficulties not only in operating but also in maintaining British and Russian submarines in these conditions are obvious.

Crew members of USS *E2* (similar to *E1* which operated from Ireland) after return from a war patrol in American home waters.

The outstandingly successful *U-XXXV*, one of the 680/870-ton 'Thirties' class, at Cartagena, Spain, in June 1916 shortly before von Arnauld commenced his most destructive cruise.

A U-boat garlanded on commissioning.

A Whitehead 45cm (17.7in) torpedo being loaded into the 173/210 ton U-21 (Lieutenant Hugo Freiherr von Seyffertitz), probably in September 1917 at Pola.

HMS K3, first of the 'K' class to be completed (22 September 1916), with W/T masts, periscopes and, of course, funnels raised. Curiously, for a submarine, the Director of Naval Construction pointed out that the top of the outer hull 'formed a reasonably flat recreation deck'.

The effects of a torpedo hitting *(above)* a merchant ship and *(below)* an American decoy ship *Santee* (Captain D. Hanrahan USN).

The 'double-ended' patrol boat *Kilbride* splendidly camouflaged to make it difficult for a U-boat commander to estimate size, range and inclination or to identify the vessel.

USS *Fanning* (Lieutenant Commander Carpenter), in dazzle paint, whose depth charges forced *U-58* (Amberger) to surrender on 17 November 1917.

The luxurious wardroom in HMS *M1* with Max Horton's trophy, a silver chanticleer, on the table. Large items of furniture in any submarine had either to be built *in situ* or dismantled to bring them down the hatch.

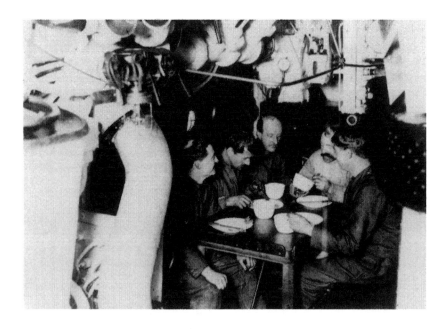

The senior ratings mess in HMS *E34*.

The bow tubes in *U-135* (Spiess). It was this U-boat that was dispatched on 31 October 1918 by Admirals von Trotha and von Hipper to help quell mutinies in the battleships *Ostfriesland* and *Thuringen* lying in the Schillig Roads.

HMS *M1*, completed with her monstrous 12-inch gun on 17 April 1918, in wartime camouflage. The boat sank after being rammed accidentally while dived by SS *Vidar* off Start Point on 12 November 1925.

The Control Room of the minelayer *E34* with the Captain, Lieutenant Richard Pulleyne, at the periscope. She was lost off Vlieland, on 20 July 1918, on her twenty-fourth minelay.

It was in this fragile, primitive *B11* that Lieutenant Norman Douglas Holbrook set out towards the end of 1914 on the perilous task of reconnoitring the Straits up the Narrows – the ancient Hellespont. The French submariners at Tenedos had been keen to force the Straits themselves but Lieutenant Commander G. H. Pownall, the Royal Navy's Senior Submarine Officer, was determined that a British boat should show the way. He sounded out Holbrook on the subject. Holbrook enthused. 'It will be a pretty heavy strain on the battery and *B9* and *B10* couldn't possibly look at it with their old boxes. We got a new set of cells at Malta recently and *B11* is the only boat that can do it. I'm all for having a try.'

The current sweeping down through the Dardanelles varied from 2 to 4 knots: *B11* would have to battle against that, but battery endurance was not the only problem. It was known that a part of the lower Dardanelles was heavily mined.

The north-easterly pointing reach of the lower Dardanelles is like a leg held upwards at an angle of 45 degrees. At the knee – the entrance between Kum Kale and Cape Helles – the width is 2 miles. At the calf it broadens to 4 miles. The well-named Narrows at the ankle are a mere 1280 metres (1400 yards) wide between Chanak and Kilid Bahr, widening to $1^1/_2$ miles at Nagara where the foot finishes. Then, beyond the foot, there is a fairly wide stretch 20 miles long, extending to Gallipoli at the entrance to the lozenge-shaped Sea of Marmara. Constantinople, the Golden Horn and the Bosporus Canal leading to the Black Sea are at the north-eastern side of the lozenge. The full distance from Kum Kale at the mouth of the Dardanelles to the comparatively open waters of the Sea of Marmara is 35 miles; and from Kum Kale to the Narrows is about 12 miles.

At the end of 1914 Turkish minefields were laid from some 4 miles short of the Narrows and continued up to Chanak at their commencement. Intelligence indicated that the fields consisted of ten successive parallel lines comprising 373 deadly eggs in all. They were expected to be moored so as to lie at depths between 5 and 9 metres (16 and 30 feet) (with due allowance for current on the moorings) in order to catch big surface ships. But it was in that depth-bracket that a submerged submarine would need to navigate when using the periscope for fixing its position, a frequent necessity in the tearing current.

There was yet another hazard. Close to the surface the water was nearly fresh, due to rivers running into the Dardanelles. But at some depth – estimated at between 15 and 18 metres (8 and 10 fathoms) – it was salt and much more dense. Passing from one stratum to another, at 15 or 18 metres (50 or 60 feet), would create havoc with the trim. Going down, the boat would suddenly seem very light, and coming up through the boundary it would seem heavy. Suspicion of a deep counter-current further complicated matters.

Eleven Turkish forts guarded the Narrows and their approaches. The two largest were at Chanak on the Asiatic side and at Kilid Bahr on the opposite bank. Numerous searchlights, seventy-two guns and a series of torpedo tubes were positioned so as to bear on warships coming upstream; and in November 1914 the Germans added eight howitzers, augmented the searchlights and laid the minefields.

The natural and man-made barriers were formidable. In a submariner's terms an expedition up the passage was going to be fraught with interest.

Until now the Allied submarine flotilla – British and French boats – had done no more than keep a dreary dawn-to-dusk watch off the entrance to the Dardanelles. The patrol was established too late to prevent the German battleship *Goeben* and the cruiser *Breslau* (which had escaped the shamed Royal Navy's Mediterranean Fleet) gaining safety far up beyond the defences in the Golden Horn at Constantinople, but it might be possible for submarines to pursue them in the Marmara.

There was healthy rivalry between the two halves of the Allied flotilla. When one of the Frenchmen reached just past Sedd-el-Bahr on the northern shore of the entrance, Holbrook capped the feat by chasing a Turkish torpedo-boat 4 miles beyond Kum Kale on the southern point, but minor 'stunts' like these did nothing except relieve boredom. Now *B11* was to go much further – as far as she possibly could – to see

Daring the Dardanelles (December 1914 – January 1916)

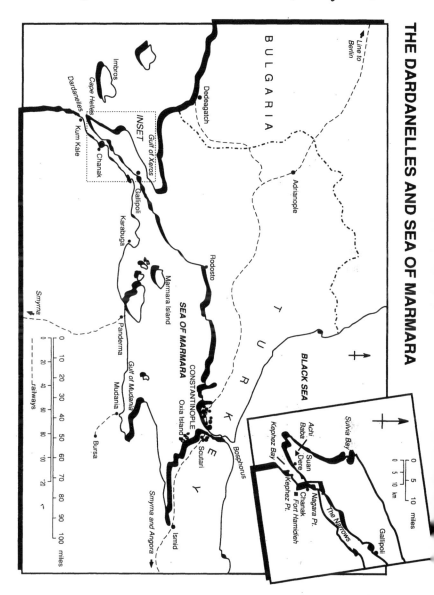

THE DARDANELLES AND SEA OF MARMARA

what targets might be lying hidden up the channel. The lower stretches around Eren Keui Bay, easily visible from Kum Kale, were empty of shipping. Beyond Kephez Point, though, there were intriguing signs of movement; the masts of patrol craft and the superstructures of larger ships beckoned invitingly. But by day it was clearly impossible to face the guns, by night searchlights swept the water, and at all times the minefields, which worried Pownall and Holbrook most, lay in wait.

Experience in the North Sea had shown that a submerged submarine could push mooring wires aside so long as something was done to prevent them being caught on projections. The newer boats had guards around the hydroplanes and a jumping wire running from stem to stern over the top of the periscope supports or standards. *B11* had no such guards and she fairly bristled with projections. A jumping wire and curved steel 'streamliners' for the hydroplanes were therefore extemporised on board the *ad hoc* tender *Blenheim* at the island of Tenedos. When these new fittings had been installed a heavy sinker, suspended by a wire, was hung out under water from the *Blenheim*'s main derrick. *B11* charged this several times and each time the wire was duly pushed aside by the guards without tugging the derrick. Holbrook reckoned that everything was satisfactory: if the submarine did foul a mine-mooring the mine itself would not be pulled down to strike the hull by reason of the boat's forward movement.

Early in the morning of Sunday 13 December *B11* slipped from alongside *Blenheim* and by 4.15 a.m. she was 3 miles from the gateway to the Dardanelles. At dawn, within a mile of Cape Helles, the Second Captain, Lieutenant Sydney Winn, trimmed the boat and dived. Nobody on board had any doubts about what the submarine was undertaking: every man had written a farewell letter home the night before sailing and scarcely anyone had been able to sleep properly. The letters would only be posted if *B11* failed to return.

Alone in the tiny conning tower, Holbrook watched through the scuttles as the grey light of pre-dawn slowly shaded to dark green while the submarine slid beneath the surface. The shore was just distinguishable through the periscope – enough to navigate by anyway – but the lens was shaking even more than usual at 5 knots; and when he climbed down into the control room, his eyes momentarily dazzled by the bright lights after the gloom of the tower, he could feel a curious vibration through his feet. It persisted even when he ordered Slow Ahead: something was wrong and the trouble had to be outside the hull.

The enemy searchlights had been switched off at 5 a.m.: dawn was fast approaching and in a little while it would be full daylight. If *B11* had to surface she must come up instantly. Holbrook opened the hatch and climbed on to the casing himself. Sure enough, the guard on his port forward hydroplane had come loose and was twisted into a hook, ideally shaped for catching and holding a mine-mooring wire. It was impossible to bend the metal straight, but it was a calm morning and two artificers, hanging on with water up to their waists, were able to disconnect the now extremely dangerous guard with spanners. The port forward hydroplane thereupon became a mine-trap, but Holbrook refused to consider turning back.

There was no sign of movement on the sombre shore but it was certain that *B11* was being watched with great interest. Resignedly, Holbrook sent his men below and then followed. Pulling the hatch shut and clipping it, he gave the order to flood main ballast.

By 6 a.m. the submarine was again on her way, less than a mile from the European shoreline to the North. Holbrook's plan, to avoid mines, was to stay down at 15 metres (50 feet) save for an excursion to periscope depth every three-quarters of an hour to check position. Unfortunately, that was just about where the boundary lay between fresh and salt water. Adjusting the trim, particularly when coming shallow, wasted precious electricity on the pumps; and every scrap of energy stored in the battery was needed for propulsion while *B11* struggled along at four knots against the current, barely making two knots over the ground. The hand-worked hydroplanes were always abominably stiff but Holbrook had persuaded Pownall to lend him the Spare Crew Coxswain[1] so that he and the boat's own Coxswain could work in shifts at the all-important 'diving wheel'.

Life in a 'B' boat was once described as like living under the bonnet of a motor car, but the oily and petrol-laden atmosphere actually sharpened submariners' appetites. A breakfast of cold tea, cold ham, bread, butter and jam was consumed with relish when *B11* dived; and Holbrook himself enjoyed half a cold lobster which one of the French officers had given him at the last minute.

By 8.30 a.m. one-third of the battery capacity had been used: the specific gravity, checked every two hours, was dropping steadily. Nevertheless, *B11* was on schedule and was now approaching the first known minefield lying across the submarine's track between Kephez Point and the northern shore. Holbrook took a careful fix and then ordered the submarine deep to 24 metres (80 feet). That should take *B11* well below the mines themselves, but whether or not the port forward hydroplane would snag a mooring wire was a matter of luck. The next hour was uneventful, but the minute hand on the control-room clock was painfully slow.

At 9.40 Holbrook's estimated position put him near the Narrows. Coming shallow again, he found that *B11* had made better headway than expected. Over on the starboard bow and less than a mile away lay the little port of Chanak. There was nothing interesting there, but the indentation to the right, forming Sara Siglar bay, was occupied – and by a Turkish battleship. It was the *Messoudieh* at anchor. The huge target was on the submarine's starboard quarter little more than a mile away, but the current was sweeping *B11* across the bay. Due allowance would have to be made for current when firing a torpedo: it was imperative to get close to the enemy to minimise its effect. Holbrook went deep, speeded up and held on for five minutes to halve the range. When he next had a look he was less than 900 metres (1000 yards) away and a little abaft the battleship's beam. It was now or never. During a torpedo's running time – about one minute at that range – current would take it between 60–90 metres (2–300 feet) off the point of aim, that is, towards the battleship's stern; so

Holbrook manoeuvred carefully to point the tubes exactly at the target's bow. Then: 'Stand by One . . . Fire!' The characteristic noise of discharge, a sibilant 'tschoof', told the crew that a tinfish was on its way.

Winn, trying to avoid the bows breaking surface, slightly overcompensated for the loss of weight, and Holbrook in the tower found the periscope dipped. No matter: less than 60 seconds later *B11* was shaken by a violent explosion. The single torpedo was sufficient. When the Coxswain brought the boat back up Holbrook could see that the *Messoudieh* was mortally stricken. But the giant was not dead yet. All guns that could be brought to bear opened fire on the slender periscope at point-blank range. Shells could be heard exploding on the water all around while Holbrook put his helm to starboard and swung away, deliberately dipping the periscope. When he next risked a look the battleship was settling by the stern and the guns had ceased firing.

But *B11* was herself in trouble. The explosions had fogged the compass and more shells from shore batteries kept exploding on the water nearby; there were no distinguishing landmarks to fix on; and the continent of Asia was unpleasantly close to port. Then, as Holbrook altered course away from the coast, the boat hit the bottom with the depth gauge showing only 11.5 metres (38 feet). *B11* had to make for deep water, but steering with only the faintest of faint marks visible in the compass-projector tube was not easy. However, if the boat had hit a shoal by turning in one direction it was clearly a good idea to try another.

'I put the helm hard-a-port,' wrote Holbrook in his report, 'and went on to full speed, the submarine frequently touching bottom from 10.10 to 10.20 when we got into deeper water.' Just as *B11* ceased to bump and grind along the bottom the last glimmer of light from the compass disappeared. Back at periscope depth Holbrook pointed his bow at the European shore. He would have to con the whole way back by verbal orders to the helmsman. The *Messoudieh* had disappeared and the guns on shore had no aiming point now that *B11* was clear of shoal water, no longer exposing her conning tower involuntarily from time to time.

The return passage turned out to be more touch-and-go than the way up. Holbrook decided to negotiate the mine-fields at 24 metres (80 feet). He could only hope that he was steering a straight course. Continual visits to periscope depth were essential to find the way, despite the mines. When it was safe to surface the boat had remained submerged for nine hours, much too long in a tiny 'B' boat. The air inside was so lacking in oxygen that the petrol engine would not fire until the ventilation fans had run for half an hour.

Holbrook was awarded the Victoria Cross (the first sub-mariner to win the highest honour) and Winn got a DSO. Every member of the crew received the DSM.[2] Even the French sub-mariners, who might well have been envious, were unstinting in their praise. Best of all, on 24 July 1916 a motion was put in the Prize Court before Sir Samuel Evans, President, that the Ship's company of *B11* was entitled to prize bounty[3] for the destruction of the *Messoudieh*. An award was agreed for £3500, of which Holbrook took £601 10s 2d, Winn £481 4s 2d, chief petty officers £240 12s 1d and able seamen £120 6s 1d.[4] The balance of the award went in fees to the prize agents; but the dis-tribution still represented three years' pay for an able seaman.

Holbrook's success was not important in itself: the old battleship was scarcely missed by the enemy, but the exploit served both as a demonstration and an inspiration. If *B11*, with her minimal endurance, could get that far, a more modern boat might be able to go the whole way into the Sea of Marmara.

In February 1915 Roger Keyes arrived at Mudros as Chief-of-Staff to the Commander of the Combined Fleet (Carden, to be succeeded in March by de Robeck) where he found the ex-Gibraltar submarines under Lieutenant Commander C. G. Brodie as well as the original Allied Flotilla. Pownall was placed in command of both flotillas and Brodie joined Keyes on the Staff.

Keyes, of course, pressed hard for more and better sub-marines. It took time for the Admiralty to be persuaded because their lordships believed, perhaps rightly at that time, that the

Middle East was a sideshow; but by the end of March, escorted by the depot ship *Adamant*, *E11* (Nasmith), *E14* (Boyle) and *E15* (T. S. Brodie, twin brother of C. G. Brodie) were well on their way. *E11* still had mechanical problems and Nasmith was infuriated by having to remain at Malta for repairs while the other two boats pushed on. The second Australian boat *AE2* (Stoker) was also at Malta making good damage caused by hitting a rock at the entrance to Mudros harbour – an event which Stoker described as causing 'a distinct loss of popularity with the Admiral'. Both commanding officers were anxious to return to the fray, and Nasmith took a chance and went on ahead with a cracked shaft, trusting that it could be replaced when he got to Mudros, closer to the action.

In the fourth week of March, while fresh submarines were on their way to the Eastern Mediterranean, any remaining hopes of a major Allied surface force breaking through the defile from the Aegean Sea to the Marmara and Constantinople were abandoned. Attempts in February and March to silence the forts and sweep the minefields barring the Narrows had been repulsed: plans for an amphibious landing on the Gallipoli peninsula were substituted for the purely naval thrust right through to the heart of the Ottoman Empire which ardent spirits like Keyes so earnestly advocated. The initial landings took place on 25 April.

Henceforward it would be of paramount importance to prevent Turkish reinforcements and supplies reaching the Peninsula. Turkish rail and road communications were inadequate, the latter involving camels because the Turks had no motor transport, and the only practicable route from Constantinople was by sea through the Marmara to small ports on the Gallipoli peninsula. The short but vital artery could be cut by submarines alone.

It is relevant at this point to compare the roles of British and German submarines. Generally speaking, The Trade acted as the eyes, the advance guard and the distant striking force of the fleet. By contrast, the U-boat arm seldom operated on behalf of the surface navy. Where a U-boat usually went out into the open ocean to kill, British and Allied submarines often had to go inshore to find their prey. The farther a German submarine commander went the less acute were his difficulties; the farther a British captain went the more dangerous his task was certain to become. And only submarines could venture through the necks of two particular bottles – one debouching into the Baltic, as we have seen, and the other into the Sea of Marmara.

Whether the Allied Gallipoli campaign was justifiable or not is outside the scope of this book, but once embarked upon it, the use of submarines was justified, albeit at great risk. The potential value of one or more boats in the Turkish sea was immense, quite apart from the possibility of cutting out the locked-in *Goeben* and *Breslau*.

On 14 April Keyes held a conference to discuss the possibility of a submarine forcing the Dardanelles. Somerville, Pownall, Boyle and C. G. Brodie (later to write under the pen-name Seagee) all said no, but the normally shy and diffident T. S. Brodie electrified the company with a firm 'Yes'. Keyes promptly responded, 'Well, it's got to be tried, and you shall do it.' No time was wasted. Theodore Brodie took *E15* out of Mudros at 2 a.m. on 17 April well knowing what the Staff, with the exception of Keyes himself, thought of his chances. The French *Saphir* (Fournier) had run aground and been wrecked while trying to avoid the minefields three months earlier. It was known that if a submarine were lost in such an attempt there was no way of rescuing the crew.

Some limited support, however, could be given from the air and three RNAS[5] seaplanes were sent to cover *E15* over the trickiest part of the passage. One, piloted by Commander Charles R. Samson DSO, a pioneer of naval aviation, carried Brodie's brother as a passenger. In fact, Samson had flown *E15*'s captain over the narrows five days earlier so that he could get 'the hang of the land'. Further support of a kind was given by picket boats from the battleships *Triumph* and *Majestic* which endeavoured, with only limited success, to cut the electrical circuits between the Kephez minefield and shore.

E15 remained on the surface until well up the Straits

in order to conserve the battery. The seaplanes followed, dropping an occasional bomb to distract the enemy's attention. At 4 a.m. Brodie dived, but in full daylight at 6.45 his brother, looking down from Samson's aircraft, was horrified to see the submarine aground in Kephez Bay. The conning tower was exposed and it inevitably attracted a withering fire from every Turkish gun in the vicinity. The strong current had won this time: unlike the smaller *B11*, *E15* stuck fast on the shoal. A Turkish torpedo boat raced to the scene but Samson and his team could do nothing to divert the Turks. Brodie opened the conning tower hatch and climbed up on to the bridge to survey the situation: he was killed by a shell almost immediately. Another shot pierced the hull amidships, exploding in the battery compartment. A dense cloud of chlorine gas spread through the boat and that, so far as the crew was concerned, was the end. Six were asphyxiated and the rest, after abandoning ship, were gathered up by the Turks and taken prisoner.

Lieutenants Price and Fitzgerald managed to destroy the charts and confidential documents while the shells were still battering the boat but there was still a more or less intact submarine waiting to be towed off by the Turkish navy. Somehow the submarine would have to be destroyed. First *B6* (MacArthur) was sent to torpedo the wreck, and C. G. Brodie went with him. Subsequent reports were conflicting but it seems that one torpedo was fired which sank a tug alongside the grounded submarine. At one stage Seagee claimed that *B6* came within 90 metres (100 yards) of *E15* and found her heeled over, nearly bottom up, with the underside of her port saddle-tank 'looking like a huge pink blister on her grey-green hull'. *B6*, not unexpectedly, scraped along the bottom and also came close to getting stuck; changing depth and maintaining a level trim in this particular B-boat was more than usually difficult because she had no forward hydroplanes.

Samson's aeroplanes tried to hit the wreck with bombs but anti-aircraft fire prevented them from getting low enough. Two destroyers, *Scorpion* and *Grampus*, raced by night to within half a mile of the stranded boat but the gun-crews were blinded by searchlights and the captains had to retire. The following morning Holbrook, with a none too enthusiastic crew, made another attempt to do the job in *B11*, but fog descended and he could see nothing.

At 1 p.m. on 18 April the battleships *Triumph* and *Majestic*, escorted by destroyers, steamed up past Kum Kale and opened fire with their big guns at 6 miles. Communications between the big ships and a spotting aeroplane went wrong and none of the 300-mm (12-inch) rounds hit *E15*. The battleships simultaneously engaged the shore batteries on either side but without noticeable effect, while *Triumph* was heavily struck by a howitzer shell – the twenty-third 'brick' to hit her.

By Sunday evening, 19 April, bombs, two submarines, two destroyers and two battleships had failed to blow up *E15*. The Admiral sent the following signal:

> Two picket-boats from *Triumph* and *Majestic* are to attack *E15* tonight with torpedoes fitted to dropping gear. Lieutenant Commander E. G. Robinson of *Vengeance* will be in charge of operations. Only volunteer crews to be sent.

Robinson had already been awarded the Victoria Cross for demolishing enemy guns at Kum Kale and for some further brave work in minesweeping. He was the right man to send and knew the area well. The *Triumph*'s captain openly advised his own volunteers that he did not think there was much chance of them coming back. When it came to choosing between two eager young officers they let dice decide for the honour of going on a 'good show'. The winner spilled four aces to beat his rival's four tens at the third throw.

At 10 p.m. the 15-metre (50-foot) picket-boats steamed off. Everybody wore dark clothes and had their faces painted black, but the craft themselves were all too visible. They were greeted by a hail of shot which never ceased from the moment they came within range of the shore. Shrapnel cracked menacingly overhead while Robinson in *Triumph*'s boat and Lieutenant C. H. Godwin in *Majestic*'s manoeuvred towards the shapeless lump they assumed to be the submarine. Robinson let go a torpedo and missed. Godwin closed to 180 metres (200 yards) and also missed. Just as he released his 'mouldy' a shell crashed into the wooden hull beneath the waterline aft. Godwin knew that he had mere moments left, but the engine was still working and the helm was answering, so he fired his remaining torpedo which hit *E15* just forward of her conning tower.

What was described as 'a glorious volcano of noise and demolition' signalled success. Robinson was promoted to commander and Godwin was awarded the DSO (the circumstances did not warrant the highest decoration although many felt it well deserved).

After that de Robeck needed a great deal of convincing by Keyes before he allowed another submarine operation. But on 23 April Henry Stoker was summoned to the flagship where Keyes told him that His Majesty's Australian submarine *AE2* could have a go: the captain returned to his boat 'with a grin all over his face'.

Stoker, an Irishman, was intensely proud of commanding an Australian submarine. An excellent writer, actor and games player, he was popular everywhere: C. G. Brodie spoke for the staff when he said that he was 'the very pattern of a forlorn hope leader'. He had formerly commanded *E7* at Gibraltar and in the past fourteen months he had taken *AE2* 35,000 miles, the first submarine to travel half-way round the world. He was determined that she should also be the first submarine of the British Empire to pass through the Dardanelles.

Unfortunately, *AE2* was forever breaking things. Apart from the incident on the rocks at Malta she had lost no less than three propeller blades on her journeyings. Now, when in sight of Chanak, the forward hydroplane-coupling snapped. To proceed was out of the question and Stoker had to return to Tenedos. Two days later, at 1.30 a.m. on 25 April, *AE2* was able to sail again. Apart from some light shelling which did no harm, all went well and Stoker dived just short of Kephez Point where the minefields began. Several times mine-wires could be heard scraping along the outside of the boat but Stoker blandly assured the crew that they were quite safe at a depth of 27 metres (90 feet). The tough, resilient young Australians took his word for it.

Stoker returned to periscope depth at 5.15 a.m. – which was almost exactly the time that 4000 Australian officers and men started to land, with such terrible loss of life, at what came to be known as Anzac Cove on the western side of the peninsula. The Gallipoli bloodbath had begun, but the men in *AE2* had no inkling then of how their countrymen were carrying the Turkish defences at bayonet point, nor of the gore-stained boats which returned time and again to the British ships to ferry more soldiers ashore.

At 6 a.m. Stoker found himself close to the European shore near Chanak where Keyes had directed him to search for minelayers. None were there, but there was something that looked like a battleship with a gunboat between it and the submarine. The water was like glass and Stoker could not risk a prolonged approach at periscope depth: he had to be satisfied with torpedoing the gunboat before pressing on towards the Marmara. The Turks had other ideas: other gunboats, soon joined by torpedo boats, started a hunt around *AE2's* periscope which had been sighted when Stoker was satisfying himself that his victim was sinking. The salt-water layer at 18 metres (10 fathoms) performed its usual trick of bouncing the submarine back when Stoker went deep, and then, drifting rapidly with the current, the boat twice grounded on shoals – the second time with a steep bow-down angle and the depth gauge showing only 2.5 metres (8 feet). However, luck was still with Stoker at this juncture: the gunners on the nearby fort proved to be rotten shots and full-ahead power took *AE2* back into deep water before any damage was done.

When Stoker next showed his periscope Point Nagara was abeam. He was through the Narrows, but the battery was dangerously low. Stoker decided to lie on the bottom at 29 metres (95 feet) and wait until nightfall to surface and put on a charge. Being Sunday, it was the captain's duty to read prayers. After breakfast all hands were called to the fore-ends for that purpose, and then everybody, except for a couple of watchkeepers in the control room and engine room, turned in.

At 2 p.m. the crew went to diving stations and Haggard, the First Lieutenant, went through the usual procedure for coming off the bottom but, as soon as the submarine started to make headway, still a trifle heavy, the depth-gauge needle swung round alarmingly – so fast, in fact, that it bent against the stop at the 30-metre (100-foot) limit. The boat had evidently been sitting on a ledge. Only a blast of high-pressure air into the main ballast tanks – not very effective at that depth where the pressure was about 3.5 kilos per square centimetre (50 pounds per square inch) – saved *AE2* from plunging deep, possibly to crushing depth.

Trim was regained after a few anxious minutes and Stoker cautiously steered shorewards in order to bottom again, thinking that the crew had had enough excitement for one day. Sleep would have been welcome, but a persistent Turkish patrol boat continually passed backwards and forwards overhead, trailing a wire. Once, it struck the hull, but if it was an explosive sweep, as Stoker assumed, the guncotton charge did not detonate.

By 10 p.m. all sounds had died away and Stoker decided to come up. No lights were visible through the periscope. *AE2* had been submerged for eighteen hours, the air was thick and a substantial pressure had built up inside the boat because of leaks from the HP air system and the earlier torpedo discharge. Stoker warned the crew to mind their ears when he opened the hatch. The immediate drop in pressure produced a thick white mist throughout the submarine. It cleared soon enough when the diesels were started, the port engine for propulsion and the starboard for charging, but the fresh air was drawn aft towards the hungry cylinders so that for a long time the atmosphere forward of the control room remained foul. Everyone longed for a smoke but matches would not strike.

At 3.40 a.m. next morning the engines were stopped: enough amps had been put back in the box to go on submerged. Twenty minutes later Stoker fired at a Turkish battleship but missed and was chased by the escorting gunboat. This delayed progress because he reversed course for a while to throw his pursuer off the scent, but at 9 a.m. *AE2* passed the town of Gallipoli. Forty minutes afterwards Henry Stoker achieved his ambition and slipped into the Sea of Marmara: it was indeed an Australian submarine that was the first to reach it.

Stoker continued to be incautious with his periscope. It was sighted too often and he had to shake off another gunboat (which he fired at fruitlessly) besides ducking under shells from the fort at Gallipoli. A succession of ships passed by and each was visited by a Turkish gunboat, obviously warning of the submarine danger. When all was clear Stoker surfaced again, out of range of the shore guns, and commenced a full charge. There was no point in concealment any longer: the Turks knew that a submarine was loose in the Marmara but it was a trifle rash, with ensign flying, to pass close to a pilot boat even if the occupants (evidently Christians) did no more than cross themselves.

The night was spent on the bottom. The following day, refreshed, the crew went to diving stations to attack a big transport escorted by two destroyers. The torpedoes did not run, and spirits rather than the target sank. Some shallow-draught vessels appeared occasionally, one crowded with soldiers, but Stoker had used up all eight torpedoes – only one with effect – and *AE2* had no gun to deal with them.

On the following evening Stoker returned shorewards in order to transmit by wireless. This had to be passed to a receiving ship in the Gulf of Saros, which was stationed there specifically to relay messages back to Keyes and de Robeck on board HMS *Queen Elizabeth* at Mudros. The signal had to be cut short because of an approaching Turkish destroyer, and the fact that *AE2* was out of fish was not included in the message.

De Robeck and his staff were gathered gloomily around the big table in the Admiral's 'cuddy' discussing the increasingly dismal situation ashore when the signal arrived. Keyes gleefully read it aloud. 'It is an omen,' he announced proudly. 'An Australian submarine has done the finest feat in submarine history and is going to torpedo all the ships bringing reinforcements, supplies and ammunition to Gallipoli.' Keyes was unaware that all *AE2*'s torpedoes had been expended and that she would have to be restocked, with all the attendant difficulties, by another submarine, but, as he remarked in his memoirs, the report could not have been received at a more opportune moment. An eternal optimist, he was oblivious to the dangers created by his own spontaneous and infectious enthusiasm.

The council of war on board the *Queen Elizabeth* was in the middle of discussing, in the light of heavy casualties on the peninsula and the likelihood of the situation worsening, whether the troops should be withdrawn from the beachheads. The good news from Stoker, so resoundingly trumpeted by Keyes, apparently gave fresh heart to the dispirited senior officers: submarines in the Marmara might prove a dominating factor in what promised to be a long and costly campaign.

Whether or not that one signal from one submarine really influenced the decision to hold on, as Keyes implied later, is impossible to say, but if it did the consequences were unimaginably more dreadful than any officer at that late-night conference could contemplate. The final casualty list for Gallipoli would total 25,279 killed, 75,191 wounded and 12,451 missing on the Allied side alone. The enemy suffered even more severely with 218,000 casualties including 66,000 dead. By the time the peninsula was evacuated at the turn of the year the Turks and Germans were said to be demoralised – maybe, but it was a shockingly high price to pay.[6] At any rate, Stoker's signal opened the Dardanelles door for another seven British submarines and one French boat.

Boyle set out from Tenedos in *E14* on 27 April, having taken the greatest care to plan the route. Particular attention was paid to the gyro compass: Edward Stanley, the First Lieutenant, was the only man on board allowed to touch it. Lieutenant Reginald W. Lawrence, the RNR navigator and, of course, the captain himself (who had gone on one of Samson's reconnaissance flights) had made themselves thoroughly familiar with every aspect of the geography. Their meticulous attention to detail paid off: *E14* ran into no navigational difficulties on either the way up or the way down.

While passing Chanak, Boyle took an accurate potshot at a torpedo gunboat from 1500 metres (1600 yards). He just had time to observe 'a large column of water as high as her mast' when he had to dip again because 'some men in a small steamboat were leaning over trying to catch hold of the top of my periscope'. That was the only incident of note in Boyle's patrol report; but his second-in-command's private account makes it clear that the passage was not entirely straightforward.[7] On the surface the captain stood on the bridge by himself with all the loose gear unrigged and instantly ready to dive, giving orders down the tower to Stanley at the foot of the ladder who in turn passed them to the Coxswain at the wheel. The engines made 'a horrible din' by night between steep cliffs: a fore-endman said the noise was like 'a full brass band in a railway cutting' but Boyle stayed up whenever possible to save the precious battery which, like the gyro, was the First Lieutenant's personal responsibility. A stray shot from a small destroyer soon after they gained the open Marmara shattered the top window of one periscope, which was a nuisance but not crippling.

During the late afternoon of the 29th Boyle met *AE2* and the two captains spoke. Stoker said he had sunk a gunboat in the Straits, but otherwise no luck had come his way. The truth was that *AE2*, after a long time making repairs, was left no opportunity to 'work up' properly. The Australian crew was keen but out of practice.

Either inefficiency or a valve defect contributed to the submarine's loss the following day. When Stoker dived to attack a torpedo boat, the boat was wildly out of trim. According to one crew member, Able Seaman Wheat, the forward trim tank was full when it should have been about half empty, but Stoker's story, written a long time after the event, differs diametrically. He remembered that, after diving,

Suddenly, and for no accountable reason, the boat took a large inclination up by the bows and started rising rapidly . . . all efforts at regaining control proved futile . . . she at last broke surface. Through the periscope I saw a torpedo-boat a bare hundred yards off, firing hard . . . I ordered one of the forward tanks to be flooded, and a few minutes later the submarine took an inclination down by the bows and slipped underwater . . . we endeavoured to catch her at fifty feet but . . . she went to sixty and seventy and was obviously quite out of control . . . water ballast was expelled as quickly as possible but down she went, eighty, ninety, and a hundred feet. Here was the limit of our gauges; when that depth was passed she was still sinking rapidly . . . I ordered full speed astern on the motors. In a few moments there was a cry from the Coxswain – 'She's coming up, sir!' – and the needle seemed to jerk itself reluctantly away from the hundred-foot mark and rise rapidly.

The submarine 'jumped to the surface' where Stoker found the torpedo-boat circling round and a gunboat coming up fast. Two torpedoes missed their target as Haggard struggled to get her down again. When *AE2* did get under it was with an exceedingly steep angle. Loose fittings and furniture slid forward before emergency blowing brought her back up, stern first this time, to the surface.

It seemed that the valves on the 'main line' trimming system and tank suctions had been inadvertently left open, allowing water to pass freely forward to aft and vice versa. Three shells holed the hull and made it impossible to dive again. Stoker had no choice: he ordered all hands on deck and overboard. Haggard remained below with the captain to make sure the boat was properly scuttled while the Third Officer, Pitt-Carey, stayed on the bridge watching the rapidly rising water. When the boat had settled right down he shouted a warning but as Stoker clambered up the ladder, he could see through the conning tower scuttles that there was still a minute to spare. He jumped down once more and had a last look round – because, he said, he was fond of *AE2*.

Pitt-Carey shouted again, more anxiously, 'Hurry, sir, she's going down!' Stoker snatched up his private despatch case which contained some money and darted up the tower. Most of the crew were already in the sea and the last half-dozen, clustered on the stern, now joined them together with the officers. As Stoker swam away, he turned his head to watch as 'slowly and gracefully, like the lady she was, without sound or sigh, without causing an eddy or ripple upon the water, *AE2* just slid away on her last and longest dive'.

Australia had started the war with two submarines, and now had none. No more were acquired until after the peace in 1918, when six rather dubious J-boats were transferred by the British Admiralty which was probably glad to be rid of them.

By contrast, Boyle's twenty-one-day patrol in *E14* in the Marmara was exemplary. His most significant sinking was the large transport *Guj Djemal* carrying 6000 troops and a battery of field guns to Gallipoli. After thirteen days he had fired all his torpedoes and was deprived of an easy shot at the battleship *Torgud Reis* which passed within 365 metres (400 yards). In normal circumstances a submarine with no weapons left would return for reloads, but de Robeck ordered *E14* to stay on patrol because her mere presence athwart the Turkish lines of communication was disruptive. Boyle deliberately let himself be seen at every opportunity and had more than one narrow escape. At one point he rigged up a dummy gun using a pipe, an oil drum and some canvas. The contraption looked lethal enough to deceive several ships, and on 13 May a small steamer panicked at the submarine's appearance and beached herself.

These vigorous activities convinced the Turks that many more submarines were infesting the Marmara than actually were there, and before long the larger and more valuable vessels tended to stay in harbour while the targets which presented themselves were mainly small and not worth a torpedo. Boyle remarked at the end of his patrol report that 'a small gun would have been invaluable'. From then on guns were fitted. *E14* was given a 6-pounder.

Boyle received a rapturous welcome on his return. The victorious submarine was cheered by the Allied Fleet assembled off Cape Helles and Boyle was awarded the VC on the strength of a wire to the Admiralty which Keyes had drafted on the night of 14 May.

It was at about this time that Hersing in *U-21*, skilled

and confident, crept out of the Adriatic and into the Eastern Mediterranean. On 25 May he created consternation by slipping in unseen among the British ships off the peninsula and torpedoing the battleship HMS *Triumph*. Two days later he sent HMS *Majestic* to the bottom off Cape Helles. He cruised around for a couple of days but, finding no more big targets and with fuel running dangerously low, Hersing entered the Straits on 1 June. He arrived without fuss at Constantinople on the 5th with just $1/2$ ton of diesel oil remaining.

We have already seen the strategic effect of those two sinkings; but, even before Hersing's arrival on the scene, reports of a U-boat in the area resulted in de Robeck, with the Admiralty behind him, removing half the heavy ships to Imbros. The author Compton Mackenzie, involved in intelligence during the war, wrote scathingly of the withdrawal, 'It is certain that the Royal Navy has never executed a more demoralising manoeuvre in the whole of its history.' The retreat made the soldiers ashore feel abandoned, and the British submarines were left to salvage the honour of the Service if they could. Meanwhile, back in Whitehall Admiral Fisher resigned the post of First Sea Lord in a huff, nominally over the Dardanelles issue but actually in opposition to the markedly different personality of Winston Churchill.

Martin Nasmith in *E11* took *E14*'s place in the Marmara. No gun was available before he sailed but, typically, he devised a scheme for restocking with torpedoes. By international law torpedoes were normally set to sink at the end of a run if they failed to find a target. Disregarding the law, Nasmith ordered the automatic sinking-valve to be blanked off on all his torpedoes so that any which missed would surface. He was twice able to recover errant fish by this means. On the first occasion he himself dived into the water to render the torpedo safe by removing the firing pin before it was hoisted inboard by the standard derrick and lowered down into the fore-ends on rails through the fore-hatch. It was a dangerous procedure because the submarine could not dive with the fore-hatch jammed open by rails which took several minutes to dismount.

The next time he had a chance of recovering a quiescent tinfish he trimmed the boat down aft and invited D'Oyly Hughes, his number one, to lead a team of six swimmers and guide the weapon into the stern tube. The stern cap was then shut, the tube drained down, the rear door opened and the torpedo hauled into the stern compartment for doctoring and topping up. It sounds very simple and for Nasmith and his expert team it was, but nobody else ever attempted to play this kind of game with armed warheads and long cylinders weighing two-thirds of a ton.

Some of Nasmith's doings in the Marmara, where he carried out three long patrols in May/June, August/September and November/December 1915, smack of gambling with fate, but he took no more than calculated risks. Everything was very carefully planned, thought through and discussed with his officers. Besides industriously hunting for targets two things were constantly on his mind – the morale of his men and the state of his battery. As successes mounted, morale was not wanting, but welfare at sea was notably absent in the oily confines of *E11*. Nasmith took the unprecedented step of allowing hands to bathe, three at a time for ten minutes, in a quiet corner of the sea which was fast becoming 'his' just as the Baltic was said to belong to Horton. Even if a swim was not practicable he gave the crew a proper make-and-mend – half a day off – for washing clothes, relaxing and 'a spot of Swedish drill'. A brief respite was marvellously refreshing, and officers and men alike were all the more efficient for it.

As for the battery, Nasmith determined to patrol as far as possible on the surface to keep the box topped up. With this in mind, two days after entering the Marmara he captured a small sailing vessel and lashed *E11* alongside, trimmed down so that only the conning tower was above water; the engines could then be run with little chance of the submarine being spotted from afar. This ruse had the added advantage of enabling a sailor to look for shipping from the involuntary host's high mast, but Nasmith felt uncomfortable as a parasite – casting loose in a hurry might have proved difficult – and the ploy was not repeated.

There seemed nothing much of interest in the south and eastern part of the Marmara so Nasmith took *E11* north towards the Bosporus and Constantinople. En route, and while his boarding party were searching a sailing ship, he sighted a large merchant ship heading for the Turkish capital. Recalling the boarding party he gave chase, only to find his way blocked by the little Turkish gunboat *Pelenk-i-Dria* anchored not far off the Golden Horn. Naturally, he dived to attack. It is sometimes thought that an anchored target must be the simplest of all but it is actually embarrassingly difficult, especially in a tideway with a single torpedo. However, luck was in and the fish hit fair and square, but the gallant little gunboat retaliated. Luck was in for her too: a shell passed clean through the submarine's periscope and almost severed the top section. *Pelenk-i-Dria* sank a few minutes later but she left *E11* blind in one eye.

E11 prudently retired so that the artificers could plug the periscope tube. D'Oyly Hughes, in a First Lieutenant's role of head housekeeper, took the opportunity of turning the hands to and cleaning ship. The sinking of the *Pelenk-i-Dria* released Nasmith from his pledge not to drink or smoke until he had destroyed a warship. D'Oyly Hughes and Brown presented him with a box of cigars and half a dozen bottles of beer to celebrate the event, and their captain resumed his old (very moderate) habits with unashamed enjoyment.

When Nasmith had written out a signal to report the damaged periscope and events to date, he felt able to get his head down, leaving Brown on the bridge with two lookouts. The destroyer *Jed* was the link ship, well within wireless range in the Gulf of Saros (or Xeros) on the Mediterranean side of the peninsula. With the wireless mast rigged, contact should have been made straightaway but there was no acknowledgement from the destroyer. Nor had messages been coming in on the previous two nights. Something had to be wrong, either with *E11*'s apparatus or the *Jed*'s. Nasmith guessed that the fault lay with *E11* and so it proved. The aerial was defective and the telegraphist had not checked it.

Nasmith was harsh when necessary. He called the crew

to the control room and pointed to the unfortunate wireless operator as an example of how the carelessness of one man could wreck the chances of success and, indeed, expose the submarine to danger because vital intelligence signals were not being received. With the crew ordered to attention by the First Lieutenant he spoke his mind clearly and deliberately:

I consider a man of this type more deserving of the death penalty than the unfortunate individual who, from work and fatigue, drops asleep at his post of duty. Personally, I think I could forgive the man who fails in his duty because he falls victim to his outraged nature. But a man who accepts a post of importance as the member of a submarine's crew knowing, as this man must have known, that he was not fully capable of meeting any emergency that might arise, either as a result of enemy action or ordinary wear and tear on his equipment, is a menace to his shipmates and a traitor to his cause.

He did not spare himself either. 'I am ashamed to confess that, owing to my own inefficiency I am unable to tell this man how the repair should be made.'[8] The repair was then made swiftly and the matter dropped. At 2 a.m. the signal got through with blue sparks flashing from the recalcitrant aerial, and the missing messages came back by return.

On the morning of 24 May a small steamer was stopped by rifle fire. As *E11* came alongside to board, a nonchalant figure on deck introduced himself as Mr Raymond Gram Swing of the *Chicago Daily News*.[9] He announced that he was very glad to make acquaintance with the British submariners but that he had paid for a passage to Gallipoli where he intended to do some war reporting. Nasmith expressed his regrets but ensured that the reporter had a place in one of the ship's boats which pulled back to Constantinople. There the crew spread the most alarming tales. Their ship had been blown up – which was true because D'Oyly Hughes had set to work with demolition charges, sending the cargo, ammunition and guns (including one from the *Goeben*) to the bottom. And there were eleven, yes, eleven British submarines roaming the Marmara. That was far from true, but Gram Swing did not contradict the mathematics. It would be a long time yet before the United

States entered the war but his sympathies were decidedly with the Allies.

The next steamer's captain was made of sterner stuff. Instead of stopping he tried to ram the submarine but misjudged his aim and then ran himself ashore. Intent on repeating the demolition trick, Nasmith followed him but was driven off by a cavalry patrol which opened fire with rifles from the top of a nearby cliff.

Nasmith now decided to try a new gambit. Boyle had discovered that the salt water layer in the Marmara, at between 18 and 27 metres (60 and 90 feet), was sufficiently dense for a submarine to 'sit' on just as if it were on the bottom. Nasmith made full use of this convenience, which allowed a boat to remain stopped and conserve amps while most of the crew slept. Battery-charging time was thereby greatly reduced and there was no need to desert the shipping lanes for long periods.

Nothing would satisfy Nasmith but to enter the Golden Horn itself, the very heart of the Turkish Empire at the entrance to the Bosporus. Constantinople harbour was packed with shipping, some of it anchored in the Bosporus and some of it alongside the wharves and jetties. Unfortunately, the major Turkish warships were out of reach, beyond the Galata swing bridge, and Nasmith had to content himself with lesser prey. His subsequent report of the affair was, very properly, bald and factual, but D'Oyly Hughes was more descriptive:

We dived into the harbour on a windless day with a glassy surface which did not help periscope work. The crew were asleep except for those actually on watch. Nothing of any note occurred until we arrived just short of the entrance to the Bosporus when we saw a large merchant ship loading up alongside the Arsenal ahead of us. We could then clearly see the Sultan's Palace on the starboard bow and Galata Bridge to port of us.

We fired two bow torpedoes at the ship alongside the Arsenal, one of which hit and sank her, but we did not know this. The other torpedo was our one failure in fifty-one war shots. It did not blow out its tail plug at once and therefore the gyro capsized. Nasmith saw it floundering around the periscope and thought the Turks were controlling a Brennan torpedo and that we had better go deep.

179

At this moment our bows must have got into a strong tide running out of the Bosphorus for, as we went deep, we spun round in an amazing way, and the compasses went to hell and we didn't know which way we were pointing. We struck the bottom at 200 feet and then heeled over violently and bumped up and up and up until only 29 feet were on the diving gauge. We made her very heavy and stayed at this depth while we stopped to consider the situation. Depth-charges now began but none very close. Now Brown, our Third Hand, woke up and got out of his bunk, saying he was sure that we had bumped on the starboard side of the ship and therefore must be on the starboard side of the channel. We reversed the helm and screws and this pushed us gradually into deeper water, proving that he was right and we were wrong. After a few minutes we found ourselves still on the bottom at about 150 feet.

For the next two hours we tacked backwards and forwards across the channel hitting each side in turn, slowly tacking out of the place, mostly on the bottom. The battery got pretty low but the tide helped a lot. By 2 p.m. we were out in deep water and had a squint and found all clear. The second torpedo had done wonders. It made two big circles in the main harbour just missing the liner *General* with all the Turkish HQ Staff on board; then it turned and ran dead straight, as though guided, under the middle arch of Galata Bridge; then, still dead straight, up the Golden Horn for about a mile, turned hard-a-port and sank a decent sized merchantman alongside a wharf. This was also seen by an agent of ours called Slade, who was watching from Pera Cemetery at the time.

We afterwards went in several times, sank several ships, took photographs etc. without any excitement at all. Once we went nearly inside on the surface at night.

D'Oyly Hughes wrote this when the full facts became known long after the event. He might have added that the Turks were thrown into utter confusion. Troops were hurriedly disembarked from transports waiting to sail and the civil populace believed that invasion was imminent. Life in the great city was chaotic and all sailings were cancelled.

The strange thing, to a submariner, is that the crew were at 'watch diving' during this extremely tricky operation – that is, only about one-third of the hands were closed up (at their stations). Nasmith was certainly a one-man band and was criticised by a rugger-playing contemporary for 'holding on to the ball too long'. It could be that he felt more comfortable in an uncrowded control room with just his First Lieutenant to assist and sufficient men at the tubes forward. Although men would doubtless have raced to their stations quickly enough if called to 'diving stations' in an emergency (equivalent to a surface ship's 'action stations'), he was taking a chance in the Golden Horn without a full team on the field, but the main thing was that he was successful. On 23 June 1915 the announcement was made of the award of the Victoria Cross to Lieutenant Commander M. E. Nasmith of HM Submarine *E11*.[10] He was thirty-two years old.

Aircraft were becoming a nuisance by May, and during one of the bathing breaks *E11* was nearly caught. D'Oyly Hughes, always imaginative, had devised a decoy raft with a dummy periscope made from a broom handle, and he launched the decoy while the hands were swimming. The swimmers were still clambering on board when a seaplane, appearing from nowhere, zoomed overhead. *E11* dived with commendable speed before three bombs were dropped: they exploded harmlessly some distance away and D'Oyly Hughes proudly claimed that his invention had saved the day. Nasmith and Brown thought otherwise and pulled his leg unmercifully but it was fun to try new ideas, to surprise the enemy and to do things which nobody had done before. Nasmith told Keyes that he thoroughly enjoyed himself in the Marmara, and he meant it.

E11 was equipped with a gun for her second patrol from 5 August to 2 September. It was every bit as useful as Nasmith thought it would be. Apart from its great value in stopping or sinking small vessels it could be used to bombard shore installations. A prime objective – the railway line to Baghdad which in places ran along the coast – was too well defended by guns to permit prolonged bombardment, nor were *E11*'s 5-kilo (12-pounder) shells sufficient to do lasting damage. D'Oyly Hughes therefore suggested attacking a viaduct with demolition charges. Nasmith thought it a splendid scheme – yet another way of getting at the enemy unexpectedly.

The plan was hatched on 19 August, when *E11* chased a dhow and took on board a quantity of wood before destroying her. On the following day the wood was hauled up onto the casing and made into a raft. The submarine surfaced at 2 a.m. next morning, and it now became clear that the First Lieutenant, equipped with 7.3 kilos (16¼ pounds) of gun-cotton, a pistol and an electric torch, a whistle and a 'very sharp' bayonet, was going to blow up the railway viaduct single-handed.

It was beginning to look as if the Second Captain (the term still used by most of the ship's company) was regarded by the Captain as expendable but that was not true: Nasmith had the highest regard for his right-hand man, nine years younger than himself, and had grave qualms about letting him go. The story is told in Nasmith's own patrol report (slightly abridged) which led to a DSO for D'Oyly Hughes:

E11 proceeded towards the shore. At 3.30 a.m. D'Oyly Hughes dropped into the water and pushed the raft carrying the charge, his accoutrements and clothes some 60 yards on the port bow of the boat. The cliffs proved unscaleable at the first point of landing. He relaunched the raft and swam along the coast to where a less precipitous point was reached. Half an hour later he reached the railway line. He then proceeded slowly with the charge towards the viaduct. Having advanced some 5–600 yards voices were heard, and three men were observed sitting by the line. He decided to leave the charge and go forward, making a wide detour inland to inspect the viaduct. This detour was successful. He decided that it was impossible to destroy the viaduct, so returned to the demolition charge and looked for a spot to blow up the line. He found a low brickwork support over a hollow and placed it underneath. It was not more than 150 yards from the three men [sentries seen earlier]. He muffled the fuse-pistol but the noise was very loud: the men heard it and stood up. They came running down the line so a retreat was made. After running a short distance he turned and fired two shots to try and check the pursuit . . .

Soon after, two or three ineffectual shots were fired from behind. In view of the fact that speed was necessary, Lieutenant D'Oyly Hughes decided that to return down the cliffs at the place of ascent was impossible . . . He plunged into the water about three-quarters of a mile to the eastward of the small bay in which the boat [E11] was lying. The charge exploded as he entered the water, fragments falling into the sea near the boat, between one quarter and half a mile away from the charge. After swimming for four or five hundred yards straight out to sea he blew his whistle, but the boat, being in a small bay behind the cliffs, did not hear it.

Day was breaking very rapidly so, after swimming back to the shore and resting for a short time on the rocks, he commenced swimming towards the bay in which the boat was lying. At this point he discarded his pistol, bayonet and electric torch, their weight making his progress very slow. It was not until he had rounded the last point that the whistle was heard, and at the same time he heard shouts from the cliffs overhead, and rifle fire was opened on the boat. As the boat came astern out of the bay the early morning mist made her appear to him to be three small rowing boats, the bow, the gun and the conning tower being the objects actually seen. He swam ashore and tried to hide under the cliffs, but on climbing a few feet out of the water he realised his mistake, and shouted again before entering the water.

We picked him up in an extremely exhausted condition [at about 6.45 a.m.] about 40 yards from the rocks, after he had swum the best part of a mile in his clothes.

The personal reports on D'Oyly Hughes, while commenting on his ingenuity and commonsense, hint heavily at ill-health a couple of years after this exploit. It could well be that the swim did him no good although he went on to command *E35* with distinction.[11]

Besides the captain, four crew members kept their own diaries and it is remarkable how these stick to the bald facts of *E11*'s three epic patrols, totalling ninety-six days in hostile waters, without betraying the tension that must surely have accompanied them. A few entries from the diary of Signalman George Plowman for 1915 give the tone:

22 May. We sighted a sailing vessel and decided to take charge of her. We went on board her, taking three hens and eighty eggs. Much sport . . .

24 May. Being Sunday we made a glorious start at 8 a.m. by sinking a gunboat, that being our first ship. Captain earns his smoke and a bottle of beer . . . Bathing also enjoyed.

26 May. Very exciting, as at daylight we dived at the entrance of the harbour of Constantinople and commenced to go up for the Grand Splash . .

7 June. We start our homeward journey and have good luck until we reach the Narrows. Then we return to torpedo a transport which we do in fine style. Then we have to make a fresh start back . . . we get caught up . . . Lieutenant Hughes goes into the conning tower and first spots a mine hanging on to us so calls Captain and Navvie up to have a look. They keep it quiet until we are about to rise when I am sent to get some flags out of the tower. I see the mine and go to inform the captain who laughs and tells me to get a hammer. . . .
  So ends our first trip.

4 August. Start by torpedoing a troopship off Nagara after which we dive to go through the net at 110 feet down, tearing a lump off it as we hear the wires, we being the first boat to get through safely as the French submarine 'Marriot' (sic) was caught and the crew taken prisoners a week before.[12] [D'Oyly Hughes was appointed lookout in the conning tower whenever *E11* had to crash her way through nets at speed. He peered through the scuttles with the deadlights raised on the return journey and was able to report that the two-and-a-half-inch wires in a ten-foot mesh parted on impact – an encouraging piece of intelligence.]

7 August. As usual for Sunday we accomplish the feat of sinking the Turkish battleship *Hairedin Barbarossa* with one torpedo off Gallipoli . . . we come to the surface and find *E14*. We give her the news. Much joy. Later. *E14* runs a transport on the mud and we both bombard it. *E14* with 6pdrs and *E11* with 12pdrs, with good results. We set her on fire and she burns for two days. We had to pack up firing as our gun breaks and shoots the crew into the ditch. [The gun mounting was repaired with cold chisels, bolts and superhuman efforts by the engine-room staff.]

4 December. 3rd Wash indulged in.

8 December. Had a battle with an aeroplane which dropped two bombs rather too close to be comfortable. Captain opens fire with rifle.

9 December. Captain misses the chance of attacking a hostile submarine. She and us were diving and he sees her periscope through ours but dare not fire because we are to meet *E2* today, just outside the harbour.

14 December. Enter Constantinople again and to our delight we sink a large Transport right inside the harbour. We go aground at 19 feet with our periscope showing but get away without being fired upon. Turks send a destroyer out but we cannot attack her owing to high speed and changing course.

21 December. I break all records and have a bath. Lots of water sculling, second coxswain serving it out.

22 December. Still looking for *E2*. No joy. Sink another sailing vessel and start rigging gear [net cutters and jumping wires] ready for returning the next day.

During those unsurpassed patrols from May to December 1915 *E11* destroyed 122 ships. Most of them were small, but Nasmith's boat was rightly named the 'Scourge of the Marmara'.

Other submarines which followed also did a deal of scourging. *E12* (Bruce) nearly fell victim to a decoy in June – the Turks had begun to copy Q-ship tactics – but conducted a devastating patrol lasting a record six weeks in September and October. On the return run *E12* ran into a net at 24 metres (80 feet), passed through but ended by towing a large portion of it astern. She thereupon achieved another record by going down to 75 metres (245 feet) out of control. The conning tower glasses burst under the pressure, filling the tower; serious leaks developed in the fore-ends; and the fore-planes had to be operated, with great difficulty, by three men using the local hand-control wheel. Bruce was very shaken, according to Keyes, but was awarded the DSO and promoted to commander. *E12*'s bag amounted to three large steamers, one small steamer and thirty-three sailing vessels.

E7 had a fine time when Cochrane, great-grandson of Lord Dundonald, displayed a penchant for shore bombardment. In Keyes's words he 'worthily upheld his ancestor's reputation for conducting war offensively'. The crew were in high spirits when *E7* set off for another patrol on 4 September: they sensed that 'Archie' Cochrane had a scheme up his sleeve that would astound 'Johnny Turk'. Unfortunately J. Turk had his own scheme for trapping *E7*. Too many submarines had been charging virtually unscathed through the barriers off Nagara; so the wire mesh had been strengthened (with German help) and extended down to 60 metres (200 feet).

Cochrane, as usual, took his boat at full speed into what he believed to be a light obstruction and was netted like a giant fish. One long strand of wire entangled the starboard propeller. Cochrane put the helm hard over but this manoeuvre only resulted in the boat paralleling the net, catching forward and aft. At 8.30 a.m., one hour later, a mine exploded a few hundred feet from the boat and at 10.30 came another, much closer this time. Cochrane hoped that the last explosion might have partially freed the submarine and he decided to lie low until nightfall. In the meantime all confidential papers were burned although the smoke did nothing to improve the increasingly stale atmosphere.

At 6.40 p.m. another mine went off a few feet from the hull. The explosion was very violent: most of the electric lights and small fittings were broken. Tradition has it that this mine was let down from a rowing boat by a man who knew his business – Heino von Heimburg, captain of *UB-14*. Heimburg had already established his reputation in *UB-15* before that boat was transferred to the Austrian Navy: on 9 June 1915 he sank the Italian submarine *Medusa* and on 17 July he despatched the armoured cruiser *Amalfi* off the Istrian coast. Then, in *UB-14*, he sank the 11,117-ton troopship *Royal Edward* in the Aegean before going on to join the newly formed half-flotilla at Constantinople. While there he heard from the Turks that a submarine was caught in the net and took his boat down at full speed through the Marmara and into the Narrows where he anchored at Chanak. Here, so the story goes, he procured a dinghy and, with the U-boat's cook Herzig, rowed out to where Turkish patrol vessels were watching the line of buoys supporting the net.

The cook swung a weighted line over the side and before long found the trapped E7. A fused mine was then lowered and it was this that spelled the end for Cochrane and his men. Main ballast was blown and Cochrane signalled surrender but managed to scuttle the submarine with a time-fused charge when the crew were clear, before either the Turks or the German submariners could get on board. Heimburg watched while the water closed over the conning tower. A final figure jumped out into the water: it was the captain, the last man to abandon ship.

E2 (Stocks) and H1 (Pirie) were the other two British boats to 'run amok' in the Marmara but the French submarine *Turquoise* (Ravenel) came to grief on 30 October and her captain's negligence directly caused the loss of another boat. *Turquoise* ran aground in the Marmara under the guns of a Turkish fort for reasons which have never satisfactorily been explained: her excessively complicated equipment gave constant trouble and this may have been a contributory factor. It was also said that Ravenel was over-endowed with élan. Pirie, at the periscope in *H1*, had watched in wonder when *Turquoise* surfaced on entering the sea: Ravenel called the crew on deck and lined them up to sing the 'Marseillaise' by way of celebration.

Not only did Ravenel allow the Turks to capture his command undamaged (she was renamed *Mustadieh Omombashi*)[13] but failed to destroy his papers. The Turks immediately passed these to the local German authorities who thereby learned that *Turquoise* was due to rendezvous with E20 (Warren) near Rodosto on 5 November. *UB-14* was by this time undergoing maintenance at Constantinople but, by dint of great exertions, she was made ready for sea in less than twenty-four hours; and, instead of the French boat, she kept the appointment with E20.

Heimburg fired a single torpedo and E20 went to the bottom. Only nine men were saved, including Lieutenant Commander Warren who had been at his ablutions when the torpedo struck. The German captain recounted that Warren was asked if there was anything he wanted when he was hauled on board the U-boat, stunned but conscious. 'Yes,' replied the prisoner, 'a toothbrush please,' and continued brushing his teeth.

Heimburg refused to ratify the veracity of this tale later, but it was well received in the U-boat arm where it demonstrated that the grey humour of submariners was pretty much the same on both sides.

While the British were intent on operations in the Marmara, German U-boats based at Constantinople worked mainly in the Black Sea (without any notable results) and occasionally made their way down the Straits to seek targets in the Aegean.

Hersing had been the first to arrive at the Golden Horn. His spectacular successes in *U-21* (temporarily renamed *U-51* to confuse Allied spies) brought relief and encouragement to the Turks who believed, with good reason, that British troops clinging to the hard-won tip of the Gallipoli Peninsula would be disheartened by the loss of *Triumph* and *Majestic*. In July, August and September *U-21* passed down the Narrows in the opposite direction to the British boats coming up but at the end of September intelligence indicated that Allied minefields barred the way back, so Hersing made for Pola in the Adriatic where *U-21* was laid up for repairs until 22 January 1916. If a man of Hersing's calibre had interfered with the Allied evacuation of the peninsula on 19/20 December from Suvla and Anzac Cove, or from the last foothold at Cape Helles on 8 January 1916, the remarkably smooth withdrawal might well have been attended by more losses than the three casualties actually suffered.

In military terms the Dardanelles campaign was the disaster it has been painted, although there were mitigating political and strategic factors. It caused the Germans to cancel their offensive in the West, originally planned for the spring of 1915; it brought Italy to the Allied side; and it delayed the entry of Bulgaria into the war. The preoccupation with Constantinople distracted attention from the Suez Canal and relieved the Russians from Turkish pressure in the Caucasus. And, by destroying the best of the Turkish army, the campaign prepared the way for Lord Allenby's victory in Palestine.

The small band of British submariners played a significant part in redeeming the honour of the navy: the great surface ships had little to be proud of. Kitchener had sent an army to

188

the Dardanelles on the understanding that a naval force would attack the Narrows simultaneously but the fleet, apart from the submarines, provided little more than transport and support facilities.

Four British and three French submarines were sunk, either in the Straits or in the Marmara, but the Turks lost a battleship, a destroyer, 5 gunboats, 9 transports, 30 steamers, 7 ammunition and supply ships and 188 smaller craft besides the havoc created by submarine gunnery against shore targets.[14] Seaborne traffic through the Marmara was reduced to a trickle and the Turkish army came close to being starved of both food and ammunition. Submarines materially assisted the Allied soldiers ashore – and to a much greater extent than the big naval guns.[15]

The German General Liman von Sanders, commanding the Turkish Fifth Army of 60,000 men on the peninsula, concluded: 'Had the British managed to increase their undersea offensive the Fifth Army would have starved.'

CHAPTER 10

The First War on Shipping
(February–September 1915)

Drama in the Dardanelles tended, at first, to draw the British public's attention away from the deadly campaign that Germany first launched against merchant shipping in February 1915 but it was not long before the grave danger in which Britain's supply routes stood became apparent to all. The first victim had been the 866-ton steamer *Glitra*, stopped, searched and scuttled in gentlemanly fashion by *U-17* (Feldkirchner) off Stavanger on 20 October 1914. The crew were allowed to take to their boats in accordance with Prize Regulations before the sea-cocks were opened. Six days later, however, Kapitänleutnant Schneider in *U-24*, patrolling off Cap Gris Nez, gained the unenviable distinction of being the first submarine commander to attack an unarmed merchantman, the *Amiral Ganteaume*, by torpedo without warning. The 4,590-ton vessel was carrying 2500 Belgian refugees. Fortunately she did not sink although about forty lives were lost.

Feldkirchner brought *U-17* back to Helgoland fearing censure, but was relieved to find that his action was formally approved. Neither, apparently, was Schneider reproved: presumably the *Amiral Ganteaume* evidence as seen in Germany was not damning. In any event he went off to send the battleship HMS *Formidable* to the bottom of the Channel on New Year's Day 1915 with the loss of 550 lives. After the triple cruiser sinking by Weddigen's *U-9* in the previous September the other ships in company were ordered not to approach the doomed pre-dreadnought.

On 29 January Hersing appeared again in *U-21*, shelling Barrow. The Vickers ship and submarine building yard was

190

virtually unscathed, but he destroyed three merchantmen with charges, allowing the crews time to escape, on the following day. Meanwhile Spiess, in *U-19*, had similarly destroyed a steamer off the Dutch coast. Dröscher in *U-20*, however, used torpedoes on three unsuspecting steamers in the Channel on the 30th: one sank with all hands. On 1 February he fired at, but missed, the large hospital-ship *Asturias*. Although it was a dusk attack Dröscher must have been aware of his target's role because she was brilliantly lit and painted the regulation white with green bands punctuated with red crosses.

It seems that at this early stage of the war U-boat commanders played the game according to their own individual rules; and a score or more interpreted the underlying intention – of frightening neutrals away – by taking terrorism to its limits.

Up to 18 February 1915 a total of eleven British and one Allied merchantmen had been sunk by U-boats and five had escaped by flight. More seriously, torpedoes had robbed the Royal Navy of one battleship, four cruisers, one light cruiser, a 'seaplane-platform' (the converted cruiser *Hermes*), an old gunboat and one submarine (*E3*). All this for the loss of seven U-boats (a fifth of all boats completed by then) which would quickly be made up now that the German naval staff appreciated the intrinisic war-value of an underwater arm. Fifteen new boats had been commissioned since August 1914 while twenty large and twenty-three small coastal and minelaying submarines were on order.

It was now possible for German naval leaders to consider a full-scale trade war (*Handelskreig*), the demand for which was loudly voiced in the High Sea Fleet in November 1914 after the *Glitra* attack.

Admiral Fisher, assisted by (then) Captain S. S. Hall, had prepared a memorandum in 1913 prophesying that the Germans would use their submarines for attacking commerce – and if that was the view of the Kaiser's most expert enemies it can hardly have been otherwise among his own more prescient officers. On the other hand, First Sea Lord Prince Louis of Battenburg (of noble Hessian birth) and First Lord Churchill (grandson of the Duke of Marlborough) refused to accept that the German nation would be capable of such an ignoble practice. Prince Louis wrote to Churchill that Fisher's brilliant paper 'was marred by this suggestion' and Churchill told Fisher that he did 'not believe this would ever be done by a civilised Power.'[1] Alas, the pragmatic Fisher, with no pretensions to nobility (and respecting a father-in-law 'in trade'), was right and the aristocracy, with strong German connections (like the King himself), wrong.

According to Gayer, *Flottillenchef* of the Third *Uboothalb-flottille* at the time,[2] an anti-shipping onslaught was discussed in September 1914 but rejected, not because of possible inhumanity but because there were then insufficient U-boats for the purpose. That statement has a ring of truth about it, while still allowing it to be said that there were no positive pre-war plans. Nonetheless, plans were soon to be formulated.

In November 1914 Germany launched a polemic to the effect that Britain was completely disregarding international law and there was not the least reason why Germany should exercise any restraint in her own conduct.[3]

The alleged British violation referred to the prevention of contraband from reaching Germany, whether carried in neutral or in enemy ships. However, the British Government had not ratified the Declaration of London (1908), foreseeing that its definitions of contraband and free goods, together with restrictions thereon with regard to interception, would make effective blockade impossible. There was never any question of 'absolute contraband' – war material – not being intercepted but on 20 August 1914 the Allies declared that 'conditional contraband' – foodstuffs, fodder, fuel, bullion and specie – would be liable to capture if its ultimate destination was Germany, whatever its offloading port. Copper, rubber and iron ore were added to the 'conditional' list in September.

The northern entrance to the North Sea – the gateway to Germany – could not be adequately patrolled, and on 2 November Britain declared the whole of the North Sea up to and beyond the Shetlands a closed military area and forced neutral traffic for Norway, the Baltic, Denmark and Holland to pass through the Straits of Dover and up the east coast of England to the Farne Islands (off Northumberland) before making for the Dutch ports or the Skagerrak. It was this tightening of the screw that finally persuaded the German Commander-in-Chief, von Ingenohl, that submarines could and should be used against Britain's seaborne supply routes. Included in his memorandum to the Chief of Naval Staff, von Pohl, were the following sentences:[4]

A U-boat cannot spare the crews of steamers, but must send them to the bottom with their ships. The shipping world can be warned of these consequences . . . that the lives of steamer's crews will be endangered will be one good reason why all shipping trade with England should cease within a short space of time. . . . The gravity of the situation demands that we should free ourselves from all scruples which certainly no longer have justification.

On 7 November von Pohl formally proposed a German counter-blockade to Bethmann-Hollweg, the Imperial Chancellor; but the Chancellor, fearing inevitable political reactions if neutral shipping was destroyed, stood firm against the naval faction. On 27 December he ruled that, although a trade war would be legal, the time was not yet ripe for such violent measures. In his view success in the field by the army had to precede total war at sea. When Germany's hold on the Continent was secure no neutral would dare pick a quarrel with the Fatherland. On the contrary, insisted the admirals, success on land could only be achieved by unrestricted warfare at sea to frighten neutral ships from British waters.

The controversy was settled by a German defeat on 24 January 1915 when Admiral Hipper, acting under von Ingenohl's orders, led a force of battle-cruisers, light cruisers and destroyers across the North Sea to reconnoitre the Dogger Bank and do what damage they could to light craft and fishing vessels suspected of acting as observation posts. The object was presumably to clear the way for a more formidable operation – very likely a third raid on the English east coast (which Zeppelins had recently begun to bomb) or on the Firth of Forth.

The reason was never confirmed because Hipper was driven back, losing the battle-cruiser *Blücher*, by the British fleet under Admiral Beatty. Beatty had, incidentally, been alerted by the interception and rapid deciphering of von Ingenohl's signal to Hipper ordering the sortie. The latter was sent at 10 a.m. on 23 January and a decryption was read in the Admiralty by noon.

The defeat brought to a close the shore bombardments which had been the keynote of German surface operations since November 1914. It cost von Ingenohl his command which passed to von Pohl. Von Pohl was by now convinced that commerce raiding by submarines was Germany's solution to the war at sea and, indeed, to the war in general. There was no way in which he could employ the High Sea Fleet more aggressively than his predecessor because the Kaiser had, in effect, refused permission for the C-in-C to act on his own initiative. The Kaiser's decision read:

. . . it must not be lost sight of that the main portion of the High Sea Fleet must be preserved as far as possible as a political instrument in the hand of the All-Highest War Lord. Advances on a large scale into enemy waters must be reported beforehand to His Majesty.

Meanwhile the war on land was bogged down. It looked as though neither side, despite great sacrifices and horrendous casualties, would ever break the stalemate and achieve victory. The arguments against U-boats and their usage were now cast aside. On 4 February 1915 the Kaiser inspected the fleet at Wilhelmshaven and the U-boat commanders were presented to him. On the same day von Pohl issued one of his last announcements as Chief of Naval Staff before becoming Commander-in-Chief:

1. The waters around Great Britain and Ireland, including the whole of the English Channel, are herewith declared a War Zone. From 18 February onward, every merchant ship met within this War Zone will be destroyed, nor will it always be possible to obviate the danger with which the crews and passengers are thereby threatened.

2. Neutral ships, too, will run a risk in the War Zone, for in view of the misuse of neutral flags ordered by the British Government on 31 January and owing to the hazards of naval warfare, it may not always be possible to prevent the attacks on hostile ships being directed against neutral ships.

3. Shipping north of the Shetland Islands, in the eastern part of the North Sea, and on a strip at least 30 nautical miles wide along the Dutch coast is not threatened with danger.

The reference to neutral flags arose from the action taken by the master of the Cunard liner *Lusitania* because of *U-21's* raiding activities in the Irish Sea in January. Carrying a heavy American passenger list, Captain Turner had flown the Stars and Stripes, a common enough ploy. Some effort would be made, it was said, to spare ships flying neutral colours unless there was evidence to suggest these colours to be false. But the memorandum to U-boat commanders was slanted differently:

The first consideration is the safety of the U-boat. Rising to the surface to examine a ship must be avoided . . . there is no guarantee that one is not dealing with an enemy ship even if she bears the distinguishing marks of a neutral . . . Its destruction will therefore be justifiable *unless other attendant circumstances indicate its neutrality.* [Italics added]

While the British statement declared the passage north of the Shetlands to be particularly dangerous, the third paragraph of von Pohl's announcement advocated the northabout route as the only safe one. Naturally, America was both alarmed and confused. Stiff notes passed between Washington, London and Berlin, but President Wilson was determined that the United States should keep out of the struggle. In this he succeeded until April 1917, when American public opinion had become increasingly inflamed by successive incidents. The British Government did everything possible to fuel the fires.

On 10 April 1915 the British 5940-ton *Harpalyce*, a Belgian

relief ship and clearly marked as such, was torpedoed by
UB-4 (Gross) without warning, close to the North Hinder Light
Vessel (just outside the strip of water declared safe by von
Pohl). The ship was en route to the United States to collect
food for the starving Belgians. The sinking outraged American
citizens who were already angry at the death of Leon C.
Thrasher, one of fifty-seven passengers and forty-seven crew
members drowned when the Elder-Dempster liner *Falaba* went
down to a torpedo from *U-28* (Freiherr von Forstner) on
28 March.

Baron von Forstner was a particularly ferocious officer:
a little earlier, while engaging the *Aquila* with gunfire and
furious at the master's attempts to escape, he cold-bloodedly
continued firing while lifeboats were being lowered and thereby killed the stewardess and a lady passenger among others. It
was alleged that the Baron called his men on deck to jeer,[5] but
that sounds like needless British propaganda. The action itself
was atrocious enough for the record. For some reason von
Forstner was not listed by Great Britain among the eighteen
declared war criminals; nor, although he sank more than thirty
ships, did Germany count him one of the forty-five aces.

Von Forstner survived the war but *U-28* came to grief
in a most unusual manner: she was sunk by a motor lorry.
On 2 September 1917, patrolling off North Cape, *U-28* (now
under Kapitänleutnant G. Schmidt) encountered the 4649-ton
SS *Olive Branch* laden with stores and munitions for Archangel.
The steamer was to prove misleadingly named. When Schmidt
inadvisedly opened up with his gun from 250 metres (270
yards) the second shell exploded in the ammunition hold.
A large truck, together with other debris, was blown into the
air and by vengeful chance it landed on the U-boat's hull. The
steel plating was holed and the crew had to abandon ship. Not
surprisingly, the *Olive Branch*'s people refused to take them into
their already overladen boat: Schmidt perished in the Arctic
water.

The *Harpalyce* debt was settled more promptly. On 15
August 1915 Gross in *UB-4* was beguiled in the North Sea by
the 93-ton trawling-smack decoy *Inverlyon* and sunk by the

diminutive Q-ship's puny 1.4-kilo (3-pounder) gun. (*Inverlyon* was herself destroyed by much superior gunfire from a U-boat on 30 January 1917.)

But it was the *Lusitania* affair followed by the *Arabic* sinking which precipitated the most violent reactions in the United States – just as the German Chancellor feared and the British Government wanted. The *Lusitania* story is so well known that it can be summarised briefly before laying bare one hitherto unpublished reason for the sinking. The 30,396-ton Cunard liner left New York bound for Liverpool on 1 May, with 1257 passengers of whom 197 were American citizens. The multi-millionaire Alfred G. Vanderbilt occupied the best suite. A week earlier notices emanating from the German embassy in Washington had appeared in the American press warning passengers not to embark on the great luxury liner. More general advertisements about shipping's 'liability to destruction' in Germany's declared war zone appeared on the morning of the departure, immediately next to a notice of the *Lusitania*'s sailing time. Nobody could have failed to take such heavy hints, which were prompted as much by German-Americans in the United States, who dreaded personal reprisals if American lives were lost, as by the German embassy on behalf of Chancellor Bethmann-Hollweg, who was fearful of national retaliation.

It was obvious (from a trail of destruction left by U-23 and U-24) that *Lusitania* would be entering a zone of serious danger as soon as she approached Ireland. It was the liner's hundred and first round trip: she did not complete it. On 5 May 1915, *U-20*, formerly under Dröscher but now known as the 'Happy U-20' under Walter Schweiger, was off the south-west coast of Ireland. In Germany everyone spoke of Schweiger, one of the comparatively few officers in U-boats when war began, with regard, affection and (after the *Lusitania* sinking) a trifle of pity. With well-cut features, blond hair, a happy temperament and a pointed wit he was a general favourite and in no way callous.

The approximate position of *U-20* was known to the Admiralty from radio intercepts. On the following evening Admiral Sir Charles Coke, responsible for the area from the

Queenstown base, wirelessed to shipping: 'Submarines active off south coast of Ireland.' The Admiralty repeated the warning an hour or so later. The master of the *Lusitania*, Captain 'Bowler Bill' Turner, received the messages at 7.30 p.m. and 8.30 p.m. He ordered the lifeboats to be swung out, watertight doors to be shut and external lighting to be switched off. Extra lookouts were posted and he reassured passengers that tomorrow 'we shall be securely in the care of the Royal Navy'. Turner cannot have believed that – he knew that he was on his own – but he was said to have described the passengers as 'a lot of bloody monkeys' and he wanted to keep them quiet.

The liner cleared the Fastnet well to seaward, as advised, on the morning of Friday 7 May in calm weather with occasional fog patches. Once more the Admiralty issued a warning of submarines but Turner reduced speed from the normal 21 knots to 18 knots (which made the ship a somewhat easier target) in order to cross the Mersey bar when the tide served. Turner reasoned that to proceed more slowly now was safer than waiting in the Irish Sea.

Meanwhile Schweiger, short of fuel and – although he had crammed in an extra weapon before sailing – with only three torpedoes left after a series of depredations, had moved slowly eastwards to a position at the entrance to St George's Channel 15 miles south of the Old Head of Kinsale. The U-boat was on the surface and Schweiger was eating his lunch on the bridge (potato soup and German sausage) when, at five past one, he sighted what he at first took to be masts and funnels of destroyers on the horizon to the south-west. Soon the mass resolved itself into the shape of a large vessel with funnels painted black.

Schweiger was broad on the target's starboard bow but by running at top speed (a little more than 15 knots) on a northerly course he succeeded in closing the track to a firing position before diving to fire a single torpedo at 2.15 p.m. from 700 metres (765 yards) on a 90-degree track. The weapon hit the Cunarder just abaft the bridge and a second internal explosion (possibly due to the substantial quantity of munitions carried) occurred moments afterwards.

The huge ship immediately listed to starboard and plunged to the bottom eighteen minutes later. A fleet of rescue boats from Queenstown hurried to the scene, but 1198 lives were lost, 94 of them children and 128 of them Americans, including Vanderbilt who displayed extraordinary courage in endeavouring to save youngsters.

Schweiger was killed on 5 September 1917 when his next command *U-88* went down in the Horns Reef minefield. The Allies were therefore unable to bring him to book for what was cited as a crime against humanity. Former President Theodore Roosevelt denounced the *Lusitania* sinking as 'piracy on a vaster scale than any old-time pirate ever practised'. British feeling, summarised by Walter Page, American Ambassador in London, was that the United States 'must declare war or forfeit European respect'. The United States and President Wilson were lampooned as cowards, but still Wilson was not ready to fight.

Whether Schweiger really knew what his target was has never been formally established. According to his own statement, as reported in Germany, he did not recognise the liner until after firing and he denied delivering a second torpedo (as accused) when the ship did not break up immediately. That was confirmed by his torpedo officer, Weisbach, who also questioned, as late as 1966, if Churchill did not risk the great ship deliberately in the hope that an attack on her (which was predictable) would swing the United States towards the Allies.

However, recent research points strongly to a deliberate attack on a known target for a very good reason and it can be conjectured that the excuse attributed to Schweiger emanated from Chancellor Bethmann-Hollweg to offset the American furore. The simple fact, apparently missed by historians and media investigators over the years, is that the *Lusitania* was openly described in Brassey's *Naval Annual* as a merchant cruiser. In 1908 the *Annual* noted that both she and the *Mauretania* were 'built under special subvention [government subsidy] for the Cunard Line' with a top speed of about 25 knots and an armament of eight 15-cm (6-inch)

guns. In 1913 Brassey's showed the liner as still being sub-
sidised annually and noted that she was permitted to fly the
Blue Ensign (which evidently she did not in the event) to
denote her Royal Naval Reserve status.

Germany can be fairly blamed for many things – including
the First World War itself – but it is hard, for a submariner
anyway, to agree that the commander of *U-20* was guilty of a
crime in this particular case. A trade war around the British
Isles had been declared; passengers had been warned; and the
target – even if not fully armed as shown in Brassey's – was
clearly not an ordinary liner. Indeed, from all the evidence
available to the German Naval Staff she was an RNR combatant and was certainly serving Britain's interests. If anyone
was at fault it was arguably the British Admiralty for not taking
a firmer grip on the situation and offering more protection. In
any case, *Lusitania* was only one of many victims in the first
war on trade: she simply happened to be larger than the rest
and had more passengers on board.

Unwisely, someone in the German Government arranged
for grim medallions to be struck to mark the sinking. These
were copied (with the German word for 'May' misspelled) in
huge numbers by the great English department-store owner
Gordon Selfridge: about a quarter of a million were sold in
the United States and Britain to display the 'beastliness' of
German submarine warfare – which they did with notable
success – and raise money for charity.

In August Rudolf Schneider in *U-24* was at work, together
with *U-27* (Wegener) and *U-38* (Max Valentiner), between
Ushant and St George's Channel. Several ships went down
to his attacks and on the 19th he was shelling the 4930-ton
SS *Dunsley* 50 miles south of Kinsale when a large steamer
approached from the east. She was prudently zig-zagging but
Schneider thought that she was trying to ram. The ship was
the 15,801-ton White Star liner *Arabic* bound for New York. *U-24*
dived, loosed off a torpedo, and the target sank in ten minutes,
taking with her forty-four of her passengers and crew. Again,
there was great indignation in the United States; again, Wilson
refused to act.

Elsewhere there was rage as well – in the Q-ship *Baralong* commanded by submariner Lieutenant Commander Godfrey Herbert, 'set a thief to catch a thief'. The 4192-ton 'three-island' tramp decoy was well suited to her task and mounted three concealed 5.5-kilo (12-pounder) guns; but so far she had steamed more than 10,000 miles without meeting a U-boat. Herbert (the officer dogged by bad luck, described earlier in *D5*) was determined to make his name, and so he did: by his first Q-ship action he attracted both glory and execration.

Decoys or Q-ships in the Royal Navy probably took their best-known title from so many of them being based at Queenstown, Ireland. For a few months in 1916/17 some were unwisely given specific Q numbers as well as names, which immediately revealed that there was something odd about them. For example, *Q13*, which was really the disguised 'Flower'-class sloop *Aubretia*, was also named *Kai*, *Winton* or *Zebal* at various times. To confuse the enemy still further (to say nothing of friends), *Q14*, properly the sloop *Viola*, was in turn the *Aubretia*, *Cranford* and *Damaris*. Meanwhile, the three-masted decoy schooner of the same rightful name *Viola* was variously called *Vereker* and *Violetta*.

A total of 225 decoy ships in the Royal Navy from 1915 to 1918 has been counted but there may have been more. Essential secrecy at the time still makes the records hard to penetrate.[6] Sometimes they were known as 'special service vessels' (and crews appointed to them were drafted for 'special service') which conveniently abbreviated to 'SS' as for a steamship. More than a few people in ports and dockyards might know that the master of SS — — was actually a naval officer and that guns and gadgets were fitted, but not many identified their task correctly. If they were referred to as 'mystery ships', as they often were, no great harm was done.

German espionage found out about the decoys quite early because Irish citizens who saw them in the Queenstown area were certainly not all British patriots, but the conversion programme was so extensive and the names – even the appearances – of the mystery ships were changed so often that it was generally impossible for a U-boat commander to differentiate a decoy from a legitimate target.

The only real answer to the question of what was legitimate prey for the grey steel sharks was, surely, that war was war; that the purpose of war was (and is) to break down the resistance and fighting ability of the enemy. Since ordinary merchant ships were being equipped as rapidly as possible with defensive armament (albeit usually inadequate and with its use hedged around with many provisos) and large areas had been declared a war zone, an objective observer could reasonably understand Germany's point of view: why should any holds be barred unless 'frightfulness' (another well-worn term employed by the Allies) threatened to bring America into the war?

By mid-1915 the U-boats were up against deliberate traps. Their commanders could not risk the prolonged examination of a potential victim before despatching it. They shot, if possible, before the target could retaliate. But the decoys – like poisoned bait – were just as underhand, if that is a proper term for such activities, as U-boats themselves or, for that matter, the German cruiser *Emden* masquerading with a false funnel and friendly ensign when she attacked Penang in October 1914.

Lieutenant Mark-Wardlaw, commanding the 373-ton Q-ship *Prince Charles*, made the first strike on 24 July 1915, submitting to gunfire from *U-36* (and pretending to abandon ship) until the enemy had closed to 550 metres (600 yards). At that range the volunteer crew uncovered their 5.5-kilo (12-pounder) and 1.4-kilo (3-pounder) Hotchkiss guns and opened an accurate fire. Fifteen of the U-boat's crew were rescued by Mark-Wardlaw after the boat sank, and they yielded interesting intelligence. In particular, it was learned that *U-36* had 6-kilowatt Telefunken-type wireless equipment which could transmit messages to Kiel from up to 100 miles away and which could receive from Nordeich, in East Friesland, at 120 miles. Of greater importance was the fact that torpedoes were rationed and that the two 88-millimetre (3.5-inch) guns on this type of submarine were used whenever possible.

Although seven torpedoes were carried (in *U-36*) a captain had to give good reasons if he expended more than four on one patrol. One man swore that the weapons on the boat were manufactured in 1896, but weapons of that date had a range of only 800 metres (875 yards). It is more likely that they came from a large batch of G6 36-knot 6560-metre (7175-yard) 'eels' issued from 1906. Another prisoner, amazed and full of gratitude at being rescued, blandly remarked that if the action had gone the other way the *Prince Charles*'s 'civilian' crew would have been shot as *Francs Tireurs*.

That little episode passed off well. Even if Mark-Wardlaw seems to have been rather ingenuous in his interrogation technique, he did the gentlemanly thing by hoisting his colours (the Red Ensign because his ship was not commissioned) before shooting back – in fact, he 'warmed the bell' unnecessarily by several minutes in his determination to get it right.

Meanwhile Godfrey Herbert in the *Baralong* and his assorted crew, which included men of the Royal Marine Light Infantry, were incensed by the *Arabic* sinking and some of them had earlier watched the bodies of drowned children from the *Lusitania* laid out on the front at Queenstown before being carried to a makeshift mortuary. It was said that the *Baralong*'s crew had held a meeting there and then and vowed to give no quarter to German submarine crews.[7] The Q-ship men were echoing the outrage felt throughout Great Britain and the Royal Navy (whatever the truth about the *Lusitania*) at these infamous acts by a U-boat.

Herbert himself desperately hoped that he might fall in with the perpetrator *U-24*. The afternoon of 19 August 1915 found *Baralong* plodding eastwards across the stretch of water south of Ireland where the *Arabic* had gone down. At 3 p.m. Herbert sighted a large steamer to the south-west: it proved to be the 6396-ton *Nicosian* laden with mules for the British army. The merchantman was observed to make a major alteration of course and, simultaneously, the master broadcast a W/T signal on distress wave: 'SOS, being chased by enemy submarine . . .'.

Herbert altered course towards, at *Baralong*'s best speed

of 10 knots, and soon saw a submarine heading towards the *Nicosian* which had apparently stopped. He ordered the international flag signal VIC-QRA ('Save Life') to be hoisted and continued towards the threatened vessel whose master, under heavy fire from the U-boat, had ordered his ship to be abandoned.

Lifeboats were a couple of hundred yards ahead of the stationary mule-carrier when Herbert contrived to manoeuvre his ship so that the *Baralong* was hidden from the U-boat by the *Nicosian* itself for a crucial minute or two. During these fleeting moments, Herbert later insisted, he struck his neutral colours and ran up the White Ensign while going to action stations. Sworn statements from witnesses tell a different story: they say that the American flag was kept flying throughout the ensuing action. Herbert's formal report has to be questioned in several respects in light of both direct and circumstantial evidence.

Herbert reported that most of his thirty-four 5.5-kilo (12-pounder) shells fired took effect and that his marines' rifles accounted for several of the U-boat's gun-crew before they could return the fire. The submarine, which turned out to be Wegener's *U-27*, heeled hard over and sank within a minute. Twelve survivors swam to the *Nicosian* and started climbing up the rope ladders, which had been left hanging after abandoning ship. Herbert ordered them to be shot away (his words) but six succeeded in getting aboard.

Herbert now placed his ship alongside the merchantman and 'put a party of marines on board, under Corporal F. G. Collins RMLI, warning them to be careful of snipers in case they found the rifles which I [Herbert] was informed by *Nicosian*'s captain had been left in the charthouse'.

Herbert continued, 'A thorough search was made (by the marines) which resulted in six of the enemy being found, but they succumbed to the injuries they had received from a lyddite shell shortly afterwards and were buried at once.'

The laconic statement is not supported anywhere. Descriptions of what happened differ wildly but there is little doubt that a massacre took place in the *Nicosian*'s engine and boiler rooms whither the U-boat survivors had fled. Kapitänleutnant Wegener was shot in the water by one account and on deck by another. The official Admiralty version made no attempt to gloss over what was reckoned by Germany to be a cold-blooded atrocity – a useful counterpoise to the accusations levelled at the Fatherland:

A number of Germans got on board. The danger of losing the ship therefore continued and as soon as possible Lieutenant-Commander Herbert placed his ship alongside the *Nicosian* and ordered a party of marines to board her and recover possession. . . . The Germans were nowhere to be seen. They had made no signs of surrender, and in the charthouse rifles and ammunition had been left readily accessible. He therefore warned the men to be on their guard against surprise and to be careful to get in the first shot. Over what happened next he had no control. It would seem that after a short search the Germans were found in the engine room; and the marines, in hot blood and believing that they had to do with the men who had so wantonly sunk the *Arabic* in the morning, shot them all at sight.[8]

Hot blood, cold blood, what did it matter? The Admiralty loyally tried to shield the *Baralong*'s captain by announcing that he was a Mr William McBride, but German intelligence knew better.

The *Baralong* business scarcely changed the picture of the war at sea, but the more notorious U-boat depredations made broad brush-strokes on the canvas. In the three-month period up to January 1915 Allied mercantile losses due to U-boats had amounted to about 75,000 tons; from January to April the figure rose to 130,000 tons; and from April to July it passed 250,000 tons. The figure was still rising when, in the interests of expediency alone, the Kaiser called a halt to the first unrestricted war on merchant shipping around the British coasts on 20 September 1915. The question, debated vigorously between the naval authorities at Berlin and Wilhelmshaven on the one hand and Chancellor Bethmann-Hollweg on the other, was simple. Which policy would best serve the Fatherland: to hold the U-boats in check, mollify America and so prolong that great nation's neutrality or to deploy U-boats en masse without any restrictions and thereby hope to win the war before American joined the battle?

The Chancellor thought that a continuing ruthless onslaught on shipping (*Handelskrieg*) would not bring about a swift enough conclusion. He was convinced that diplomacy, to avoid the active hostility of the most powerful neutral State, was preferable by far to risking further provocation. Bethmann-Hollweg won his case against the admirals, and for more than a year Britain's direct trade routes were afforded some respite.

All this time, the U-boat arm was gathering in strength. On 1 January 1915 there were twenty-six boats. During the ensuing twelve months twenty were lost and sixty-two added, giving a total of sixty-eight hulls at the end of the year. Relatively few, however, were available or suitable for an anti-shipping campaign around Great Britain. Little 'UC' minelayers from the Flanders Flotilla comprised a fair proportion of the total (laying 648 'pineapples' in the latter part of the year and claiming 94 victims); half a dozen boats were in the Baltic and up to a dozen more at Constantinople. A substantial force was preparing in the spring for deployment to the Adriatic and, towards the end of September when the first deliberate *Handelskrieg* ceased in the west, only four of the remaining thirteen North Sea boats were fit to carry out the sort of destruction which *Führer der Uboote* Bauer's submarines had wrought in focal areas around Great Britain for the past nine months. The remainder were in sore need of extensive overhauls, which may have helped to overcome the bellicose arguments advanced by Bethmann-Hollweg's opponents.

CHAPTER 11

Mayhem in the Med (August 1915–December 1917)

U-boats had little difficulty in passing by night through the Gibraltar Straits into the *Mittelmeer*. Heavy merchant traffic masked the intruders, and substantial anti-submarine forces in the shape of trawlers and other patrol craft could not be spared to guard the Mediterranean entrance until very late in the war.[1] Contraflowing currents and density layers added to the difficulties that anti-submarine (A/S) forces and their hydrophone listening devices faced in trying to detect and localise submarines in the 15-mile wide gap. The gate was never effectively closed: U-boats could deploy more or less at will.

However, aside from four UB-boats and three UC-boats routed from Pola to Constantinople for work in the Black Sea, Hersing in *U-21* was alone in the Eastern Mediterranean until the late summer of 1915. But then, on 23 August, *U-34* (Rücker) and *U-35* (Kophamel) arrived from Germany at the secure landlocked Dalmatian port of Cattaro (now Kotor) halfway up the eastern side of the Adriatic from where operations in the Mediterranean were to be mounted. *U-33* (Gansser) and *U-39* (Forstmann) followed through the Straits and set about molesting shipping off Algeria before resuming their eastward voyage to Cattaro. Max Valentiner brought *U-38* past Gibraltar in November.

At the end of the year Kophamel, after a productive and exciting three months ranging between North Africa and the Aegean, handed *U-35* over to the man who was to become the 'ace of aces', Lothar von Arnauld de la Perière. Although de la Perière's name is always associated with *U-35*, Kophamel did great execution while in command. The troopship *Marquette* and some lesser vessels went down to him; and he showed himself to have more than a spark of compassion by towing lifeboats from the British armed boarding-patrol steamer *Tara*, torpedoed on 5 November off Solum, to Bardia on the North African (now Libyan) coast.

Kophamel became *Flotillenchef* at Cattaro where he was soon promoted to *Korvettenkapitän* to make plain his seniority over the U-boat commanders who were actually senior to the former half-flotilla leader Kapitänleutnant Adam. Adam remained in command of the German Naval Special Command at Pola to liaise with the Austrian authorities, to take charge of the UB/UC assembly line at Pola and oversee the quarterly U-boat overhauls undertaken at Pola and Fiume. A secret advance base was also set up at Budrum (today usually styled Bodrum) on the Turkish side of the entrance to the Aegean Sea.

Although U-boat operations in the *Mittelmeer* were initiated *faute de mieux*, so to speak, communications through the inland sea were crucial to the Allies who were ill-placed to defend them against submarine attack. A continuous procession of merchantmen, transports, supply ships, support vessels and colliers was required to maintain 400,000 British troops in Egypt and around Salonika (where there was also half that number of French troops) as well as the large force at Gallipoli. That was in addition to the normal throng of cargo vessels plying to and from East Africa, India, the Far East and Australia via the Suez Canal. Practically none of this shipping had direct American connections, so the German Government believed that U-boats on the rampage would not be unduly inhibited by political consequences of their actions.

Nor was there much need to seek out the targets: as a rule their paths were easily predictable. That was just as well for the Germans, because although there were nominally five U-boats and two UC-minelayers assigned for work in the Mediterranean at the beginning of the campaign in October 1915, fewer than half the force could be kept at sea. And even when more boats came to swell the flotilla, proportional availability was seldom improved.

The relatively few boats available, concentrating on known routes, inflicted mayhem in the Mediterranean during the autumn of 1915. Allied losses from October through December amounted to eighty ships (including one sunk by a submarine-laid mine) for a total of 293,423 tons representing 82 per cent of shipping losses in all theatres for the period. Those figures exclude attacks on warships.

For various reasons, notably diversionary operations against warships and, for a spell in spring 1916, some unusually effective Allied countermeasures in the Aegean backed by good intelligence, there were troughs in the U-boat success rate. The percentage of Mediterranean sinkings out of the total naturally decreased when the full fury of underwater warfare was unleashed around the British Isles in 1917. However, with scarcely ever a pause, the submarine onslaught on Mediterranean trade and supply lines continued with devastating effect almost to the end.

Two pirate kings stood out among the band of buccaneers and of this pair Korvettenkapitän Max Valentiner was branded the most bloodthirsty, appearing (unlike his colleague de la Perière) on the list of war criminals compiled by Great Britain as No. 3 out of eighteen. The dubious distinction arose from what might be called a specimen charge – the sinking by *U-38* of the P & O liner *Persia* on 30 December 1915 between Crete and Port Said. That act, resulting in the loss of 334 lives, aroused a series of protests from neutral countries which did not win sympathy for Germany's cause.

Valentiner was an astonishingly profligate pirate although the total tonnage destroyed by *U-38* – 292,977 tons resulting from 136 ships – came third in the ultimate list after *U-35* and *U-39*. It did not seem to matter much where Valentiner was sent: he invariably scored because of his determination to let nothing stand in his way – neither the hated enemy nor scruples. He had joined Submarines in 1911 after an important posting to the weaponry school at Kiel and had

considerably more U-boat experience than most of his colleagues, taking command of *U-38* in December 1914 on his
thirty-first birthday. He trained his crew to the highest pitch,
and his personal skill in attacking with torpedoes was possibly unequalled. No technical detail escaped his attention:
the engines always worked well in *U-38* and navigation was
precise. Resourcefulness was another of his strengths: to save
fuel on one occasion (after his Mediterranean tour), he stopped
a Norwegian ship west of Gibraltar and forced her to take the
U-boat in tow for three days towards Madeira, where he sank
three ships in Funchal Roads and bombarded the harbour.

Before going to the *Mittelmeer* Valentiner destroyed no fewer
than thirty ships in the South West Approaches during just
five days of August 1915 – a clear record. In September *U-38*
was ordered to operate from the south-west of Ireland across
the Bay of Biscay to the mouth of the River Gironde. It was a
vast area of sea but Valentiner always seemed to know exactly
where to find a fresh victim. At least five more vessels, including the 10,920-ton liner *Hesperian*, went down to him between
4 and 8 September, all without warning.

Once inside the Straits of Gibraltar, Valentiner evidently
decided (initially, anyway) to change his tactics. It is not
clear why he gave warning to the SS *Woodfield* and ordered
the master to 'abandon ship immediately' on 3 November. It
may be that he had been cautioned about growing sensibilities
by Korvettenkapitän Spindler, *Flottillenchef* of the Second High
Sea Fleet Flotilla at Helgoland, during a short refit, or perhaps
he was anxious to investigate the nature and destination of the
ship which was carrying a cargo of Allied motor vehicles and
thirty-one soldiers. If he did have good intentions they were
frustrated by Captain A. K. Jones of the *Woodfield* who swung
the ship stern-on to the U-boat and started shooting with a
little 1.3-kilo (3-pounder) gun.

A running chase ensued. Valentiner opened fire with
his heavier 10.5-cm (4.1-inch) artillery while keeping out
of range of the little transport's guns. At 8.15 a.m., an
hour after the *Woodfield* was first sighted, the shells from
U-38 began to hit. Within fifteen minutes eight men had

been killed and Captain Jones was wounded: he ordered the remaining crew to abandon ship and set about destroying all confidential documents.

At 10.15 *U-38* dived and fired a single torpedo which struck amidships, sending a column of water 60 metres (200 feet) into the air. Valentiner then surfaced, 'borrowed' one of the lifeboats and sent an officer across to the waterlogged steamer to recover the ship's papers. Nothing was left apart from the log book. After completing the vessel's destruction by gunfire, Valentiner handed the survivors a bottle of brandy and promised he would tell the first ship he encountered about them.

At 2 p.m. on the same afternoon, still off the Moroccan coast, *U-38* encountered the 6305-ton SS *Mercian*, outward bound from Gibraltar with troops. Valentiner opened fire and did some damage but the *Mercian*'s master skilfully zig-zagged away while his crew replied so effectively with machine guns that, after an hour and a quarter, Valentiner decided to call it a day. *U-38* had fired one hundred shells, killing twenty-three men and wounding another fifty, but the vessel escaped and was able to put into Oran for repairs. It was probably this incident, combined with his disappointment at finding no important papers in the *Woodfield*, that hardened Valentiner's heart again.

On the following morning the French SS *Calvados*, unarmed and with no wireless but carrying Singalese troops from Marseilles, was sunk with a loss of 740 lives. The French reaction was temporarily to suspend all navigation between France and Algeria.

A few days later, still making his way eastwards, Valentiner sank the empty French transport *France IV* off Sardinia and then came across the Italian liner *Ancona*. Germany was not at war with Italy, so Valentiner ran up Austrian colours. His accusers said that he deliberately fired at the passengers when they took to the boats, but it is more likely that he simply disregarded them in his efforts to finish off the liner quickly.

Valentiner gave his own version of events which is plausible enough. He claimed that the *Ancona* was at first believed to be a troopship, which was possible although she was carrying passengers from Messina to New York. He went on to say that he had given the captain forty-five minutes to abandon ship and had only fired a torpedo because another, and possibly threatening, vessel was seen approaching. Moreover, it was the fault of the Italian crew that so many lives were lost: they had taken to the boats without regard to rescuing the passengers – all of them civilians as it turned out – although plenty of unused lifeboats remained which would have been quite sufficient to save everybody.

Robert Lansing, the US Secretary of State, took a different view. He described the action as 'more atrocious than any of the submarine attacks which had previously taken place. For cold-blooded inhumanity the conduct of the submarine commander scarcely found an equal in the annals of modern war.'[2] (We might wonder how Lansing would have received Admiral Jacky Fisher's advice to The Hague Peace Conference in 1899: '. . . hit your enemy in the belly, and kick him when he is down, and boil his prisoners in oil – if you take any – and torture his women and children. Then people will keep clear of you . . .')

It is difficult to judge whether Valentiner really sought to justify himself or whether his explanation was no more than a perfunctory gesture to cover a conviction that justification was not necessary. On the whole, it seems that he and many of his fellow U-boat captains were not unduly bothered about the legitimacy or otherwise of targets flying an enemy flag: they just got on with the job. Nor was there ever much time to deliberate. As the historian Professor G. Halpern[3] has said, 'The question of atrocities in wartime, particularly in regard to submarines, is sometimes a matter of perspective.'

On 9 November, two days after the *Ancona* incident, *U-38*, still under Austrian colours, torpedoed the 3960-ton Italian steamer *Firenze* after a short chase. A full-scale diplomatic row ensued. The Austrian Admiral Haus signified his readiness to accept responsibility, at least for the *Firenze*, and proposed to vindicate the *Ancona* sinking without stating categorically that an Austrian submarine had done the deed.

However, on 11 November, the Austrian Foreign Office demanded to know from Haus exactly what agreement existed with the Germans about flying the Austrian flag. The pro-German Haus was obliged to admit that there was no formal agreement; he believed German U-boats intended to fly the Turkish flag when attacking Italian shipping in the Aegean Sea and the Austrian flag in the western Mediterranean, but this answer satisfied nobody. Nor was it considered relevant that Haus blamed the captain of *Firenze* for loss of life because he ordered lifeboats to be lowered while still under way, thus capsizing them, or that Italian papers had been found which required Italian merchant captains either to flee or to ram a U-boat rather than obey orders to stop.

The United States was not prepared to ignore the crucial question of which nation had caused the death of some twenty American citizens in the *Ancona* and probably more in the *Firenze*. Under pressure from Lansing the Italian Government demanded to know from the State Secretary of the German Foreign Office whether the submarine that had sunk the *Ancona* really was Austrian. It was a direct question and the reply had to be considered very carefully.

There was nothing for it but to cheat. *U-38* was formally entered into the Austrian list of warships backdated to 21 October 1915. This crafty move, which had no substance in practice, came just in time: on 16 November Lansing required Frederic C. Penfield, American Ambassador in Vienna, to call for the Austro-Hungarian list of U-boats and report whether the submarine attacking the *Ancona* appeared thereon. It seems that Penfield did not probe deeply and that neither the name Valentiner nor the number of his boat was offered up, but Lansing persisted, and took the same view as the Italian Government – that the *Ancona* sinking bore the stamp of a Prussian rather than an Austrian act. Baron Zwiedinek, Austrian chargé d'affaires in Washington, rashly endorsed this comparison with his government's ally and declared that 'no Austrian officer is capable of an inhumane act', a sanctimonious statement which left him in a difficult position when his government finally assumed responsibility for the sinking. The Austrians clearly feared Berlin's displeasure more than Washington's wrath and were still not prepared to go into details, let alone respond satisfactorily to an American note dated 6 December, which demanded that the Austro-Hungarian authorities denounce the sinking, punish the U-boat captain and make reparations by paying a sum in respect of the American victims. Presenting nothing more than 'a quibble', as the United States saw it, about the facts, the Austrians were bluntly told by Lansing that they must duly punish the captain or as a government assume the whole mantle of guilt.

Powerful personalities were put in play on all sides. On the one hand Germany was anxious that Austria took the blame for Italian ships sunk by German U-boats flying the Austrian flag (on at least one occasion shifting flags in mid-attack), and on the other Chancellor von Bethmann-Hollweg dreaded the effect on America of German U-boat commanders being unmasked – as, in effect, Valentiner had been. Meanwhile, the Austrians resented being portrayed as soft: Admiral Haus termed the conduct of *U-38*'s captain as 'utterly irreproachable' and defended the *Ancona* affair with a lengthy hard-line statement which included a claim that the U-boat commander had gone beyond his obligations by allowing so long for the passengers and crew to abandon ship – quite long enough for everybody to be saved if the Italian crew had done their duty by their passengers. The latter point was again emphasised by the Austrian government in a note to the United States dated 29 December. At the same time, however, Austria backed down to the extent of saying that the officer concerned had been punished 'in accordance with the Rules in force in this matter for exceeding his instructions' (Rules, whatever they were, which left Valentiner unscathed) and an indemnity was apparently paid.

The day after this note was written Valentiner torpedoed, from submerged, the British P & O liner *Persia* 70 miles south of Crete, with a loss of 334 lives including two Americans. There was no warning and no flag issue to debate; the identity of the underwater pirate could not positively be established and denials were received from the Austro-Hungarian, Turkish and, not surprisingly, the German governments, but there could never be any real doubt about who perpetrated the deed. In fact, as we have seen, it was the *Persia* that resulted in Valentiner being listed as a war criminal – although any number of other vessels in his huge bag might equally well have been cited. On the single expedition which accounted for the *Persia* (which went down very quickly because her boilers blew up) *U-38* destroyed five British ships, a French merchantman and a liner and the large Japanese liner *Yasaka Maru*, all between 27 December and 4 January and with the loss of more than 500 lives.

The diplomatic to-ing and fro-ing continued, with flat accusations, bland assurances, open disbelief and much drivel. Germany was, frankly, playing for time: the aim was to cripple Britain by *Handelskrieg* economic warfare before President Wilson came to her aid. That was an eventuality brought nearer when the French cross-channel packet *Sussex* (supposedly mistaken for a troop transport because of her crowded decks or, alternatively, a sloop of the 'Arabic' class) was torpedoed on 24 March 1916 in the English Channel by *UB-29* (Pustküchen); several more American citizens were killed. Fragments of the torpedo, found embedded in the hull when the steamer was towed to Boulogne, belied initial German excuses that a mine had done the work. Coming after the Mediterranean carnage which Germany hoped would pass unnoticed, the *Sussex* outrage, if that was the word for it, sparked the most violent American reaction yet.

Meanwhile, some token restrictions were imposed on U-boats in the *Mittelmeer*. The rules changed frequently. Kophamel complained on behalf of his flotilla that orders from the naval staff (following the *Persia* incident) for passenger steamers not to be attacked were impracticable. The crux of his argument was that most merchant vessels, whether belligerent or neutral, were being armed with guns: the *Persia* carried a 120-mm (4.7-inch) gun on her stern and Valentiner, if he had troubled to make the point, could have argued that she appeared to be an armed transport and with a gun larger than his own 105-mm (4.1-inch) weapon. How could submarines surface in order to investigate without exposing themselves to undue risks? Flags by themselves were by no means proof of national identity; the *Baralong* incident had proved that conclusively.

The Kaiser was, to a degree, persuaded. On, 11 February 1916 he signed an order permitting armed British and French ships to be attacked whenever their armament was clearly seen. However, the relaxation was rescinded because of diplomatic wrangles before it could take effect. Passenger liners, whether equipped with guns or not, were to be allowed to pass. This was a matter of particular concern to the Cattaro Flotilla because, even with the excellent enemy silhouettes provided to U-boats, it was often impossible to distinguish between a forbidden liner and a legitimate troop transport or even an auxiliary cruiser. Nevertheless, the spring of 1916 saw a measurable diminution of traffic destroyed in the Mediterranean, and, with Austria increasingly disenchanted with the role of scapegoat, German captains – with some notable exceptions – observed Prize War Regulations in the theatre. For the remainder of 1916 they allowed passengers and crew time to take to the boats before their ship was destroyed.

Rules of conduct, albeit continually shifting, and a blockade of the Straits of Otranto leading to the Mediterranean appeared to be a considerable hindrance. But the Otranto barrage (described in the next chapter) was less than a stopper, and Kophamel was soon able to regain the upper hand for his boats with a marginally revised strategy. Some reinforcements arrived; commanders were given a free hand to torpedo passenger liners in the Aegean north of Crete (where they could only be troop transports); and Lothar von Arnauld de la Perière in *U-35* worked up to full brilliance.

While in command of *U-35*, Kophamel had brought the crew to a superb state of efficiency. Doubtless both he and his successor recognised the credit due to the engine-room staff. It is impossible to exaggerate the worth of thoroughly good engineers as well as torpedo technicians in all the successful

U-boats. The German handbook on torpedo firing ended, in heavy print: 'For a successful hit with a torpedo, part of the credit is invariably due to the technical personnel!' It is also relevant that the very best U-boat commanders were mature men. Kophamel was thirty-five when he took command of *U-35*, and von Arnauld was nearly thirty when he relieved him. Both were highly intelligent officers with extensive staff experience and a thorough approach to their duties. Just before war broke out von Arnauld had even gone to England to perfect his knowledge of the English language, a knowledge that was invaluable in understanding merchant wireless traffic and gaining intelligence quickly from prisoners and documents seized at sea. He had also served for two years as Adjutant (Flag Lieutenant) to Admiral von Pohl, Chief of Naval Staff, and it is likely that he was given preference in matters of replacement personnel and weaponry. Indeed, his appointment to such a good submarine suggests privilege. It may have been this association with the naval aristocracy that made him notably reserved towards his crew, while solicitous of their health.

De la Perière considered his tactics in the Mediterranean with great care. He decided to use artillery as much as possible. That implied giving warning of attack although it would be wrong to attribute his decision to feelings of humanity. Although in British terms von Arnauld was a gentleman by comparison with Valentiner and other cut-throats, the fact was that torpedoes were scarce and only half a dozen could be taken on patrol. Since he had gone virtually straight to the U-boat command school in April 1915 (instead of the zeppelin service for which he had volunteered) and had no previous operational experience in submarines, it can be conjectured that initially torpedo-fire control was not his strong point.

Shells were plentiful and up to 1000 could be stored (with some discomfort for the crew) throughout a submarine. With gunnery in mind, therefore, and presumably with the support of friends on the Naval Staff, a picked gunlayer from the High Sea Fleet was sent to join the boat. On at least one cruise a professional cinema operator accompanied the boat to film sinkings, which must have contributed to 'gentlemanly' conduct.

Kapitänleutnant von Arnauld de la Perière set off at the beginning of 1916 on the first of his *Handelskrieg* cruises with a more or less free hand. He was determined to exploit intelligence reports and follow the directions dictated by that sixth sense with which 'aces' were endowed.

The Cattaro boats, in resuming the *Handelskrieg*, were in no doubt that the only way to bring Britain to her knees was to strangle her supply line. Von Arnauld well knew that a high percentage of essential commodities such as rubber, jute, tea (without which the British could not survive), gasoline and manganese passed through the Mediterranean in numerous fair-sized ships which trekked daily from Suez to the Straits of Gibraltar.

The tactics of the most successful U-boat captain of all were simple enough. It was his persistence in looking for targets, his perceptiveness in interpreting clues (such as indiscreet merchant wireless messages) when doing so, his engineers' devotion to the diesels and his gunlayer's unshakeable competence under all conditions that were remarkable. *U-35* was also well supplied with intelligence from shore – the wireless equipment was particularly good – and she was heard to communicate at 1 a.m. daily.

The preferred procedure in *U-35* was to open fire at 6000 metres (6500 yards), close to 3000 metres (3300 yards), wait until the target's crew abandoned ship, and then finish off the victim with carefully aimed shots at the bow and stern. Torpedoes were seldom used: only four were fired (one ineffectually at the French cruiser *Waldeck Rousseau*) during one of his most successful expeditions in the summer of 1916 but 900 rounds were expended.

The record cruise seems to have been from 31 March to 6 May in the western basin where twenty-three ships, totalling 67,989 tons, were destroyed. Altogether, *U-35* sent 224 ships – 535,900 tons – to the bottom of the Mediterranean Sea. All but a sloop, a gunboat, five troopships and possibly one auxiliary cruiser were merchantmen; sixty-two sailing vessels were included in their number. Von Arnauld, awarded the 'Blue Max' (*Pour le Mérite*), accounted for most of them, although Kophamel had done great execution in a short time. Adding his successes in *U-139* (which he commanded from March 1918) to those in *U-35*, von Arnauld was credited with 194 merchant ships (453,716 tons) and two warships. He might reasonably be called a genius at his trade and, like Hersing, he survived the war.

By August 1916 *Handelskrieg* sinkings in the Mediterranean had passed the million-ton mark, although it had not been possible to keep, on average, more than one large submarine (that is, one of the 'Thirties') at sea at any one time. Kophamel asked for more boats and in September the Kaiser approved the naval staff's proposal to send *U-32*, *U-63* and *U-65*. At the same time the All Highest sent the *Chef* at Pola a congratulatory telegram.

Some shuffling of German boats took place between Cattaro and Constantinople (for the Black Sea), but towards the end of 1916 there were usually five of the 'Thirties', five slightly newer large torpedo-type boats, three small UB-boats (*UB-44* having been lost in August, cause unknown), the two slow and clumsy minelayers *U-72* and *U-73* of the 'Children of Sorrow' class, and seven assorted tiny and middling 'UC' minelayers. There would have been another of the latter highly effective little pineapple-planters (which put paid to a number of Italian ships) if *UC-12* had not run on to one of her own mines at the entrance to Taranto harbour on 16 March.

The loss of *UC-12* (Fröhner) had extensive repercussions. The boat was quickly salvaged and repaired to become submarine *X-1* of the Royal Italian Navy but it was discovered that *UC-12* had been constructed in sections by the Weser Company of Bremen, then shipped by rail and assembled at Pola, that her crew was German and that both Austrian and German colours were carried. This, once and for all, scotched the farcical pretence that Austrian submarines had been responsible for sinking Italian ships. There could be no excuse for a German submarine mining the close approaches to a foremost Italian port, and the Italian Government, already influenced by events in the Dardanelles, could no longer dither. At last it formally declared war against Germany on 27 August 1916. Italy's entry into the war should have put an end to the misuse of the Austrian flag, but a few German U-boats continued to masquerade under Austrian colours, partly to conceal the true number of German boats at large in the Mediterranean and partly not to afford the Allied press the satisfaction of pointing to the salvage of *UC-12* as final proof that this was going on.

The assault on shipping in the Mediterranean continued unabated. On the Allied side, anti-submarine concentrations, independent patrols, improved intelligence from radio intercepts, continued attempts to safeguard assigned routes by the British, endeavours to find U-boat coastal hiding places by the French, the variation of shipping lanes and 'jinking' from them at night, and the provision of more and more A/S craft (mostly trawlers and drifters) did little more than inconvenience the crack U-boat commanders. In fact, the movements of patrol vessels often indicated a prospective merchant route for the next day. Zones of anti-submarine responsibility were assigned to the British, French and Italian navies. At one point there were eighteen zones but these were later reduced to eleven. The dividing lines sometimes resulted in U-boat movements not being reported properly to the next authority, and U-boats naturally took advantage of gaps.

Despite the arrival of a strong and efficient Japanese force in April 1917, there were never enough anti-submarine patrol craft. A year earlier Admiral Sir Arthur Limpus at Malta had pointed out that the number of Allied merchantmen circulating each day in the Mediterranean – there could be more than 100 British ships under government charter alone – was infinitely greater than the escorts that could be provided. Escorts were therefore given only to especially important ships – transports, for example – and even these found it difficult to remain with their charges along the whole passage because the average destroyer's machinery and fuel were simply not adequate. In the main, routes rather than ships were protected and protection was a wildly over-optimistic word.

When convoys were at last instituted by the extraordinarily dilatory Admiralty in 1917 the sinkings gradually
declined but were by no means halted. In some months
losses continued to be high. Geographical limitations in
the Mediterranean partially robbed the convoy system of its
greatest value elsewhere – which was, of course, to present
fewer opportunities for submarines to find and attack their
targets. Without an A/S air opposition a U-boat commander,
acting on informed guesswork or intelligence information,
could use speed on the surface to get himself into the 'grain'
of a group of ships and then dive to attack. However, he had
to remain submerged from then on and reloading torpedoes
took so long that he could only take one or two shots before
the convoy passed on. Nevertheless, he was not in much
danger of effective counter-attack from the relatively weak
escorting forces in the Mediterranean, and when on the
surface again, he would find more smoke and another forest
of masts soon appearing somewhere on the horizon. Thus it
was a matter of judgement as to how long he could stay up
to gain a favourable firing position. If his earlier betting on a
convoy's route was not far out there was usually sufficient
time to shorten the range and dive. Gunnery, though, was out
of the question. Von Arnauld avoided convoys and continued
to seek independently sailed merchantmen, transferring his
attentions from April 1917 mainly to areas outside the Middle
Sea west of Gibraltar. There, his favourite technique was to
halt a vessel with gunfire (or the threat of it) and despatch it
with demolition charges.

Britain's solution to the submarine problem anywhere was
convoys, but the U-boats based in the Adriatic had other difficulties to contend with as well. Torpedoes were scarce, and
long, arduous cruises took their toll of machinery. Repair and
supply facilities became increasingly inefficient, and by the
end of 1917 the Mediterranean campaign was in decline.

Extensive refits had to be undertaken in Germany – a
4000-mile voyage through enemy-infested seas – and in January
1918 (the worst period) only five boats of the Cattaro Flotilla
were waging war on commerce; the other twenty-eight were in

undependable dockyard hands at Pola or alongside at Cattaro making good a host of defects. Generally, during the last year of the war, no more than a quarter to a third of the Adriatic Flotilla could be kept on patrol. Mechanical breakdowns and the inability to put them right quickly were probably as much responsible as convoying for eventually bringing down the number of Allied ships lost to U-boats in the Mediterranean.

CHAPTER 12

The Sound of Music – Whiteheads in the Adriatic (1915–18)

The home for *Mittelmeer* German U-boats, the Adriatic was also the scene of sundry minor submarine activities by the French, British, Italians and Austrians. Operations in the narrow island-strewn sea devolved into games of hide-and-seek, ambush and counter-attack, with aircraft playing an increasing and sometimes ambivalent and unreliable role.

The French submariners were early on the stage. Towed initially from Toulon to Malta, they moved successively to coves and bays in the Greek Islands before finally establishing themselves at Brindisi when Italy joined the Entente in May 1915. The submarines deployed were mainly of the 'Pluviôse' (1907–9) and 'Brumaire' (1911–12) classes, similar in displacement at about 398/550 tons; but the former were steam driven on the surface by two du Temple boilers, the latter by diesels. At the time steam for submarines was regarded with suspicion by submariners elsewhere, but it was the French diesel boats which were plagued with breakdowns, not the 'Pluviôse' class.

The Frenchmen had an exciting time, and displayed an extraordinarily aggressive spirit at variance with their performance in the Dardanelles and Sea of Marmara. The driving force was undoubtedly Capitaine de Vaisseau (in effect Commodore) Henri-Thimoléon-Marie-Joseph de Cacqueray, a veritable fire-eater who commanded the mixed French Adriatic Flotilla destroyers and submarines. De Cacqueray disliked the Italians and, according to the British Senior Naval Officer (SNO), Rear-Admiral Cecil F. Thursby, the antipathy was mutual. Thursby himself preferred to work with the French who were 'gallant and good seamen' although they could 'not stick at sea for long', while the Italians, in his opinion, lacked initiative and avoided responsibility.[1]

Les sous-mariniers were duly spurred to distinguish themselves despite their usual handicaps of external torpedo cradles and Drzewiecki systems, 1904-model torpedoes and problematical propulsion. Their courage in the face of *matériel* difficulties was never in doubt but prudence was not a prevailing characteristic and losses were severe.

The Commodore insisted on a meticulous *compte rendu* for each operation (would that British submarine records were presented in such a neat and concise form). Analysis of the time spent on patrol gives the lie to claims frequently made by senior British officers (de Robeck at Gallipoli and Thursby in the Adriatic being the most vociferous) that the French were not pulling their weight.

The most audacious ventures were directed against the Austrian ports of Pola and Cattaro where, besides German U-boats, submarines and surface vessels of the Austro-Hungarian navy were to be found. On 17 December 1914, at the suggestion of her French-Irish *commandant* Gabriel O'Byrne, the new diesel boat *Curie* (of the 'Brumaire' class) set out from her temporary island base in the Ionian Sea to force the Pola defences. She was towed half-way up the Adriatic by the armoured cruiser *Jules-Michelet*, which slipped her sibling when there were 150 miles to go – a distance that could be covered in twelve hours at the top surface speed of 13 knots.

December 18 was spent reconnoitring the approaches to the port (unknowingly in the middle of an Austrian minefield) and on the 19th O'Byrne inspected the boom and harbour defences as best he could from submerged. Believing that he had noted the gate correctly on his chart, he dived early the following day and at a little after noon set course for the entrance at a depth of 20 metres (65 feet). Very soon chains and wires could be heard and felt, scraping along the submarine's side, but the noise ceased after half a minute and O'Byrne took *Curie* up to periscope depth. He then saw, all too clearly, the buoys supporting another barrier close ahead. Allied intelligence had failed to learn that the Austrians had reinforced the defences during the previous three months. The second net was too close to avoid and the boat was quickly caught in the heavy meshes. Pumping, flooding, racing the crew from forward to aft and back again were to no avail. Both propellers were entangled by wires and only turned jerkily; the electric motors overheated; the crew became listless in the increasingly foul air and the unfortunate dog that invariably sailed with *Curie* as a mascot died of asphyxiation,[2] which did nothing to help the crew's morale. At 4.20 p.m. one last attempt was made to escape the net's clutches, but the only result was to pitch the submarine 30 degrees bow down, whereupon acid started to spill out of the battery cells.

The Captain decided to bottom and destroy secret documents before surfacing to abandon ship. Enemy torpedo-boats, attracted by swirls of water above the net, were quickly on the spot: at 5.05 p.m. they opened fire as the submarine broke surface and the shore battery at Punta Cristo joined in. One shell penetrated the kiosk and another the hull. At that point main vents were opened to scuttle the submarine while the crew, in admirably disciplined fashion, climbed on deck and jumped overboard.

O'Byrne, wounded like three of his men, wanted to go down with his ship but a quartermaster persuaded him to jump with the rest. The second-in-command was killed outright and the wounded Coxswain died in hospital; the remaining twenty-six men were rescued and treated as heroes. One cold and half-drowned French sailor took pains to reassure his captor, Linienschiffsleutnant Linhart,[3] in French: 'I am your friend, I am no longer your enemy – you [sic] are safe. We are alone.'

Curie was salvaged by the Austrians, refitted with better 330 hp motors, a new battery, an 88-mm (3.5-inch) gun and extra fuel tanks which increased her radius of action from 1200 miles to 6500 miles on the surface. There were no more tows for *U-XIV*,[4] as she was styled on being recommissioned in the Austro-Hungarian navy under Lieutenant von Trapp (of whom more later) but she was recovered by France after the war and awarded the Croix de Guerre pennant – posthumously, so to speak.

Out in the open Adriatic many attacks were attempted, but French torpedo failures were common and the clarity of the water favoured Austrian anti-submarine aircraft. Hence there were a good many aborted efforts to hit the enemy and casualties were high. *Curie, Circé, Monge, Fresnel, Foucault* and *Bernouilli* were all lost on Adriatic operations and *Artémis* was nearly sunk mistakenly by British aircraft.

Nevertheless there were some significant successes, as well as daring endeavours which failed but deserved better fortune. In 1915 the 'steamboats' *Ampère, Cuignot, Fresnel* and *Monge* all slipped through the bottleneck and into the bulging bay at the end of which lay Cattaro harbour. It was an extraordinary feat and, what is more, they got out again, but none of their torpedoes hit. The diesel boat *Bernouilli* had another try on 4 April 1916 and blew the stern off the destroyer *Csepel*.

Monge was patrolling off the entrance to Cattaro Gulf on the night of 28 December 1915 when, frustrated by failure inside the Bay, her *commandant* Roland Morillot sighted an old adversary escorted by five destroyers. It was the scouting cruiser *Helgoland* which he had missed four months earlier in August. Determined that his tubes should take effect this time he manoeuvred his submarine much too close. Just as he was about to fire, 4000 tons of speeding steel crashed into the kiosk. The collision was accidental: the watch on board the cruiser never saw the periscope and, happily, the immediate damage was not catastrophic. However, the crew thought all was up and reacted with the *'Vive la France'* expected on such occasions. Electrical power failed, the boat was plunged into darkness and Morillot felt he had to surface. Not unexpectedly, he was greeted with gunfire when he reached the bridge. Retreating down the ladder and shutting the conning-tower hatch smartly, he ordered the main vents to be opened even though power had not been fully restored. The submarine settled down in agonisingly sluggish fashion – the class was notorious in this respect – made even worse by the safety weights ('drop keels') having been released at the initial impact. Then a shell pierced the hull. The torrent of water that followed promised to speed up the diving process uncontrollably and Morillot wisely ordered main vents to be shut again, at the same time telling the crew to open hatches and abandon ship. For some reason, only the forward hatch could be opened but the crew, passing their captain in the control room, were able to make their way, one by one, onto the casing and swim for it. The Austrians ceased firing and watched as *Monge* slid, rather more speedily than usual, beneath the waves for the last time.

Roland Morillot went down with his boat to make sure she flooded fully and did not fall into enemy hands. He was a heroic officer, albeit evidently not gifted with 'periscope eye', and his name was given to three successive French submarines thereafter, including two ex-German U-boats. One of the latter was *UB-26* which was discovered in Le Havre Roads trapped in nets shot by drifters, bombed by the torpedo-boat *Trombe* and forced to surrender. On board were papers which furnished positive proof that the *Sussex* had fallen victim to a German submarine and not a mine.

Archimède, which had been the first French submarine to join the British Flotilla at Harwich before deploying to the Mediterranean, was the only boat of her type: steam-driven, she was an improvement on the 'Pluviôse' class and, like her *commandant* Deville, highly regarded. While her funnels could not withstand the battering of North Sea waves, under Deville she performed excellently in the more sheltered Adriatric, although sudden storms could blow up with ferocity there too. Four large Austrian transports went down to her torpedoes, demonstrating yet again that practically everything depended upon the expertise of a commanding officer who knew his job thoroughly and possessed that certain, elusive knack at the periscope.

Ampère damaged her reputation on 18 March 1916 when Lieutenant de Vaisseau Devin torpedoed the 3199-ton Austrian Lloyd *Elektra* which had been requisitioned as a hospital ship in 1914. Devin subsequently claimed that she was not wearing the correct markings, but photographs of the ship show otherwise: the signs were prominent. There was no question of deliberate foul play, however; the periscopes fitted in *Ampère* and others of her class were decidedly not the best. Then, too, like most submarine captains – and we have to remember the accusations against U-boat commanders – Devin doubtless saw what he wanted to see. In the event, Captain Quarantotto managed to beach *Elektra* and casualties were confined to one nurse and one seaman killed. De Cacqueray, an honest man, simply noted on the *compte rendu* that *Ampère* had fired at *'un bâtiment supposé transport'*.

On the debit side *Fresnel* (steam) was surprised on the surface by Austrian seaplanes off Cattaro on 5 December 1915. Unable to dive quickly enough, she subsequently succumbed to the attentions of a torpedo-boat. Commandant Jouen was forced to beach the submarine but the crew abandoned ship before he blew her up.

The diesel *Circé*, another 'one-off' type, scored a triumph on 24 May 1917 when de Cambourg sank *UC-24*, an exceedingly difficult target only 50 metres (162 feet) long, emerging from Cattaro. Ironically, *Circé* herself, still shorter at 47 metres (154 feet), was torpedoed by the equally skilful Metzger in *U-47* off Cape Rodoni only 70 miles away, on 20 August 1918.

An obvious way of guarding Mediterranean shipping was to seal the Adriatic at its southern end and thus prevent U-boats from Cattaro and Pola reaching the Mediterranean. It was easier said than done, but in September 1915 sixty drifters arrived from England to set up a net barrier, and in 1916 another 100 joined them. The mobile barriers stretched across the 44-mile-wide gap between Otranto and Fano Island. The Chief of Staff at the Admiralty, Vice-Admiral Sir Henry Oliver, was disappointed with its achievements, and in December 1916 wrote that 'the inefficiency of this barrage is the root of all submarine troubles in the Mediterranean'. But given the difficulties under which the drifters laboured, the diversions to which they were subjected and their vulnerability to weather and the enemy, they did not do so badly. During the winter of 1915, when they first shot their nets, two or possibly more U-boats had become enmeshed.

Although they easily tore through them there was some deterrent value in these early incidents. If Oliver and his colleagues had wholeheartedly backed the barrage it might have done more than deter.

In theory the drifter line was protected by a flotilla of Royal Navy motor launches based at Taranto under the orders of the Italian C-in-C, but in practice it was virtually undefended. Worse, Italian destroyers which should have been tactically integrated with the barrage to force U-boats to dive and engage them when snagged (which is how British destroyers operated in conjunction with net vessels in the English Channel) kept themselves, for the most part, firmly in harbour. Italian submarines spasmodically – and pointlessly as they probably realised – patrolled to the north, and equally resigned French submarines kept watch to the south. When Rear-Admiral Mark Kerr (the first Flag Officer to become a qualified pilot) took command in the Adriatic in May 1916 he asked for, and got, a wing of RNAS seaplanes to reinforce the barrage although they did not arrive for nearly a year. Kerr was modern in his ideas and committed to the concept of bottling up the U-boats not only by blockade but by attacking them at source.[5] Alas, little came of his enthusiasm and he was worried about the drifters being open to attack.

The barrier was clearly a misnomer: it was not even a sieve. There were never enough drifters to form a continuous line and by no means all necessarily had their nets out. Currents displaced individual vessels during the night when navigational fixing was impossible, leaving gaps up to 10 miles wide. U-boats generally had little difficulty in finding gaps or passing over the top of the nets on the surface under cover of darkness, preferably in the foul weather which accompanied a westerly gale. Von Arnauld in *U-35* liked to start the run at 10 p.m. and stay up. Alternatively, at near the limit of their safe diving depth, boats could slide beneath the curtains which seldom reached down more than 43 metres (140 feet), or could even, on occasion, charge straight through the relatively fragile strands which were designed to catch fish rather than steel sharks.

Kerr's fears for the barrier-watchers were realised. The drifter *Restore* had already been shelled and sunk by *U-39* on 12 October 1915. On the night of 31 May 1916 two Austrian destroyers and the scouting cruiser *Helgoland* sped down from Pola and sank the *Beneficent* – not a very profitable result for their efforts and attended by some risk of interception; but on 9 July Captain Horthy de Nagybanya, a rising star in the Austro-Hungarian Navy and commanding the 27-knot scouting cruiser *Novarra*, sank two drifters and damaged two others, unchallenged by supporting naval units. The raid caused alarm and despondency and strengthened Kerr's case for reinforcements. His pleas were answered in part but the barrage had no strategic effect on the conduct of the war and there were endless internecine squabbles among the Allies about who should command it.

Naval back-up forces suffered as well as the drifters. On 23 June 1916 the Austrian *U-XV* (Schlosser) torpedoed the Italian auxiliary cruiser *Città di Messina* 20 miles east of Otranto and then sank the escorting French destroyer *Fourche*, whose captain had dropped depth-charges, seen an oil slick and wrongly assumed a kill. Stopping to pick up survivors from the cruiser, *Fourche* took a torpedo amidships. Then, on 10 July, *U-XVII* (Hudeček) sank the Italian destroyer *Impetuoso* which was also endeavouring to guard the drifters. After this, Italian anxiety to protect the frail line waned, and protection was further reduced. The western end of the barrage was rotated southwards by some 30 miles, to the bottom of Italy's heel, in the hope of a little added security. That hope was to prove vain.

Several submarines fouled the nets in 1916 but only two paid the ultimate penalty. The Austrian *U-VI*, with a predominantly German crew under von Falkenhausen, was destroyed with certainty on 13 May by the gunners of *Evening Star II*, summoned by the two unarmed drifters that made the haul between them. *UB-44* (Wäger) can be counted as a near certainty: she was caught on 30 July by the *Quarry Knowe*'s nets and *Farrigil* came to assist. Two depth-charges were dropped; it appeared that an underwater explosion followed and a dead weight continued to drag down the nets. The *Quarry Knowe's* master steered for shoal water, much encumbered, to try and strand the catch but it broke loose and, since Wäger failed to return to Cattaro, he and his men presumably perished in deep water. The Austrian *U-XXX* was lost in the following year and may have been another victim.

Although the catches were meagre the barrage was seen as an inconvenience by German and Austrian U-boat men alike. On the night of 15 May 1917, determined to clear the annoying obstacles out of the way, three Austrian light cruisers, with Horthy commanding the squadron in *Novarra*, swept down upon the line. The drifters fought gallantly when, rather late in some cases, they recognised the enemy ships; but 2.7-kilogram (6-pounder) and 57-mm (2.3-inch) guns were outclassed by multiple 100-mm (4-inch) weapons and fourteen of the forty-seven drifters on duty were sunk.

Such ships as the Allies could muster immediately put to sea from Brindisi bent on retribution, but the subsequent action was inconclusive. On the way back, the cruiser HMS *Dartmouth* was totally disabled by a torpedo from *UC-25* (Feldkirchner) which, a couple of days earlier, had planted 'pineapples' off Brindisi. The French *Boutefeu*, steaming to the rescue, ran straight into the field and swiftly disappeared beneath it. Once again a submarine had hit harder, more humiliatingly and with more hurt than any of the splendid surface ships.

A popular American assessment of 1919 was that the Otranto Barrage had been a great success; that more submarines had been sunk than was generally supposed; that it had a serious effect upon the enemy crews' morale; and that the American Chasers – thirty-six of them, all equipped with listening devices – which worked on it from June 1918 were 'feared most of any barrage craft'.[6]

Those beliefs were unfounded. But even Vice-Admiral William S. Sims USN in London, a realist, was deceived into thinking that the Chasers under Captain Charles P. ('Juggy') Nelson USN and Captain Richard H. Leigh USN turned the tide; that the danger they presented in the Otranto Straits was such that, after a mere two weeks, Austrian crews refused to penetrate the Straits, and that German morale dropped to a point where officers had to urge their men on through the hazardous waters at pistol point. All this was nonsense. True, a series of mutinies took place in Austrian ships at Cattaro from 1 to 3 February 1918 but the revolt had nothing to do with the blockade. (The cause was Communism which was beginning to spread rapidly from Russia.) Nelson, on the spot, reckoned the Chasers had destroyed nineteen submarines in thirty-seven hunts; but careful post-war analysis did not credit a single kill to them.

Ineffectual though the barrage was, important ships no longer had necessarily to patrol the Straits and thereby expose themselves to submarine attack. The danger of that had been emphasised a little after midnight on 26/27 April 1915 when the armoured cruiser *Léon Gambetta* took two torpedoes from the little Holland-type *U-V* commanded by von Trapp. All the officers and most of the men were killed: out of a company of 821 only 137 were saved. The cruiser was just south of the Straits and moving at an economical speed of 6 knots (von Trapp reckoned 4 knots) with no destroyer screen. The lessons learned so painfully by the British about evasive tactics had not been hoisted aboard by the French.

Lieutenant Georg von Trapp had a unique right to be foremost in the underwater business because of his family connection with Robert Whitehead who had invented the free-running 'locomotive' torpedo.[7] Von Trapp rapidly became known as the Austro-Hungarian navy's torpedo ace. Aged thirty-four when the war began, he was no exception to the general rule that mature submarine captains were better than youngsters. Moreover, he thoroughly understood the mechanics of his trade, which was just as well because *U-V* had many faults. The twin petrol engines were unusually prone to fill the boat with poisonous fumes, more so even than British 'B'- and 'C'-boat engines. Ventilation was a continual matter for concern: it was dangerous to dive without running the fans after stopping the engines. The periscope hoist was another major problem: the motor was so slow that it was best to leave the periscope raised and take the whole boat up and down on the hydroplanes, trusting to a proficient planesman, rather than lower the heavy instrument between looks.

That was doubtless why von Trapp's periscope was glimpsed (without reaction) by the *Léon Gambetta*'s lookouts on 25 April: it was impossible to show it for just a few seconds at a time in the way that the Germans and the British so strongly advocated. However, the slender stalk was a great deal more difficult to spot, even by moonlight, when the cruiser resumed her beat, like a ponderous overweight policeman, at nightfall. Twice more in the succeeding twenty-four hours she appeared and disappeared, but von Trapp had a shrewd idea of her movements. On the evening of the 26th he stayed on the surface and made for a position close to the coast of Italy's heel. With the moon rising over the sea to the south-west *U-V* would be hidden against the land while any ship to seaward would be silhouetted, and thus it transpired; the cruiser loomed up at 12.10 a.m.

The U-boat's battery was three-quarters charged, the compressed air bottles were topped up and the engines had been stopped for half an hour. It was, in fact, the last night on patrol and the fuel tanks were almost empty. The attack had to be now or never.

Von Trapp dived, hoping against hope that his feeble periscope lens would enable him to discern the unlit target. For tantalising minutes he could see nothing. Then, at an estimated 3000 metres (3280 yards), a monstrous black shape appeared in the eyepiece – without question, with its two distinctive funnels, a ship of the 12,550-ton 'Victor Hugo' class, steering a most convenient course that would take it within easy reach of *U-V*'s two 449-mm (17.7-inch) Fiume 'Wet Heater' bow torpedoes.

Taking each funnel group as his point of aim (because U-boat commanders were taught, with Teutonic precision, to try to hit a target's boilers) he fired first the starboard and then the port tube at a little under 500 metres (550 yards). The first of the Whiteheads, accelerating up to its full 44 knots, struck home twenty-five seconds later and the next followed with devastating effect. The appalling loss of life has already been recounted; von Trapp wrote later, in his memoirs, that he left the scene with a heavy heart. There was no way that he could have helped to rescue the struggling survivors: if he had taken some on board, crowding a handful on the tiny bridge perhaps, *U-V* would have been unable to dive – and his first duty was always to his own crew.

After the destruction of *Léon Gambetta* all French big ships were withdrawn to the southward – another strategic victory by a lone submarine. In August *U-V*'s Whiteheads claimed two more victims, the Italian submarine *Nereide* and a Greek steamer.

On 14 October 1915 von Trapp was transferred to command the much bigger *U-XIV* (ex-French *Curie*), probably because of his technical skill since the boat was becoming notorious for breakdowns. Careful nursing brought *U-XIV* to a reasonable state of reliability by 1917 and von Trapp succeeded in making at least some of her odd assortment of torpedo systems function properly. He torpedoed nine merchant ships, including the 11,500-ton liner *Nilassa*, between July and October, all outside the Adriatic where he and his comrades were supposed to be bottled in.

The Austrian submariners did very well. Besides a number of small vessels captured or sunk with demolition charges, an astonishingly high proportion – possibly 90 per cent – of torpedoes fired during seventy-nine attacks hit their targets. Occasionally one torpedo out of two fired in a salvo missed or failed to run; but every target engaged was hit by at least one fish.[8] Expatriate Robert Whitehead, who died in 1905 after creating the torpedo as a practical weapon, might have viewed such outstandingly good results against his countrymen and their allies with mixed feelings.

The other resident denizens of the Adriatic deeps, the Italian submariners, did not fare nearly as well. The narrow sea was something of a disaster area for them, compounded by own goals. On 10 March 1917 the sloop HMS *Cyclamen* rammed the *Alberto Gugliemotti*, which had strayed across an Allied convoy route off the island of Capraisa, and on

17 April 1918 HMS *H1* (Heaton) accidentally torpedoed the Italian *H5*, which was miles out of position in *H1*'s patrol area.

The quite large Italian underwater flotilla, which looked so good on paper, had little bearing on the battle. With the Austrian fleet based at Pola, only 60 miles across the Adriatic from Venice, it might reasonably have been expected that the Italian boats would blockade the enemy harbour and torpedo whatever endeavoured to come out. This did not happen.

Rear Admiral Thursby, flying his flag in HMS *Queen* at Brindisi, reported that the Italians seemed to place little reliance upon the efficacy of their submarines. Their boats were 'quite incapable of keeping the sea during the bad weather of which so much was experienced during the autumn and winter. Even during the summer weather, after a day or two at sea, they returned to harbour and required a week's repair'. With only two submarines exceeding 300 tons and, as elsewhere, a lack of peacetime operational preparation, the Italian submariners were not on a war footing.

The Italians claimed that their *E-12* sank the *U-XX* – but their records are mistaken. *U-XX* was also supposed to have been caught on 17 December 1916 in an Otranto net cast by the drifter *Fisher Girl* who called the *Guerdon* and *D.H.S.* to assist.[9] Depth charges were scattered and oil welled up so generously that it calmed the choppy sea. Thereafter an inert weight hung in the net, but the wires gave way when *Fisher Girl* tried to drag the mass shorewards. It was assumed that the submarine dropped like a stone to the bottom, but not so: Austrian records insist that *U-XX* was in dock at the time. The boat, under Ludwig Müller, was actually destroyed by the Italian *F-12* (A. Marengo di Morindo) on 9 July 1918 off Venice.

Six Italian submarines were lost, *Medusa* going down to *UB-15* and *Nereide* to *U-V*. The balance of success weighed heavily against the Italian submariners, perhaps because, as arguably demonstrated in the Second World War, the Latin temperament was not well suited to teamwork. They performed outstandingly well, however, as individuals or in very small groups when it came to midget submarines and 'human torpedo' operations, the first of which – outside the scope of this story – took place at Pola on 1 November 1918.[10]

Submarines on a Shoe-string: British 'B' boats in the Adriatic

Captain Herbert Richmond, British Liaison Officer with the Italian battle fleet at Taranto until Autumn 1915, was caustically critical of his hosts:

> They have admitted that the Austrians have command of the sea in spite of inferior force and without fighting an action [he must have meant a full fleet action]. They had better sell their fleet and take up their organs and monkeys again, for, by Heaven, that seems more their profession than sea fighting.[11]

'Until', concluded Richmond, 'we have some good submarines there, it will be the enemy who commands in the important northern zone [of the Adriatic].'[12]

'Good' was not exactly what he got – at least, not at first. On 22 September 1915 the Admiralty told Rear-Admiral Thursby that *B6, 7, 8, 9, 10* and *11* would be joining the British Adriatic Squadron and would be based primarily at Venice. Thursby arranged for the cruiser *Marco Polo* to serve as depot ship. Commander Wilfrid Tomkinson, a non-submariner but a favourite of Keyes, was despatched to command what Keyes described as 'five [sic] broken down B-boats' broadly directed by the Italian Staff. Tomkinson 'failed to see' why he should be 'taken out of a good seagoing job and dumped in a shore job with absolutely no chance of going to sea'.[13] He was convinced that Commodore Hall deliberately got rid of him once Keyes was out of the way. His state of mind augured ill for the happiness of the small long-in-the-tooth squadron which started to assemble at Venice on 11 October, *B8* colliding with an escorting tug off Ancona en route.

Tomkinson quickly started to express disquiet to Thursby. The accommodation in *Marco Polo* (laid down in 1890) was satisfactory for officers but 'for the Petty Officers and Men not entirely so at present. The messdecks are cold and damp and

236

not worth sitting in,' reported a Petty Officer from *B9*. An Engine Room Artificer (ERA) in *B7* had slept on watch, Tomkinson continued, and was 'very strange in his manner'; the spare crew (reserve men in the depot ship) was inadequate; the Bora wind made practice attacks and torpedo recovery very difficult (and later, in December and January, dense fog often prevented boats leaving harbour); *B9* had a hole in her battery tank and several cells were contaminated but no sulphuric acid was available to change the electrolyte; and realistic exercises were hard to arrange because they were 'unusual with the Italian submarines'. On the other hand, the local pigeons despatched to sea in little cages, for submarine-to-shore communications, were very reliable in homing back to Venice, which exuded a powerful effluvium for their sense of smell to follow.

Tomkinson did not point out when commencing operations (and failed to grasp later) that enemy submarines patrolling on the western side of the Adriatic were geographically advantaged. The waters on the Italian side were dark, muddy and concealing, but clear on the Austrian side, allowing Allied submarines to be more easily seen submerged, especially from the air. Another factor was the coastline: the Austrians could keep watch from high cliffs but Italian defenders had few vantage points.

The Commander's opening address to the men did not go down well. Petty Officer Victor Westall of *B9* complained in his diary entry for 11 October:[14]

At 5.30 p.m. we were all before the Commanding Officer (Tomkinson Commander) for what we must do and what we must not do. We must first have the submarines ready for sea and action. Leave is only a secondary consideration. Why? We might not do justice to the British Navy. . . .

B9 was the first boat to set out for war, on 18 October 1915. Lieutenant Jermyn Rushbrook took her to the Istrian coast close to Trieste, for a three-day patrol. During the day the submarine lay trimmed down, retreating to seaward by night to bottom in 13 metres (7 fathoms) where all hands 'got a fat head after ten-and-a-half hours doggo'.

Thirteen patrols were mounted by the 'B' boats before the end of 1915 without any result, but at great risk from floating enemy mines and some erratically charted Italian defensive minefields. They withstood the short, steep winter seas better than the bigger Italian submarines which were not ordered out when a storm was brewing on the grounds that their hydroplanes would be damaged. Tomkinson was sceptical about that: 'The fact is they give any excuse for not going out.'

A quaint incident occurred on 11 November. *B11* (Gravener)[15] was attacked by the Austrian flying-boat *L42* armed with 150-kilo (330-pound) bombs and one 8-mm (3/10-inch) machine gun; but the 145 hp Hiero engine failed just when the pilot was preparing to release his load. The aircraft was forced to come down a quarter of a mile from *B11*. Gravener ordered up the portable Maxim gun, which promptly jammed. Calling for full speed – all 12 knots – he steered to ram, but the flying-boat's two-man crew miraculously managed to restart the engine and take off in a shower of spray. *L42* did not have another go at the target.

A couple of months later, on 17 January, *B11* again encountered an Austrian aeroplane. Gravener had been watching Austrian destroyers and torpedo-boats searching for something, but was unable to attack because of an unserviceable periscope. Frustrated and not knowing what the ships were looking for, he headed back for the Italian coast and surfaced when he felt it was safe to do so. At about 3 p.m. an object sighted low in the water revealed itself as another enemy flying-boat. *B11* had found what the Austrian force was looking for – *L59* which had force-landed on the water after a raid on Ancona. The seaplane's crew at first convinced themselves that *B11* was one of their own boats, but, realising their mistake, they knocked holes in the floats and tore up their charts. The machine did not sink immediately, but it was impracticable to tow the foundering wreck. Gravener had to be content with rescuing the two airmen and taking them back to Venice. *B11*'s feat was duly acclaimed by the Italian C-in-C but rather coolly reported by Tomkinson to Thursby.

At the end of January 1916 Commander Martin Nasmith of *E11* took time off after his exploits in the Dardanelles before moving to HMS *J4*[16] as a four-stripe captain. He visited Tomkinson and talked of the opportunities for a modern submarine in the Gulf of Fiume and among the Dalmatian Islands. He obviously hoped to bring *E11* to fresh, exciting hunting grounds but de Robeck (whom Nasmith had failed to importune beforehand) refused to spare the boat from the Eastern Mediterranean. Tomkinson desperately wanted better submarines than the 'B' boats: their ten-hour maximum endurance dived at the most economical speed was far too little for patrolling in enemy waters watched over from the air, surface and shore, especially in the summer months. The 'E' class, by contrast, could stay submerged for twenty-four hours, dive in less than one minute (compared with three minutes for a 'B') and had quite good periscopes which the 'B' boats, with the captain viewing from a cramped conning tower, certainly did not. Thursby digested Nasmith's carefully considered points culled from hard experience. Unimpressed by The Trade, he marked Tomkinson's forwarding letter 'No action'.

Austrian aircraft were beginning to be a menace by the end of March 1916. On the 29th *B9* was machine-gunned and bombed while on the surface, trimmed down, 15 miles from Pola. Rushbrook dived to 18 metres (60 feet) but an hour later had great trouble with the trim. He had to blow individual ballast tanks three times between 30 and 33 metres (100 and 110 feet) and blamed density layers. Tomkinson, however, thought that the forward auxiliary tank must have been filled inadvertently and that was surely due to carelessness rather than the earlier bombing.

Somebody had indeed made a mistake in the fore-ends but failed to report it. Yet Rushbrook neglected to investigate. In fact, if we believe Petty Officer Westall, the lieutenant was 'not fit to be in charge of a boat'. When the submarine took a 20-degree bow-down angle it was he, Westall, who proposed the corrective action – blowing trimming water forward to aft and blowing Number 1 Main Ballast – while Rushbrook 'was lost for words' and only able to repeat the orders 'parrot like'.[17] Not long afterwards, although reported as possessed of 'a highly sociable nature and dedicated to improving Anglo-Italian relations', poor Rushbrook was 'hit on the head' in Venice and 'sent home with a bad case of nerves'. The records do not reveal who did the hitting.

The spring of 1916 heralded no more action than before. *B10* (Michell) was given a higher-capacity battery which enabled him to dive for sixteen hours but 'breathing was rather difficult . . . frequent shifts on the diving rudder and steering wheel were necessary'. Michell was thrice sent to the Gulf of Fiume (Quarnero) with his new 'box', but he may as well have stayed at home for nothing happened. In the same area *B11* lost her rudder and had to be rescued while *B8* (Tufnell) was fired at, but missed, by *U-XI* (ex–German *UB-15*).

B7 (Ouchterlony) was also fitted with a better (but still feeble) battery but on 4 June, instead of maintaining a dived patrol by day, the Captain decided to keep watch off Pola on the surface, trimmed down, in a heavy swell but calm sea. Lieutenant Oliver North took the watch with just his head and shoulders out of the conning tower, an impossible position for one man to search the sky all round efficiently, particularly with the swell rocking the boat and obscuring the horizon. It would have been a lot safer, albeit hard work for the planesman, to have alternated between, say, 18 metres (60 feet) and periscope depth, keeping beam-on to the swell when the periscope was up. Predictably, two seaplanes saw *B7* before North saw them, and homed in with Austrian accuracy. The first bomb blew in the glass scuttles of the conning tower and jammed the hydroplanes. The next half-hour was unpleasant, and on the way back, when the crew were at last congratulating themselves on a lucky escape, the engine broke a connecting rod. A pair of pigeons was loosed to call for a tug which arrived within the hour – another triumph for pigeon post – but Thomas Ouchterlony was in an even worse state than his command by then. He never again went to sea in a submarine.

By this time fifty patrols had been carried out by the squadron and not one torpedo had been fired in anger. Michell in *B10* now blazed the way with a shot at the paltry little 100-ton steamer *Alsa* from 275 metres (300 yards), but the fish, set to 1.8 metres (6 feet) and having no time to acquire its proper depth, ran under the shallow-draft target.

On 9 August eight Austrian aircraft from Trieste, led by Gottfried Freiherr von Banfield ('the Eagle of Trieste') and thirteen machines from Pola, raided Venice. *B10*, secured to *Marco Polo*, was hit and her hull ruptured. *B8*, lying alongside, was damaged. *B10* foundered without casualties, the first submarine ever, albeit in harbour, to be destroyed from the air. (The French *Foucault*, destroyed in the Adriatic by flying-boats *L132* and *L135* on 15 September, became the first submarine to be sunk at sea by aircraft.) Tomkinson was upset by the air attack. He would 'not have minded in the least' if *B8*, due for annual refit, had gone down but *B10* was 'our most valuable craft'.

The last of eighty-one patrols by the 'broken-down 'B' boats', with nothing of note to show for them, was conducted by *B9* from 18 to 20 October 1916 off the Istrian coast. The remaining four seaworthy boats (*B11* was in refit at Malta) were cheered by the Italians out of Venice, bound initially for Brindisi, on 30 October. Tomkinson thankfully left for London the next day with the Order of the Crown of Italy on his chest. Like his eight submarine commanding officers (including Ouchterlony) he also became a Chevalier of the Order of St Maurice and St Lazarus. But for what?

The duties of Senior Naval Officer Venice were transferred to the experienced Commander Charles G. Brodie in HMS *Adamant* and sound 'H'-class replacements were soon on their way. HMS *H2* and *H4* arrived in early November 1916; *H1* was in refit at Malta and would join later. However, HMS *Adamant* could not, after all, be spared for the new Venetian squadron and Brodie was ordered to sail for Mudros on 12 November. With typical British inattention to submariners' needs, while paying scant regard to paymastering formalities, *H2* was commissioned as the nominal depot ship at Venice and her quite junior captain, Lieutenant D. W. Fell, was appointed Senior British Naval Officer there instead of Brodie. He was evidently not a forceful character.

By June 1917, with some twenty or thirty patrols completed and a great deal of time wasted in harbour, Rear-Admiral Kerr (Thursby's relief) was sharply taken to task by the Admiralty.

Their Lordships' attention has been drawn to the three 'H'-class submarines attached to the Italian Fleet at Venice. It has been noticed from several recent reports from the Senior Officer that for a long period they have carried out no offensive operations and, although this was partly due to the weather, it is not understood how they should have been continuously prevented from movements to the extent reported.

You are to arrange to pay a visit to Venice and take such steps as may be practical to induce more active employment of the British submarines against the enemy.

Kerr, rather lamely, pointed out that not only was bad weather to blame but that frequent gales dispersed floating mines widely over an area which was, in any case, limited by Italian and Austrian minefields. The question was not repeated.

H1 (Owen) had fired at the Austrian torpedo-boat *78T* off Pola on 11 May 1917, but he raised the periscope too far and for too long and the feather was spotted. The captain of the TB (Rossel) turned to comb the twin torpedo tracks (a fish passed down each side of his ship) and opened fire at the still visible periscope with his bow 66-mm (2½-inch) gun. No blood was drawn by either side. *H4* (Smyth) was next with a pass at *U-X* (ex-*UB-1*), a tiny but new boat built at Kiel in 1915 and put together at Pola. He fired two fish spread (by the pre-angling gear unique to 'H' boats for the Royal Navy) five degrees apart at 365 metres (400 yards). Smyth concluded that he overestimated the length of the U-boat – 28 metres (92 feet) – and that he had just missed ahead and astern because 'in each case the track of the torpedo was clearly seen practically touching the end of the submarine's jumping wire'.

Five degrees subtends 30 metres (100 feet) at 365 metres (400 yards), so Smyth saw himself robbed by a hairsbreadth, but, as noted earlier, torpedo tracks were not a correct indication of the position of fish relative to the target.

The *H4* and *U-X* encounter was the last between the Royal Navy and the Austro-Hungarian navy in the northern Adriatic. The small flock of 'B' boats and three modern 'H' boats had achieved little by the end of 1917, and now it was not safe to patrol anywhere close to the Austrian and German bases because of even more drifting and moored mines. Accordingly, the 'H' boats were transferred south to Brindisi in the hope of strengthening the Otranto Barrage. HMS *Adamant* returned to mother her brood and at various times six 'E' boats attached themselves to the squadron as advocated by Nasmith. The task for all Allied submarines was to catch U-boats short of the so-called Barrage. In rotation, the British did a five-day spell, then the French five and the Italians three.

On 23 May Oliver North, promoted from *B7* to command *H4*, found himself ahead, but off track, of *UB-52* (Launburg) inward bound. North used full speed submerged to close the track and fired two torpedoes at 11.15 p.m., by moonlight, from what he reckoned was 228 metres (250 yards) although he probably underestimated the range – a common mistake for a novice in semi-darkness. The fish ran true; for the past eighteen months the 'H' boats had been fitted with a low-pressure firing system and this was paying dividends. Discounting the unfortunate 'own goal' by HMS *H1* against the Italian sister-boat *H5*, North's success was the only contribution by submarines of the British Adriatic Force to the war effort.

CHAPTER 13

The Bloodless Bear (1916–17)

The year of 1916, presaged by a winter of boredom and monotony, was both frustrating and ominous for British submariners in the Baltic.

Francis Newton Allan Cromie, thirty-three years old and now Senior Officer, was a very different man from Max Horton: in contrast to the overtly carefree, buccaneering manner of Max, he had an air of flourish tinged with foppery exemplified by long side-whiskers, an astrakhan collar on his uniform great-coat and a predilection for displaying his medals at every opportunity. He got away with it – just – in the Baltic because this was the fashion of Tsarist officers with whom he communicated reasonably well in struggling Russian acquired by hard study. His success as a submariner, although not seen as equal to that of the legendary Horton, earned him the respect of his own crew in *E9* and, grudgingly, of the Russian officers too.

Even so, first-hand accounts of Cromie hint faintly at his blarney and inconsistency as well as a suspicion of professional carelessness. For example, he fired a salvo at a ship which he had gleefully told his men was a fully laden transport, but when there was no bang he said that the torpedoes must have run under because the target was light and riding high. Once, for some reason he personally shut off the control-room depth-gauge and forgot to reopen the cock, with near-disastrous results, although the crew all laughed – a good sign in itself of course; and to charge over the Revel boom instead of passing through the gate was careless, to say the least.

There were no saints in the submarine service, but Cromie was no sinner either. His minor weaknesses were irrelevant when measured against his doings on patrol and his political stature among the Russians (despite his being teetotal and a non-smoker – an incomprehensible feat of asceticism in their eyes). 'Our Captain', wrote *E19*'s navigator Cecil Mee[1] after a Russian admiral's visit, 'looked fine, the other chaps were not in it, he has a look and air of breeding about him which the others lack and only yesterday a Russian officer passed a similar remark. I feel rather proud of him and the men have great faith in him.' This was from a man whose fixing and dead reckoning were continually called into question by his captain – unjustly one would guess, knowing that Royal Naval Reservists like Mee were usually a good deal more expert in this regard than regular RN submarine officers.

E19 had sent the light cruiser *Undine*, a destroyer and ten steamers to the bottom of the Baltic between October and December 1915. But 1916 wore on with nothing to show for Cromie's efforts; and his position *vis-à-vis* the discontented, ineffectual Russian fleet became more and more delicate.

E18 (Halahan) was inexplicably lost after damaging the German destroyer *V-100* at the end of May. She was presumed to have run on to a mine but may have had an internal accident. It was a bad year for the remaining boats, and Cromie expressed his feelings frankly to Commodore Hall:

. . . oh, the begging and the weeping I have had to get the [Russian] staff to move, and the lies they keep putting me off with, with what idea I never discovered. Now I am doing my best to keep at least two boats always at sea in two positions having direct offensive bearings on any naval movement against Riga, viz, Libau and Steinort. I reconnoitred [in *E19*] these positions last trip and located the swept channels, patrols and courses used, and went right up to Libau, counting five cruisers inside, but they never stirred out.

And later:

There is very little for us to do at present beyond the eternal 'stand by', as I have failed to persuade them to let us hunt Fritz off the entrance to the Gulf [of Riga].

While Cromie was trying to make his 'E' boats useful, the Russians were doing very little. During the whole of the war in the Baltic, with forty-two boats on the books (it is impossible to say how many were fit for service), only five boats scored. They were all of the same 650/782 'Leopard' class armed with twelve tubes and external launchers as well as either one or two 57-mm (2.2-in) guns. No German warships suffered their attentions but seven merchantmen were sunk, four by *Volk*, two by *Vepr* and one by *Gepard*. All (except *Gepard*'s perhaps) were torpedoed. *Alligator* and *Kaiman* each took a prize but whether the crews received prize money is doubtful. Six Russian submarines were lost.

Set against this meagre haul, German U-boats torpedoed the Russian armoured cruiser *Pallada*, a minelayer, six transports or auxiliaries and a minesweeper. The last went down to an exceptionally skilful shot by Spiess, who had been well groomed by Weddigen in *U-9* and commanded the boat himself from 12 January 1915. Mines laid by UC-boats accounted for a minelayer, seven minesweepers and one German sweeper (an own goal by *UC-57*'s field), two destroyers, two torpedo boats and five submarines. Two U-boats and one UC-boat were lost in the Baltic, all on mines. Summarising the British successes, two German cruisers were torpedoed and sunk by *E9* and *E19*, and sixteen merchant ships went down (or were damaged beyond repair during the war) to *E19* (nine), *E9* (five), *E8* (one), and *C27* (one). There were two submarine losses – *E18* and *C32*. It is clear who bore the brunt of the Baltic war. The Russian submarine contribution was disappointing, especially since they were playing a home match.

It is possible that the Russian submarines would have done better under more inspired leadership, and this was provided at the end of 1916. The vacillating C-in-C Admiral Kanin was relieved by Admiral Nepenin, a much more energetic man who had previously headed the Naval Intelligence Service. At the same time a new Russian submarine flotilla captain, Verderevsky, arrived. Like Cromie, but totally unlike most other Tsarist officers, he was a man of boundless energy. The two got on well together and Cromie took heart for the coming year. But with that came the Revolution.

Dissatisfaction throughout the lower deck of the Russian navy was obvious and understandable. The officers were, in the main, effete, arrogant, insensitive, immoral, inefficient and (a horror when they joined the 'E' boats for liaison duties) scented. The ratings, paid a pittance, ill-fed and forbidden alcohol, were, in the view of their superiors, no better than ignorant and superstitious peasants from the steppes – which in truth many of them were.

British seamen and stokers sharing the messdecks in the depot ship *Dvina* with Russian crews – one nationality one side and one the other – were appalled at what the latter had to eat. It consisted 'of only the barest necessities – tea, black bread and a combination of soup-stew in which floated gobbets of meat and vegetables'. There was no butter or jam, never an egg or a proper meat dish, while pay for the average seaman was a miserable five roubles (about ten shillings) a month.[2]

Lieutenant L. H. Ashmore (ex-*E18*) gave a telling account[3] of the underlying reasons for the eventual revolt which would almost certainly have occurred even if the Revolution had not been the immediate overwhelming cause:

The harsh discipline and degrading rules of conduct for ratings, which fixed a fathomless gulf between officers and men, undoubtedly contributed to placing the sailors of the fleet in the forefront of any violent revolutionary movements and to leading them on to such savage excesses as had occurred in 1905 and were to be repeated in 1917 and 1918.

Conditions of life for Russian ratings were of a standard that no western nation since the early nineteenth century could have conceivably imposed on their sailors. . . . Their relations with their officers were such as to deny them all sense of self-respect. Speaking to an officer, a Russian rating had to use such obsequious forms of address as 'Excellency' or 'High-born'. Throughout the conversation he had to stand at the salute, a custom hardly conducive to encouraging communication between officers and men or the mutual respect on which good discipline must rely.

Punishments were appallingly harsh by our standards. Sentences of banishment for years to Siberia or imprisonment in some grim prison such as the fortress of Sts Peter and Paul might be meted out for offences which would have earned ninety days' detention with us.

The only relaxations that a Russian sailor could enjoy were his music, singing and dancing. At the slightest encouragement the balalaikas or harmonicas would be brought out, and soon the glorious sound of Russian male voices in perfect harmony and the wild exhilaration of Russian dancing would bring an air of gaiety and sentiment to a community that had been, a moment before, languishing in the depth of deadly depression.

It was always a source of wonder to me, the way any group of Russians seemed able to harmonise a song or even a concerted greeting. Often I listened with delight to the Ceremony of 'Divisions' in a Russian ship. It would open with the arrival on deck of the Captain who would salute and greet his ship's company with some phrase such as 'Good Health, my brave sailors'. In perfect unison, the whole ship's company would reply 'Good morning, Excellency. We are happy to serve under you.' It was always a most impressive little scene. Morning prayers would follow and, in the absence of a priest, an officer would intone the prayers most beautifully.

Morning prayers were just one of many ceremonies dispensed with in March 1917. Cromie was on leave in Petrograd when the Revolution broke out in the middle of that month. He remarked, without intentional sarcasm, 'I have never seen better-tempered people – both troops and mob – they always seemed sorry to kill and very jovial over any little jest.'[4] 'Jovial' and 'sorry to kill' they may have been in Petrograd, but, as Ashmore said with feeling, there was little joviality or compunction in the way the sailors treated their officers in the fleet when their turn came.

The *Dvina* became the most revolutionary of all the vessels at Revel. This depot ship, which supported the British submarines and housed their crews, was the first to hoist the Red Flag aft together with a black flag at the main. The conditions under which Russian sailors would serve in future were laid down by the Central Committee. Those officers who were not dealt with summarily were forced to abide by them:

1. No man to be removed from a ship without the approval of the ship's Committee.
2. Undesirable officers to be removed at the demand of the Committee. Any new officers to be approved by the same body.
3. Officers to be elected and promoted by the crew.
4. Work to start at 9 a.m. and cease at 3 p.m.
5. No saluting.
6. Officers and men to have equal rights ashore.
7. All summary punishments to be awarded by a committee of three men and one officer.
8. All matters of routine and internal organisation of the ship to be run by the Committee.
9. Food and pay to be improved.

According to Ashmore:

Some of the results of the new regime were simply ludicrous, others most alarming. Many of the Russian sailors were quite childish in the way they exercised their new liberty, returning on board when they felt inclined, dressed in weird garments – lavender gloves, boots with grey cloth uppers or spats, straw hats – anything to show their independence. They succeeded only in making themselves ridiculous. It has to be remembered, of course, that many of them had come to the navy straight from some dim hovel in a distant village of the vast primitive spaces of the interior. With discipline and guidance they were the kindly, simple people that we got to know as our sailor servants. But many of them were transformed, under our eyes it seemed, into ravening savages as soon as the bonds of authority were loosed.

Cromie, hastily returning to the *Dvina*, was determined to prevent bloodshed and protect not only the British crews but the Russian liaison teams attached to his submarines. He was not entirely successful but insisted that, because these Russians had been awarded their proper portion of the prize bounties gained by British submariners, they must be deemed to be serving under the White Ensign.

By April 1200 Tsarist officers had been murdered, but a

handful of Russian submarines continued to patrol spasmodically. *Vepr* sank the 873-ton German steamer *Friedrich Carow* on 8 August 1917 but this was their only achievement after the start of the Revolution, and four Russian boats were lost on mines during the year. In addition, *AG-15* dived with the hatch open at the cost of eighteen men drowned. She could have been saved if the crew had stuck to their posts but, although the First Lieutenant behaved properly, the Captain was the first to quit and bob to the surface.

On the one hand Cromie's position as Senior British Officer became more and more difficult while on the other he became virtual head of the Russian submarine service when the appointed head was murdered. He gave up command of *E19* in May 1917 by which time the *Dvina* had been renamed *Pamyat Azova*. The British Admiralty granted him the rank of Acting Captain in belated recognition of his flotilla command. No Russian officer dared to accept such high rank, and Cromie found himself the mediator between the Russian C-in-C and the Sailors' Committee.

One division of Russian submariners refused to go to sea, but in Cromie's opinion a German attack might recall a sense of duty among the fleet which was rapidly losing all sense of patriotism. 'Pray God,' wrote Cromie, 'the Huns are foolish enough to make it.' A German amphibious force did, in fact, launch a new offensive and Riga was captured on 3 September. But by then Russian morale had evaporated.

In May Kerensky moved from the Justice Ministry (which had ceased to function save in name) to become Minister of War and Marine. Cromie described him as 'an insignificant-looking man of thirty-three' and – prophetically – 'not likely to live long'. Admiral Maximov, succeeding Nepenin as C-in-C, decided to play to the gallery and dismissed Verderevsky, the only strong man on the staff, who had been the submariners' direct commander. Conditions at Revel, a veritable hotbed of agitators, became insupportable during the month of May. The British and Russian submarine depots therefore shifted to the Finnish port of Hango.

In October the Germans, already in possession of Riga

itself, followed up with Operation Albion against the Gulf of Riga. Only five out of seventeen seagoing Russian submarines were serviceable by now, and these were held in reserve for last-ditch defence against a prospective attack by the German surface fleet. HMS *C26*, *C27* and *C32*, working from their advanced base in Moon Sound at the northern entrance to the Gulf, made a valiant attempt to check the invasion but without significant effect. The little boats were bombed and depth-charged; with a damaged compass *C32* (Satow) was forced to beach in Vaist Bay. Satow sent his men ashore and blew up the boat, only to find the area still in Russian hands. Cromie was not complimentary.

C27 (Sealy) went too close to the German battleship *König* and his torpedoes ran under the target. A second salvo damaged the transport *Indianola* but the vigorous German counter-attack was even more damaging to the submarine which just managed to limp back to Hango.

C26 (Downie) did his best to intercept a particularly strong German force south of Moon Island within the Gulf but ran aground before he could fire. Energetic efforts to reach deep water failed, and Downie had to take his boat, with jammed hydroplanes and a fouled propeller, into Pernau. Here, aided by a team of British ERAs and stokers sent post-haste by Cromie, makeshift repairs were urgently put in hand, but while testing the refitted gear just outside the harbour someone started a petrol fire in the engine-room. Eventually, in December with the ice closing in, *C26* was made sufficiently seaworthy to risk the passage to Hango 120 miles away and thence to Helsingfors where the rest of the flotilla had moved in October. Downie brought her back looking like a seagoing sieve full of Heath Robinson devices: her petrol pump was driven by a wooden pulley.

In November 1917 the Bolsheviks seized power, and in the middle of December the Sailors' Committee announced its intention of going to Kiel to bargain with the Germans. Cromie not only managed to persuade the Committee that this would not be a good plan but also obtained a personal guarantee from Lenin himself that, whatever happened, British men would be unharmed and that the submarines could be scuttled or blown up if necessary.

The end of the year saw the Germans in undisputed control of the entrance to the Gulf of Finland. The Admiralty refused permission for the British flotilla to try breaking out so, in January 1918, the flotilla personnel, shepherded by a Bolshevik Able Seaman Commissar, departed for a ten-day journey by an unlit, unheated train to Murmansk. A care-and-maintenance party of two officers (including Downie) and twenty-three men remained precariously in the *Pamyat Azova* at Helsingfors while the Bolsheviks struggled to reach an accommodation with Germany at Brest Litovsk.

Cromie also spent a good deal of time at Helsingfors when he was not attending to new and unwelcome duties as Naval Attaché at Petrograd. From here, on 3 April, it was his sad task to ratify Downie's decision to destroy the four 'E' boats and three 'C' boats in the face of a German landing at Hango 80 miles down the coast. The job was effectively executed by 5 April, and Downie and his team prepared to leave. Cromie originally intended to go with them but conscience would not allow: as Attaché now, with exceptional experience and influence, he felt bound to stay if only to help three British merchant ships which had been trapped in the Baltic since 1914. In that respect he was not successful, but he did prevent them falling into Red hands by ensuring that they were scuttled.

At one stage Cromie refused a Finnish bribe of £50,000, offered in the hope that he would prevent Russian sailors interfering while anti-Bolshevik Finns dealt with the Reds ashore; he also rejected no less than £5 million which Finnish Whites were willing to pay for the British submarines while they were still afloat. He did, however, engage in several cunning ventures, which succeeded in preventing the Germans from laying their hands on substantial quantities of valuable copper and other metals.

In May he went (twice) to Moscow, where the increasingly influential Trotsky was suspicious but not unfriendly, until Allied intervention against the Red Bolsheviks in early

August cost the Allied missions, consuls and Cromie himself the immunity they had hitherto enjoyed. Back in Petrograd, Cromie moved secretly from place to place, over the rooftops on one occasion, to avoid arrest or worse.

On 31 August 1918, he interrupted a fugitive existence to discuss matters in the embassy. At 4 p.m. he was asked to collect a letter from the chancery, a side-room at the top of the grand staircase. There are several versions of what happened next. According to one by a young army nurse attached to the embassy,[5] members of the Cheka (the secret police and ancestral KGB) or German agents, or perhaps both, forced their way into the embassy and held the staff at gunpoint on the ground floor. Cromie, knowing nothing of this, started to walk back down the staircase from the chancery with his letter when he came face to face with one of the intruders whom he seemingly recognised. He immediately bounded down the stairs while the intruder – whose identity has never been established – fired his pistol at him from the top. Cromie was mortally wounded. An alternative account, traced to Assistant Paymaster Lieutenant Hayward,[6] says that a deputation came to the embassy for some quite peaceful reason but that Cromie drew his pistol and started shooting first. (Hayward escaped.) The facts will probably never be established with certainty. Practically every contemporary of Cromie's was convinced that he died a martyr's – indeed a hero's – death.

An unwitting tribute to the Royal Navy's submariners in the Baltic over those long, comfortless years of war came in an instruction by Prince Henry of Prussia to German U-boats when British guns and torpedoes were crippling German lines of communication:

I consider the destruction of a Russian submarine as a great success. I regard the destruction of a British submarine to be as valuable as that of a Russian armoured cruiser.

CHAPTER 14

Merchant U-Boats (1915–16)

While still questioning the political risks of unrestricted sub-marine warfare against transatlantic shipping, Germany was feeling the results of the British blockade on her own ports. Virtually from the outset of war, the Royal Navy's minefields, surface patrols and submarines effectively debarred neutral, let alone German, merchantmen from carrying goods needed for the efficient running of German war-making machinery and the economy.

There was no way that food could be imported across the North Sea, and the Kaiser's people had to make do with home produce and whatever could be brought overland from neighbouring countries or wrung out of occupied territories. Rations were short and supplies to shops were irregular; racketeers in black markets flourished; country folk fared better than town-dwellers; the gaps between rich and poor widened; and, in due course, Communism, spreading out-wards from Russia, inevitably took root.

The dreadful state of affairs in Germany, worsening year by year as the war ground on, tends to be forgotten in the light of Britain's desperate struggle against the U-boats. But it was the pitiful plight of the Fatherland's half-starved civilian population – far worse than Britain's population even at the height of *Handelskrieg* – that bred such bitterness among many U-boat commanders and their crews.

There was nothing the U-boat men could do except fight ruthlessly, with the single aim of forcing Great Britain to her knees and bringing the war to a speedy conclusion. The con-sequences of that determination will be apparent in the next chapter. Meanwhile, a novel scheme was devised to import certain essential commodities – although not food – covertly by sea.

International law forbade ships of war, which obviously included U-boats, from embarking commercial goods in neutral ports. Neutral countries, the United States in particular, were not prepared to flout that law. One possibility offered by politicians in Berlin was to transfer merchandise, notably rubber which would float, from neutral merchant ships to U-boats far out at sea which would then evade (diving when necessary) the British Cruiser Squadron off the east coast of America and the vigilant cruisers, destroyers, submarines and light craft patrolling the approaches to the German Ocean. The Imperial Navy rejected the scheme as impractical, but the admirals were prepared to listen to Herr Alfred Lohmann, a businessman, who suggested building unarmed underwater cargo vessels.

The 1440/1820-ton *Deutschland*[1] and a sister vessel *Bremen*, at a cost of 2.75 million marks (£137,500) apiece, were the result. In September 1915 Lohmann persuaded the out-of-work merchant-marine Captain Paul König, of North German Lloyd, to command the *Deutschland*. König was well acquainted with Chesapeake Bay and, since the American trading port selected was Baltimore, he would stand a better chance than most of navigating the 120 miles of pilotage waters with an effective draught (submerged) of some 20–25 metres (65–80 feet). Nobody knew for sure what political or naval reactions to the *Deutschland*'s appearance would be but König, an equable character, shrugged off the potential problems facing him.

On 23 June 1916 *Deutschland* sailed from Kiel carrying mail and a cargo of 700 tons including 163 tons of concentrated dye worth $1.4 million on the American market, as well as precious stones. Four patrol boats escorted her into the open sea and then left König and his men, in fair comfort and high spirits, to forge their way across the mine-strewn sea, known to U-boat men as the Rose Garden, around the heavily patrolled coast of Scotland and out into the Atlantic at an economical speed of $9\frac{1}{2}$ knots. The 'merchant' seamen (all hand-picked and some from operational U-boats) were issued with superb leather coats and warm uniforms which, together with ample provisions and a generous allowance of luxuries such as cigars and gramophone records, made life on board unusually tolerable.

It was imperative to avoid discovery by any other ship or submarine. Quite apart from the danger of attack with no means of retaliation, *Deutschland*'s mercantile identity must not be revealed until she reached neutral America. Here, König was assured, friends awaited her. The crew's attitude was pragmatic: when König asked the gigantic Bos'n Humke what he thought was the purpose of the voyage, the reply came with a broad grin, 'Why, to make money, of course!'

König's theme, well rehearsed, ran differently. The goods they were carrying would prevent envious British traders not only from damaging German imports and exports but also from injuring American manufacturers and American trade. Without carrying guns or torpedoes the *Deutschland* would revolutionise trans-ocean commerce and international law. Even armed U-boats were only employed to protect the Fatherland against the barbaric methods of starvation adopted by the British contrary to all international law. Yet the British armed their merchant ships and bombarded every U-boat which approached them for the legal purpose of sinking contraband. That, said König contemptuously, was what the British called defence. Although Germany was compelled to sink British merchant ships without warning, that was only so that U-boats might not be sunk by ramming or gunfire.

Now, continued König, the British had begun to whine for help, and, with existing international law, had contrived to win over the Americans to their point of view. Germany only desired peace with the great American people, so the Government did not argue. But the *Deutschland* was both an *Unterseeboot* and a merchant vessel and defenceless merchant vessels could not be sunk without warning. It followed that a merchant submarine had to be examined before being sunk – and that would be very difficult as long as it was capable of diving.

So, if the *Deutschland* was not to be searched before being attacked, *all* merchant ships could be sunk without warning – including British vessels. Thus, concluded König grandly, the *Deutschland* would bring about the collapse of what was a one-sided interpretation of the former law, and the laws of warfare would once more be justly balanced by means of a peaceful unarmed merchant submarine.[2] It was a plausible argument and plenty of people in America were glad to listen to it. There is no record of the crew caring one way or the other about such issues.

Out in the Atlantic, Humke rigged a dummy canvas funnel fastened to the periscope. The disguise was completed with smoke from an oily wad of cotton waste whenever a ship loomed in sight. On one occasion the Bos'n ('a simple soul') thought this was not enough and backed it up with a lump of tar, thereby giving a passable imitation of a ship on fire which attracted a helpful but unwelcome merchantman. The steamer sheared off smartly when the shape revealed was undeniably that of a U-boat.

When he was 100 miles from the American coast, König could not afford to take risks, and dived whenever smoke or masts were sighted on the horizon. Unknown to him, however, *Deutschland* had already been identified (on 24 June) and reported to British Intelligence as a very large submarine. The Dutch steamer *Westerdyk* reckoned it was 120–150 metres (4–500 feet) long, double its actual length.

Vice-Admiral Sir George Patey, C-in-C North American and West Indies Station, did not hold the same views as König. When apprised of the merchant U-boat's coming he told the Admiralty: 'I cannot conceive that any enemy's submarine can have any status except that of a belligerent enemy and I shall treat her accordingly if met. The fact of flying a merchant flag, or any other flag, would be no guarantee.'

As it happened, the Royal Navy's patrols went to the wrong place to intercept the blockade-runner (Room 40 OB had miscalculated for once) and König slipped into American territorial waters without being challenged. The local pilot was expecting the boat, and his first words were, 'I'll be damned, here she is.'

At 11 p.m. on 9 July the first mercantile submarine in the world anchored off the Quarantine Station at Baltimore. König and his crew were welcomed rapturously. The Press and 'movie men' were there in shoals and when the boat finally came alongside, a German-American band struck up suitable airs from the Fatherland while a crowd of enthusiastic girls rained flowers on the deck. König's initial ride in an automobile to the North German Lloyd Agency in Baltimore City was like a triumphal procession and the city police wearily recognised the vehicle thereafter as an inevitable traffic obstruction. The crew were greeted, wherever they were, with the 'Wacht am Rhein' sung (apparently with the right words) in German.

In short, the Kaiser's Ambassador Bernstorff and the German Club had prepared the ground well; when Patey instituted patrols, late in the day, off the Chesapeake the American press angrily reported that the British were violating American waters.

The cargo was unloaded and replaced with 348 tons of rubber (257 externally), 341 tons of nickel and 93 tons of tin. The rubber alone was worth $17.5 million, several times more than the building costs of *Deutschland* and *Bremen* together. Humke's assessment of the voyage was correct.

Despite Patey's efforts, König sailed on 2 August to arrive safely back at Bremen, without notable incidents, on 24 August. The Chief Stoker of the battleship *Posen* was moved to pen a congratulatory poem of nine verses. In the evening a state banquet for König at the Rathaus was accompanied by a hymn of thanksgiving: 'To the God of Justice we offer our Prayers'. *Deutschland* had covered 8450 sea miles, of which 190 critical miles were submerged.

A second successful cargo trip was made between October and December to New London, Connecticut, but the companion U-freighter *Bremen* disappeared en route to Norfolk, Virginia, probably after being rammed while dived – accidentally it was said – by HMS *Alsatian* and HMS *Mantua* south of Ireland. Both ships modestly declined to take any credit for *Bremen*'s loss.

At the turn of the year it was decided, with all-out

Handelskrieg imminent, to convert *Deutschland* to a fighting U-boat, and the navy adopted her as *U-155* on 18 February 1917. Her exploits as one of the U-cruisers, for which she provided a very useful foundation, will be examined later.

Nevertheless, the Royal Navy also profited. The diplomatic wrangling that followed *Deutschland*'s voyages resulted in a sop to Great Britain. Ten H-class submarines (*H11* to *H20*), built in America but held under the neutrality laws in Boston, were released. Six went to Chile in exchange for Chilean ships taken over in British yards. It became clear from *Deutschland*'s first merchant venture that a strong pro-German feeling, doubtless backed by commercial considerations, existed in the United States, and this would be a formidable obstacle in the way of bringing the USA into the war on the Allied side.

CHAPTER 15

No Holds Barred (1917)

At the beginning of 1917 Chancellor Bethmann-Hollweg at last surrendered to those who pressed for a ruthless submarine campaign. The Kaiser bowed to his most militant advisers and accepted the risk of war with the United States: U-boats were commanded to resume unrestricted attacks on merchant shipping – 'with the utmost severity' – from 1 February. A note to that effect (with a specious preamble about the Allies rejecting peace terms) was delivered to Washington on 31 January.

Even before the Kaiser's order Britain had lost 154 merchantmen between October and December 1916 – more than 300,000 tons a month. The Mediterranean was infested by U-boats, and in northern waters a specific onslaught had been directed against neutral Norwegian ships[1] engaged principally in bringing timber for pit-props, a vital import. Another commodity that occupied a vast amount of cargo space and suffered heavily, especially in the Eastern Mediterranean, was horse and mule fodder.

Berlin was aware that Jellicoe, Commander-in-Chief of the Grand Fleet, had recently cautioned the Admiralty that if such wastage continued Great Britain might be compelled, by the summer of 1917, to conclude a peace very different from that which she had a right to expect. The pessimistic but rational Jellicoe was to be greeted with his own prediction when he moved to Whitehall as First Sea Lord and became responsible for anti-submarine policy.

The case presented by the German naval staff for no holds being barred rested on statistics. Out of a British total of some 20 million tons of shipping only 8.5 million tons remained for cargo-space after deduction of military and other Allied requirements. An outside figure of 2 million tons might be added for neutral shipping. If the U-boats went all out they ought to sink at least 600,000 tons a month. After five months (say in mid-1917) Great Britain would have lost 39 per cent of her available total, that is, of the ships which could be kept at work, allowing for repairs and so on.

In addition, said the financiers who primarily compiled these figures (ship-owners and economists had little to do with them), the failure of the American wheat harvest in 1916 would drop transatlantic imports from 92 per cent to 64 per cent of the total required. This would have to be compensated in 1917 by imports from more distant India, Australia and the Argentine, requiring twice as many ships. Meanwhile, U-boats would almost entirely cut off supplies of butter and fats from Denmark and Holland which normally provided half of Britain's needs.

The British Government had, for some time, been extremely uneasy about U-boat depredations but on paper the situation seemed fairly favourable despite the warnings of men like Jellicoe. After two and a half years of war the total merchant tonnage was only 5 per cent less than at its outbreak, but this was self-deception. The civil servants did not make allowance for military services and support for the Allies as the Germans did; they included a million tons captured or seized in port from the enemy and they failed to note, let alone remedy, the declining rate of mercantile ship-building which had only reached a miserable 539,000 tons in 1916. They also did not foresee the reluctance of neutrals to bring in cargoes (in February and March 1917 neutral entrances and clearances were a quarter of those for the same period in the previous year) and neither did they appreciate the decline in efficiency caused by the best masters and officers being transferred to the Royal Navy or the difficulty in replacing those who were killed.

In the main, the German figures were much closer to the truth. During the five months from February (when the U-boats were unleashed) to June 1917, sinkings in all areas averaged just over 650,000 tons monthly; damage requiring extensive repairs amounted to a further 100,000 tons monthly. The sinkings represented about 580 tons per U-boat day with between forty and sixty boats at sea at any one time. As Jellicoe pointed out,[2] the increased size and hence greater radius of action of enemy submarines enabled them to work in waters so far afield as to make it increasingly difficult to trap them.

Moreover, U-boats were attacking more frequently from submerged with torpedoes, which prevented the use of A/S 'surprise' weaponry applicable to submarines which came to the surface – that is, guns on Q-ships and armed merchant ships, and bombs from airborne units. Those U-boats that did still surface for gun action carried such heavy and comparatively long-range armament that it was seldom possible for a merchantman to retaliate. Not one merchant vessel actually destroyed a U-boat by gunnery; and throughout the war only ten Q-ships enjoyed success out of some 180 motley craft that served at various times, four of them sinking a couple apiece. In fact, it is arguable that putting guns on decoys and merchant vessels was counter-productive in that U-boats, for entirely practical reasons of self-protection, were even more ruthless as a consequence.

If no holds were barred on the German side the Allies had only the flimsiest of bars to hold back the underwater hordes in 1917. Although depth-charges were beginning to take effect (and becoming safer for the user) technology was definitely on the side of submarines. The most promising underwater detection devices, based on multiple hydrophone arrays and towed hydrophones (to reduce noise from the operating ship), were American – and that begged the big question. When, if ever, would the United States enter the war?

The declared German danger zone for all traffic, irrespective of nationality, ran from the Dutch coast up to Norway, thence to the Faroe Islands and down to Cape Finisterre with a western ocean-boundary 400 miles out into the Atlantic from Ireland. Greece and Spain were permitted narrow access channels, and two American ships every week were allowed to sail between New York and Falmouth, provided that they identified themselves by, of all things, the American convict markings of vertical red and white stripes.

No Holds Barred (1917)

German admirals and generals were prone to sophistry; and they were encouraged by Gerard, the American ambassador in Berlin, to hope that President Wilson would confine himself to a diplomatic rupture. They deluded themselves that if war was actually declared even the great American nation, menaced by a conflict in Mexico and still so unprepared, would be unable to bring sufficient weight to bear against the Central European Powers within five or six months, by which time the U-boats would have decided the issue.

Bernstorff, German ambassador in Washington, held no such delusions. He had constantly warned that the United States would declare war if further provoked and that her resources were inexhaustible. In his view Germany's only hope lay in a peace negotiated through the offices of President Wilson.

Bernstorff received his dismissal almost immediately after the German 'unrestricted warfare' note was delivered. But Wilson was still unwilling to declare war until 'an overt act' had taken place. In March, however, events gathered pace. Five more American merchantmen were sunk with loss of life and, more important, British Intelligence decoded what came to be known as the Zimmermann Telegram. This, from the German Foreign Office to Mexico on 19 January, suggested a German–Mexican alliance such that, if the United States entered the war against Germany, Mexico's army would march northward, and that at the subsequent peace settlement (which Zimmermann predicted) lost territory in New Mexico, Texas and Arizona would be restored to Mexico. Zimmermann also implied that Germany was seeking to induce Japan to change sides and to attack American bases in the Pacific.

The telegram was, of course, passed across the Atlantic, albeit after some delay – presumably while 40 OB[3] was double-checking its authenticity. On 2 March the contents were released to the press in Washington where they provoked widespread and, to the British Government, welcome protests. Fury in the United States was fanned by the indisputable fact that the Germans had used a privileged wire assigned to them by the State Department specifically for peace proposals.

263

In the event neither Mexico nor Japan collaborated with Germany but Congress, more than a little hesitant before, was now reconciled to the inevitability of open conflict. The northern and western states, which had been indifferent or in some cases favourable towards Germany, were embittered and the 'German Club' that had greeted the *Deutschland* so enthusiastically on the east coast found itself outnumbered. The pro-German feeling of the preceding year was rapidly evaporating.

On 2 April President Woodrow Wilson, with masterful measured eloquence and carefully adjusted pince-nez, spoke in the House of Representatives, demanding war with Germany:

To such a task we can dedicate our lives and our futures, everything that we are and everything that we have, with the pride of those who know that the day has come when America is privileged to spend her blood and her might for the principles that gave her birth and happiness and the peace which she has treasured. God helping her, she can do no other.

Thus the United States, pledging to use 'force to the uttermost, force without stint or limit' finally entered the war.

While the President was speaking, underwater warfare was sharply rising to a climax. In April 1917 802 tons of shipping were sunk per U-boat day (the realistic German method of calculating submarine effectiveness) and Allied merchant ships totalling 860,334 tons (about 810 vessels) were lost in all theatres. However, the tonnage per U-boat in that month would have been 21 per cent less had it not been for von Arnauld de la Perière's spectacular Mediterranean cruise, which underlined the fact that a few submarine commanders did the most.

There were still at this late date many influential officers in the Admiralty (and also in the American and French navies) who believed that a convoy presented the ideal opportunity for U-boats, and that large groups of ships would lead to even greater losses. Nevertheless, convoying of a sort – but called 'controlled sailings' to avoid the controversial word – had been

working very well since February for coal exports to France.
Large numbers of colliers were involved in the trade and losses
had been mounting until the French asked for protection in
the light of their dire need. Not many escorts were available
but the little ships sailed in groups: no more than sixteen out
of 8871 sailings were sunk in the next six months.

However, John Terraine has pointed out[4] that there was a
much more important example of convoying going on under
the noses of their lordships at the Admiralty from August 1914,
but disregarded by them – and by most historians – since.
During the war nearly $5^1/_2$ million men were transported by
sea to France for service on the Western Front. Not one was
lost to the German High Sea Fleet or the Flanders U-boats,
simply because the continual procession of transports was
guarded throughout the final crossing by the Royal Navy.
As Terraine says, the gigantic army was, in effect, escorted
in convoy.

Five years after the Armistice, Winston Churchill put
the case for convoying succinctly:

The size of the sea is so vast that the difference between the size of
a convoy and the size of a single ship shrinks in comparison almost
to insignificance. There was in fact very nearly as good a chance of
a convoy of forty ships in close order slipping unperceived between
the patrolling U-boats as there was for one single ship; and each time
this happened, forty ships escaped instead of one . . . [5]

That was the main point: U-boats had nothing to see for
days or weeks on end. But Churchill added, correctly:

. . . the destroyers, instead of being dissipated on patrol over
wide areas, were concentrated at the point of the hostile attack,
and opportunities of offensive action frequently arose.[6]

In other words, convoying brought into play at least three long-
proven principles of war: offensive action, concentration, and
economy of force. Until now, in nearly 150 actions between
German submarines and British anti-submarine vessels, twenty-
three U-boats had escaped for each one destroyed.

It took time for the new convoy organisation to be established, and in April there were huge shipping losses. On the 17th 34,000 tons went down, 32,000 tons on the 19th, 28,000 tons on the 20th and 30,000 tons on the 21st. During the whole of April 1917 sinkings averaged thirteen ships every day against the daily average of three throughout 1916. (It was to fall again to 3.6 in 1918 but nobody could foresee that.) For the moment, the collapse of the British Isles and with it the collapse of the Allied war effort 'began to loom black and imminent'.[7]

During May there was a significant drop in shipping losses of about one-third compared with April, partly because about 20 per cent fewer U-boats were at sea: they simply could not maintain the April pace.

Unfortunately for Britain, though, the underwater enemy was refuelled, rearmed and refreshed by June when sixty-one U-boats (out of 132 in commission) were at sea, forty of them in focal areas around the British Isles. It was the second worst month for merchant sinkings at about 690,000 tons – 23 per cent down on April but more than 15 per cent up on May. Losses of that magnitude were not sustainable: Jellicoe, First Sea Lord, stated flatly that it would be impossible to continue the war in 1918. Nor were U-boat losses proportional: only two boats were sunk in June while eight new submarines were commissioned.

The decision to adopt convoys did not provide an immediate panacea because it took a while for all concerned to get used to the system, which was not applied forthwith in all areas. North Atlantic convoys did not start until July, South Atlantic convoys not until September, and through-Mediterranean convoys not until November. Moreover, right up to the end of the war a large number of ships were sailed independently, and it was these that, predictably, suffered the greatest losses – 85.5 per cent (1500 ships) of the total shipping destroyed by U-boats (1757 ships) between April 1917 and October 1918 or 5.93 per cent of 'independents' sailed. Meanwhile, during the same period no more than 257 ships in convoy were sunk out of 83,958 convoyed sailings – 0.3 per cent. In short, convoys were indeed the solution wherever and whenever they could be efficiently organised. Would that the Admiralty had seen sense earlier.

As it was, shipping losses continued at an alarming rate with sinkings running at more than a $^1/_2$ million tons a month, the great majority 'independents'. The tide showed signs of slackening in September, but that was probably due to *Flottillenadmiral* Michelsen (who had relieved Bauer in June) redeploying his boats which – because of convoys – now looked over mostly empty waters in the Western Approaches. Some went to the Bay of Biscay, but more concentrated in the eastern Channel and North Sea, quite close inshore where no convoy system had been instituted either for ships dispersing from and joining ocean convoys or for regular coastal traffic. About two-thirds of the successful U-boat attacks in the latter part of 1917 took place within 10 miles of land – albeit at great risk from mines, mine-nets and submarine torpedoes as well as depth-charges which took an increasingly heavy toll. Seaplanes of the Royal Naval Air Service also became a danger in restricted waters close to home, while air escorts proved effective in deterring submarine attacks anywhere. In fact any convoy with air escort and support (only possible by day in reasonable weather conditions and within a limited range of land) proved virtually immune. Eventually coastal convoys were assembled – the first in December 1917 – but, again, they should have been organised much earlier.

In December 1917 the number of U-, UB- and UC-boats at sea again peaked at sixty, of which twelve were in the Mediterranean and forty-four in the approaches to, or around, the British Isles. However, their success rate was declining although this was not yet apparent to the Royal Navy. It was not until spring 1918 that merchant losses dropped to the point where new construction overtook them and Britain could breathe easily.

Germany, on the other hand, had been promised that unrestricted U-boat warfare would bring about peace before the 1917 harvest – by 1 August to be specific.[8] Austria had cried in April (when the United States entered the war) that it was essential to have peace before the summer was out, the

Foreign Minister adding that 'submarine war would damage but not ruin [England]'. July and August witnessed serious disaffection in the High Sea Fleet, and in July socialists in the Reichstag openly declared that submarine warfare had failed[9] and that Germany should strive for 'a peace of understanding, for a durable pacification of peoples'.[10]

The High Command would have none of this. Chancellor Bethmann-Hollweg, who might well have supported the Peace Resolution and who had long opposed unrestricted U-boat warfare, was forced to resign on 13 July, when the High Command Prussian puppet Michaelis took his place. Field-Marshal Hindenburg and General Ludendorff established what was virtually a military dictatorship which thenceforth directed the political course of the war, and submarine policy remained firm despite heavy casualties.

It has been said, or implied, by strategists and historians[11] that the defeat of U-boats did not depend on sinking them; that the point was to get vital cargoes through. While this was true, the submariners took a different and justifiably more subjective view. The aggregate of U-boat losses grew rapidly. It had been forty-six by the end of 1916 but was 107 by the end of 1917. As far as hulls were concerned these figures were not important: the building programme exceeded losses by a wide margin. It was the loss of experienced men, the dilution of crews, the inefficiency that aces had to contend with and the greater odds that run-of-the-mill commanders had to face that ultimately resulted in diminishing and unprofitable returns for the underwater raiders. Other factors were the difficult night – as opposed to easy day – attacks that had so often to be made in the last twelve months of war (although even harder for A/S forces to counter), the frequent denial of surface running, and, above all, the frustrations of an empty sea. From the end of 1917, whether or not perceived in Germany and England, the U-boat arm could not achieve victory before the United States weighed down the balance on the Allied side.

CHAPTER 16

The Yanks Are Coming
(April 1917–November 1918)

In April 1917, after nearly three years of bloody conflict in Europe, the Yanks were coming. The Kaiser's staff was right in thinking that the United States was not ready for war, but America's industrial muscles were flexed; European productivity paled by comparison. The Bethlehem Steel Company, for example, declared – and demonstrated – that it could build a large destroyer in just six weeks, while the same ship could not be turned out by a British yard in less than eighteen months.

Nevertheless the superb American production methods would still take time to influence the course of war even if put into top gear. There was no way, in the short term, of meeting the British Admiralty's stated requirements for 55 destroyers, 41 light cruisers, 4 battleships, more than 100 aircraft, 100,000 mines, 250 minelayers, numerous anti-submarine patrol vessels and any number of merchant ships.

Whitehall could be confident that ships and war materials would be steaming across the Atlantic from now on. Nobody doubted America's capacity for swelling a trickle into a torrent in due course, but it was estimated that she might have helped to save the Allies some 600,000 lives and £3 billion – equivalent to about £60 billion today – if she had been less tardy.

President Wilson was determined that America should be an independent co-belligerent, not an ally of Britain and France in the strict sense but an 'associated power'. He eventually advocated war not, it seems, to defeat Germany (except incidentally) but in order that he, for the United States, should dictate ideal conditions of peace. His own emissary to Britain, Professor M'Laughlin of Chicago University, made it plain a year later, in 1918, that Wilson had found it intolerable 'that all the great world questions were going to be decided and America have no voice – that was more than flesh and blood could stand'.[1] In other words, Woodrow Wilson – very properly – put America's interests before those of Britain. Old England and her Allies had to be supported in sufficient strength not so much to win the war but to achieve security through favourable treaties on both sides of the Atlantic. Wilson reserved the right to negotiate a separate peace at any time. Initially, therefore, the USA's war effort lacked wholeheartedness. It was the unenviable task of Rear-Admiral William Sowden Sims, US Navy, to get things moving.

When Ambassador Walter Page in London called for an officer of relatively high rank to command US Navy forces in Europe, and learn how best to cooperate with the Royal Navy, Secretary Daniels of the Navy Department selected Sims, who was then President of the Naval War College at Newport. Daniels made an excellent and perceptive choice when he sent Sims, who had known First Sea Lord Jellicoe since 1906 when both were captains. The two officers had formed a strong and frank friendship, freely exchanging information on gunnery matters; they trusted each other. Sims thought that 'simplicity and directness were Jellicoe's two most outstanding points', there was 'nothing of the blustery seadog' about him.[2] Jellicoe saw the American rear-admiral, his junior by two ranks, as 'a man of great sea experience and expert knowledge, of broad views and charming disposition . . .'.[3]

Four days after the United States had formally entered the war, on 9 April, Sims arrived at Liverpool by steamer in plain clothes and incognito as Mr V. J. Richardson. Straight away he was taken to London by special train, and there he met Jellicoe at the Admiralty. The First Sea Lord's revelations, kept from the still cheerful British public, could be summed up in a few words: German submarines were winning the war. Among those few who knew the truth, the beginning of November 1917 (some said the end of December) was sombrely mooted as the limit of British endurance. This was, of course, a later date than Berlin had counted upon 'in this life and death struggle by hunger';[4] but, as Ambassador Page declared: 'What we are witnessing is the defeat of Britain.' Jellicoe could see no immediate or guaranteed solution to the U-boat menace, but he wanted to impress the value of early assistance from the US Navy – and in doing so he strove to paint a picture that was dark yet not black.

Sims did his utmost. Cable after cable to Washington emphasised that, unless all available patrol vessels, especially destroyers, were sent over quickly, there would be no war remaining for the United States to join. 'I think', he wrote later, 'that history records few spectacles more heroic than that of the British navy fighting this hideous and cowardly form of warfare in half a dozen places with pitifully inadequate forces, but with undaunted spirit which remained firm even against the fearful odds. What an opportunity for America!'

The United States did not exactly seize the opportunity, but on 4 May six destroyers from Boston joined Admiral Bayly's dozen sloops at Queenstown: 'Sure, and it's our own boys coming back to us,' a delighted Irishwoman exclaimed. There were another dozen British destroyers at Devonport so the US Navy's contingent brought the total number of fair-sized A/S vessels in the Western Approaches to about thirty. This was soon raised to forty by detaching sloops and destroyers from the East Coast and from the Grand Fleet (at some risk) but it was calculated that eighty-one were needed to deal meaning-fully with U-boats threatening that crucial area. Thanks to Sims another twelve destroyers were sent to Queenstown later in May. The total number of American destroyers in European waters would rise to seventy-nine in 1918.

Meanwhile, *Handelskrieg* continued relentlessly. The British Government ceased to publish the tonnage sunk, simply giving out the number of British vessels above and below 1600 tons while ignoring Allied and neutral losses. By cleverly allowing the German lists to appear, however, the public was induced to think that they were wildly inaccurate. They were, in fact, on the high side as regards the tonnage actually sunk because

U-boat commanders seldom stopped to observe the fate of a damaged vessel. A torpedo hit was assumed to result in a sinking and that was not true in about 35 per cent of torpedo attacks. There was also a natural tendency to exaggerate the size of a target. But German intelligence was often ignorant of the serious losses caused by submarine-laid mines and heavy damage from submarine guns or torpedoes could put a ship out of action for so long that it might as well have been destroyed.

Since the answer was convoys the Admiralty was emboldened by American promises to withdraw A/S ships from fleet protection and assign them to convoy-escort duties in the hope that numbers would eventually be made good with the help of the US Navy. The battleships and heavy cruisers of the fighting fleet were less important than merchantmen in this critical hour, although there is no record of that being openly admitted. However, the Grand Fleet was by no means denuded of protection: Sims understood the necessity of retaining 100 destroyers to guard it. Indeed, Admiral Beatty in due course, and in the face of the German surface warfare threat which Sims correctly predicted, regularly attached a battle squadron to the covering forces of Scandinavian convoys in 1917 – and that demanded an A/S screen.

Passionate protests against convoys continued. It is worth examining these because, although most were unjustified, the system had its disadvantages. In brief, the arguments were:

- Even with American backing the required number of escorts was unprocurable. This was not so, although the Admiralty Convoy Committee was very demanding, wanting eight destroyers (a loose word including sloops and P-boats) for convoys of twenty-two ships and over, seven for sixteen to twenty-two ships, and six for fewer than sixteen ships. The total number of 'destroyers' required for convoys predicted in mid-1917 was eighty-four, and with substantial American help ninety-one were available by July, rising to 195 (115 proper destroyers) in April 1918. However, it was calculated that no fewer than fifty-two cruisers or other fairly large ships were also needed to replenish Atlantic Ocean escorts. These seem to have been provided although actual numbers are uncertain.

- Much time – amounting in effect to 20 per cent or more of available cargo space – would be lost while convoys were assembled. This was true.[5]

- Losses would be greater when U-boats succeeded in finding a convoy because there would be many targets in a relatively small area. This was not true, as previously discussed, for lone wolves who were lucky to get in one shot, but it was fortunate that the few attempts at 'wolf-pack' tactics, involving several U-boats, failed – mainly by reason of inadequate radio communications.

- The speed of a convoy would be determined by that of the lamest duck. This was true, but ships could be separated into fast or slow convoys.

- Merchant skippers would not submit to the necessary discipline. They could not keep station by night with their crude instruments, and smoke from just one careless engineer could give away the position of the whole convoy to a submarine over the horizon. This was partially true, but in the event merchantmen did much better than expected despite difficulties such as the lack of a voicepipe between bridge and engine room (to order precise speed alterations) and the strain on engines designed for steady plodding, caused by frequent changes in speed. Smoke, however, was certainly a constant problem and the shepherds were constantly chasing black sheep.

- There would be collisions and straggling, especially when a zig-zag was ordered. This was true, but acceptable. However, the German U-boat *Torpedo Firing Manual* of 1918, based on the experience of 1917, remarked uncharitably on the 'indescribable irregularity in station-keeping at the point of assembly . . . threatening mutual ramming'. Doubtless that was not a bad description of unpractised ships; but merchant captains underestimated their own ability to learn and they soon mastered the skills required.

Even Jellicoe had doubts, although he took Sims's point that if the Grand Fleet was immune to torpedo attack by virtue of its destroyers the same immunity could be enjoyed by merchant convoys. Sims, with sound war college reasoning, had a stronger point to make which evidently filtered through to Prime Minister Lloyd George who was all for experimenting with anything that might save the situation.

The traditional patrol system required a destroyer (or, often, a smaller craft) to cruise around in a quite large given area, ready to assist vessels in distress, escort ships through her own parish and attack submarines when the opportunity came – which was seldom. Patrolling was essentially a defensive strategy: a U-boat had only to submerge and keep quiet when a destroyer hove in sight, bobbing up again to resume its appointed deadly task when danger was past. Nor could a destroyer hope to reach a submarine reported by, say, the coastguard or an airborne unit because either the datum would be stale or the submarine – which was almost bound to see the enemy before being sighted itself – would simply duck. Hydrophones were not good enough to search a large expanse of sea even if a submerged boat was noisy. Not only did patrols offer scant protection to ships in practice, but they seldom brought U-boats to action. As President Wilson sourly remarked, looking for U-boats with wandering patrols was as futile 'as hunting hornets all over the farm'. (Wilson extended this philosophy by saying 'he despaired . . . when he knew where the [hornet's] nest was'; but attacks at source, save for the temporary blocking of Zeebrugge in 1918, were not seriously contemplated by the Allies.)

An escorted convoy, on the other hand, made combat between escorts and submarines inevitable – although who won an engagement was, of course, another matter. Convoying as an offensive strategy appealed both to Sims and the British Admiralty.

In Sims's words[6] the system

should compel any submarine which was planning to torpedo a convoyed ship to do so only in waters that were infested with destroyers. In order to get into position to discharge its missiles the submarine would have to creep up close to the rim that marked the circle of these destroyers. Just as soon as the torpedo started on its course, and the tell-tale wake appeared on the surface, the protecting ships would immediately begin sowing the waters with depth-charges. Thus, in the future, the Germans would be compelled to fight for every ship which they should attempt to sink, instead of sinking them conveniently in waters that were free of destroyers, as had hitherto been their privilege.

Sims could have added that convoy escorts denied U-boats the use of gunnery while the number of torpedoes carried was strictly limited and the best of those were sometimes rationed.

The convoy system saved England, but it would scarcely have been practicable without destroyers from America, at least not on a grand scale. By the time of the Armistice in November 1918 more than 88,000 vessels had been convoyed with the loss of 436 – less than half of 1 per cent against an average of 4.7 per cent in the months immediately preceding the wholesale adoption of convoys.[7]

There were other factors at work when U-boat successes began to decline, such as the diluted crews in operational submarines, worsening dockyard facilities and improved depth-charges. Some convoys, particularly on the narrow Mediterranean routes where ships had little room to manoeuvre, still suffered heavily from submarine concentrations but there was no doubt that Sims was right. Offence – bringing the enemy to battle – was the best means of defence. Depth-charge usage was one measure of the new offensive: in July 1917 production was still only 140, but by the end of the year it reached 800 and went on mounting. During the year of 1917 depth-charge usage climbed from 100 to 300 a month and in the final six months of 1918, when convoys were well escorted and A/S vessels had learned the knack, 2000 charges per month, on average, were expended. Only a tiny fraction of these was dropped during calculated and hopefully accurate attacks. The point was that a cluster kept a U-boat commander's head down, and if he could not see he could not shoot.

American destroyers looked strange to the Royal Navy, not at all like British ships. On the whole they had better anti-submarine equipment and their companies, although initially inexperienced, were quick to adapt to war. Their commanding officers showed themselves willing to work under British admirals: give or take a few misunderstandings, due to a supposedly common language, they were both helpful and flexible. For example, USS *Davis* thought nothing of replenishing the larder of *E54* (Raikes) at sea off Gibraltar, an occasion when bureaucratic accountancy was notable for its absence – one advantage of operating 3000–4000 miles from home.

USS *Fanning* (Lieutenant Commander Carpender) accompanied by USS *Nicholson*, escorting eight merchantmen westward-bound from Ireland, scored the first wholly US Navy kill on 17 November 1917. 'Ash-cans' forced Amberger in *U-58* to surrender after dropping, perilously out of control, to 85 metres (280 feet). Sims wirelessed Carpender to 'go out and do it again!'

An Atlantic submarine flotilla (Lieutenant Chester W. Nimitz) had been established at New London on 5 March 1912 but the Submarine Force Atlantic Fleet was not inaugurated until 19 June 1916. Before that the three 'D'- and two 'G'-class boats, with the monitor *Ozark* acting as tender, were somewhat informally organised. A school for officers, actually termed informal with plainclothes the order of the day, was established at New London on 1 July 1916.

The US Navy was astern of station in underwater warfare. USS *Skipjack* (later *E-1*, *SS-24*), the first diesel boat, did not commission (under Chester Nimitz) until 14 February 1914, not long after Germany's diesel *U-19* but five years after HMS *D1*. The performance of US submarines was generally patchy: speeds were slow, ventilation was poor, periscopes were inferior (*K1* had the first American-designed instrument in 1916) and realistic exercises were unknown. In short, the 'pig-boats' were unprepared for war.

In October Submarine Division Four, consisting of four 392/521-ton diesel 'K' boats, was despatched from New London to Ponta Delgada in the Azores. Only one boat had the luxury of a proper bridge, and the two-week Atlantic crossing was sheer misery. The task of these submarines was to search for German surface raiders and U-boats believed (correctly) to be operating in mid-Atlantic. The boats were not suited to ocean work and no contact was made with the enemy during the whole year.

On 4 December a more promising group of six 450/548-ton 'L' boats and the tiny 287/342-ton *E1* from Division Five

(Commander R. C. Grady) sailed from Newport for Berehaven in Bantry Bay, Ireland, via the Azores. The 'L' class, however, was specifically designed (as stated by the Act of Congress of 22 August 1912) for coastal defence 'at or near the mouth of the Mississippi River and the United States seaports of the Gulf of Mexico'. These submarines rolled abominably in heavy weather: *L-10* went over to 69 degrees in a storm and the captain, Lieutenant junior grade (jg) James C. Van de Carr recorded 'about one half the men are sick, a few very sick'. *E-1* (ex-*Skipjack*), with Lieutenant (jg) Eric L. Barr commanding, was the smallest submarine to cross the Atlantic under its own power. That she reached Ireland was a minor miracle, performed by an exceptionally experienced crew. During the storm, which nearly rolled *L-10* over, Barr reckoned his helmsman was doing well if he kept within a point and a half either side of the set course.

From Berehaven the 'L' boats, or 'AL' boats as they were now designated to avoid confusion with the British class, did their best, but their best was not good enough and some 'own goals' were narrowly avoided. Van de Carr, in *AL-10* on the surface, sighted what he took for a U-boat of 'an unusual grey' colour on 25 March 1918. It was an American destroyer, but this was realised too late. Diving as quickly as possible the submarine took a pounding before Van de Carr blew main ballast and exchanged signals with the destroyer captain, Jack Simpson, who chanced to have been his room-mate at Annapolis. Lieutenant (jg) Paul F. Foster made a similar mistake in *AL-2*, when a 'U-boat' turned out to be a British trawler. 'Go ahead and shoot anyway, Captain,' a crewman said (or so the story goes), 'and if it isn't a German submarine we'll never tell on you.'

On the same evening *AL-2* was herself attacked by a couple of 'friendly' trawlers; two months later she was twice fired upon by US destroyers and bombed by British aircraft. These incidents underlined the frighteningly inadequate mutual recognition signals in force and the lack of information disseminated – to those with a 'need to know' – about Allied submarine movements.

Yet another case of mistaken identity caused HMS *H5* (Forbes) to be fatally rammed in the Irish Sea by the steamer *Rutherglen* on 6 March 1918. The master believed she was a U-boat, and was not disillusioned after the event because the Admiralty, just as U-boat commanders claimed, did not wish to discourage merchantmen from aggressive tactics. The crew were given the usual monetary reward. Ensign Earle F. W. Childs USN, on board *H5* for experience, was the first USN submariner to be lost on active service.

Lieutenant (jg) G. A. Rood in *AL-1* had had a shot at a U-boat on 22 May – 'a perfect broadside at ideal range' – and was so confident that he told his men to 'save a dinner for Captain Smaltz'. Unfortunately, due to lack of realistic exercising, Rood's engineer did not compensate for the sudden loss of weight forward when two fish were fired. *AL-1* broke surface; the U-boat opened fire with her gun (but missed) and 'Captain Smaltz', warned in time to avoid the torpedoes, failed to arrive for the dinner date.

Andreas Michelsen, who succeeded Bauer as *Führer der U-boote* (FdU) on 5 June 1917 to become *Befehlshaber* (C-in-C) *der U-boote* (BdU), would not have considered the USN contingent as *Frontboote* – that is, fully operational front-line submarines; and he would certainly not have sent them across the Atlantic. For that purpose he deployed the big 1510/1870-ton *U-151* (Heinrich von Nostitz und Jänckendorff) to the American east coast in April 1918.[8] Von Nostitz made his landfall on 21 May. Within sight of the bright lights along the coast he laid a small minefield off Cape Henry, pausing only to allow an armoured cruiser to pass placidly by. Another large cruiser was seen returning from target practice. No anti-submarine precautions were being taken on that occasion, although *U-151* was struck by depth-charges later, going down to 83 metres (270 feet) – 33 metres (108 feet) below test depth. Twelve months of quietude in the western Atlantic had lulled the US Navy into a sense of false security, while the American public reassured itself that all the fighting was 'over there' in and around Europe. The truth was that Michelsen had until now other priorities for new but scarce cruiser submarines down on the South

Atlantic trade routes. Their appearance on the American sea-board came as a shock, especially since Sims had predicted in April 1917 that U-boats were unlikely to forgo successful operations in the English approaches for forays to the United States.

On 21 May 1918 *U-151* penetrated Chesapeake Bay (as the *Deutschland* had two years earlier) and laid mines off Baltimore. Von Nostitz then went on to lay a few more mines in Delaware Bay where defensive nets had been carried away during the severe winter and not replaced. One of these mines destroyed a 6000-ton steamer on 3 June, throwing the shipping organisation into great confusion.

The U-cruiser was equipped with a cable-cutting device. At 12.35 p.m. on 28 May the Commercial Cable Company's line went dead between New York and Canso, Nova Scotia. At about 3.30 p.m. the Central and South American Cable Company's New York–Colón cable became faulty and the connection failed entirely six hours later. Finding, snagging and severing seabed cables was not easy; the navigating quartermaster, in particular, must have been very skilful.

By the time *U-151* returned to Kiel on 20 July 1918, after ninety-four days at sea and with 10,915 nautical miles behind her, von Nostitz had sunk twenty-three ships totalling 61,000 tons while his mines had accounted for another four. The submarine also brought home a quantity of copper from the Norwegian steamer *Vindeggen*, jettisoning iron ballast to take on board this much-needed commodity.

The aristocratic and doubtless politically aware commander took great pains to ensure that survivors from his victims did survive. He sent wireless messages, towed lifeboats and took people on board, but he had none of the pressures under which U-boats operated around the British Isles. He could afford to be charitable while other U-boat captains in dangerous waters could not.

The six boats which visited North American waters destroyed 166,907 tons of shipping there – ninety-one assorted vessels of which forty-five were American and fourteen Canadian. Eleven more ships totalling 30,655 tons, were lost in accidents arising directly from confusion in the threatened shipping lanes. They sank either as the result of collision (while running at night without lights) or went down to mistaken gunfire from 'friendly' US Navy ships. Five of them were minor war vessels; the only major warship sunk was the armoured cruiser USS *San Diego* which hit a mine laid by *U-156*.

However, what the U-boats failed to accomplish against American interests is more significant than their achievements. From 1 May to 11 November 1918, 1142 ships carried 2,079,880 American soldiers to France: only one of these heavily escorted transports, in convoy, was successfully attacked eastward-bound during this critical six-month period although two British transports, returning empty to the United States for more troops, were sunk.[9]

The US Navy and American merchant skippers were just as resistant to local convoying as the Europeans had been, even though convoys were unquestionably a success. And for their instigation Britain was indebted largely to the persuasive Rear-Admiral William Sowden Sims US Navy.

CHAPTER 17

U-Cruisers (1917–18)

The *U-Kreuzer* was conceived to carry the underwater war far afield, primarily across the Atlantic and well outside the traditional hunting grounds where, by 1917, anti-submarine vessels, aircraft and dirigibles were making life difficult. In September 1916, when the U-boat Inspectorate (UI) proposed converting existing and prospective cargo U-boats like *Deutschland* for war, it was not foreseen that comprehensive transatlantic convoy systems would be instituted by the Allies, but Germany clearly intended to broaden the scope of U-boat operations to encompass very distant areas – 'in all the seven seas' according to a memorandum from the naval staff to the Kaiser dated 6 January 1916 – where protection of shipping was bound to be sparse. That commendably far-sighted paper,[1] which detailed all aspects of submarine warfare for prosecuting an economic war of destruction (*Handelskrieg*) against Britain, looked beyond the immediate Continental conflict to a future, final confrontation with Britain.

Some extracts from the memorandum illustrate the strategical and political esteem in which U-boats were now held – a sharp contrast to their estimated worth in 1914. They also show just how ominously far ahead the All Highest was prepared to think when two and a half years into the current war.

1. Our war aim, apart from destroying the English Fleet as the principal means by which Britain controls its Empire, is to reduce its total economy in the quickest possible time, bringing Great Britain to sue for unconditional peace. To achieve this it will be necessary:

    a. To cut off all trade routes to and from the British Isles.

    b. To cripple, in all the seven seas, all ships flying under the

British flag and all ships under neutral flags plying to and from Great Britain.

c. To destroy military and economic resources and, by means of air attack, disrupt the trade and commerce in the British Isles, showing its population quite mercilessly the stark realities of war.

2. The shutting-off of the British Isles from all incoming and out-going passenger and mail supplies in such a way that the British Isles are encircled by blockade and forbidden to neutral shipping: any ship attempting to breach the blockade will be destroyed. This blockade will be enforced in the inner waters, as far as our resources allow, by minelaying from mine-carrying U-boats and in the more distant approaches by U-boat operations. It is antici-pated that defensive operations on the part of our opponents will compel our U-boats frequently to avoid the immediate vicinity of the coast and to move from place to place, and all this will mean that a very extended territory will need to be patrolled. It is not advised that surface ships be used for this blockade on account of danger from English submarines and other warships.

3. The German Bight is the main starting-point for U-boat operations. The coast of Flanders is the natural starting-point for operations against the mouth of the Thames and the English Channel. Most important for the carrying on of the U-boat campaign in the North Atlantic would be bases in the Faeroes and in the Azores and also on the Spanish coast. Bases in these places would reduce consid-erably the lines of approach for U-boats and facilitate greatly the task of blockading the British Isles. One cannot tell at this point in time whether, when peace is declared, the Faeroes and the Azores may be acquired and whether in the next war it will be possible to obtain the use of Spanish ports for our purposes: all this will depend completely on future political alignments. But, for the present, none of these bases can be counted upon at all for the present conflict.

(Paragraphs 4 and 5 concern the Mediterranean and Adriatic reviewed in Chapters 11 and 12.)

6. The use of U-boats and surface cruisers in the blockade of dis-tant countries depends upon the future development of U-boats and on our possessing suitable bases. There is no doubt that the

appearance of German submarines around North American harbours, in the approaches to the Panama Canal, at Cape Verde or in the Indian Ocean would be very effective. However, with the increase in operational distances and the duration of journeys, ships to keep U-boats in supplies will be needed and bases will be absolutely essential for all operations in distant waters. The number of U-boats that would be needed to maintain an economic blockade from such bases and the number of U-boats needed to defend these bases depends solely on strategic considerations and local conditions; they are not to be evaluated here. . . . The use, then, of U-boats in remote parts of the world must remain a question for the future. . . .

7. Number of U-boats: our U-boat fleets must be so numerous that a decisive victory is not only certain but can be achieved quickly. This will mean that our opponent has not time to work out countermeasures, and it will shorten the war. At the same time we must consider neutral intervention against us in the event of England collapsing at our onslaught. Reorganisation of U-boat fleets must take place in the shortest time so that we have an effective weapon to back up our policies. This building-up must be done in, at most, five years. The possible disadvantage in the building of a large number of similar U-boats, with the attendant feature that developing technology may overtake them, is outweighed by the need in which we find ourselves; we have to put up with this. As a corollary, the demands for U-boats, especially large ones, should be restricted to the number required for realising our war aims.

Of the forty-seven large U-cruisers (designated type UA) ordered, custom-built or converted from cargo-carriers in 1916 and 1917, only nine of the roaming raiders (*U-139* and *U-140* at 1930/2483 tons and *U-151* to *U-157* at 1512/1875 tons) were completed and put into service before the Armistice. At one time it was suggested that some of them could be used for fuel replenishment at sea (as relatively big boats were to be tasked ad hoc in the Second World War) or specifically for minelaying – and, as we have seen, *U-151* laid mines in American waters – but their powerful guns won the day for the prime purpose of distant commerce raiding. Bauer, while still

FdU, had proposed employing one or more of the cruisers with W/T intercept and D/F (Radio Direction-Finding) equipment, manned by cipher experts and linguists, for controlling mass attacks against convoys; but wolf-pack tactics, apart from the experiments already mentioned, did not find favour with the High Command during the first great underwater war.

The ex-merchant designs *U-151* to *U-157*, similar to the original *Deutschland (U-155)*, were very slow, although at about 9 knots the range was a prodigious 13,130 nautical miles on the two little 400 hp diesels, or even 25,000 miles at 5.5 knots. Top speeds of 5.3 knots for one hour or so submerged and 12.4 knots on the surface were predicted but not realised. By using an engine and an electric motor on the same shaft each side 11 knots could be achieved, but it was a fuel-greedy and battery-draining method of propulsion. However, these cumbersome submarines could cover 65 miles at 3 knots dived, implying nearly twenty-four hours underwater, with the auxiliary electrical load kept to a minimum – which was not at all bad for the day. They therefore had a reasonable chance of making their escape if detected.

U-155 had six external torpedo tubes in two tiers under the casing, angled out at 15 degrees. The other six boats in the class had two internal bow tubes and carried eighteen torpedoes. Gunnery, though, was the main means of destruction in remote parts of the world where interference from air or surface A/S units was not expected.

The *U-139* class (only two boats operational), 92 metres (302 feet) long overall and a military design from the start, was better in all respects. Four bow and two stern tubes were fitted for the twelve Type G6 torpedoes carried, but the main armament consisted of two 150-mm (5.9-inch) guns with mechanical ammunition supply for 1000 shells and a range-finder on the after part of the bridge. The kiosk command centre in the conning tower was sheathed in protective armour: its walls were 90 mm (2.5 inches) thick, shell-proof against the guns on merchantmen. This was a prudent precaution because the time to dive was a laborious two minutes. The pressure hull was thicker than usual at 25 mm (0.7 inch) for a safe diving depth of 75 metres (246 feet). The superstructure was raised, by an average 2 metres (6.5 feet), to ensure that an enemy shell exploding on it would not rupture the pressure hull. In addition there was some measure of internal compartment separation for what today would be called damage control.

Speed on the surface was a little better than 14 knots on the twin 1750 hp MAN diesels[2] and in *U-140* at 10 knots the range was well over 12,000 nautical miles. Forward hydroplanes were retracted into the casing on the surface to avoid battering by the sea. Top speed submerged was 7.6 knots and dived endurance was 53 miles at 4.5 knots or considerably more at 3 knots.

There were fifty-six men (six officers) in the complement with another twenty (one officer) for prize crews. With such a large number on board for prolonged cruises (plus 'sample' prisoners) great attention was paid to habitability: fresh-water distillers, heated by engine-exhaust gases, were installed.

A *U-139*-type submarine cost 8.7 million marks or £435,000, about £8.7 million in today's terms – 8 per cent of the price of a modern diesel-electric submarine of similar size where a huge proportion of the money goes into weapon systems. In a U-cruiser the principal gun armament accounted for 7.7 per cent of the final bill.

The cruisers fulfilled their task well, roaming southwards across the Equator and far to the west across the Atlantic. Their independent operations so far from home demanded particular skills and the best commanding officers were appointed to them.

When he relinquished command of *U-35*, Lothar von Arnauld de la Perière[3] took *U-139*, defiantly named *Korvetten-kapitän Schweiger* after the man who had sunk the *Lusitania* and who now lay entombed in *U-88*. Under von Arnauld from May 1918, *U-139* sank five smallish ships but then nearly came to grief attacking a convoy off Finisterre on 1 October 1918. Retaliatory gunfire forced the *U-Kreuzer* to dive deep and it was (ineffectually) depth-charged.

Von Arnauld was not a man to be deterred by near misses, so he returned to periscope depth and found himself well placed to torpedo a waterlogged ship which he had earlier shelled. Uncharacteristically he miscalculated the range – the sun had just set – and went far too close before firing. He was practically alongside his victim when the warhead detonated, so the explosion did quite serious damage to the submarine and water flooded into the conning tower. The 'ace of aces' was probably badly shaken – and very likely tired and war-weary anyway – because he allowed his boat to pass slowly under the sinking target which actually settled down on top of the submarine, forcing it down to a perilous depth. Tanks were blown and the victim slid off, but the cruiser's superstructure and periscopes were seriously damaged.

Von Arnauld made light of the affair and the crew were able to make repairs well enough to continue to patrol but in mid-Atlantic they received Admiral Scheer's signal ordering cessation of hostilities. *U-139* returned to Kiel on 14 November to find the Red Flag flying over the base.[4]

Waldemar Kophamel, who commissioned *U-140* on 28 March 1918, had been the other brilliant captain of *U-35* and he had also spent a busy five months in *U-Kreuzer-151* (*Oldenburg* when in merchant guise) during the latter half of 1917. The Kaiser's navy was not apt to let talent go to seed. *U-140*, named *Kapitänleutnant Weddigen*[5] after the first ace, took a toll of 30,612 tons in American waters, bringing Kophamel's total to fifty-four ships amounting to 148,852 tons of which 35 per cent went down to his two U-cruisers.

Kophamel did not have it all his own way in *U-140*. The destroyer USS *Stringham* gave him a bad time off Cape Hatteras and his guns were damaged by depth-charges. Two U-cruisers failed to return: *U-154* was torpedoed by HMS *E35* (D'Oyly Hughes) west of Gibraltar in May 1918 and *U-156* struck a mine in September off Bergen in the northern barrage.

Admiral Sims USN denigrated the U-cruisers, saying that they accomplished little during the war, that they sank very few merchantmen and did not divert anti-submarine craft from the main theatre of operations. They accounted for only 174 ships representing little more than 3 per cent of the overall tonnage destroyed by U-boats throughout the war, but they were operating during a period of decline elsewhere in U-boat successes caused primarily by the convoy system,[6] and for Britain their achievements were serious enough. It was well for the Allies that the corsairs started their raiding late and never attained the numerical strength planned, but they foreshadowed something of what was to come – during the intended final conflict – less than a quarter of a century later.

CHAPTER 18

K for Catastrophe (1917–18)

Naval architects recognised from the start that the bigger a
submarine was the further and faster it could go. The twin
requirements of speed and endurance required a large hull,
and that is why the U-cruisers were twice the size, or more,
of most standard U-boats. But while the Germans were clear
that the only purpose of these big boats was to carry heavy
armament to distant seas, weaponry came a poor second to
propulsion when the Royal Navy embarked on sizeable submarines.

The extraordinary thing about submarine construction over
the years, outside Germany, is that the vehicle has almost
invariably taken precedence over the weapon system. The first
consideration has been speed linked with endurance; next,
propulsion machinery formulated to generate the necessary
power; then a hull designed to accommodate the necessary
machinery and fuel in a shape suited to speed; and, lastly,
weapons chosen to fit the hull. It has hardly been a logical
process. The first consideration should have been the weapon
system appropriate to a particular task, and the second, the
best kind of submarine to carry it. Instead, with Keyes anxious
for submarines to work with the Fleet – for no clearly defined
reason – speed was the dominating factor in design. Disregarding nugatory steps on the way – the steam *Swordfish* completed
in 1916 and the diesel *Nautilus* in 1917 – the calamitous 'K'
class was the result.

On 1 June 1913 Admiral Lord Fisher declared in a letter
to Jellicoe (then Second Sea Lord) that 'The most fatal error
imaginable would be to put steam engines in a submarine.'
Fisher had observed the French kettle-boats and he was right.
Unfortunately he changed his mind within months, persuaded

288

on the one hand (by incorrect intelligence) that new German U-boats were credited with 22 knots and on the other that the Grand Fleet, without submarines in company, was being deprived of a vital arm. Steam was the only way to achieve fleet speed. The 'J' class (completing in 1916) was intended for fleet work with three diesels and three shafts but top speed would be more than 4 knots short of the 24 knots required so, even before the 'J's had undergone sea trials, Vickers forwarded a design for a large submarine with boilers and turbines. In June 1915 the Admiralty placed an order for two submarines of this type with the Barrow firm as lead yard: *K3* and *K4* were commissioned in August 1916 and January 1917 respectively. *K1* came into service from Portsmouth dockyard in May 1917 and *K2*, also from Pompey, in February 1918.

Seventeen 'K' boats were completed during the war and one more, *K26* (a greatly modified version), appeared in 1923. They were probably the most hazardous, and certainly the most notorious, submarines ever built. Eight of them suffered disasters and there were sixteen major accidents together with an uncounted number of lesser mishaps. One historian[1] stated pointedly that they 'were asked for by the Grand Fleet and were not the product of the Submarine Branch', but he was forgetting Keyes and his admission, when losing his job as Commodore Submarines, in early 1915: 'I do not think that *matériel* is much in my line.'

By 1915 British submarines and German U-boats had already proved their effectiveness as lone wolves. There was neither precedent nor reason for thinking that they could work with surface units in battle – at least, not without grave danger of mutual collisions and attacks.

There is scant evidence that the tactical problem of how exactly these new Fleet submarines were to be employed in action was thought through, either by Keyes, who initiated the idea, the Admiralty or the Commander-in-Chief Grand Fleet. Yet despite the lack of purpose and planned tactics, the big, fast 'K' boats were undeniably regarded as prestigious at the beginning of their short service. That they became objects of extreme dislike and that 'K'-boat men were known collectively as the Suicide Club did not detract from the glamour of command. The quality of the officers appointed to 'K' boats was exceptionally high: size more than purpose dictated rank, and 'K'-boat captains were usually full commanders with four other officers and sixty-four ratings. 'K'-boat command was a matter of pride in 1917, but it became a cachet allied to catastrophe before the year was out.

Among the commanders were Kellett who had made a German trawler tow him back to Harwich when the engines of his *S1* had packed up in the North Sea in 1916; Laurence, ex-*E1* and *J1*, the only man to hit two battleships with one salvo; Layton, the escaper from *E13*; Harbottle who had disguised *E21* as a U-boat in a spy-catching operation off Crete; Dobson who, in *C27* towed by a trawler-trap, had despatched *U-23*; and Calvert, reported by his flotilla captain in 1917 as 'one of the best all-round officers I know'. Then there was Bower who wrote professionally under the pen-name 'Klaxon', with brilliant humour that is still not out-dated; and Shove (pronounced to rhyme with stove but often called Push) who, at a time when officers outside their submarines took pains with their appearance, stood out from his contemporaries with 'matted, dishevelled hair' and a 'high-water mark above his collar'. On one occasion on board Shove was heard to remark to his third hand: 'Sub, I must wash. I can smell myself.' When commanding *E29*, he had harboured a small pet rodent called Ratto which spent a good deal of time up one sleeve of his monkey-jacket; the creature had a habit of obeying quite frequent calls of nature without leaving its warm nest, whereupon its owner would shake the droplets out of his sleeve with apparent unconcern. It may have been this practice which defeated the Bishop of Stepney whom Shove, a man of notable intellect matched by an equally notable irreverence for authority, chose to engage in profound theological argument at Harwich one day. 'The more I see of Shove,' a fellow officer was moved to remark, 'the better I like his rat.'

Nobody could say that the 'K' boats had dull commanding

officers or that leadership was lacking – at first. But by June 1918 Calvert was 'suffering the stress of "K"-boat life'[2] with all that implied about command. He was not alone: too many officers and men were formally reported as suffering from neurasthenia (which, synonymous with bad morale, was a popular diagnosis by doctors and captains alike) but very few were transferred out of 'K' boats or given adequate medical examinations. The Coxswain of *K7*, for example, was observed by a visiting officer to have trembling knees while he was sitting at the hydroplane controls, yet no one save the visitor commented.

Comprehensive medical reports about such problems were not compiled until after the war ended. When they did emerge they tended to gloss over the danger signals that must have been apparent. In those days of muscular public-school Christianity and stiff upper lips, no sympathy was wasted on men with 'cold feet' who today would be recognised as a menace to their messmates as well as themselves and be given proper treatment.

Reactions must, in some cases, have been slow and contributed to the dreadful record of this steam-driven submarine class. Also, after their excellent former careers in command of 'C', 'D' and 'E' boats, the captains – like Germany's von Arnauld – were probably worn out by danger, discomfort and sheer fatigue. There was, not surprisingly, some exceptionally heavy drinking in 'K'-boat wardrooms even judged by the lavish standards of the day. Whisky and gin were the antidotes for officers and could easily be afforded at duty-free prices. Less attractive beverages were to be had in ratings' messes where only the standard ration of one-eighth of a pint of rum a day was officially allowed. Boot-polish, heated and strained through bread, provided alcohol of a sort, and magnetic compasses floating in spirit mysteriously tended to run dry in harbour.

The problems that beset the officers and men of 'K' boats were, first, that there was not enough 'proper' submarining work to do: co-operating with the fleet did not appeal. Second, Scapa Flow, where the 'K's initially spent a lot of time with the Grand Fleet, was a dismal place (Layton started a garden ashore to divert the crew) and witnessed some unpleasant social occurrences. Third, the 'K' design was inherently dangerous. Throughout 1917 rumours of operational problems and mechanical failures filtered through the two 'K'-boat flotillas; they were entirely believable in the light of *K13*'s sinking (with the ill-starred Herbert, of *D5* and *Baralong*, in command) on acceptance trials in January.

With a length-to-beam ratio of nearly thirteen-to-one (the ideal is about seven-to-one for underwater control) 'K' boats were bound to be difficult to manoeuvre when they dived. There is the well-known story of one Captain telephoning his First Lieutenant in the distant fore-ends: 'I say, No. 1, my end is diving – what the hell is your end doing?' It illustrates the point. Once a bow-down or bow-up angle developed beyond a gentle few degrees, it tended to increase because the broad flat casing itself started to act like a gigantic hydroplane. Then it was difficult if not impossible to level the boat without recourse to flooding and blowing tanks or, in desperation (but against instructions at the time), using full power astern on the motors.

To make matters worse the hydroplanes themselves had a habit of jamming when set to hard-a-dive when things looked like getting out of control. A prudent captain or officer-of-the-watch learned to avoid full angles and so did the hydroplane operators – the Coxswain of *K7* had obviously learned the hard way – but they often did not realise the dangers quickly enough, and bounces on the seabed were the inevitable result. With a length of 100 metres (330 feet), a design depth of 60 metres (200 feet) – but a normal operating depth of 30 metres (100 feet) to avoid damage to inadequate hull-fittings – the risk in deep water was clear enough: a steep angle could take the bow to a dangerous depth in seconds while the control-room depth-gauge amidships still indicated plenty of feet to spare.

The general opinion was that 45 metres (150 feet) was just permissible if necessary, but 'K' boats frequently dipped inadvertently below that. In shallow water most of them hit the seabed at one time or another. It was claimed, not altogether jokingly, that visitors to the Firth of Forth (when the flotillas were at Rosyth) would, as an almost daily occurrence, see parts of a 'K' boat projecting above the water: sometimes there would simply be two propellers idly whizzing around and sometimes a large sinister bow looking like a basking whale. The twenty-one-year-old Prince George was not much impressed with the efficiency of the submarine service when the Arch-Thief Leir performed this trick in *K3* with the future monarch on board. Nor were the admirals amused when Leir, unabashed, lowered his funnels in salute while passing Beatty's flagship on rejoining the Grand Fleet at Scapa Flow. 'K'-boat captains tried to make light of their troubles but jocularity was more evident than humour.

The danger from 'too many damned holes' in the pressure hull was constant, as a contemporary submariner complained. The largest, for the four air-intakes in the boiler-room, were 1 metre (3 feet) in diameter. It was these that were left open (though verbally reported shut) when *K13* dived in the Gairloch on 29 January 1917. The boat sank with the loss of 25 lives.

The funnels were lowered electrically, while a telemotor-operated (hydraulic)[3] top-door hull-valve and a secondary lower door sealed off the uptake. The time specified to shut down the boiler-room and secure it was nominally thirty seconds but, with plenty of time available while the clumsy submarine struggled to submerge, it would have been a very unwise engineer officer who endeavoured to hasten the drill for the sake of smartness. Meanwhile, it was not unknown for the captain to press the hooter (klaxon) and then wander around, perhaps climbing down from the bridge on to the casing, to reassure himself that everything was shipshape before going below and shutting the conning-tower upper lid. There was not the slightest reason to hurry.

The diving arrangements were immensely complicated, with twenty external and eight internal main ballast tanks. With 40 vent-valves and several Kingstons (bottom flood-valves) involved, even assuming that the new centralised telemotor controls were functioning correctly, a very careful drill was needed to flood the tanks evenly and avoid a list or a longitudinal angle. The fastest diving time ever recorded from full buoyancy (by *K8*) was three minutes twenty-five seconds, but four minutes was considered good if sea and swell were favourably on the beam and five minutes was more usual. An enemy U-boat with a small silhouette on the surface could travel a mile in that time so it is difficult to understand how a 'K' boat was expected to sight a suitable target and submerge in time to waylay it before being seen itself – even if funnel smoke had not already given it away. Most U-boats (except for the U-cruisers) could get down in between thirty and forty-five seconds, while the UBs and UCs were even quicker to vanish from the surface.

Nor could the 'K' boats lie in wait for long periods submerged, whatever their expected targets might be: at a maximum of 8 knots their batteries were drained after an hour and at 4 knots their endurance was limited to little more than seven hours. It was difficult to know how they could contribute sensibly to a fleet action when heavy units, to say nothing of destroyers, were moving around the sea in all directions at 20 or 25 knots.

Alternatively, if they were employed on independent patrols, they would have to restrict their periods on the surface to hours of darkness. Even though their endurance was extended at extremely low speed, in practice, other than in flat calm conditions, they had to make close to 4 knots to avoid either broaching or dipping the periscope.

During a major Grand Fleet wartime exercise their diving difficulties were tacitly recognised. The 'K' boats attached to their respective sides were not allowed to dive at all: they had to stay on the surface and fly a red flag while being deemed invisible. As it happened, the giants all around them were so occupied in looking at each other through binoculars that *K8* came within a mile of the opposing fleet without being seen by anybody. But that was worrying in itself because the submariners were led to believe that, in a real mêlée, the big ships and their escorts would know who they were and where they were, and neither run them down nor shoot at them. Happily, a realistic situation never arose because it became obvious that the German High Sea Fleet would not seek another major engagement after Jutland.

'K' boats were therefore almost wholly employed, or rather wasted, on anti-submarine patrols. Those, too, carried a risk from friendly forces: Kellett in *K7*, watching and waiting in the Fair Isle Channel, was chased by the destroyers *Observer* and *Rocket* who were convinced they had a U-boat in view until, after dodging depth-charges, Kellett was able to surface and signal that he was on their side. This incident occurred during the massive 'Operation BB' in June 1917. Naval Intelligence had predicted that a succession of U-boats would pass outward-bound through the North Sea between 15 and 24 June, and Admiral Beatty accordingly flooded the area around the northern part of Scotland with four flotilla leaders, forty-nine destroyers and seventeen submarines. The surface ships were deployed in such a way as 'to force enemy submarines to dive through certain areas occupied by destroyers so they would be on the surface while passing through adjacent areas occupied by our submarines'.

This optimistic large-scale effort reaped absolutely no results – as usual the Staff simply did not understand the ways of submariners, friendly or otherwise – although the force claimed to have sighted U-boats on thirty-seven occasions and struck eleven. The attack on *K7* was one of the few that nearly succeeded. The passing U-boats, wholly undeterred, picked off eight merchantmen and an armed trawler.

Beatty and his Staff doubtless drew some comfort from Kellett trying to attack *U-95*. When *K7* was left alone and had submerged following the fracas with *Observer* and *Rocket*, Kellett was fortuitously presented with a submarine target. He fired six torpedoes altogether; one hit, but failed to explode.

It would have been sensible for some intrepid Grand Fleet staff officers to go to sea in a 'K' boat on patrol. They would then have appreciated for themselves the facts of life in these monstrosities.

Few diversions relieved the tedium, whether at Scapa

Flow or at Rosyth where the 'K'-boat flotillas were lodged from December 1917. Lady Beatty, the Commander-in-Chief's wife, concentrated her formidable abilities in ensuring that baths, recreation facilities and a reading room ashore were provided for submarine officers and men who still lived in the supposedly self-sufficient boats, but many officers and men continued to seek solace in the bottle – legitimately in the wardrooms (where gin was 2d a glass and vintage port only 10d) and illicitly in the messes when the delights of Scottish hostelries palled.

Morale remained low at Rosyth, and the better-educated sailors began to question methods of operating with the fleet. George Kimbell in *K17*, a qualified signalman, felt uneasy about formation orders. These laid down that the Twelfth and Thirteenth Submarine Flotillas, consisting of four and five 'K' boats respectively and each led by a light-cruiser leader, were to follow astern of the battle-cruisers when leaving harbour in daylight but were to precede them in line ahead during hours of darkness. Kimbell's unease was well founded.

No account was taken of the difficulties in station-keeping and maintaining a good lookout from the bridge of a 'K' boat at sea and it seems that the submarines were wrongly credited with the same capabilities in this respect as a destroyer. In theory the formation on leaving harbour was sound since the submarines were intended to surprise an enemy which evaded the guns of the surface fleet. In the open sea the idea was for the 'K'-boat flotillas to submerge and lie in wait, generally in pairs, spread across the enemy's line of advance or on one bow of approaching German heavy units, ready to fire torpedoes while the British battle fleet engaged with guns on the other bow.

High-speed fleet manoeuvres in formation can be difficult at the best of times for novices. Surface ships graduated from basic manoeuvres by day to complex evolutions at night, but no such exercises were planned for the inexperienced and ill-equipped submarines, now part of the well-rehearsed fleet. It was just the sort of omission that, in retrospect, might be expected in view of the widespread ignorance about submarine capabilities and the unwillingness of submarine officers to make plain their limitations.

On 31 January 1918, the ships in the Firth of Forth were ordered to sail at dusk and rendezvous in the North Sea with the remainder of the Grand Fleet from Scapa Flow for a full-scale exercise designated 'ECI'. Vice-Admiral Sir Hugh Evan Thomas, wearing his flag in the battle-cruiser *Courageous*, devised the departure plan and placed himself at the head of the line leaving Rosyth. *Courageous* was followed at 5-mile intervals by the leading ships of battle-squadrons and submarine flotilla leaders. The light cruiser *Ithuriel*, Commander (S) XIII – Leir, no less – led five 'K' boats; *Fearless*, Captain (S) XII (Little), led four. The two flotillas were sandwiched, in line ahead, between *Courageous* in the van and the Second Battle-Cruiser Squadron's flagship *Australia*, and between the Second Squadron's rear ship and the Fifth Battle-Squadron bringing up the rear. With escorting destroyers, the long procession included more than forty vessels strung out over some 20 miles and all proceeding at the ordered speed of 16 knots. *Courageous* was to increase speed to 20 knots (later amended to 21 knots) on reaching a position north of May Island (which marked the mouth of the estuary) and alter course eastwards for the rendezvous. The ships and submarines in her wake were to conform.

A U-boat was reported off May Island; the night was pitch black with patches of mist; the Fleet was darkened with only dimmed blue stern-lights showing; wireless silence was enforced; the swept channel was narrow; the 'K' boats were by no means expert at station-keeping; and a group of armed trawlers engaged in minesweeping from their base on May Island were not informed of the Fleet's movements. It was inevitable that something would go wrong.

Courageous increased speed and altered course, as planned, on passing May Island. Although *Ithuriel* had lost sight of the flagship in the mist, she conformed by dead reckoning at 7.30 p.m. but, unknown to Leir, only three of his flotilla followed. The captain of *K14* had put the wheel hard over a few minutes earlier to avoid two of the unwarned mine-sweepers and, typically, the helm jammed for six minutes. From then on, with submarines altering course in all directions to avoid each other and to avoid the battle-cruisers and destroyers coming up fast astern, confusion reigned. *K22* sliced into *K14* at 19 knots and *Inflexible* (last in the Second Squadron line) rammed *K22* in turn.

Although severely damaged, both submarines eventually returned safely to Rosyth. Others were not so lucky. Leir in *Ithuriel*, by now well to the east of May Island, received garbled and inaccurate news of the collisions in two successive coded signals (which took time to translate into plain language) when wireless silence was eventually broken. Impulsively, unwisely, but understandably, he decided to turn back with his three remaining 'K' boats and do what he could to help. Reversing course to the west back towards May Island, with *K11*, *K17* and *K12* following in line astern, turned out to be a terrible mistake. Leir ordered navigation lights to be switched on to minimise the risks of collision but he assumed that the huge company of ships following an easterly course would all be following identical tracks. Alas, he was wrong. Finding *Australia* dead ahead on an opposite course, he jinked the flotilla to port, by ill chance right across the path of Little in *Fearless* with his four 'K' boats which were offset a mile to the south of the main fleet.

At 8.32 p.m. *Fearless* collided with *K17* which sank eight minutes later. *K4*, directly astern of *Fearless*, veered away to port and stopped. *K6*, third in line, also went hard-a-port, stopped engines and went full astern but, with way still on, hit *K4* a little forward of amidships. It was a mortal blow. Layton, in *K6* with the bows buried deep in her sister submarine, had difficulty in pulling clear as *K4* settled in the icy water, threatening to take *K6* with her. *K7*, last in line, bumped hideously over the sinking wreck as Gravener drew slowly up, without any clear picture of what had happened, to pick up such survivors as there were: he rescued eight and, while doing so, was nearly run down by the escorting destroyers which passed on, still at high speed, straight over the spot where *K17* had gone down, washing away or cutting down the men who had swum clear. Apart from the handful rescued by K7, there were no survivors from the two submarines sunk at what came to be called the Battle of May Island: 103 officers and men lost their lives.

First Lord of the Admiralty Sir Eric Geddes (notorious after the war as wielder of the 'Geddes Axe') blamed the submariners: 'I cannot but think, as a layman, that this chapter of accidents looks as if there was something wrong with the standard of efficiency of the officers.' Those same officers – or rather, those who survived – took a different view, but the underlying fault lay with the submarine service for not protesting at the 'K'-boat design and the conditions under which the submarines were operated with the Grand Fleet. It was the old problem, stemming from the time that submariners retreated into a private navy in the face of disdain from their brethren on the surface: communications up the chain of command to the admirals was lacking. One submarine officer summed up the cause of the disaster: 'The "K" boats came to grief because they had the speed of a destroyer but the turning circle of a battle-cruiser and the bridge control abilities of a picket boat.'[4]

The 'K'-boat project was encouraged in the light of false intelligence about forthcoming 22-knot ocean-going U-boats, but Germany had no such fast submarine cruisers. Doubtless the U-cruisers would have liked high speed but they preferred reliability. Nor did the U-boat arm ever contemplate submarines which could keep up with the High Sea Fleet: the German navy was nothing if not logical.

Signalman George Kimbell summed up the 'K'-boat concept for the average submariner. On seeing his new chimneyfied home, K17, in the Gairloch with smoke coming out of two stubby funnels, he was moved to remark, 'That's never a submarine, surely?'

CHAPTER 19

The End (1918)

The Great Underwater War was won by the German U-boats, very nearly. That there was no outright victory at any point was the fault of weak decisions and half-measures adopted by German politicians and statesmen.

The U-boat men themselves were not to blame for Germany's eventual collapse. Indeed, although the Kaiser was beaten militarily, the spreading influence of the Russian Revolution of 1917 was a significant factor in the collapse being so complete and so sudden in ships of the High Sea Fleet. It was ironic that the German General Staff itself had provided the 'sealed train' that took Lenin back to Petrograd after the Revolution in the hope that he would sow disaffection among the Russian soldiery; the seeds were scattered beyond Russian borders. Communism left U-boat crews largely unaffected, however, and they were still prepared to fight on at the end. Fresh tools were being prepared for them to continue the battle at least until 1921: 226 boats were building in November 1918 and a further 212 were projected.[1]

Following the appointment of Admiral Scheer as Head of the Naval Staff in August 1918 the Naval War Staff (SKL) was moved, to be integrated with the Grand Strategic Headquarters at Spa on 10 September. The move came too late, but for the first time the navy could have expected to harmonise with the Supreme Army Command (OHL) and with the wishes (perhaps manipulated) of the Kaiser himself.

At HQ the so-called Scheer Programme for a massive U-boat building effort could be given top priority. Here, the OHL could be persuaded to part with workers in their thousands, and from here the whole might of German industry could be subordinated (Scheer's word) to the task.[2]

The End (1918)

On 12 September, two months before the Armistice, Scheer demanded 333 boats for the year 1919 and 36 boats monthly thereafter; eleven building yards were assigned.

Although these ambitious plans were never realised, Scheer reasoned that:

In the light of the present military situation the U-boat arm is the only offensive weapon open to us. If we go over to the defensive we shall not achieve a worthwhile peace settlement. It is therefore absolutely necessary, and there must be no delay, that we develop our sole offensive means with all the capacity that Germany possesses, so that the goal of achieving a worthwhile peace is achieved.

British submariners, too, were prepared to go on with the struggle although the most experienced commanding officers were war-weary and the 'K' boats were not war-worthy. The Royal Navy should have kept to medium-sized, simple and reliable designs for independent patrols, and Keyes's idea that submarines should be built to work with the fleet cost The Trade dear.

Important German targets – capital ships and transports – were never plentiful and it was clear that few would be at sea from the beginning of 1917. It is strange that all submarine efforts, including minelaying, were not more wholeheartedly devoted to destroying the U-boats which by then were so obviously the only significant strategic menace. As it was, sixteen relatively modest British submarines, four tiny antiquated 'C' boats among them, were responsible for the loss of seventeen U-boats; all but five of those sinkings took place during the last two years of the war. From late 1917 ten 420/500-ton 'R' boats were completed specifically for anti-submarine work, with an unprecedented underwater speed of 15 knots, six bow tubes and advanced hydrophones to detect submerged as well as surfaced U-boats. Developed under Commodore Hall's regime, they were a technological marvel for the period but they did not arrive in time. Only one got into position for an attack, which was frustrated by torpedo failure.

301

The sinkings by submarines were creditable, given the extremely difficult target presented by a surfaced U-boat (none were attacked submerged), but more dedicated anti-submarine deployment, making full use of the usually reliable intelligence available, should have created many more attack opportunities than there actually were against the prime foe. German U-boats torpedoed five British submarines in chance encounters; they also scored two 'own goals'.

British wartime developments like the 'L' class were, on the whole, sound if pedestrian – the 'K' and 'J' designs excepted – and the potentially valuable 'R' boats were far ahead of their contemporaries. However, there was one radical departure from tradition. Since torpedoes were unreliable and their tracks apt to be seen and avoided by alert ships, it was thought that a really big gun might perform better, bearing in mind The Trade's continuing hopes of engaging substantial surface targets and its increasing interest in shore bombardment stemming originally from operations in the Marmara. On 5 August 1915 a plan for 'a submarine Dreadnought' with a 300-mm (12-inch) gun mounted forward of the conning tower in addition to normal torpedo armament was put by Jacky Fisher (then chairman of the Board of Invention and Research) to Arthur Balfour (First Lord of the Admiralty). The eventual result was three submarines of the 'M' class – M for monitor or, as sailors preferred, for 'mutton boat' because of the leg-of-mutton appearance it presented.[3] HMS *M1* was completed in August 1918 with the renowned Max Horton in command.

The snag with the 300-mm (12-inch) gun (a sawn-off version of the main armament in 'King Edward VII' battleships) was that, although it could be fired from semi-submerged, the submarine had to surface fully to reload. Nevertheless, one hit from a 390-kilo (863-pound) shell would probably have been enough for all but a heavily armoured target; Max would doubtless have fired, with the benefit of surprise, from point-blank range. Unfortunately there were no worthwhile targets at all by 1918, and shore bombardment was forbidden by the Admiralty lest the Germans follow suit, either with rapidly improvised big-gun fittings or with the standard 150-mm (5.9-inch) weapons carried on U-cruisers.

German decision-makers stand accused by their own people of vacillation, lack of unity and lack of a strong cohesive U-boat policy,[4] but it cannot be claimed that the Royal Navy had a clearcut, single-minded aim for its submarine service either, at every stage of the war. Nevertheless, British submariners did, by their own exertions, achieve some remarkable results which had a considerable strategic impact in specific areas, notably the Sea of Marmara and the Baltic. Alas, the same cannot be said of the French and Italian allies. Nor did the American submariners (accent on the 'i')[5] contribute anything worthwhile because their pre-war purpose was singularly ill-defined, and when they eventually joined the fray they were simply not ready in terms either of material or training.

An underwater arm could neither be constructed nor operated effectively without an unequivocal objective (which might change with circumstances) and an unambiguous mandate, but this lesson was not learned until the Second World War except by a scattering of men, notably one Karl Dönitz. However, there was another factor which neither Dönitz nor anybody else appears to have acknowledged. This was that only a small proportion of submarine captains could be expected to make full use of the tools they were given. From August 1914 to November 1918 4 per cent of U-boats destroyed 30 per cent of all shipping that went down to U-boat attacks; alternatively, twenty-two of about 400 German commanders accounted for over 60 per cent of Allied merchant vessels lost. On the British side, some 150 submarines saw service during the war under a great many more commanding officers, but just nine captains were responsible for the fourteen enemy surface warships actually sunk (Nasmith four, Horton three) and fifteen captains destroyed seventeen U-boats (Raikes two and, in command of two different boats, Phillips two). Forty-six British captains sank, captured or damaged 346 assorted enemy vessels of which 212 were small craft but of that grand total eight captains (with Nasmith far out in front) claimed 281.

These bald statistics cannot be taken entirely at face value: opportunity was a key to success. Nevertheless, some captains seized opportunities – or created them by vigorous patrolling – much more readily than others, and whether for geographical reasons or because of 'easy' targets or sheer skill, a few achieved the most. Since exceptional qualities were required of a first-class commanding officer on both sides it is not surprising that 'aces' were so rare.

One British commanding officer was called upon to exercise the particular qualities of leadership and determination in an extraordinary way, but the considerations which led to the heroic action by Sandford and the crew of HMS C3 in April 1918 must first be explained.

At a time when U-boats were mounting what proved to be their final offensive, often ranging into distant waters by circuitous routes in the face of stronger and stronger A/S forces in the air, on the sea and under it, Keyes was appointed as a Rear-Admiral to the Dover Command. He relieved Bacon on 1 January 1918 and immediately started to plan a characteristically daring operation. The intention was to deny the Germans 'for an indefinite period' their advanced naval base at the inland port of Bruges, reached by a $6^1/_2$-mile canal, and their 'harbour of refuge' at Ostend. The 'forty or fifty submarines that would probably be resting or refitting at these two places' would thereby be immobilised.[6] These ends would be achieved by sinking simultaneously, by night, blockships at the seaward end of the Bruges–Zeebrugge canal and between two piers which flanked the entrance channel to the port of Ostend.

Something on these lines could have been done much earlier in the war, but apparently few men (and no generals) actively sought an answer to President Wilson's despair, voiced in 1917, at 'hunting hornets all over the farm' when the hunter knew where the nest was. It is that point which makes the affair historically important. The Royal Navy had never, throughout its long history, managed to sink a blockship in exactly the right place in the face of opposition, but Keyes was not deterred and as usual his enthusiasm converted doubters.

To anticipate subsequent events the twice-attempted Ostend venture failed: navigational problems, mechanical defects, dense fog and intense fire from coastal batteries prevented the ships concerned from reaching their objective. The Zeebrugge raid, though, was another matter, and a submarine played a crucial part in this.

Admiral Hall, Director of Naval Intelligence (and concerned with much other intelligence, counter-intelligence, and 'disinformation' emanating from Room 40 OB) persuaded Keyes that, contrary to popular belief, a steady stream of U-boats was still passing the Straits of Dover despite the 'Dover Barrage' of nets, mines and A/S units. Hall's assertion was confirmed by a scrap of paper discovered in *UC-44* (Tebbenjohanns) which had been blown up and sunk by one of her own mines off Waterford. Tebbenjohanns was a cunning man: *UC-44* had escaped once, when depth-charged, by discharging oil and ejecting chairs from the stern torpedo tube to feign death. But on 4 August 1917 he succumbed to something like a practical joke. The Royal Navy had let it be known that a former minefield had been swept when in truth one patch of mines had deliberately not been cleared away in the certain knowledge that another U-boat would come along to replenish the field. Tebbenjohanns fell for it, and when he was picked out of the water he was a very angry man, complaining bitterly about British carelessness in not clearing the area properly.

Due to this grim little jest, Keyes was able to read *UC-44*'s instructions, forwarded by Hall, for avoiding the Dover net defences:

It is best to pass on the surface. If forced to dive, go down to 40 metres. . . . As far as possible pass through the area Hoofden-Cherbourg without being observed and without stopping. On the other hand, the boats which in exceptional cases pass round Scotland [a much longer passage] are to let themselves be seen as freely as possible in order to mislead the English.

The inference was obvious; it also begged the question of whether the costly northern barrage (see Chapter 5) was a wasted effort. The English Channel was unquestionably the preferred route to the Western Approaches; and Bruges, via Zeebrugge, was 300 miles closer to Dover than German home ports in the Helgoland Bight. The canal from Bruges thus had to be blocked at Zeebrugge.

Zeebrugge was protected against the sea by a vast crescent-shaped concrete and granite mole; it was guarded against enemy ships by heavy guns which could keep a hostile vessel under continuous fire from the moment it was sighted until it reached the entrance to the Bruges canal more than a mile inside the artificial harbour mouth. Blockships would have to pass extremely close to the mole to reach the canal. The guns there would first have to be immobilised by a shipborne assault force of bluejackets and marines and it was vital that the Germans should not be able to reinforce the garrison until the British force had re-embarked.

The mole was connected to the shore by a steel viaduct 275 metres (300 yards) long and 12 metres (40 feet) wide, carrying a double railway line. The tided raced through its piers. If the viaduct could be destroyed the mole would become an unreinforceable island. Lieutenant Commander Francis H. Sandford DSO, a torpedo specialist serving on Keyes's staff (with a 'Pension for Wounds') hit on an idea for blowing a gap in the viaduct. An old submarine with a low silhouette would stand a fair chance of approaching the viaduct unobserved until the last moment. Its slim shape would be perfect for penetrating the piers, and if it came under fire most of its vitals would be underwater. Keyes immediately agreed and selected, without deliberate irony, Sandford's younger brother Dick, then twenty-seven years old, to do the job with his expendable boat *C3*.

Lieutenant Richard Douglas Sandford, known as 'Uncle Baldy' for his mock-old manner and thinning hair, seemed undaunted by the hazardous one-way prospect. The operation was set for 23 April: Keyes's wife Eva reminded him that it was St George's Day and begged her husband to use 'St George for England' as his battle cry. Keyes duly transmitted it by semaphore to the armada, led by himself in HMS *Vindictive* with two other assault ships, *Iris* and *Daffodil*, followed by five converted cruisers for use as blockships. In the rear came *C3*, packed with 5 tons of time-fused TNT in the bows, towed by a destroyer. It is doubtful whether her captain received the inspiring message. None of the five men with him was a signalman. Sandford's crew consisted of First Lieutenant John Howell-Price DSC, RNR, Petty Officer Harner, Leading Seaman Cleaver, ERA Roxburgh and Stoker 1st Class Bindall.

Two small motor dinghies hung from the submarine's tiny conning tower, one on either side, for eventual escape. A gyroscopic control was installed to enable the boat to steer itself, when on course for the viaduct, so that the crew could abandon ship before collision.

Incredibly, everything went according to plan. Under heavy fire, HMS C3 reached a position from where the automatic steering gear could be engaged, but Sandford had no intention of trusting to a 'gadget'. Petty Officer Harner continued to steer by the bridge wheel. Stoker Bindall described the next few minutes graphically:

With her engine running smoothly the submarine glided into the shoal waters of Zeebrugge at midnight, the whole crew of six being on deck. The mole, looming up black in the darkness, and the viaduct joining it to the shore were clearly seen.

It was a silent and nervy business. She was going at full tilt when we hit the viaduct. It was a good jolt, but you can stand a lot when you hang on tight. We ran into the middle of the viaduct and stuck there as intended. I do not think anybody said a word except, 'We're here all right.'

It was only at this point, with the boat's bows jammed firmly in the ironwork, that Sandford lit the fuses. There were just two minutes to get clear. One skiff had been smashed by gunfire but the crew shoved off in the other although the propeller of that had unluckily been wrecked by fouling the submarine's exhaust pipe. They had to row with only a couple of oars under the glare of searchlights and a hail of machine-gun fire. German soldiers on the viaduct could be heard laughing, evidently thinking that C3 had lost her way and would be captured intact. Their merriment was short-lived.

Sandford and two of his men were severely wounded and the little dinghy was perforated, but the other three men succeeded in pulling about 180 metres (200 yards) away before C3 blew up with a tremendous explosion, hurling 30 metres (100 feet) of the viaduct and a crowd of jeering Germans into the air. The searchlights were immediately extinguished and the firing ceased. Debris showered the sinking dinghy. But the crew, to their amazement, were quickly picked up by none other than Dick's elder brother who had brought a picket boat 80 miles from Dover in the hope of effecting a rescue. After all, it had been his idea in the first place.

The submarine's diversion was invaluable and the mole could not be reinforced. British losses among the ships and landing parties on the mole were nevertheless high: total casualties in killed, wounded and missing amounted to 635 when Keyes withdrew after satisfying himself that no more men could be re-embarked. But the canal was sealed by the cruisers *Iphigenia* and *Intrepid* with their bottoms blown out. Forty or more German submarines and destroyers were imprisoned at Bruges, or so the British Admiralty believed. But the following day the small *UB-16* worked her way past the blockships, and within three weeks it was business as usual. In principle the scheme was brilliant, but the suspicion arises that again Keyes did not apply himself to detailed staff work. The blockage could and should have been effective, and yet the German official history simply remarked that 'the conduct of the war suffered only minor and temporary restrictions'.

The Victoria Cross for Sandford's gallantry was gazetted three months later, on 23 July 1918, together with the DSO for Howell-Price and the Conspicuous Gallantry Medal for the rest. 'Well done, Uncle Baldy' telegraphed a friend, glad to know that Sandford was recovering from his wounds. There should have been a happy ending to the gallant episode, but

Dick died the following year from typhoid fever. It was a sad way to go after braving the dangers of St George's Day on a strange job for a submarine.

Surface fleet strategy

During the course of the war the big ships of the German High Sea Fleet and the British Grand Fleet with their great guns provided a show of power which stabilised – or perhaps stultified is a better word – traditional maritime strategy, although the Royal Navy maintained *surface* command of the seas. But the only significant action in which they were engaged – the Battle of Jutland (or the Battle of the Skagerrak in German parlance) – was inconclusive.

Jutland should have resulted in a victory for the Royal Navy, bearing in mind the marked British preponderance in ships (151 to 99) and generally superior gunpower. It must surely have been clear at the time that if the day was won the way would be cleared for aggressive action without undue risk against U-boat bases. At least some of the vast resources devoted to the fleet could be rechannelled to support the army, and entry for a seaborne force into the Baltic would be a practicable proposition. The prizes therefore gleamed, yet the Grand Fleet declined to steer for glory. It was the ubiquitous threat of mines and torpedoes (the latter carried by destroyers as well as submarines) that effectively deterred the Commander-in-Chief who, on 14 October 1914, had written to the Admiralty, 'it is quite within the bounds of possibility that half of our battle fleet might be disabled by underwater attack before the guns opened fire at all. . . .' In the event, Admiral Scheer's escape by night across the rear of the main British fleet had nothing to do with underwater weaponry. However, earlier, at the Battle of the Dogger Bank on 24 January 1915 – the first engagement between 'dreadnoughts' – Beatty's conviction that German submarines were present had made him alter the course of his battle-cruisers at a crucial moment (10.45 a.m.), putting them hopelessly astern of the fleeing Germans. In reality the nearest U-boat was 60 miles away. When Beatty 'personally observed the wash of a periscope two points on the starboard bow' of the flagship HMS *Lion* (heavily hit by gunfire) he was imagining things, but the statement in his despatch illustrates his state of mind.

In this way, therefore, submarines – which could covertly lay mines as well as fire torpedoes – exercised a disproportionate influence not only on fleet tactics but on maritime strategy generally – even when, as at Jutland, they played no active part. Their mere suspected presence (together with possible minefields) was enough – another factor of naval warfare that came to be forgotten.

It was admitted by Scheer that the diversion of dock-yard and shipyard labour to High Sea Fleet repairs after the Skagerrak-Jutland battle seriously impeded U-boat con-struction and put the programme in arrears from the autumn of 1916 – one fortuitous result that Jellicoe and Beatty could have set down on the credit side of their account book.

Jutland offered conclusive proof, if further proof was needed, that Jacky Fisher, Percy Scott and the handful of other underwater-minded prophets at the beginning of the century had been right. Fisher, the creator of 'dreadnought' battleships, foresaw the limitations that would be forced on surface fleets and that the submarine would revolutionise naval warfare.

Fisher – a lone voice in 1913 – had also been right in saying that trade would be the target of England's enemy. Churchill was wrong to assert, in reply, that submarines would not be used to sink merchant vessels, that this would never be done by a civilised power, that such outrages could be compared with the spreading of pestilence and the assassination of individuals.[7] Equally, Churchill's stout denial of the post-war belief that unrestricted U-boat warfare nearly succeeded was specious: to say that 'the seafaring resources of Great Britain were in fact and in the circumstances always superior to the U-boat attack' and that the 'attack was inherently of a char-acter so gradual that their superior resources could certainly obtain their full development'[8] was misleading. It was the entry of the United States into the war, convoys and, not least, the individual efforts of Admiral Sims, that enabled Britannia to continue ruling the waves – more or less – in 1918.

But were the U-boat commanders pestilential assassins? Was submarine warfare, as practised by Germany, unadulterated devilry?[9] Were the Germans somehow different from the British in their conduct of the underwater war? The German task was different. Once U-boats had proved their capabilities, the Kaiser's aim (albeit more than once deflected by German–American political considerations) was to starve England into submission. Any ship that was furthering Britain's ability to survive and fight had to be destroyed. Being cautious and selective in the choice of targets did not meet the objective, nor was it practicable, in the face of armed merchant vessels, Q-ships and escorted convoys, to sink ships in such a way that the crews would have a reasonable chance of escape. Moreover, it was often extremely difficult, amid the fog of war and through clouded periscopes, to distinguish between legitimate targets and purportedly innocent passers-by.

However, bitterness among the German submariners was evident: they counted their work as retribution for the 'starvation blockade' of the Fatherland and records exist which speak of gratuitous cruelty. It is alleged, for example, that after sinking the British MV *Torrington* on 8 April 1917, Kapitänleutnant[10] Wilhelm Werner deliberately drowned the crew. According to the Master's testimony, given long afterwards at Bow Street police court on 31 August 1921, the men from one lifeboat were taken on board the U-boat and he himself was sent below. The remainder – twenty of them – were lined up on the slatted deck and deprived of their lifebelts. Werner then gave the order to dive. It was further alleged that the crew of the MV *Toro* suffered the same fate four days later, 200 miles to seaward of Ushant.

The mysterious thing about the *Torrington* incident (and perhaps that of the *Toro* as well) was that one lifeboat was let go although it was never seen again. If that is so, Werner was not trying very hard to follow a policy later recommended by Count Luxburg, German chargé d'affaires at Buenos Aires: in May 1917 the Count advised that two small Argentinian steamers, *Oran* and *Gauza*, then nearing Bordeaux, should either be spared or else sunk without a trace – *spurlos versunkt*. In any event, although sinking neutrals without a trace could conceivably have been the order given to U-boat commanders – tacitly, no doubt, for no such directive has been discovered – there was scarcely any need to observe the dictum in the case of vessels like the *Torrington* belonging to a combatant. In other words, it is impossible to find an excuse for Werner's actions if the testimony against him was true.

Kapitänleutnant Helmut Patzig, on the other hand, had good reason to eliminate all evidence when his *U-86* sank the hospital ship *Llandovery Castle* 116 miles west of the Fastnet on the night of 27 June 1918. The 11,423-ton ship was en route to Halifax, and Patzig knew her identity because he questioned the Master, found in one of the lifeboats, about eight American airmen who were supposed (from intelligence) to be on board. The accusation was denied. Thereupon, according to collated accounts, Patzig rammed some of the lifeboats and opened fire on survivors. Twelve shots were said to have been heard but *U-86* failed to sink the ship without trace because the twenty-four survivors in the Master's boat were subsequently picked up by the destroyer *Lysander*. Other crew members and medical staff, including fourteen nurses, perished. Patzig and two of his officers, Boldt and Dittmar, were arraigned for trial at Leipzig in July 1921. None of them served a sentence: Patzig fled to Danzig before the trial took place and his lieutenants escaped after conviction, certainly with the connivance of the authorities.

The Royal Navy was not confronted with moral problems because its targets were warships or, almost always, plainly recognisable supply vessels of one kind or another. It is pointless to speculate on how submarine commanding officers would have reacted if required to conduct a British form of *Handelskrieg*; but 'Seagee' Brodie, looking back on the war in which he was a distinguished submarine commanding officer,[11] was convinced that 'Frightfulness' did not pay. He was a deeply respected man with a strong religious faith and unshakeable ideals which he had shared with his brother

The End (1918)

'TS', killed when *E15* grounded on Kephez Point,[12] and his view was applauded by the Naval War College. In brief he believed that 'barbarous and forbidden methods' demoralised the personnel concerned; that sacrificing agreements and honour to expediency was not warranted even if national existence was deemed to be at stake; and that 'the Germans more or less openly admitted that it [unrestricted submarine warfare] could only be justified by success'.[13] These admirable sentiments took scant account of reality. Worse still, Seagee lulled his listeners into complacency:

Although submarines may have improved in various directions, and may have the benefit of air reconnaissance in future, I think the pendulum has swung very markedly against them. Detection devices have vastly improved, and the complete immunity enjoyed by a well-handled submarine against all attack, unaided by mishap or remarkable luck, will never recur . . . I consider the submarine menace against our commerce definitely dead as a decisive factor.

Alas, Seagee's hopes were pious and his beliefs were false: no adequate solution had been found by the end of the First World War to combat the hidden threat. The German U-boat men never admitted defeat. In the second Great Underwater War from 1939 to 1945 it was proved yet again that submarine warfare is either total warfare or not worth pursuing.

The words of a former First Lord of the Admiralty, Lord Selborne,[14] written to Jellicoe on 28 April 1915, predicted the real outcome of the Great Underwater War:

Supposing that there is another war in a generation hence and that Germany then has 500 submarines of immense power and able to keep the sea for weeks, what is going to be our success? At the present moment there is no known way of surely protecting our mercantile marine from such a fleet of submarines. . . .

Selborne was saying, in effect, that the 'war to end all wars' was perhaps a rehearsal for even more powerful submarine warfare against Great Britain. In the event, Germany's U-boat arm barely had to wait a generation before it was called upon

313

afresh. Just seventeen years after the Armistice there was to be a new beginning for the German U-boat arm; four years later, on 3 September 1939, the boats were back in business.[15]

Meanwhile, the Royal Navy's submarine service was maintained at quite a high level between the wars, with fifty to sixty boats at any one time. That says much for the tenacity of each successive Rear-Admiral (Submarines) at Fort Blockhouse, and the respect for The Trade (a title soon forgotten) engendered by the first Great Underwater War. Wartime submarines had proved themselves, in the main, to be flexible, economical weapon systems with far greater surface range and endurance than destroyers; their crews were of necessity exceptionally professional. Yet submariners still failed to make their needs, capabilities and limitations properly understood in the Admiralty. In general their purpose in any future conflict was unclear, and in particular the invaluable anti-submarine role was largely neglected.

So far as a new breed of German U-boat was concerned Great Britain was to find herself once more unprepared, in 1939, for the coming onslaught.

Notes

Prologue

1. Accounts, times, numbers of survivors vary widely. For example, most texts say that *Stag* was alongside *Pathfinder* before she finally sank and that 259 men perished. Research from original sources show, however, that *Stag* did not arrive on the scene until 5.15 p.m.; and the memorial register (Commonwealth War Graves Commission) insists that the death toll was 256, of whom 245 belonged to the Port of Chatham.

2. Lieutenant Commander (T) Favell.

3. German instructions for 'torpedo firing from submarines' held in Royal Navy Submarine Museum (RNSM). The periscope was, of course, exposed as briefly as possible: the instructions were not intended to imply leaving the 'Asparagus' up for more than a few moments at a time.

PART I   WAYS AND MEANS

Chapter 1   'The Trade'

1. Fisher to Knollys (Private Secretary to King Edward VII), 20 April 1904.

2. These are the figures given by Admiral Scheer who commanded the 'pre-dreadnought' Second Battle Squadron in August 1914 and should have known the Order of Battle accurately. In this case there was no need for him to prevaricate. Historians have sometimes added another battle-cruiser and two 'pre-dreadnought' battleships but these were not ready for service. The balance was anyway to shift further in favour of the Royal Navy with the completion of four more battleships (two of them *Queen Elizabeths*) with 380-mm (15-inch) guns, a calibre 76 mm (3 inches) larger than the latest German 'dreadnoughts'.

3. Lothair Persius, *Warum die Flotte versagt*, p. 20 (Leipzig, 1925) and Lothair Persius, *Die Tirpitz Legende*, p. 17 (Berlin, 1918).

4. Hermann Bauer, *Als Führer der U-boote im Weltkrieg* (Leipzig, 1940).

5. Alfred Thayer Mahan, *The Influence of Sea Power upon History* (1890).

6. R. H. Gibson and M. Prendergast, *The German Submarine War* (Constable & Co Ltd, 1931), an invaluable and thoroughly well-considered assessment.

7. *German Official History (GOH)*, pp. 50–54 in the English translation, held by the Naval Historical Branch.

8. Bauer was promoted to *Fregattenkapitän* (F.Kpt) on 16 April 1915 and then styled *Kommodore*, as *Führer der Uboote* in overall command of the U-boat arm. Bauer was relieved by Kapitän-zur-See/Kommodore Michelsen on 5 June 1915 who became *Flottillenadmiral*.

9. Unpublished reminiscences of Captain Oswald Hallifax, DSO, RN (First Lieutenant of *A7*, *E7*, 1912–15, and in command of *B5*, *D7*, *E55*, *R11*, *K6*, 1916–24. He was also in command of the depot ship *Lucia* when the crew mutinied in 1931, but was highly regarded during his submarine service).

10. Ibid.

11. Churchill to Fisher, 24 December 1914, RNSM.

12. Keyes's principal technical assistant was Commander, later Admiral Sir, Percival Addison. Others on the committee of experts assembled by the Inspecting Captain were to become famous names in war: Commander Charles Little; Engineer Commander Reginald Skelton; Lieutenant Martin Nasmith; Lieutenant Noel Laurence; and Lieutenant Charles Craven. Keyes and the committee worked closely with Arthur Johns of the Department of the Director of Naval Construction (DNC).

13. The Inspecting Captain of Submarines was for a while nominally under the Admiral Reserve Fleet at Portsmouth, but this rather curious and purely administrative anomaly made it somewhat easier to forge links with Whitehall.

14. *The Naval Memoirs of Admiral of the Fleet Sir Roger Keyes, Volume 1* (Thornton Butterworth 1934).

15. Ibid.

Chapter 2   Living in a Can

1. Alas, the story of *E54* (Raikes) torpedoing *U-81* while the crew were at their ablutions on the upper deck and one man was using the bucket ('I saved him the trouble of using toilet paper,' said Raikes) is untrue: *U-81* was at action stations because the boat was engaged in sinking a steamer when the torpedo struck.

2. A Lieutenant's basic annual pay was £172 10s 0d (£172.50 in decimal currency), equivalent to about £3800 today; submarine pay was 6s (30p) per day. An AB normally drew £30 8s 4d per year or 1s 8d (16p) per day: submarine pay added another £36 10s 0d a year or 2s a day. In the United States Navy a submarine sailor was paid $5.00 a month extra and also $1.00 for each day his boat dived up to a maximum of $20.00 a month.

3. There is a hilarious true story in the RNSM archives of a depot ship Chaplain endeavouring to catch a couple *in flagrante delicto* in a 'K' boat. Bulkhead doors were slammed and clipped successively by a loyal sailor as he endeavoured to reach the wardroom, while the lady and the poodle escaped up the engine-room hatch.

4. British submariners were issued with the same clothing as divers, but German U-boat men were given no less than twenty-two separate kinds of carefully chosen clothing with two sets of the more intimate items.

5. Captain E. M. C. Barraclough, CBE, RN, *I Was Sailing*, unpublished memoirs, RNSM archives. He was, in fact, describing post-war US Navy submarines but the design differential between the US Navy and the Royal Navy, as far as comfort was concerned, was evident before then. 'Pigboats' were so called not because of sty-like conditions but for the habit of early submarines porpoising to the surface for the captain to look through glass shutters in the conning tower when periscopes were cumbersome to raise – and 'sea pig' was the mariner's name for a porpoise.

6. Held in RNSM archives.

7. Four-per-cent hydrogen in air constitutes an explosive mixture. It was a common cause of accidents in all navies.

8. This was, of course, exceedingly bad for the hull as well as for health. Battery compartments with their own bilge-pumping arrangements were built into later boats.

9. Ex-U-boat captain Pastor Martin Niemöller *From U-boat to Pulpit* (William Hodge & Co., 1936).

Chapter 3   Mechanics

1. Unpublished memoirs in RNSM of Lieutenant (later Vice-Admiral Sir) Robert Ross Turner.

2. Records held in RNSM.

3. The German mark at the beginning of the war was equivalent to one shilling, that is, 20 marks to the pound sterling.

4. *Instructions for Submarine Officers*, RNSM (1918).

5. 'Professional Notes' in USNIP, volume 41 (1915), extracted from the *Journal of the American Society of Engineers* and the *United Service Gazette*, RNSM.

6. *War Lessons and Experiences* compiled by staff of flag officer submarines in manuscript in 1919, RNSM.

7. Confidential reports on officers, RNSM.

8. It has just reached about the same level today (1990) after falling off after the First World War.

9. Confidential reports on officers, RNSM.

Chapter 4   Finding the Enemy

1. Until 1933 steering orders given to the helmsman gave, by long-established custom, the direction in which the tiller was to be moved – that is, the opposite direction to that which the ship's head (and rudder) was to move. On 1 January 1933 direct steering orders were introduced in the Royal Navy, with a six-month transitional period in which the words 'wheel to' were included in the order. Thus the former order 'Starboard 20' became 'Wheel to port 20' and on 1 July 1933 simply 'Port 20'.

2. A diesel engine could not be run astern and had therefore to be unclutched from the common shaft connecting the engine motor and propeller before the motor could drive the screw astern. HMS *G14*, laid down in 1916, was the first Royal Navy boat to have reversing diesels (made by Fiat). They were only thereafter installed in 'P'-, 'O'- and 'Porpoise'-class minelayers built between the wars.

3. Chief LTO – Chief Leading Torpedo Operator in charge of electrics under the First Lieutenant.

4. Lieutenant R. R. Turner attributed this tale to Lieutenant Tom Triggs in *A6*, but by common consent it was Feilman. Ferdie was probably an alcoholic and was relieved of his command (*K14*) in 1917. His commander (S) – Somerville – remarked that he had 'taken to the bottle again after promotion [to Commander], had done the Submarine Service a great deal of harm and should never be re-entered'.

Chapter 5   Mouldies, Bricks and Deadly Eggs

1. By Nicholas A. Lambert as part of a thesis. Lambert is probably the only person ever to have looked in detail at hits, misses and torpedo failures in the First World War: his conclusions, summarised in this chapter, are fascinating. The RNSM is much indebted to him for such painstakingly objective research and I am extremely grateful for his permission to use the figures he has compiled.

2. A parting shop was, in effect, the repair and maintenance garage for torpedoes where mouldies were taken apart and put together again

before being 'prepped' – made ready for running before being embarked in submarines. The submariners then completed the preparation by topping up their air chambers with high-pressure air and setting the depth.

3. 40 and 45.5 knots, the latter predominating, were the usual post-war and Second World War speed settings in the Royal Navy.

4. Named after a (rather unpopular) submarine CO.

5. HMS *Thetis* sank on trials in Liverpool Bay on 1 June 1939, after a rear door was opened when the bow cap was already open.

6. Ernst Hashagen, *The Log of a U-boat Commander* (Putnam, 1931).

7. Research by Brian Head to whom I and RNSM are much indebted.

8. Organised by Admiral Earle US Navy and Commander Fullinwinder US Navy.

9. *U-92* (9 September 1918), *U-156* (25 September 1918) and *UB-123* (19 October 1918) were the victims deduced from circumstantial evidence.

10. A. J. Marder, *Dreadnought to Scapa Flow* II, p. 249 in particular (Oxford University Press, 1965).

11. The British minelayers were *E24*, *E34*, *E41*, *E45*, *E46* and *E51*.

Chapter 6   The Enemy All Round – Anti-Submarine Measures

1. They were also called 'catchers' or 'hunters'.

2. Quoted by Henri le Masson in *Du Nautilus (1880) au Redoutable (1969)* (Presses de la Cité, Paris, 1969).

3. Although the craft was only awash (trial dives had proved disastrous), the first successful submarine attack is credited, fairly, to the Confederate semi-submersible *Hunley* which sank the Federal ironclad *Housatonic* at Charleston, Carolina, on 17 February 1864. The gallant little *Hunley* went down with her giant adversary because the spar torpedo was, in these circumstances, a suicidal weapon.

4. Bushnell's *Turtle*, a one-man barrel-shaped contraption with a fused charge for affixing by means of an auger to the bottom of a 'wooden wall' battleship, attempted to sink the British flagship HMS *Eagle* at New York in September 1776. The exploit failed (probably partly because Ezra Lee, the pilot, was asphyxiated by carbon dioxide), but subsequent inventors were undoubtedly inspired by the 'effort of genius' as George Washington called it. The 'genius' may well have lain in Washington recognising that a small, covert craft could not only attack big ships but also deter those ships from operating or anchoring in the threatened areas.

5. The top of *E11*'s periscope, almost severed by a ragged hole, is preserved in the Imperial War Museum, London.

6. Most historians, the author included, have believed that the acronym

ASDIC stood for Allied Submarine Detection Investigation Committee; but research by Willem Hackmann, discussed in his definitive and strongly recommended work *Seek and Strike* (HMSO, 1984), revealed no committee of that name. It is much more likely, as Hackmann suggests, that it stood for 'pertaining to the Anti-Submarine Division' (or Anti-Submarine Division -*ics*), the Admiralty department which had initiated research.

7. Memorandum, significantly without a BIR reference number, noted in *Submarine Menace* (Lord Fisher) PRO CAB 21/7.

8. A BIR minute dated 27 March 1917 suggests that Hall was rebutting accusations of non-cooperation.

9. Winston S. Churchill, *The World Crisis*, Volume II, chapter XIV (Odhams Press n.d.).

10. German depth-charges weighed only 50 kilos (110 pounds).

11. From German records. British records do not show a depth-charge attack on *U-49* at this time, but it was of course usually impossible to know which U-boat was being attacked if it was submerged throughout – or even if the contact was indeed a submarine and not a school of fish.

12. Fisher, letter to Controller of the Navy, 20 April 1904.

13. The relevant archive is available in the RNSM for serious researchers.

PART II   THE ACTION

Chapter 7   Opening Shots in the North Sea (1914)

1. Where tonnages are given in this way (e.g. 660/800) they refer to surface and submerged displacements. The difference between the two figures is the reserve buoyancy.

2. Diary of Lieutenant Ingleby S. Jefferson (RNSM).

3. Cheese – *der Käse.*

4. *Naval Memoirs of Admiral of the Fleet Sir Roger Keyes*, Volume 1 (Thornton Butterworth, 1934).

5. Ibid.

6. The two flotillas (four half-flotillas) available for service at the outbreak of war were later expanded into four flotillas. The staff for the First was at Brunsbuttel, for the Second at Wilhelmshaven, for the Third and Fourth at Emden. Eventually the organisation became more complex, with flotillas and half-flotillas operating in the Baltic, Mediterranean, Adriatic and Black Sea as well as the U-cruiser group ranging far afield from Kiel. The bases at

Notes

home were Kiel, Helgoland, Brunsbuttel, Emden, Wilhelmshaven, Borkum, Bremerhaven, Danzig and Libau in occupied territory at Flanders and Zeebrugge; and overseas at Constantinople, Sevastopol, Pola and Cattaro. Each area had its own *Führer der Uboote* who enjoyed considerable autonomy.

7. This quite common type of accident probably caused the disappearance of HMS *AE1* off the coast of German New Guinea on 13 September 1914, while searching for the German cruiser *Geier* – despite theories about running on to an uncharted reef. It was the first Australian submarine and the first Allied boat lost on active service.

8. Scheer, Reinhardt, *Germany's High Sea Fleet in the World War,* p. 224 in the English translation (Cassell, 1920).

9. *Conclusions of the German Fleet Command* quoted in (British) Naval Staff Monographs, CBQ17(H) Volume X (RN Submarine Library).

10. Heligoland was the usual English spelling (and was used in the original) but Helgoland is correct.

11. 'Make-and-mend' – naval expression for an afternoon off.

12. Reported in *The Times* (London), 24 December 1914.

Chapter 8   Boats for the Baltic (1914–16)

1. *E9* was the first of the 'E' class to have two bow tubes and she carried ten torpedoes. *E1* to *E8* had only one bow tube and carried eight torpedoes.

2. Corbett, Sir Julian, *Naval Operations*, Volume III, p. 137 (Longmans, Green & Co., 1923).

3. Scheer, Reinhardt, *Germany's High Sea Fleet in the World War* (pub. in translation by Cassell, 1920).

4. *Moltke* was again hit, by Allen in *E42*, on 26 April 1918.

5. This account is taken from unpublished memoirs by Geoffrey Layton in the RNSM.

Chapter 9   Daring the Dardanelles
(December 1914–January 1916)

1. Spare Crew: for each flotilla or squadron of submarines a number of extra officers and ratings was provided to fill gaps caused by casualties, sickness, unexpected leave and so on. The number seldom amounted to a complete crew but at least one officer and key ratings were included.

2. DSM: Distinguished Service Medal (for ratings only).

3. Prize bounty had an interesting history: it benefited submariners more than anybody else during the war. In previous wars it had been customary to make periodical distributions both of prize money – proceeds of the capture of enemy property – and prize bounty which was a bonus provided by the Government 'for the capture or destruction of armed ships of the enemy'. The first Prize Act was passed in 1708, declaring that 'if in any action any ship of war or privateer shall be taken from the enemy, five pounds shall be granted to the captors for every man which was living on board such ship or ships so taken at the beginning of the engagement between them'. King George V renewed the bounty at the historical level by Order-in-Council on 2 March 1915; but the value was nothing like so great as in the old days when, in 1762 for example, the captains of HMS *Active* and HMS *Favourite* were each awarded £65,000 – which would have made them millionaires today – for capturing the Spanish *Hermione* carrying coin and precious metals amounting to £519,705. In action between surface ships during the First World War the numbers of men involved were so large that individuals gained little. On the other hand, submarines with their small crews sometimes did very well out of the system, and the President of the Court was sympathetic towards them. In *B11*'s case Sir Samuel assessed the complement of the Turkish battleship at 700 – hence the bounty of £3500 payable – remarking that 'nobody can say that I am wrong, and I hope I am right.'

4. Holbrook's share would be worth about £14,000 today and an Able Seaman's about £2750.

5. Royal Naval Air Service, the forerunner of the Fleet Air Arm founded on 1 April 1918.

6. The evacuation took place between 10 December 1915 and 9 January 1916.

7. RNSM archives.

8. Nasmith had himself been court-martialled and reprimanded for 'by default hazarding' HMS *A4* when commanding the primitive boat in 1905. The submarine was the target for underwater signalling trials in the Solent with Torpedo Boat *No. 26* and was required to show a red flag, poked up through a ventilation tube, to mark her position submerged. A passing steamer's wash poured down the tube and sent the boat to the bottom with the ventilator-valve still open. The crew, choked with chlorine gas, got her back to the surface after three and a half very anxious minutes, and the boat was taken in tow to Portsmouth Dockyard; but three explosions occurred as she was about to enter the dock gates and she sank. Along with the court-martial came a commendation from the C-in-C to officers and crew for their 'pluck and devotion to duty'.

9. The famous correspondent and journalist.

10. He eventually added a family name to become, at the end of his career, Admiral Sir Martin E. Dunbar-Nasmith, VC, KCB, Vice-Admiral of the United Kingdom and Lieutenant of the Admiralty.

11. D'Oyly Hughes was Captain of HMS *Glorious* during the Second World War when he was killed while bringing the carrier back to court-martial two of his commanders.

12. The French 530/627-ton *Mariotte*, known as 'The Toothbrush' because that was the appearance of her superstructure above water, was trapped in nets and destroyed by Turkish gunfire on 27 July 1915.

13. The Turks, perhaps encouraged to think they could now embark on submarine warfare, relaunched the *Abdul Hamid*, renamed *Yunusbaliği* (Porpoise) in August 1916. This was one of the two appalling Nordenfelt steam submersibles sold to Turkey by the Reverend George William Garrett Pasha in 1887.

14. There are some discrepancies in the figures compiled by both sides because some of the ships were beached, salvaged and refitted.

15. For ease of reference, the key dates in the complex interwoven story of the Dardanelles campaign are given below:

1914

11 August	*Goeben* and *Breslau* take refuge in the Marmara.
13 December	B11 (Holbrook) sinks the *Messoudieh*.

1915

15 January	Churchill proposes a naval expedition to force the Dardanelles with Constantinople as its objective. French submarine *Saphir* mined in lower Dardanelles.
18 February	Keyes arrives at Mudros as Chief of Staff to Rear Admiral Carden in flagship *Inflexible*.
19 and 26 Feb	Bombardments of Turkish defences in Lower Dardanelles and attempted passage up the Straits by Anglo-French fleet.
16 March	Rear Admiral de Robeck relieves Carden.
18 March	Fleet's further attack on Turkish defences results in heavy losses due to mines and gunfire. Battleships *Irresistible*, *Ocean* and *Bouvet* sunk; battleships *Gaulois* and *Suffren* and battle-cruiser *Inflexible* badly damaged.
14 April	Submarine penetration of the Dardanelles agreed.
17 April	E15 (T. S. Brodie) stranded in Kephez Bay.
25 April	Allied landings on Dardanelles Peninsula.
26 April	AE2 (Stoker) enters the Sea of Marmara; lost on 30 April.
25 May	U-21 (Hersing) sinks battleship *Triumph* off Gaba Tepe.
27 May	U-21 (Hersing) sinks battleship *Majestic* off Cape Helles. Arrives at Constantinople 5 June.
27 July	French *Mariotte* trapped and sunk.
4 September	E7 (Cochrane) lost.
20 October	E20 (Warren) sunk by UB-14 (von Heimburg).
30 October	French *Turquoise* stranded and surrendered.
19/20 December	Evacuation of Allied troops from Sulva and Anzac Cove.

1916

3 January	*E2* (Stocks), the last submarine in the Marmara returns.
8/9 January	Evacuation of Allied troops from Cape Helles.

1918 (Not included in narrative)

20 January	*Goeben* and *Breslau* emerge from the Dardanelles. *Breslau* sunk; *Goeben* re-enters the Straits and runs aground.
27 January	*E14* (White) enters Dardanelles to ensure *Goeben* is immobilised; destroyed in the attempt on 28 January. White awarded VC: *E14* a 'double VC' submarine.

Chapter 10   The First War on Shipping
(February–September 1915)

1. The various quotations in this section come from Admiral of the Fleet Lord Fisher, *Records* (London, 1919) and W. S. Churchill, *The World Crisis* (Odhams Press, n.d.).

2. A detailed, albeit not very conveniently arranged, list of commands and U-boat histories is given in *60 Jahre Deutsche Uboote 1906–66* by Bodo Herzog (Munich, n.d.) which is an invaluable reference book for both world wars. John Terraine's *Business in Great Waters* (Leo Cooper, 1989) is outstandingly good for the period 1916–45.

3. Paraphrased from a memorandum addressed by Fleet admirals to Chief of Naval Staff, Admiral von Pohl, in November 1914. (Also quoted in Scheer's *Germany's High Sea Fleet in the World War* (Cassell, 1920).)

4. Ibid.

5. This allegation about jeering is made in Gibson and Prendergast's classic *The German Submarine War 1914–18* (Constable, 1931) but no source reference is given, nor can one be found.

6. Excellent references are Carson I. A. Ritchie, *Q-ships* (Terence Dalton, 1985); Admiral Campbell, *My Mystery Ships* (Hodder & Stoughton, *c.* 1929); and E. Keble Chatterton, *Q-Ships and their Story* (Sidgwick & Jackson, 1922).

7. Commander G. C. Steele RN, formerly first lieutenant of the *Baralong* as an RNR lieutenant, quoted in E. Keble Chatterton, *Gallant Gentlemen* (Hurst & Blackett, 1931).

8. Sir Julian Corbett, *Official History of the War – Naval Operations* (Longman, 1923).

Notes

Chapter 11   Mayhem in the Med
(August 1915–December 1917)

1. The Straits were never sealed during the Second World War either.

2. *War Memoirs of Robert Lansing* (Indianapolis, Ind. 1935), quoted by Halpern (see note 3 below).

3. Professor Paul G. Halpern, Professor of History at Florida State University, edited *The Keyes Papers* (very valuable in the preparation of this book) for the Navy Records Society and produced his classic work *The Naval War in the Mediterranean 1914–1918* (Allen & Unwin, 1987), strongly recommended for further reading.

Chapter 12   The Sound of Music – Whiteheads
in the Adriatic (1915–18)

1. R. A. Thursby, letter dated 12 May 1916 to Admiral Sir Henry Jackson, First Sea Lord.

2. From the account by *Commandant* Thomazi recorded in Henri le Masson, *Du Nautilus (1800) au Redoutable* (Paris, 1969).

3. The abbreviation for the rank is *Lschlt*. Unlike German ranks and abbreviations which are in the main pronounceable to English readers, the Austrian ones are not. Hereafter English equivalents will be used.

4. The convention of using roman numerals for Austro-Hungarian submarines has been adopted to distinguish them from German U-boats with similar numbering.

5. This excellent strategy was adopted in 1916 by the Italian Mas (*Motobarca armata silurante*) – small, fast motor torpedo-boats which scored their first triumph in Durazzo Harbour on 7 June and laid the foundations for the outstandingly good surface and submerged harbour-penetration craft employed by Italy with such notable effect in both world wars.

6. Report by Ensign H. W. Blumenthal USNRF, known as 'The Blumenthal Report' dated 30 November 1919; US National Archives.

7. Whitehead married Frances Maria Johnson in 1845, twenty-one years before his own invention, produced at Fiume, successfully replaced the crude floating torpedo designed by Captain Lupius of the Austrian Navy. The couple had three sons and two daughters. The eldest son, John, helped to run the Whitehead factories, and his eldest daughter Agathe, one of seven children, continued to live at the Villa Whitehead overlooking the Fiume Works after her father's death in 1902. Here she met the handsome, aristocratic Georg who had been posted to Fiume as a serving naval officer to study torpedoes and submarine construction. In 1909 Agathe launched *U-V* which the lieutenant was in due course to command. It was obvious

325

to all that the couple were destined for each other but (following a long engagement period, mandatory in those days) they did not marry until 1911.

The Fiume torpedo factory was evacuated to St Polten during the war, and in 1918 Austria was left without a coastline. The submarine captain's promising career in the navy was thus abruptly ended and he had to seek commercial employment. Agathe died in 1922, leaving Georg to bring up five children. Georg thereupon engaged a governess, Maria Augusta, the Baroness von Kutschera (a former nun) whom he married after a decent interval, and several more children were added to the family. Maria taught the girls and boys to sing and their remarkable talents brought them widespread fame as the Trapp Family Singers, immortalised by the book of that name and to a greater extent by the Hollywood musical *The Sound of Music*. Five of the singers were, of course, great-grandchildren of Whitehead; hence the rather laboured connection sometimes made (and perpetuated in this chapter) between the compositions of Rogers and Hammerstein and the markedly less mellifluous sound of a torpedo running.

8. The hitting percentage of 90 per cent for torpedoes fired without missing a single ship was unprecedented for a submarine arm anywhere and unequalled subsequently. It is natural, therefore, to think that the results, summarised in G. W. Aichelburg, *Die Unterseeboote Osterreich Ungains*, Volume 2 (Graz, 1981), are suspect; but research has failed to prove them wrong.

9. The Italian records say 4 July and the *Kriegsarchiv* Report (Vienna, 1930) says 1 May when *U-XX* was almost certainly in harbour. Italian and Austrian records often fail to match.

10. Richard Compton-Hall, *Submarine Warfare – Monsters and Midgets* (Blandford Press, 1985) tells the story.

11. Diary of Captain Herbert Richmond RN, 18 August 1915. A. J. Marder, *Portrait of an Admiral: the Life and Papers of Sir Herbert Richmond* (Cape, 1952).

12. Ibid., 8 July 1915.

13. Diary of Vice-Admiral Wilfred Tomkinson, 26 November 1915. Quoted by Paul Kemp and Peter Jung in their excellent article *Five Broken Down B Boats*, a copy of which is held in the Submarine Museum and Churchill College, Cambridge. This article has given several invaluable pointers to sources and offers an exceptionally lucid and succinct assessment of British submarine warfare in the Adriatic from October 1915 to August 1917: it is highly recommended to researchers.

14. Diary in RNSM archives.

15. Holbrook had relinquished commanding soon after the award of his VC and was wounded in a scuffle in Egypt on 16 August 1915.

16. Nasmith took D'Oyley Hughes with him to *J4*.

17. Records and Westall diary in RNSM archives.

Notes

Chapter 13   The Bloodless Bear (1916–17)

1. The son of Lieutenant C. H. Mee generously gave his father's diary to the RN Submarine Museum. It reveals an objective, dependable officer with high moral standards and a clear conscience. Generally, he praised Cromie; but he also had the unusual capability of criticising his captain very occasionally in a private, gentle, understanding, loyal sort of way. That loyalty, however, was not always reciprocated by Cromie, as demonstrated in his collected letters held in the Museum archives.

2. Quoted in the unpublished memoirs of Vice-Admiral L. H. Ashmore CB, DSO (ex-*E18*) held in the RNSM.

3. Ibid., supported by other accounts held in the RNSM.

4. Cromie letters in the RNSM.

5. Mary Britneiva's *One Woman's Story*, quoted by Michael Wilson in his excellent book (mandatory for researchers and a good read in its own right) *Baltic Assignment* (Leo Cooper, 1985).

6. Quoted by Lieutenant Commander R. L. Burridge RN in his letter dated 13 July 1979 to the RNSM.

Chapter 14   Merchant U-Boats (1915–16)

1. As usual the tonnage refers to surface and submerged displacements. These figures are given to indicate the size of these submarines compared with normal U-boats. The use of merchant gross tonnage seems unduly confusing and is, anyway, very difficult to calculate in this case.

2. The speech is recounted in *Voyage of the Deutschland* by Captain König. This was published by Hearst in translation so soon after the event and in such a carefully groomed style that one is forced to believe that the book was ghosted by a highly professional writer dedicated to the German cause and doubtless rewarded accordingly.

Chapter 15   No Holds Barred (1917)

1. In the course of the war more than 3000 Norwegian sailors lost their lives because of U-boats and mines. Just over 50 per cent of the Norwegian mercantile marine was destroyed.

2. Jellicoe, Admiral Sir John, *The Submarine Peril* (Cassell, 1934).

3. It was the secret centre of British Naval Intelligence and counter-espionage directed by Admiral Sir Reginald Hall (not to be confused with Commodore S. S. Hall). This exceedingly efficient organisation scored notable triumphs during the war and concerned itself with many matters not directly connected with the navy. For example, it was able to give warning of Zeppelin

attacks, and it dispensed what today would be called disinformation. Some of the Allied submarine successes and many German U-boat losses can, at root, be credited to Room 40 OB with its associated staff of cryptographic experts (notably Sir Alfred Ewing), linguists, photographers, chemists and intelligence analysers working for Hall. It was not physically linked with the Intelligence Division but was situated, with a number of adjoining offices, in the Old Building of the Admiralty (hence OB). Very few people, even Cabinet Ministers, knew about the organisation which worked closely with Sir Basil Thomson's police team – a forerunner of the Special Branch – at Scotland Yard. The intriguing book *40 O.B. or How the War was Won* by Hugh Cleland Hoy (Hutchinson, London 1932) raised eyebrows when it was published and is well worth reading.

4. John Terraine, *Business in Great Waters – The U-boat Wars 1916–1945* (Leo Cooper, 1989) is arguably the best book in the field.

5. W. S. Churchill, *The World Crisis*, Volume II, pp. 1234–5 (Odhams, 1938).

6. Ibid.

7. Ibid., p. 1233.

8. Specifically by Admiral von Holtzendorff.

9. Deputy Gustav Hoch, 5 July 1917.

10. From the Peace Resolution drafted by the left–centre amalgamation in the Reichstag led by former Centre Party leader Mathias Erzberger. The Resolution was passed, to the fury of the High Command, on 19 July 1917.

11. Professor Mandin and Patricia Beesly among them.

Chapter 16   The Yanks are Coming
(April 1917–November 1918)

1. Speech by Professor M'Laughlin of Chicago University at Oxford on 10 May 1918 and statement by Spenser Wilkinson in 'Security', *Nineteenth Century*, April 1927.

2. Rear Admiral W. S. Sims US Navy in collaboration with Burton J. Hendrick, *The Victory at Sea* (John Murray, 1920).

3. Admiral Sir Reginald Bacon, *The Life of John Rushworth Earl Jellicoe* (Cassell, 1936).

4. Dr Karl Helfferich, Imperial Secretary of the Interior, February 1917.

5. Sims reckoned that 15–20 per cent of shipping space would in effect be lost. In the event the amount sometimes proved much higher. For both world wars, bearing in mind the time taken to load and unload a large number of ships at one time in one port, some authorities have quoted an effective loss in excess of 30 per cent or even 50 per cent on occasion.

6. *Victory at Sea*, op. cit.

7. There are alternative figures for Atlantic convoys from 26 July 1917 to 5 October 1918, not counting convoys actually on passage on the latter date. Of 14,968 transatlantic ships convoyed, 118 became casualties (two-thirds of them inward bound) – 0.79 per cent. If gross tonnage instead of the number of ships lost is calculated, the figure becomes 0.85 per cent. The average daily loss of ships worldwide declined from 10.43 per cent in the second quarter of 1917 (i.e. including the black month of April) to 6.2 per cent in the third quarter and 5.04 per cent in the fourth. The year 1918 started with an average of 4.5 per cent, reducing to 3.37 per cent in the second quarter and 2.91 per cent in the third quarter. *Handelskrieg* was deemed to cease on 26 October 1918.

8. The 720/902-ton *U-53* (Kptlt Hans Rose) had crossed the Atlantic and visited Newport, Rhode Island, on 7 October 1916 while America was still neutral. The U-boat's arrival under her own power caused a sensation which startled the world and greatly impressed USN officers. Rose (whose conduct towards survivors was invariably impeccable) was evidently an excellent ambassador for Germany, but he sank three British steamers in the vicinity of Nantucket lightship on his way back to Helgoland. Shortage of fuel compelled him to return to base before he could do any more damage – hence the need expressed by Bauer for longer-range boats. In fact, *U-53*'s courtesy call at Newport was counter-productive in the sense that Congress was persuaded, appreciating the danger if war came, to pass a supplemental naval appropriation bill – but even so there were those in power who scoffed at proposed measures for coastal protection.

9. The armed merchant cruiser *Moldavia* (9500 tons) was torpedoed in the Channel, not in ocean convoy, with the loss of 56 American troops.

Chapter 17   U-Cruisers (1917–18)

1. Memorandum from Department B111 of the Naval Staff to the Kaiser dated 6 January 1916. Significant extracts can be found in the invaluable reference book *The U-boat* by Eberhardt Rössler published in English (Arms and Armour Press, 1981).

2. *U-139*, first of class, had twin 1650 hp GW two-stroke diesels; the 1750 hp MANs in *U-140* were four-stroke. There was also an auxiliary diesel-generator beneath the control room and isolated from it.

3. Lothar von Arnauld de la Perière rose to the rank of Vice-Admiral in the German Navy and was killed during an air raid on 24 February 1941. Hitler's Mediterranean group of U-boats was named after him in November 1941.

4. *U-139* was handed over to the French Navy after the Armistice, when

she became the *Halbronn*. Her new owners were rather disdainful about her performance but she served until 1932.

5. Most of the U-cruisers were given names:
   U-139 *Kapitänleutnant Schweiger*
   U-140 *Kapitänleutnant Weddigen*
   U-145 *Kapitänleutnant Wegener*
   U-146 *Oberleutnant-zur-See Saltzwedel*
   U-147 *Kapitänleutnant Hansen*
   U-149 *Kapitänleutnant Freiherr von Breckheim*
   U-150 *Kapitänleutnant Schreider*

6. The U-cruisers destroyed 174 ships totalling 361,496 tons, with *U-155* (ex-*Deutschland*) under Meusel and then Eckelmann taking 42 ships totalling 118,373 tons.

Chapter 18   K for Catastrophe (1917–18)

1. Commander F. W. Lipscomb, OBE, RN, in *The British Submarine* (Adam & Charles Black, 1954, subsequently reprinted).

2. Officers' Confidential Reports held in RNSM.

3. The hydraulic system was known as telemotor until the 1960s.

4. Quoted, as well as elsewhere, in Don Everitt's excellent *K-boats* (George Harrap, 1963, reprinted in paperback). This is an invaluable reference and makes entertaining reading. However, the information for this chapter has been drawn from original records mostly held in the RNSM archives. Some sections have been paraphrased, amended as necessary and updated with later research, from one of the author's earlier publications *Submarine Warfare – Monsters and Midgets* (Blandford Press, 1985).

Chapter 19   The End (1918)

1. Several interpretations can be placed on the numbers reportedly building or ordered. The figures quoted are taken from Gibson and Prendergast and they compare well with other references. However, there were so many 'ifs' and 'buts' attending the construction programme from 1917 onwards that specific figures are not very meaningful: they simply indicate that U-boats in large numbers were intended to wage the anti-shipping war for as long as necessary to achieve either victory or, much more likely in realistic minds, favourable terms for peace.

2. Scheer's plans were summarised in a memorandum following a meeting with the great industrialist and ship-builder Hugo Stinnes at Spa on 12 September 1918. The memorandum is most easily found, more or less

in full, in Rossler's invaluable *The U-boat*, published in English (Arms and Armour Press, *c*. 1982).

3. Chapter 3 of the author's *Submarine Warfare – Monsters and Midgets* (Blandford Press, 1985) tells the full story.

4. Self-criticisms of this nature are stated or implied in most responsible post-war German records. They are neatly summed up in the Epilogue of Ernst Hashagen, *The Log of a U-boat Commander*, published in English (Putnam, 1931).

5. Submariners to avoid confusion with below-par mariners – further evidence, perhaps, of the 'chip on the shoulder' carried by underwater sailors.

6. *The Naval Memoirs of Admiral of the Fleet Sir Roger Keyes* (Thornton Butterworth, 1934); *The Keyes Papers* (edited by Professor Paul G. Halpern and printed for the Navy Records Society in 1972); Cecil Aspinall-Oglander, *Roger Keyes* (Hogarth Press, 1951); records in RNSM.

7. Various sources but Winston S. Churchill, *The World Crisis 1911–18*, Volume II (Odhams Press, date of first publication uncertain) is the most convenient reference for these and other relevant quotations concerning Fisher and Churchill.

8. Ibid.

9. The view of *The Morning Post* towards submarine warfare generally on 8 August 1904.

10. Werner may still have been an *Oberleutnant* at this time.

11. See Chapter 9 and elsewhere.

12. See Chapter 9.

13. The lecture by Captain C. G. Brodie RN to the Royal Naval War College, Greenwich, on *Frightfulness – the post-war view and its effect on the navy* was delivered on 1 February 1928 and is held in the RNSM archives.

14. First Lord from 1900–5.

15. In 1932 the German Naval High Command made covert preparations for a resumption of U-boat construction. In 1935 the building programme was under way with 45 per cent – 24,000 tons – of the British submarine strength (fifty-seven boats by the outbreak of war) permitted by the Anglo-German Naval Agreement of that year.

INDEX

Index

Cattaro, 207–8, 216–22, 224, 226, 228, 231–2
Central and South American Cable Company, 279
Chanak, 155–7, 160, 167–8, 172, 186
Channel, English, 49, 82, 86, 90, 132, 215, 229
Charlton, Edward F.B., Rear-Admiral, 71
Charmes, Gabriel, 89
Chasers, American, 231–2
Chatham, 112
Chesapeake Bay, 279
Chicago Daily News, 178
Childs, Earle F.W., Ensign USN, 278
Chile, 259
China station, 112
Churchill, Winston: Baltic strategy, 134–6, 138–9, 154; Battle of Helgoland, 122; convoy system, 265; Dardanelles campaign, 93, 154, 175; Fisher relationship, 93, 175, 191–2, 310; *Lusitania*, 199; mines, 83; on role of submarines, 19; opinion of Keyes, 17; Q-ship strategy, 98; submarine living conditions, 26; successor, 92; test mobilisation (1914), 7; U-boat attitude, 191–2, 310
Circé (French submarine), 226, 228
Città di Messina (Italian cruiser), 230
Cleaver, William G., Leading Seaman, 307
Cochrane, Archibald D., Lieutenant, 16, 186–7
Coke, Charles, Admiral Sir, 197
Collins, F.G., Corporal RMLI, 204
Colville, S.C., Admiral, 96
Commercial Cable Company, 279
Constantinople, 155–7, 163, 177–9, 184–8, 206–7, 219
convoy system, 103, 264–6, 272–6, 280
Copenhagen, 148
Courageous, HMS, 297
Cowie, J.S., Captain, 87
Cranford, 201
Craven, Charles, Lieutenant, 316
Cressy, HMS, 130–1
Cromie, Francis Newton Allan, Lieutenant Commander, 146, 148–50, 244–53
cruiser forces, 13
Csepel (Austro-Hungarian destroyer), 226
Cuignot (French submarine), 226
Cunard Line, 195, 197, 199

Curie (French submarine), 78, 224–6, 234
Cyclamen, HMS, 234

'D'-class 14, 25, 35, 109, 111
D1, HMS, 19, 45, 73, 111, 120, 276
D2, HMS, 19, 114, 122
D3, HMS, 114, 122
D4, HMS, 120
D5, HMS, 114–15, 201, 292
D6, HMS, 19
D7, HMS, 126
D8, HMS, 25, 125
D5, (German torpedo boat), 116
Daffodil, HMS, 307
Daily Mail, 8
Dal Alfoen (German steamer), 149
Dalmatian Islands, 239
Damaris, 201
Danish First Torpedo Boat Squadron, 147–8
Danzig, 145
Dardanelles: campaign, 135, 154–89, 220; Churchill–Fisher disagreement, 93; minefield, 85
Dartmouth, HMS, 231
Davis, USS, 275
decoys, *see* Q-ships
Defender, HMS, 123
Delaware Bay, 279
depth-charges, 100–1
de Robeck, John Michael, Vice-Admiral: anti-submarine strategy, 105; Commander of Combined Fleet, 162; opinion of French, 224; submarine strategy, 167, 170, 174–5, 239
'Desiderata' boats, 13, 115–17
destroyers, 19–20, 272–3
Deutschland (merchant U-boat), 255–9, 281, 284
Deville, Lieutenant, 47, 227
Devin, Lieutenant de Vaisseau, 227
D.H.S., 235
Diesel, Rudolf, 48
Dittmar, Leutnant-zur-See, 312
Dobson, Claude C., Lieutenant Commander (later Commander), 99, 290
Dogger Bank, Battle of, 193–4, 309
Dolphin, HMS, 109
Dönitz, Karl, 303
Dora Hugo Stinnes (German collier), 142
Dover, 112
Dover Barrage, 305
Dover Straits, 100, 112, 192

335

Index

Index

Index

Index

Jellicoe, John, Admiral Sir: convoy debate, 273; correspondence, 288, 313; depth charge production, 101; Grand Fleet command, 111, 134; opinion of Keyes, 17; on mines, 84–5; on submarine conditions, 32; relationship with Sims, 270; U-boat worries, 118, 260, 262, 271, 310; war predictions, 260, 266
Jeune Ecole, 12, 89
Johns, Arthur, 316
Johnson, Robert, Captain, 131
Jones, A.K., Captain, 210–11
Jouen, Lieutenant de Vaisseau, 228
Jules-Michelet (French cruiser), 224
Jutland, 117
Jutland, Battle of, 309–10

'K'-class, RN, 48, 75, 288–9, 300, 302, 317
K1, HMS, 289
K2, HMS, 289
K3, HMS, 289
K4, HMS, 289, 298
K6, HMS, 298
K7, HMS, 291, 292, 295, 298–9
K8, HMS, 294
K11, HMS, 298
K12, HMS, 298
K13, HMS, 115, 292, 293
K14, HMS, 297–8, 318
K17, HMS, 296, 298, 299
K22, HMS, 298
K26, HMS, 289
'K'-class, USN, 276
K1, USS, 276
Kai, 201
Kaiman (Russian submarine), 246
'Kaiser' class battleship, 152–3
Kanin, V.A., Admiral, 246
Kapitänleutnant Weddigen, 286
Karlsruhe (German cruiser), 13
Kattegat, 135, 136, 138, 140
Kellett, Gilbert H., Commander, 290, 295
Kephez Point, 158, 160, 167, 313
Kerensky, Alexander Fyodorovich, 250
Kerr, Mark, Rear-Admiral, 229–30, 242
Keyes, Eva, 109–10, 306
Keyes, Roger, Admiral Sir: achievements, 18–19; appointment, 17; background, 18; Baltic strategy, 134–6, 139–40, 154; Battle of Helgoland, 120–2, 125; Dardanelles strategy, 164, 167, 168, 170–1, 174,

185; K-boats, 288–9, 301; Mudros position, 162–3; opinions of, 17–18; relationship with Fisher, 17, 18; submarine exercises (1912–13), 19–21; war outbreak, 109–16; Zeebrugge raid, 304–8
Kiel, 251, 255, 279, 286
Kiel Bay, 135
Kiel Canal, 64, 110
Kilid Bahr, 155, 157
Kimbell, George, Signalman, 296, 299
Kingston valves, 35–6
Kipling, Rudyard, 17
Kitchener, Horatio Herbert, 1st Earl, 189
kites, 105
Köln (German light cruiser), 122
König, Paul, Captain, 255–8
König (German battleship), 251
Kophamel, Waldemar, Korvettenkapitän, 207–8, 215–17, 219, 286
Körting paraffin engines, 46, 115, 117–18
Korvettenkapitän Schweiger, 285
Krab (Russian submarine minelayer), 86
Kronprinz (German battleship), 153
Kum Kale, 155, 157–8, 166

'L'-class, RN, 37, 75, 302
L2, HMS, 37
'L'-class, USN, 276–7
L42 (Austrian flying-boat), 238
L59 (Austrian flying-boat), 238
L132 (Austrian flying-boat), 241
L135 (Austrian flying-boat), 241
Lake, Simon, 38
Lambert, Nicholas A., 318
Lansing, Robert, 212, 213–14
Laubeuf, Maxime, 35, 47
Launburg, 243
Laurence, Noel, Lieutenant Commander (later Commander): Kattegat scouting, 136; Libau venture, 137–9; on committee of experts, 316; promotion, 142; relationship with Horton, 151; successes, 144–6, 152–3, 290
Laurenti, 35
Lawrence, Reginald W., Lieutenant RNR, 171
Layton, Geoffrey, Lieutenant Commander (later Commander), 19, 146–9, 290, 292, 298
Leake, Martin, Captain, 1–3
Lee, Ezra, 319

339

Index

Index

Index

Index

Index

Index